| | | | |
|---|---|---|---|
| | | | |
| | | | |
| | | | |
| | | | |
| | | | |
| | | | |
| | | | |
| | | | |
| | | | |
| | | | |

Presents eight modern Spanish plays covering a wide range of subjects from fantasy to
politics.

# MODERN SPANISH THEATRE

Also by Michael Benedikt
and George E. Wellwarth

MODERN FRENCH THEATRE
POSTWAR GERMAN THEATRE

# MODERN SPANISH THEATRE

## AN ANTHOLOGY OF PLAYS

EDITED BY

*Michael Benedikt* AND *George E. Wellwarth*

E. P. DUTTON & CO., INC., NEW YORK

1968

### INDIVIDUAL COPYRIGHTS AND ACKNOWLEDGMENTS

RAMÓN MARÍA DEL VALLE-INCLÁN: *Divine Words*. English translation copyright © 1968 by Edwin Williams. Published by permission of D. Carlos del Valle-Inclán Blanco.

FEDERICO GARCÍA LORCA: *The Shoemaker's Prodigious Wife*. Reprinted from *Five Plays* by Federico García Lorca, English translation by J. Graham-Lujan and R. O'Connell. Copyright © 1963 by New Directions. Reprinted by permission of New Directions Publishing Corporation.

MIGUEL MIHURA: *Three Top Hats*. English translation copyright © 1968 by Marcia Wellwarth. Published by permission of the author.

RAFAEL ALBERTI: *Night and War in the Prado Museum*. English translation © 1968 by Lemuel Johnson. Published by permission of Editorial Losada S.A. and the author.

ALEJANDRO CASONA: *Suicide Prohibited in Springtime*. English translation copyright © 1968 by Adam Horvath. Published by permission of Aguilar S.A. de Ediciones.

FERNANDO ARRABAL: *First Communion*. English translation copyright © 1968 by Michael Benedikt. Published by permission of Christian Bourgois, Editeur.

LAURO OLMO: *The News Item*. English translation copyright © 1968 by Marcia Wellwarth. Published by permission of the author.

JOSÉ-MARÍA BELLIDO: *Football*. English translation copyright © 1968 by David Turner. Published by permission of the author's and translator's agent, Kurt Hellmer.

iv

ACKNOWLEDGMENTS

The editors would like to express sincere thanks for their invaluable suggestions to Professor Anthony M. Pasquariello and Professor Robert Lima.

# CONTENTS

   * The date in parentheses indicates the year in which the play was completed.

# INTRODUCTION

## 1.

THE EXISTENCE OF a modern theatre in Spain has not been properly acknowledged. Up to the present, the Spanish theatre has been represented heroically, if not really sufficiently, by the plays of Federico García Lorca, which English-speaking audiences have slowly come to know through the efforts of a few venturesome editors and publishers. Both before and beyond Lorca, however, there was and is in Spain a drama of extraordinary force and depth, as well as outright invention and charm. It is the intention of this book to present some of the best examples of this still virtually unknown modern theatre.

In all fairness it must be said that in view of the peculiar difficulties encountered by the new drama in Spain, one would not expect to find there a fully developed modern movement. In the style of (if not to the same degree as) Nazi Germany or Soviet Russia, Spanish drama has been subjected to the frustrations of vigilant censorship. Since the Civil War of 1936–1939, this censorship has been particularly vigorous and has involved a regular review of all forms of creative writing—including newspaper articles, poetry, and plays—obviously designed to prevent outspoken criticism of Franco's regime. Still more insidious has been the prohibition of publication or performance of works by those who fought against the Falangists during the Civil War. This ban has often been extended to those who had sought and found exile, whatever the reason. Not only political beliefs, but variations of style have been condemned. Too much playfulness or lyricism in construction, as well as too deep a critical bite, have been interpreted as either "anti-Spanish" or "immoral." Earlier, another factor contributed to the rather gnarled, erratic, growth of a truly modern Spanish drama: the difficulty of launching a vigorously experimental modern literature in Spain in the first place, even during the relatively propitious time when censorship was not so strict as it has been during recent decades.

## 2.

The wave of experimental, anti-Naturalistic plays which broke over Europe in the late nineteenth and early twentieth centuries, definitively changing the theatrical temper of the times and also laying the cornerstone for all the advanced twentieth-century theatre to come, was slow to break in Spain. Even the arrival of that international precursor-style, Symbolism, the genre which a few decades after the death of its patron saint Charles Baudelaire in 1867 virtually swept over Europe, was relatively tardy. Symbolism was to all intents and purposes introduced to Spanish literature in 1898 by the Nicaraguan poet-statesman Rubén Darío, during his second mission to Spain, rather than by any native Spanish writer.

The situation in drama was even more *retardataire* than in the rest of Spanish literature. A Naturalist theatre still prevailed, a theatre which appeared to sweep away the Romanticism of the years before, yet which ended by simply transferring the old violences and passions from grandiose to bourgeois characters. The late drama of the nineteenth century was epitomized by the socially oriented realism of Benito Pérez Galdós (1843–1920) on the one hand, and on the other, by the indulgence in "slice-of-life" sensationalism for its own sake found in the work of José Echegaray (1832–1916), generally acknowledged to be the chief dramatist of the period.

The birth of contemporary drama in Spain, as well as the birth of modernity in most other literary forms, came with the advent of the so-called "Generation of 1898." [1] In contrast to the relatively internationalist quality of Spanish Naturalism the writers of this new generation were emphatic in their use of Spanish subjects; they frequently reached back into the great ages of Spanish litera-

[1] This anchor-date for the renaissance in Spanish literature of this period derives roughly from the year in which the works of the above writers began to receive widespread notice. But it is also the date that shook all Spain out of its post-Romantic slumber: the crushing defeat it sustained in the Spanish-American War.

ture and history for the sources they cultivated. Technically, too, they were highly exploratory, for the most part rejecting the techniques of Naturalism in favor of Symbolism, and particularly French Symbolism.

At first, the resulting changes were most evident outside the field of drama. Among the many noteworthy writers of the Generation of 1898, which included Benavente, Unamuno, Maeztu, Manuel and Antonio Machado, Azorín, Juan Ramón Jiménez, and Ramón María del Valle-Inclán, only Benavente and Valle-Inclán were to become deeply committed to the drama; and only Valle-Inclán worked in the anti-Naturalistic manner. The charmingly satirical comedies of Jacinto Benavente (1866-1954) were a healthy departure from the Naturalist modes of the period; but only the changes introduced by Valle-Inclán were to prove truly prophetic. A budding writer and also an actor (among his roles was a part in a drama by his friend Benavente), Ramón María del Valle-Inclán's first play Cenizas (Ashes, 1899) was published the year in which he lost his arm in a violent quarrel, thus committing him permanently to the role of a playwright. Still, it was to be some years before even Valle-Inclán's dramas were to be performed with any frequency. Even such an indisputable masterwork of the twentieth-century theatre as Divinas Palabras (Divine Words, 1913), was not premièred until 1933.

But changes were plainly in the offing. When, in 1909, José Echegaray, the reigning dean of Spanish Naturalist drama, received the Nobel Prize for literature, a storm of protest arose among the younger Spanish writers.

3.

It was twenty years later, with the celebrated "Generation of 1927," that twentieth-century Spanish literature—and with it the theatre—came to the maturity that the Cencration of 1898 had foreshadowed. The period has been called everything from "a second Golden Age in Spanish drama"[2] to one which included the formation of " . . . the most brilliant circle of . . . Spanish

[2] Barrett H. Clark, quoted by Angel Flores in Spanish Drama (New York: Bantam Books, 1962), p. 5.

poets for three hundred years."[3] How did this virtual renaissance occur?

To a certain extent, the main concerns of this flowering can be traced back to those of '98. The emphasis on a broader and a more liberal education that the *fin-de-siècle* intellectual and literary figures helped effect had resulted in the establishment of many modern schools, chief among them being the university that was to become the showcase of Spanish culture in an era in which political and literary conservatives were otherwise mostly in control: the Institución Libre de Ensanza, in Madrid. Founded in the year 1898, by 1910 it had become potent enough to father another liberal educational establishment, the Residencia de Estudiantes—in essence a college-sized branch of the parent institution. Here gathered the entire "brilliant circle" of poets and writers. Among them were Jorge Guillén, Pedro Salinas, Gerardo Diego, and Dámaso Alonso; in 1919 Federico García Lorca arrived; shortly after this came an ex-student of painting, Rafael Alberti. Their acknowledged mentor was Juan Ramón Jiménez who, although he was by then regarded as a spokesman for literary Symbolism, was quick to encourage experiment of all kinds among his juniors. Gradually, together with such members of the visual-arts contingent at the Residencia as the future filmmaker Luis Buñuel, and a painter just emerging from his Cubist past, Salvador Dalí, this circle began to discover a literary current newer than Symbolism, but destined to become a major influence on the new Spanish drama: Surrealism. Just as the writers of '98 had learned much from French literary techniques, so this more recent group had begun, one by one, to look across the Pyrenees for inspiration and guidance. Already, both before and during World War I, Spain had made a place for itself in two heavily French-influenced movements: Barcelona had been one of Dada's international headquarters, and, of course, Picasso and Juan Gris had been instrumental in the creation of Cubism. In literature, a further fusion between the two cultures was reflected in "Creationism," a movement founded in 1919 by the Chilean poet Vicente Huidobro in collaboration with the French poet

[3] J.B. Trend, *Lorca and the Spanish Poetic Tradition* (Oxford: Blackwell, 1956), p. 19.

Pierre Reverdy; Huidobro himself frequently wrote in French. "Ultraism," a more generally inclusive as well as more lasting avant-garde literary movement, was founded in 1924—the same year in which André Breton created French Surrealism out of the remains of Dadaism—by several members of the "brilliant circle," including Alberti. It is true that Ultraism tended to give greater freedom in the use of traditional metrics and displays of "craftsmanship" than did Surrealism; still, it was similar enough to Surrealism to enable one to suppose that had the Spanish Ultraists lived in Paris, the capital of Surrealism, they would have been Surrealists.

Probably the best date to pinpoint for the literary conquest of Spain by Surrealism would be April 18, 1925. That was when one of Breton's leading associates, Louis Aragon, gave a lecture on Surrealism at the Residencia. We cannot know for sure whether the two most prominent young playwrights at the Residencia, Lorca and Alberti, heard the Aragon talk called "Fragments d'une conference" ("Fragments of a Lecture") [4] but the influence of Surrealism becomes very marked in the work of both at about this time. Some of the earliest of Lorca's plays, including *Teatro Breve* (*Pocket Theatre*, 1926–28), and *Asi Que Pasen Cinco Años* (*And Thus Five Years Pass*, 1931), and Alberti's first play *El Hombre Deshabitado* (*The Hollow Man*, 1930) are among the most firmly Surrealist dramatic creations in any language.

The full impact of advanced Spanish intellectual and literary thinking, however, was not felt in the contemporary theatre until a little more time had passed. As in 1898, the new young literary generation undertook a "Spanishizing" program, based especially on the increased use of traditional Iberian literary materials: the literature of the early 1920's is notable for a widespread resurrection of folkloristic forms and materials, clearly reflecting such popular sources as national or regional songs, nursery rhymes, folk legends, and gypsy and Arabic materials and formulations. Thus, together with such a work as the "Oda a Salvador Dalí" ("Ode to Salvador Dalí," 1927) we find Lorca bringing out his *Romancero Gitano* (*Gypsy Ballads*, 1927); Alberti's strongly Sur-

---

[4] Sections of this lecture appear in English in Maurice Nadeau's *The History of Surrealism* (New York: Macmillan, 1965), pp. 110–11.

realistic *La Amante* (*The Beloved*, 1926) was written almost simultaneously with his folkloristic *Marinero en Tierra* (*Sailor Ashore*,
1924), which won a National Literature prize.
The tendency to blend these new and old literary traditions
first came to a head in poetry—an art whose developments in
Spain, no less than in other countries, often tends to foreshadow
those of the theatre. In 1927, during the celebrations honoring
the 300th anniversary of the death of the great seventeenth-century poet Góngora, several of the "Generation of 1927" wrote
about the "modernity" of Góngora's oblique but perfectly baroque
manner. In an essay delivered first as a lecture in Granada, and
immediately afterward at the Residencia, Lorca noted:

> To place Góngora in his world, we must first take note of
> two schools of poetry struggling for mastery in the history of
> Spanish lyricism; the so-called "popular"—or the more improperly
> called "national" poets—and the poets rightly known as culti
> vated. . . . While the indigenous . . . poets of the thirteenth
> century stammered songs medieval in feeling . . . the school that
> we are going to call the "opposite" school, to distinguish it from
> the others, turned its attention to the French and Provençal.[5]

Lorca added that "As I see it, both schools are capable of a profound national feeling."[6] Lorca's thoughts on the double-edged
character of Spanish literature in the seventeenth century are
equally applicable to much of the best literature of his own
period. Rafael Alberti also acknowledged this harmonious duality,
noting in his *Autobiography* that "in the tercentenary year of
D. Luis Góngora, my passion for verbal refinement in poetry
reached its apogee. . . . All the brio and flair of my earlier
songs I stored, as in cut-crystal, in caskets and urns where all was
resilient, transparent, and colorless. I subjected my metrical line
to the utmost precision and pressure."[7]
The combining of "cultivated" and foreign modernist techniques (i.e., Surrealism) with traditional materials was soon re-

[5] "The Poetic Image in Don Luis de Góngora," in *Poet in New York*, tr.
Ben Belitt (New York: Grove Press, 1955), p. 168.
[6] *Ibid.*, p. 169.
[7] Alberti, *Selected Poems*, tr. Ben Belitt (Berkeley and Los Angeles: University of California Press, 1966), p. 48.

flected in the theatre. The rediscovery of the Spanish masters of the Golden Age was also reflected in a general revival of interest in the old Spanish theatre. It is easy to understand why the plays of the Golden Age were to prove irresistible models. The great plays of the Golden Age have in common with the finest literary works in all forms of that period a fascination with the processes of imagination, both as theme and technique. Two of its major poets, Góngora—in his *Soledades* (*Solitudes*) which found particular favor among "the brilliant circle"—and Quevedo, in his *Sueños* (*Dreams*), had sounded the visionary note. Probably the greatest work of the period, Cervantes's novel *Don Quixote*, had concentrated on the role of the imagination in life. Quixote's struggle to keep faith with a courtly ideal in the face of earthly contradictions is, as has generally been agreed, an outright confrontation between illusion and reality. Cervantes's shorter plays, or "entremeses" (several of which seem to have directly influenced Lorca during the composition of his *The Shoemaker's Prodigious Wife*) pit similar opposites: specifically those of ordinary reality and honor. Calderón's *La Vida es Sueño* (*Life Is a Dream*) demonstrated the relevance of dream and delirium to an understanding of life as it is lived. The highly "theatrical" plays of Lope de Vega, dramas whose action is constantly and emphatically interrupted by regular departures from the Naturalistic in the form of songs, dances, and mime, suggest a comparable interest in anti-realities, but in technical terms. In one form or another, contrasts between the real and the fantastic are as typical of the literature of the Golden Age as they are of the twentieth century.[8]

[8] The contemporaneousness of *Quixote*, and of the typical Golden Age themes generally, has seldom been better explored than in the writings of the great Spanish philosopher and aesthetician, Ortega y Gasset (1883-1955). In his *Meditaciónes del Quijote* (*Meditations on Quixote*, 1914), Ortega wrote: "We are carried along in the adventure as if within a missile, and in the dynamic struggle between it, as it advances on an escaping tangent, and the center of the earth which tries to restrain it, we side with the missile. . . . the important thing is . . . the osmosis and endosmosis between the two." (*Meditations on Quixote*, tr. E. Rugg and D. Marin, New York: W. W. Norton, 1961, pp. 133-34.) In a sense, even the great work on aesthetics of Ortega's maturity, his celebrated *La deshumanización del arte* (*The Dehumanization of Art*, 1925), is a discussion of modernist aesthetics in the terms evoked by Cervantes. Ortega sees the difference between the great Spanish art of the Golden Age and modernist art as a difference not of kind, but of

It is not hard to recognize the value of this renewed interest in classic Spanish Theatre. It enabled a widespread incorporation into firm theatrical structures of the extravagance of imagination that Surrealism encouraged, a kind of classicizing of Surrealist excess. It facilitated the creation of a group of plays whose solidity compares with any dramas of the modern theatre. Indeed, one can perhaps best compare them to the classic "absurdist" dramas of our time. The plays collected here are much less close to the Spanish dramatists whom translators and editors have usually regarded as good risks—Benavente, Martínez Sierra, and the Quintero brothers—than they are to such post-Surrealist dramatists as Ionesco, Genet, Adamov, and Arrabal (the latter, to be sure, a playwright born and raised in Spain, who now writes in French largely because of the impossibility of production in his native land; and whom we represent here.

It remained for an educational event to forge a permanent bond between the strain of "cultivation" and the strain of "native tradition" in Spanish literature. Soon after the liberal Spanish Republic was installed, a teaching program was undertaken which had been envisioned since 1898: the education of the vast mass of unlettered Spaniards in the formal culture of their country. By 1932, some 30,000 new schools were said to have been established. Moreover, when a Ministry of Culture and Public Information was founded in 1931, it included "Misiónes Culturales," with two touring companies among its branches. One purpose of both the "Teatro Universitario" (affectionately known as "La Barraca") and the "Teatro del Pueblo" was to educate the people, especially in the provinces, in the works of Spain's Golden Age dramatists. The new government selected the young García Lorca (along with his friend Eduardo Ungarte) to direct the "La Barraca" and to head the "Teatro del Pueblo," the equally young dramatist Alejandro Casona. Thus a connection between the classic and the modern in Spanish theatre was confirmed officially.

---

degree—specifically of the degree of what Ortega calls the modern artist's "intervention." Significantly, the dates of these two crucial essays lie a few years on either side of T. S. Eliot's well-known essay proclaiming the "presentness of the past" for modern English literature: "Tradition and the Individual Talent" (1917).

4·

The effect of the Spanish Civil War was as cataclysmic for the modern Spanish theatre as it was for virtually all other divisions of Spanish life. Many theatres were closed; shortly after the beginning of the conflict the touring theatres were officially dissolved. To some extent, this seems to have been offset by the production of plays—mostly on the Republican side—just behind the front lines. There is little of value that survives from these plays.

Not only were theatres eliminated, but the ranks of active playwrights also were winnowed. A wave of deaths, some directly traceable to the war, occurred: the mid and late 1930's saw the deaths of such beloved writers as the elder of the Quintero brothers, Serafín Álvarez Quintero, and María de la O Lejárraga, wife and vital collaborator of Gregorio Martínez Sierra (1881–1948). Two distinguished literary men who had contributed something to the intellectual density of the newer theatre were the poet Antonio Machado and the essayist Miguel de Unamuno who died in 1936. That same year saw two particularly cruel losses: the murder of Federico García Lorca by a Fascist firing squad and the death of Valle-Inclán. While the loss of the young Lorca was obviously a great tragedy, it is ironic to note that the 79-year-old Valle-Inclán was also a relative newcomer to the stage, having just begun to receive occasional production.

Because of the tide of literary exiles that increased as the Falangist forces advanced, and which included Alberti and Casona, an era of relative conformity set in. The imposition of the rule of "precensorship"—the requirement that plays be cleared with the Franco regime before either performance or publication—sharply cut down on the freedom of theatrical activity, both in the larger state-controlled theatres, and in the smaller, more experimental playhouses. Despite the fact that the work of even avant-garde playwrights was produced, the over-all atmosphere of Franco's theatre was nevertheless chilling. The new Spanish theatre, as defined by an official catch-phrase of 1943, was to be directed toward that almost inevitable goal of state-dictated theatre: "social and aesthetic purification."

In view of this goal, and the official "encouragements" by which

it was implemented, it is scarcely surprising to find that some of
the most important Spanish plays of the post-Civil War years
when the attempts at "purification" were particularly vigorous,
were not written in Spain; nor have they necessarily been performed there. This period is notable for accelerated theatrical
activity in the countries to which playwrights and, in some in-
stances, whole acting companies had fled: Mexico, the Argen-
tine Republic, and Chile. Even today the Spanish theatre is divided into three major centers: Mexico City, Buenos Aires, and
Madrid. Among the few members of the brilliant prewar generation to survive after the war, Rafael Alberti has written almost *all*
his plays in exile, while Alejandro Casona has managed to write
several of his most important plays abroad.

5.

The more recent Spanish playwrights have managed to revive
at least some of the brightness of the days when Spain produced
a group of dramatists worthy of international consideration. One
might well characterize the modern Spanish theatre according to
a formula devised by one post-Civil War playwright, Alfonso Sastre
(b. 1926), who sees the Spanish theatre as being divided between
a "Theatre of Magic" involved with themes of fantasy and a
"Theatre of Anguish" involved with political problems.[9] As might
be expected from the terms of the characterization, Sastre is on
the side of a theatre of politics, as opposed to a theatre of
fantasy. The division itself appears simplistic. As we have seen,
even the most anti-Naturalistic Spanish playwrights of this century have been preoccupied with the humblest of realities. Moreover, even Sastre's realistically oriented dramas, or those of
Antonio Buero Vallejo (b. 1916), another fine playwright
whose style was founded in Naturalism and who emerged after
the Civil War, have explored effects which draw upon the broader
traditions of avant-garde drama.

It is also noteworthy that Sastre's remarks on the post-Civil War
theatre were made in the 1950's; it has been since about 1960

[9] "Drama and Society," in *The New Theatre of Europe*, ed. Robert Corri-
gan (New York: Delta Books, 1962), pp. 136–145.

that what promises to be one of the most interesting tendencies in modern Spanish theatre has become evident.

Recent years have seen the re-emergence of a theatre comparable to the anti-Naturalistic traditions of most other modern European drama. Although it is a theatre that is theatrical in the extreme, incorporating elements of both Surrealism and Absurdism, this theatre, like the avant-garde theatre of the thirties, is marked by a concern for both tradition and "reality." This theatre is often allegorical. Its departures from reality have, as the reader will observe while reading the final plays in this book, considerable relevance to the contemporary scene in Spain. The experiments of Lauro Olmo, who speaks with an almost Surrealistic obliqueness about what he sees as the *malaise* of modern Spain, and the work of José-María Bellido, who in his *Football*, included here, has commented on the Civil War as directly as any Spanish playwright has ever dared, clearly relate to an earlier tradition of half-veiled motives of plot and character. They have much in common with the best works of Lorca, Casona, Mihura, and Valle-Inclán. This trend is strong, and it includes many playwrights as yet unknown abroad, but who are slowly becoming known in Spain in an "underground" fashion, since performance of their plays is either explicitly forbidden or obviously impossible under the present system.[10]

In view of the sparse information available on much of the "overground" theatre in Spain, it is somewhat previous to make definite predictions about the future of the Spanish theatre now "underground." It is easy to predict, however, that eventually a genuine liberalization will occur. This may well happen at the end of Franco's dictatorship. Although a new government could prove as concerned with "purification" as his, it is still encouraging to note, when considering the fate of the arts in a totalitarian state, the liberalizing "thaw" that continues to develop in the arts

---

[10] One of the most interesting surveys of the changing but still powerful system of censorship in Spain since the Civil War is the account by a pseudonymic author, Roberto Mansilla, published in the British magazine *Censorship*, Vol. 5, No. 1 (Winter, 1966). And, as this is written, an article on this point has just appeared in *The New York Times* of June 11, 1967. Entitled "New Pressures on the New Spanish Painting," and written by H. G. Wilson, it, too, describes fresh methods of censorship which have been put into effect despite certain official acts of ostensible liberalization.

in Russia. One thing seems certain from the best of its recent accomplishments, however: that when the Spanish theatre fully emerges from its temporary bonds, it will provide delights of substance. We hope that this collection will prove a prelude to this revelation.

MICHAEL BENEDIKT

# DIVINE WORDS

*A Village Tragicomedy*

*by* RAMÓN MARÍA DEL VALLE-INCLÁN

TRANSLATED BY EDWIN WILLIAMS

RAMÓN MARÍA DEL VALLE-INCLÁN (d. 1936) was born in 1866 in Galicia, the northwest corner of Spain, with whose unique folk traditions much of his work is closely associated. As a young man he traveled a great deal, following a variety of professions, including that of theatrical manager, while absorbing and transmuting the influences which he was to use in his writing. In his early works he displays the influence of French *fin-de-siècle* aestheticism, particularly in his absorption with style as such, in his fascination with artificial and archaic words and unusual syntactical constructions, many of them derived from the Galician language (which is, in effect, a development of medieval Portuguese). This fascination, although it became less prominent in his later works, never left him, and, together with another aspect of his early works—his interest in the realistic portrayal of popular and regional "lower-class" types—may be seen in *Divine Words*.

Critics have at various times tried to categorize Valle-Inclán as a "pure artist," a "decadent," a "degenerate," and a "sensualist," and while he was all of these in varying degrees, none of them adequately describes the spirit of his works. In addition, there is a *special* quality in Valle-Inclán's work, a quality so profoundly and characteristically associated with him and so exclusively the emanation of his own spirit that it is impossible to give it any name other than *valleinclanesque*. What it amounts to is sufficient to make Valle-Inclán a fulcrum in Spanish literature. The dream/reality conflict, the forced marriage of the rational and the irrational that is so characteristic of earlier Spanish literature is transmuted in his work through his habit of contrasting the beautiful with the grotesque, the everyday with the absurd, into an uncanny and prescient foreshadowing of the twentieth-century European avant-garde drama. Valle-Inclán, long before any other modern Spanish dramatist, took the lagging Spanish dramatic tradition, immured in the pedestrian and imitative style of such writers as Pérez Galdós and Echegaray, and personally thrust it forward into the mainstream of twentieth-century artistic thought. It is not for nothing that the distinguished Spanish critic Domingo Pérez Minik calls Valle-Inclán the direct forerunner of Michel de Ghelderode's grotesquerie and Ionesco's absurdism.

2

*Divine Words* was written in 1913 but remained unperformed until 1933, when the celebrated actress Margarita Xirgu, also a champion of the plays of Lorca and, later, Casona, put it on in Madrid. The play is a combination of two kinds of drama which Valle-Inclán had developed: the *comedia bárbara* and the *esperpento*. The latter term means "absurdity" and is derived from a word denoting a distorting fun-house mirror. And *Divine Words* is best described as a barbaric (in the sense of ruthless and uncompromising) reflection of reality. Contrast is the keynote of the play's structure: contrast between the idyllic rusticity of the setting and the sordid horror of the action; contrast between the warmth and beauty of the background and the callousness of the actors. Valle-Inclán constantly emphasizes the calm, almost Elysian beauty of the Galician countryside and contrasts it with the pitiful squalor of the idiot child and the unfeeling mercenary attitude of the characters, climaxing in the ghastly brutality of the scene in which the swine gnaw at the deformed child's dead body. In the magnificent character of Mary Gaila the dichotomy is personified as we see the coarseness inside the beauty she flaunts. Valle-Inclán's boldness in technique and subject matter is shown in his evocations of adultery and incest, in his blending of pagan and Christian elements, in his introduction of nudity, and in his episodic, cinematographic structure.

G. W.

# CHARACTERS

LUCERO, who at other times is called NINTH MEOW and COMRADE MEOW

POCA PENA, his woman

QUEEN JOANNA and her IDIOT CHILD

PEDRO GAILO, sexton of San Clemente; MARY GAILA, his wife, and SIMONIÑA, their offspring

ROSA TATULA, an old beggar

MIGUEL PADRONÉS, a young pottery mender

A CATTLEMAN

OLD WOMEN who fill their jugs at the fountain

MARICA REINO, with other OLD WOMEN

A DEPUTY MAYOR

A YOUNG GIRL

THE BLINDMAN OF GONDAR

THE LEMONADE VENDOR

A PILGRIM

A pair of CIVIL GUARDS

A PEASANT COUPLE with their sick DAUGHTER

THE INNKEEPER

SERENÍN BRETAL

AN OLD WOMAN in an attic window

A PREGNANT WOMAN

ANOTHER NEIGHBOR

A SOLDIER with his discharge papers

LUDOVINA the tavernkeeper

GANGS OF YOUNG BOYS full of pranks and songs

FLOCKS OF LAY SISTERS, young and old

BENITA the seamstress

QUINTÍN PINTADO

MILÓN ARNOYA

COIMBRA, a trained dog

COLORIN, a fortune-telling bird

THE GOAT GOBLIN

An anonymous TOAD who croaks in the night

A chorus of adolescent cries

# ACT ONE

## SCENE 1

*(San Clemente, in the parish of Viana del Prior. A country church situated at a crossroads, in the midst of tombstones and cypress trees. Pedro Gailo, the sexton, pinches out the candles under the Romanesque portico. He is a gloomy old man in cassock and surplice. He is poorly shaven; his face and hands are yellowed. He shakes his fingers, blows off the sooty fingertips, and scrapes them against the columns of the archway. He talks to himself constantly. His expression is furtive, his speech incoherent.)*

PEDRO GAILO: They *would* have to stop in front of the altar. Good-for-nothing tramps. They're as bad as they come. Wherever they go they parade their evil ways. Just look where they've planted themselves! Birds of a feather! Parasites! On the road night and day!

*(Pedro Gailo runs his hand over his forehead and his four remaining hairs stand on end. Cross-eyed, he looks toward the road where a pair of drifters are resting: a man and a woman with a small child—the flower of their wild oats. The woman, sad and thin, wears a short skirt and a blue scarf that covers her combs and ringlets. The man has on a cap with a visor. His guitar is in a cloth cover and his trained dog tied by a filthy reddish cord. They are sitting in the ditch, facing the portico of the church. The man is talking and the woman listens while she rocks the crying baby. The woman is known by various names and, depending upon the region, she is Julie, Rosina, Matilda, Pepa the Brunette. The man's name is another enigma, but the woman calls him Lucero. She is addressed by her lover as Poca Pena.)*

LUCERO: We ought to dump that kid some night when we're passing through a village.

POCA PENA: A hell of a father you are!

LUCERO: Well—suppose I'm not!

POCA PENA: So you admit you're a cuckold.

LUCERO: I admit that as the kid's father, the best thing I can do is not pass on any of my rotten character.

5

POCA PENA: What are you worrying about—afraid that I want something for myself? All I'm asking is that you show some affection for your son!

LUCERO: That's exactly what I'm trying to show!

POCA PENA: If the boy disappears, or if he dies on account of your abuse, I'll bury this knife between your ribs. Oh, Lucero, don't leave me without a child!

LUCERO: We can always make another one.

POCA PENA: Have a heart, Lucero!

LUCERO: Cut it out, now!

POCA PENA: Gallows-bird!

*(Lucero scowls contemptuously and slaps the girl's mouth with the back of his hand; whimpering, she wipes her lips with the corner of her handkerchief. At the sight of her own blood, she bursts into tears. The man coughs with obvious intent and makes the sparks leap rhythmically from his tinderbox. There between the columns of the doorway, Pedro Gailo, the sexton, shakes his fists.)*

PEDRO GAILO: Take your evil examples elsewhere! Don't display them before the house of the Lord!

LUCERO: God doesn't see what we do. His face is turned the other way.

PEDRO GAILO: Heathen!

LUCERO: And proud of it! For twenty years I haven't set foot in a church!

PEDRO GAILO: So you boast of being a friend of the Devil, do you?

LUCERO: We're old pals.

PEDRO GAILO: The time will come when you will gnash those flashing teeth of yours.

LUCERO: I'm not afraid of that day.

POCA PENA: Even the beasts of the jungle are afraid of it.

PEDRO GAILO: Every act brings either reward or punishment, so teaches the doctrine of Our Holy Mother the Church.

LUCERO: Don't give me that song and dance! I know an old wives' tale when I hear one.

PEDRO GAILO: My silence won't hold back the avenging hand of the Lord.

LUCERO: Fine!

*(An old woman with a dark mantilla steps from the doorway, then another, followed by a third. They walk in single file, carrying holy water in their cupped hands and sprinkling it on the graves. The last woman pulls a small trough fitted with wooden wheels; it serves as a rickety bed in which a hydro-cephalic dwarf is sleeping fitfully. Queen Joanna, a dusty, bare-foot shadow that begs in the local fairs and pilgrimages with her hideous offspring, questions the sexton, her brother.)*

THE QUEEN: Why didn't you give communion with mass?

PEDRO GAILO: There were no wafers left in the chalice.

THE QUEEN: I was counting on receiving the Lord. The earth sum-mons me.

PEDRO GAILO: You do look worse.

THE QUEEN: The pains of my womb gnaw at me.

PEDRO GAILO: The earth is your only womb, and the womb of every sinner! And my nephew, is he waking up? He is showing a bit of intelligence, sister!

THE QUEEN: The poor little thing!

*(Pedro Gailo turns his runaway eyeball toward the dwarf, who bobbles around his enormous head with its imbecilic look. His mother brushes away the flies that swarm around the creature's slobbering mouth. The downiness above his lips is beginning to grow dark. Dragging the cart behind her, she crosses the grounds and merges with the shadows of the road. The vaga-bond's dog, balanced on two feet, attempts a little dance beside that pathetic, earth-colored figure. Then, slowly, the animal returns to all fours and lowers its tail, howling the mournful cry reserved for the presence of death. Lucero whis-tles, and the dog, once again on hind legs, heads for its master, who laughs and winks his eye.)*

LUCERO: This animal has a pact with Brother Satan.

PEDRO GAILO: Until it comes face to face with someone who exorcises his evil spirits and smites it with a thunderbolt.

LUCERO: No doubt we'll both be fried in the end.

PEDRO GAILO: You try to stir up doubts with the truth.

LUCERO: Well, you've discovered my sin, then.

POCA PENA: Rubbish!

LUCERO: Here, Coimbra! Now watch how you answer this question. Your right paw for Yes, your left for No; your tail's left over for I Don't Know. Answer truthfully: The wife of our friend here, has she ever decorated her husband with horns?

*(Coimbra, still on two legs, meditates and shakes her black and yellow head, jingling the bells on the tips of her ears. Possessed by the prophetic spirit, she gradually becomes still and stares at her master. After a moment of hesitation during which the bells continue to tinkle, she begins to move her left paw furiously.)*

LUCERO: Pal, Coimbra answers no. Now she's going to tell us something else. Coimbra, do you have the power to see if our friend is destined for *future* membership in the Antlered Brotherhood? Right paw for Yes, and left for No: and you still have your tail for I Don't Know.

*(Coimbra, wagging her tail and barking, rears again on hind legs and, with an uncertain quivering in her paws, gazes at her owner. The bells on her ears set up a prolonged and hypnotic tremor. The rake smiles with a wink and the dog decides suddenly to raise her right paw.)*

LUCERO: Sure you're not mistaken, Coimbra? Go shake hands and apologize to our friend for giving him a bad name.

PEDRO GAILO: Worthless scum! The pranks of a scoundrel can hardly offend me.

LUCERO: Pal, you have to take it as a joke. Let's get moving, Poca Pena.

PEDRO GAILO: A lot you'll find to laugh at in the fires of Hell.

*(Poca Pena gathers up the child in the folds of her shawl, and the vagabond shoulders the cage of his trained bird. Off they march, as:)*

POCA PENA: Have pity as a father, Lucero!

LUCERO: Shut your mouth!

POCA PENA: I swear I'll break away from this slavery. Some morning you'll find me gone.

LUCERO: You think I'd come running after you? Don't kid yourself.

POCA PENA: You did it before; you even killed a man, too.

LUCERO: Not because I wanted to.

POCA PENA: If the blow was meant for me, how come you missed?

LUCERO: That's enough of that. Does the bird have any seed?

POCA PENA: He won't eat.

LUCERO: Coimbra, where'll we find another? Why don't we just pray for one to Brother Satan?

POCA PENA: Don't flatter yourself!

*(The child grows restless in her mother's arms, while the cage of the fortune-telling bird swings from the vagabond's shoulder. Gilded by the rays of the sun, it seems an enchanted palace.)*


## SCENE 2

*(A clump of trees at the side of the road. Queen Joanna, sheltered by the shade, begs for alms with a flowered shawl spread out on the embankment; the deformed dwarf, swallowed up by the straw mattress and the grimy blanket of the cart, makes grotesque faces.)*

THE QUEEN: A bit of charity for the poor fellow without the light of reason! Look how helpless he is!

*(Her words are intermingled with moans, and she rubs her loins. Rosa Tatula, who during summer weather and county fair-time also begs for alms, gives her a straightlaced old biddy's characteristic advice:)*

TATULA: You should be in the Santiago Hospital. The pain's too much for you.

THE QUEEN: It's been at me for years.

TATULA: Be thankful the boy brings you a bit of bread.

THE QUEEN: If he could just get off his mattress! Even if only to come at his mother with a drawn dagger!

TATULA: God the Father gave him to you that way, and so his divine will is realized.

THE QUEEN: Well? Have you ever seen me opposing it?

*(Gasping for breath and holding a pewter plate, the Queen runs to meet the well-to-do fair-goers in the middle of the road. A cattle dealer driving young bulls down from the hills, stands in his stirrups and shouts at her to get out of the way.)*

THE HORSE DEALER: Look out! . . . You'll scare the cattle!

*(The beggar, holding her sides, returns to the shade of the oak trees. Her eyes are glassy and her lips the color of the parched soil. The young bulls, covered with black spots, pass by in a cloud of dust. The obese and red-faced cattleman follows at a trot, his Roman profile outlined against the sky.)*

THE QUEEN: God, I'm dying, I'm dying!

TATULA: Is the pain bad?

THE QUEEN: A cat is eating away at the very place of my sins!

TATULA: Ah! It's your groin that's bad.

THE QUEEN: Just a little sip of brandy would revive me!

TATULA: Someone with a jug will come by.

THE QUEEN: The door of the Lord is opening for me!

TATULA: Only good deeds on earth can open the Pearly gates.

THE QUEEN: I'll never make it through the day!

*(She doubles up, mouth against the ground. Her hair covers her cheeks and her hands claw at the grass. Below the ragged fringe of her underskirt, the bare legs and feet are waxen. Rosa Tatula watches her with a frightened expression.)*

TATULA: Try to get up! You can't give up your soul at the side of this road! You have to confess and set things right with the Lord!

THE QUEEN: Oh, ah! what a banquet! Delicacies everywhere!

TATULA: The pain's making you delirious.

THE QUEEN: Gather up the scarf, all the money's spilling out! . . . Quiet, Laureano! . . . Ah, that feels good! . . .

TATULA: Good Lord! Is this what delirium is like?

THE QUEEN: Marelo, give me a glass of lemonade! There's money, Marelo, there's plenty of money!

TATULA: Queen Joanna, don't die here, you'll get me mixed up in it! Try to hold on! Let's get to the village first!

THE QUEEN: The heavens are full of shooting stars!

*(Tatula attempts to lift this agonizing relic, and the limp and lifeless body slips from her hands, flailing its arms upward like the blades of a windmill.)*

TATULA: What a holy mess!

*(In the distance, stepping out from underneath some low-lying grape arbors supported by stone posts, appears a young man, and behind him one can make out the outline of another figure lying in the shade. With the help of a stick, the youth hefts a pottery mender's rig onto his shoulder. He is Miguel Padronés, who walks the roads and who, because of his affectations, is usually run after and insulted in the fairs and marketplaces. He wears an earring.)*

THE QUEEN: Come here, Christian!

MIGUEL: If it's to help you, I'm already close enough.

TATULA: Come, for the sake of the one who brought you into the world.

MIGUEL: My mother-in-law had me.

TATULA: Enough of that nonsense. Queen Joanna just had an attack of epilepsy!

MIGUEL: Rub her with nettles.

TATULA: Come over here, you heretic!

MIGUEL: Comrade Meow's on his way.

*(The youth who was lying down in the shade of the arbors has gotten up and comes into the sunlight. He is the same hooli-*

*gan other times seen in the company of the grieving woman
who called him Lucero.)*

MIGUEL: Shall we go down, Comrade Meow?

COMRADE MEOW: What for? To see the grimace of death?

MIGUEL: How'd you get the word?

COMRADE MEOW: Coimbra got it a while back.

TATULA: What are you afraid of, cowards?

COMRADE MEOW: Since you get so personal, we're on our way.

*(The two cohorts descend toward the roadway. Miguel reaches
with his tongue for a wrinkled mole at the corner of his mouth,
while the other strikes sparks from his flint. In the shade of the
oaks the beggar lies motionless, unable to speak. Her shin-
bones protrude from the dress like two wax candles.)*

TATULA: Queen Joanna! Queen Joanna!

COMRADE MEOW: Don't bother waiting for an answer; you'd better
notify her family. You only need to tell them half the truth:
that the pain attacked her here and that it hasn't left her.
That woman is dead.

TATULA: Damn it! Having to tell the police is what I get for being
so softhearted.

COMRADE MEOW: Needless to say, you won't mention me under any
circumstances. . . .

TATULA: And who noticed that she was dead?

COMRADE MEOW: Just don't give my name.

TATULA: And if they call me to testify?

COMRADE MEOW: Just don't name me.

TATULA: So much secrecy, what does it mean?

COMRADE MEOW: If you're not careful, it could mean your hide for
a drumhead.

*(The rogue, seated in the shade of the trees, spears two cigar
butts together on his Albacetian knife. Rosa Tatula, shivering
with fear, puts on her wooden shoes at the edge of the road
and checks her knapsack. Leaning on her cane, she clumps off*

*bearing the bad news. In the shadows of the oak grove the idiot grimaces, black with flies. Miguel Padronés, with the tip of his tongue on the wrinkled mole, undulates toward the cart and slips his fat little hands under the straw mattress. He pulls out a small dirty purse, tinkling with money.)*

COMRADE MEOW: That silver voice is pretty!

MIGUEL: Like the mewing of a kitty.

COMRADE MEOW: Let's have a look.

MIGUEL: This little transaction is mine alone.

COMRADE MEOW: I didn't know you were such a miser, comrade! If you don't want it to be joint enterprise, then we'll have to air the matter.

MIGUEL: In what court?

COMRADE MEOW: Let's let Coimbra decide the case, comrade.

MIGUEL: I don't want my claim ruled on by the Devil.

*(The hoodlum stands up and rolls the cigar with his gold-handled knife. With two quick steps he seats himself on the pottery mender's belongings. With a pale, half-hearted smile, Miguel stuffs the moneybag into his belt. Comrade Meow, looking cross-eyed at a lock of hair covering his forehead, suddenly explodes.)*

COMRADE MEOW: Look, Queenie! Either you fork over that purse or I drive this blade into your heart.

MIGUEL: What ever happened to that woman who was traveling with you, comrade?

COMRADE MEOW: She's heading for home.

MIGUEL: A long trip?

COMRADE MEOW: Damned long!

MIGUEL: To the end of the earth maybe?

COMRADE MEOW: To the town square in Ceuta.

MIGUEL: Where the penitentiary is.

COMRADE MEOW: And the flower of Spain!

MIGUEL: Do you know those parts?

COMRADE MEOW: I broke out of there, Queenie. What's it to you?

MIGUEL: Just this: seeing as how you're in deep already, you'd better forget about these little odds and ends.

COMRADE MEOW: Queenie, don't give me that. I see I'll have to remind you of a certain job in the seminary in Viana.

MIGUEL: I may have been a suspect, but they let me go when they found out I was clean.

COMRADE MEOW: Remember that time we were fooling around in that bar on the new highway?

MIGUEL: Rumors!

COMRADE MEOW: Coimbra discovered you were in on that little business.

MIGUEL: All rumors!

COMRADE MEOW: Rumors, eh? She was scratching around under the window where the boys got away and she found this earring. Here—take it back, since it matches the one you're wearing. And now, let's split up that money. Of course if you don't want to accept my gift, we'll hand it over to the authorities.

MIGUEL: Oh, filthy lucre! How I detest it! To think: we were on the point of an argument, comrade! Just a little lover's quarrel.

SCENE 3

*(Another road, this one weaving its way among a group of farm houses. The yellow-green squash is ripening alongside the tile roofs, and the chains by which the dogs are tethered rattle against the bottom of the stone granaries. The road descends toward a well, half-hidden in the shadows of a poplar grove. The blackbirds are cawing. The old peasant women let their buckets overflow in order to exchange a bit of gossip about the landlord. Rosa Tatula arrives on the run, the bearer of sad news.)*

TATULA: Glory be to God! How mysterious is his divine justice! Queen Joanna is lying unconscious down the road. When I called to her she didn't move a muscle. Her skin's the color of a corpse. If I wasn't in such a hurry to get to the village, I would have gone by the house of that sister of hers who lives at Cruz de Leson. Do any of you live down that way?

AN OLD WOMAN: We live next door to each other.

TATULA: Then you can take her the bad news.

AN OLD WOMAN: Did she actually surrender her soul, do you think?

TATULA: She's the same color as a corpse, that's all I can say.

ANOTHER OLD WOMAN: For a long while the disease had been eating away inside her. Now her troubles are over: day after day, rain or shine, dragging the cart. What'll become of the child? Where will he end up?

TATULA: Depending on how you look at it, he's a burden or he isn't. Queen Joanna could down more alcohol in a day than any one of us in a year, and they don't just give liquor away. She lived off her afflicted child. You have no idea how much one can make off that cart! Nothing can match it for making somebody's heart bleed. Queen Joanna made better than seven *reales* a day. You're strong as an ox, and I'd like to see you make half that wage.

*(Two women, a mother and daughter carrying jugs on their heads, come down the path toward the shade of the well. The mother is blonde and fair-skinned. Her eyes sparkle and there is a harmony in the way she speaks and walks. The daughter is dull-witted and ungainly; in her plumpness, one sees something of the moon, a cow and a loaf of bread.)*

AN OLD WOMAN: The Gailas are headed this way. They're her relatives.

TATULA: Mary Gaila, wife of the dead woman's brother. Sexton Pedro Gailo's real name is Pedro Reino.

ANOTHER OLD WOMAN: By the looks on their faces, they haven't heard the news yet.

TATULA: Hurry, Mary Gaila, your sister-in-law had a seizure and she's lying in the shade alongside the road.

MARY GAILA: Which sister-in-law?

TATULA: Queen Joanna.

MARY GAILA: Ay, Tatula, tell me if she's gone. I can stand the shock.

16                                    Ramón María del Valle-Inclán

CHORUS OF THE WOMEN: We don't know any more than you do.

*(Mary Gaila drops the earthen jar and unties the kerchief on her head. In front of her cowering daughter, she opens her arms rhythmically, as if beginning a primeval, tragic dance. The row of heads, murmuring reverently, is turned toward the weeping woman, who, within the shadows of the fountain, resurrects an ancient histrionic beauty. Atop the crest of the road, she fuses the melodious sweep of her arms with the sensual inflections of her voice.)*

MARY GAILA: Break the jug, Simoniña! Smash it to bits! What a fate! To die like the daughter of a tyrant! Never once did she seek shelter in the bosom of her family! Ay, sister, your own kin forsook you and the dust of the highway has forever claimed your bones! Crush that jug, Simoniña.

AN OLD WOMAN: For weeping and wailing, nobody can touch her!

ANOTHER OLD WOMAN: It runs in the family.

ANOTHER: She spouts Spanish like a politician.

MARY GAILA: Ay, sister, day after troubled day on the road, making your pilgrimage through this vale of tears! Ay, sister, how you shunned your family! And how you scorned me, sister! Ay, sister, the serpents' tongues had poisoned you!

TATULA: When the bosom of the family turns out its children, what worse enemy can there be?

AN OLD HAG: Who can deny the laws of the family?

TATULA: Some can.

MARY GAILA: Not in my heart, Tatula!

TATULA: So it seems.

MARY GAILA: Even when there's not a crumb to eat, I'll take care of the cart.

TATULA: If you keep the cart rolling, it'll profit you.

MARY GAILA: A lot it'll profit me if I have to give up my housework.

TATULA: Then hire someone to do it. And, if that should ever happen, come talk to me.

MARY GAILA: I'll keep it in mind. I'm not opposed to taking the cart. The deceased was my husband's sister, and she doesn't have any closer relatives.

TATULA: The suit will be between you two and your other sister-in-law, Marica Reino.

MARY GAILA: Suit! Why should there be a suit? I'm doing this as an act of kindness, because I'm good-hearted. Who could deny the elder brother this responsibility? If it goes to court, they'll decide in favor of the male, or there's no such thing as legal justice.

TATULA: Well, if it ends up with you, remember what we've talked about.

MARY GAILA: Hold on there! I haven't promised a thing!

TATULA: Of course, you're committed to nothing, but should you want to remember . . .

MARY GAILA: I remember everything I don't want to forget.

TATULA: I'll come by your house.

MARY GAILA: A lot of good it'll do you . . .

AN OLD WOMAN: The cart represents enough to eat on.

ANOTHER OLD WOMAN: Enough to eat on at least!

MARY GAILA: What an evil fate awaited you, sister! May all wicked women learn from it! To die, without confessing your sins, at the side of a lonely highway!

*(Simoniña, pale, full-faced and bewildered, closes her eyes and mimics the wailing of her mother, spreading out her arms before the pieces of broken jug.)*

## SCENE 4

*(The oak grove beside the main road. Queen Joanna is stretched out with her ashen face toward the sky. On her chest lies a cross made of two green branches. Her bare legs and feet—both the color of wax—extend from her dress like two candles. Bastián Candás, a deputy mayor, stands over the corpse and issues orders with a raised hand, as if giving a blessing.)*

THE DEPUTY: You, hooligans, stand watch here! Not for an instant are you to leave the body of the deceased. Under no circumstances is it to be moved until the judge appears.

*(Several old peasant women approach on the run with their skirts flying. Glare of lanterns; blackness of mantillas. Among the old women comes one bent over and sobbing, her face hidden in her hands. Time and again she falls to the earth, arms outstretched, and recites the ritual-like strophes of a lament. She is Marica Reino, sister of the dead woman.)*

MARICA: Where are you, Joanna? Never again will you speak! The Lord took you away, forgetting those of us who have stayed behind! Where are you, Joanna? Where did you breathe your last, my sister?

A YOUNG GIRL: Control yourself, Aunt Marica!

*(Aunt Marica, aided by the women and covered by a cloak, stoops as she walks. When she comes to the body of her sister, she embraces it.)*

MARICA: Ay, sister Joanna, how white you are! Your eyes cannot see me anymore! And your mouth has no more words for me, your sister! Never again will you stop in my doorway to sample my hot muffins! How you loved them! Just last Monday we had some together. How delicious you said they were, spread with lard and mint leaves.

*(When her outburst subsides, she remains kneeling and sobs monotonously. The women are seated around her, recounting roadside tragedies: cases of violent death and stories of souls in agony. When they tire of these tales, Marica Reino renews her loud wailing. Across the grove comes the Gailo couple. The wife has a mantilla around her shoulders; her husband wears a long cape and carries an imposing ivory cane with a gold tip. Seeing them approach, the sister rises up on her knees and opens her arms in a melodramatic gesture.)*

MARICA: How long it's taken you to find out! I've been here most of the day, numbed by the chill of the ground.

PEDRO GAILO: A working man has his responsibilities, Marica. And how did this misfortune take place?

MARICA: Part of the divine plans!

PEDRO GAILO: Naturally! But how did it happen?

MARICA: You ask *me* that? Put the question to your dead sister, she's the only one who knows.

PEDRO GAILO: Gone forever, sister! Lo, these many years of wandering, only to have death overtake you on the highway.

MARICA: I've just made these same laments! God save us!

*(Seemingly more cross-eyed than before, the sexton wipes his eyes and stands over the idiot's cart.)*

PEDRO GAILO: Now you're an orphan, Laureano—even though you can't realize it. Your mother, my dear sister, has passed away, and you can't understand it, Laureano! I offer myself as your foster father!

MARICA: The care of that poor thing falls to me.

MARY GAILA: We don't intend to abandon him either, sister.

*(Mary Gaila, carefree and jaunty, has a provocative sparkle in her eyes. The other woman snaps her head around scornfully.)*

MARICA: I was talking to my brother, my real brother.

MARY GAILA: But I answered you.

THE DEPUTY: That's enough, now.

PEDRO GAILO: What are we waiting for, Bastián?

THE DEPUTY: We need clearance from the authorities.

PEDRO GAILO: There's hardly anything to clear up. As I see it, the victim drank some contaminated water and that's what killed her.

THE DEPUTY: Remember that spotted cow of mine?

MARY GAILA: What a beauty!

THE DEPUTY: Once she was on the brink of death, but I pulled her out of it with boiled gentian. It cost me more than seven *reales* at the apothecary.

AN OLD WOMAN: Poisoned waters do exist. . . .

PEDRO GAILO: Of course they do: and what sick, weary creature can withstand them? They eat away one's insides.

MARY GAILA: Among the rich landlords, there's a lot of complaints about brandy, but never a thought for bad water.

THE DEPUTY: They watch their brandy because sometimes certain people cut it on them with other kinds of fluids.

MARY GAILA: How awful! Watered-down brandy!

*(The judge comes into view, mounted on a silver-gray horse with showy saddle bags and tassels on its blinders. The bailiff walks alongside, like a groom. Kneeling and blowing on their fingers, the old women turn up the flames of their lamps. A solemn chant begins.)*

MARICA: Sister Joanna, if you see my husband in the great beyond, tell him how faithful I was. Tell him I refused to get married again, and not for lack of opportunities! Now I'm an old woman, but he left me in full bloom. Tell him a well-to-do Cuban courted me, and that I never gave him the time of day. A prince of a man!

MARY GAILA: Joanna, wandering flower, you are in the bosom of our Lord and Savior! After all your suffering, you have taken your place at his table! Waltzing with the angels! From this day forward your daily bread will be served with eggs and cinnamon! Ay, sister, if we too could only revel in St. Peter's wonderful stories and tales!


SCENE 5

*(San Clemente. The courtyard, with the church in the background. The moonlight filters through the foliage. Lanterns on the ground spread halos of flickering light about the corpse, whose outline is visible beneath a white sheet. Those keeping the vigil—capes and mantillas—sip brandy in the shelter of the church. The murmur of voices, the footsteps and the shadows, together produce the allusive eeriness of a fairy tale.)*

PEDRO GAILO: From the beginning I said that she died from having drunk from a poisoned well. Man and beast alike have often perished from just such a cause.

MARY GAILA: The little creature must have had the same water because he had soaked his mattress, if you'll pardon the expression. I had to wash him like a babe in diapers. And you have no idea how well endowed he is!

MARICA: Be quiet, sister! You'll not have to bother with such things since I'm going to take care of the cart.

MARY GAILA: Talk to your brother! You can settle that with him, Marica.

MARICA: What do you have to say for yourself, brother?

PEDRO GAILO: A man's arms are stronger for any burden, no matter what it is.

MARICA: The will of the deceased was that the care of the cart be entrusted to me. She herself told me that!

MARY GAILA: Where are your witnesses, Marica?

MARICA: I was talking to my brother.

MARY GAILA: But I was listening to you.

MARICA: Oh, if only the dead could make their wishes known!

PEDRO GAILO: Speak, dear departed sister! Tell us if your intention was to go against the law of the family.

TATULA: Don't expect an answer. Death forges no words.

THE DEPUTY: The bellows breathe no more, and without air there can be neither words nor fire.

PEDRO GAILO: Miracles happen!

THE DEPUTY: Perhaps in the past, but not anymore. God himself could not tear these oxen from the dead woman's wagon.

MARICA: All this yakking just because a brother and sister are having a little disagreement!

MARY GAILA: There would be no argument if you honored the rights of the elder son.

MARICA: We'll consult the lawyers.

THE DEPUTY: The minute you set foot in the lawyer's office, your problems will grow more complicated. Without leaving our own village you will find honest men who know the law.

PEDRO GAILO: What is your advice, Bastián Candás?

THE DEPUTY: If I were to give you my counsel, no one would be satisfied. Since the law is on the side of no one!

MARY GAILA: Doesn't it favor the eldest son?

THE DEPUTY: You do not understand the subtleties of the law.

MARY GAILA: But there's someone here who knows his Latin.

THE DEPUTY: My only answer to that is that the Latin of the mass is not the Latin of the law.

PEDRO GAILO: What is your recommendation, Bastián Candás?

THE DEPUTY: Unless you're willing to follow it, why should you hear it?

MARICA: We're asking for your advice and it's your duty to say what it is.

THE DEPUTY: Had the deceased left behind something other than the poor child, let us say a pair of cows, each one would simply take his cow. That much I know. If she had left two carts, each would have one.

TATULA: Nor would there be a suit.

THE DEPUTY: Now, if she leaves only one, you must divide the responsibility which it represents between you.

TATULA: It isn't a responsibility, it's a profit.

THE DEPUTY: It is indivisible wealth, as they say in court.

MARY GAILA: You can hand down a sentence, Bastián, but you can't show us how to split up the cart! How on earth can somebody wear the same shoe on both feet?

THE DEPUTY: Yet every day of the week I see mills grinding for a different owner.

A LITTLE GIRL: My father grinds twelve hours a day at Andras' mill!

MARICA: So the fair thing to do is divide the cart between the two families according to the days of the week.

THE DEPUTY: For example: You are the two operators of a mill. From Monday to Wednesday one takes the earnings, and the other, from Thursday to Saturday. On Sundays, you alternate.

TATULA: That way there's no dispute.

MARICA: It's your turn to speak, brother.

PEDRO GAILO: What this distinguished neighbor proposes is a recommendation! and it's up to us to accept or reject it. My feelings are already clear, and you should declare yours.

MARICA: I feel the same as you, and beyond that I have nothing
to say.

MARY GAILA: Your words are murky.

MARICA: As clear as day.

THE DEPUTY: Let us see if you and I are on the same track, Marica.
To me, your words indicate that you will agree with whatever
your brother decides to do.

MARICA: Precisely!

THE DEPUTY: And what do you answer, Pedro Reino?

MARY GAILA: As henpecked as *he* is, he'll agree to anything.

THE DEPUTY: Then let that be the end of it.

MARICA: So for three days I'll take charge of the cart and for the
next three my sister-in-law will have it.

THE DEPUTY: With Sunday left over.

TATULA: You see, you've taken care of things without experts.

MARY GAILA: We should celebrate it with a drink. Find the jug of
brandy, husband.

PEDRO GAILO: Don't you see it next to you, leaning up against the
corpse on the stretcher?

MARY GAILA: And we'll let the poor little idiot have some too.

THE DEPUTY: Will he drink it?

MARY GAILA: Will he drink it! You'll see how he cries out for more.
He's saturated with liquor.

TATULA: With all that traveling, in rain and shine, he would have
died without it.

MARY GAILA: Do you want a drink, Laureano?

TATULA: Offer him the jug. Words alone won't give him the idea.

*(Mary Gaila, graceful and mysterious, stands at the foot of the corpse. She fills the glass to the brim and passes it on, savoring the aroma of the brandy.)*

MARY GAILA: Bastián, you should be the first to drink since you resolved the dispute.

THE DEPUTY: To the health of everyone present.

MARY GAILA: Next, the child. Now you can have some, Laureano.

TATULA: First have him sound like thunder. He can do it just right!

MARY GAILA: Sakes alive, look at him! He sticks out his tongue like a whistle!

THE IDIOT: Hoo! Hoo! Gimme it!

MARY GAILA: Who gives it to you?

THE IDIOT: Da ... da ...

TATULA: What is it, Laureano?

THE IDIOT: Hoo! Hoo!

MARY GAILA: How do you ask for it?

THE IDIOT: Shit! Hoo! Hoo!

MARICA: Give him the drink and don't make him swear any more.

MARY GAILA: You have to make it thunder if you want a drink.

THE IDIOT: Meow! Foo! Meow!

MARY GAILA: No, silly, that's the cat.

TATULA: Laureano, be a firecracker, then you can have some.

MARICA: Don't make him swear.

THE IDIOT: Hiss! ... Boom! ... Boom! ... Boom! ... Hiss! ... Boom!

THE DEPUTY: Now he can have a drink.

MARY GAILA: He's a world of fun!

PEDRO GAILO: He's pitiful!

MARICA: The dead woman had him well trained! Just because she was our sister didn't mean she couldn't make money. Ay, Joanna, what an evil fate you've had.

MARY GAILA: Oh, sister, save your tears for the morning and finish your drink. My arms are tired of holding up the jug!

*(The other woman sighs and before drinking the brandy wipes her lips with a corner of her mantilla. Then, in a single gulp and with a look of disgust, she downs the brandy. Mary Gaila drinks the last glass and takes her place in the circle. An old woman commences some story or other and the Idiot, his enormous head rocking back and forth across the straw pillow, cries out in the humid darkness of the cemetery.)*

THE IDIOT: Hoo! Hoo!

A TOAD: Cro! Cro!


## ACT TWO

### SCENE 1

*(Lugar de Condes. An old hamlet. Canopies of grapevines in front of the granaries and haystacks. Atop the walls, barking dogs. The first rays of dawn, fading stars, clear morning voices, the lowing of cows and bleating of calves. Shadows with lanterns come and go in the dark stables, carrying armfulls of hay. Cornbread is being baked in an oven, and the smoke from the wild rockrose perfumes the waking village. Marica Reino, huddled in the doorway of her house, has a bowl of cabbage for breakfast.)*

A NEIGHBOR: Waiting for the cart I'll bet, Aunt Marica.

MARICA: I've been waiting for it since yesterday.

THE NEIGHBOR: Your sister-in-law, Mary Gaila, is overdue.

MARICA: Sister-in-law! That word makes me gag. The thief! Now that she has some money in her purse, she stays out till all hours and spends the night carousing in bars and cheap hotels.

THE NEIGHBOR: She's amusing after a drink or two. By God, you should have seen us laugh at her a while back at Ludovina's roadhouse! The blindman of Gondar, who was three sheets to the wind himself, wanted her to take up with him. She shut him up everytime she spoke.

MARICA: The blindman is pretty sharp himself.

THE NEIGHBOR: Well he wasn't clever enough for her. They sang everything and made it rhyme: the blindman with a hurdy-gurdy and she with a tambourine.

MARICA: Miracles of wine and dissipation.

THE NEIGHBOR: She doesn't even have to buy all her drinks. Many offer to pay just to listen to her wit and the hilarious songs she makes up.

MARICA: That's a new talent I never knew about! It's no way to take care of the poor little idiot! She neither looks out for him, nor changes the straw in his mattress, nor washes his privates. He has more sores than Saint Lazarus. Oh, what a black soul!

THE NEIGHBOR: The cart's turning a nice profit just the same. There's quite a few would like to have it!

MARICA: She makes that much because it doesn't bother her conscience to keep moving, rain or shine, from one fair to the next. With me it's different. Since he's a blood relation I take pity on him and all I gain is a lot of worry. Pulling the cart for a whole day, I never made more than one *peseta*.

THE NEIGHBOR: Well, your sister-in-law makes more than that in liquor alone.

MARICA: My decency ties me down.

THE NEIGHBOR: And when she drinks, she offers some to the kid, too.

MARICA: That's the least she can do! Believe me, he earns it.

THE NEIGHBOR: Brandy can hardly be very good for the little thing.

MARICA: A little won't hurt him. If he has worms, one drink will get rid of them.

THE NEIGHBOR: If he would only be satisfied with one . . .

MARICA: You don't need to tell me!

THE NEIGHBOR: And you needn't wait for your sister-in-law today either.

MARICA: Don't mention that word to me! Sister-in-law! Sister-in-law! I curse the day that good-for-nothing became my sister-in-law! And my brother, so terribly deceived!

THE NEIGHBOR: Pedro sings at funerals and his wife sings in the roadhouses.

MARICA: How true it is that we women are the Serpent's daughters! And that brother of mine, blind to his shameful deception!

THE NEIGHBOR: He sees only the money.

MARICA: Not even that!

THE NEIGHBOR: I'll bet Mary Gaila took the cart to the fair at Viana. She wouldn't miss out on a chance like that!

MARICA: And she's robbing my daily bread from me! Well, she's finished now! I'll rescue the cart and she'll never get it back. Let me tell you a secret: the ghost of my sister came to my doorway. She sees how the child of her sin is suffering, and she told me she doesn't want him in the hands of strangers. She ordered me to take charge of the cart, and she prophesied iron shackles for that intruder, in this world and in the hereafter. If I'm lying may God strike me dead!

THE NEIGHBOR: You must have dreamed these things.

MARICA: I was wide awake.

THE NEIGHBOR: You mean you actually talked with the dead woman's soul?

MARICA: Just the way I'm talking to you! But don't breathe a word of it.

THE NEIGHBOR: I'll be silent as the tomb.

(*The neighbor goes into her house to look after the fire. Another hen, accompanied by her chicks, scratches in the doorway. Three small children, dirty, their skin showing through their clothes, eat breakfast near a fig tree.*)

## SCENE 2

(*A grove of chestnut trees. The caravan of beggars, tinkers and winnowers who every August travel to the fairs at Viana del Prior, stops for a rest. Mary Gaila, delighting in her new venture, is pulling the cart along the main road, bathed in blinding sunlight. She arrives out of breath but smiling.*)

MIGUEL: That cart's worth a fortune to you, Mary Gaila.

MARY GAILA: Not a red cent.

THE BLINDMAN OF GONDAR: Since you started showing the little fellow's privates, you've been making money hand over fist!

MARY GAILA: Money isn't flowing these days.

THE LEMONADE VENDOR: Money is always "flowing," even when you can get your clutches on it. And that isn't very often for those who live by their wits.

THE BLINDMAN OF GONDAR: You don't have to tell us!

MIGUEL: There's no money, and what little there is is under Comrade Meow's spell.

MARY GAILA: You mean Ninth Meow! I've heard of him and his trained dog Coimbra. From what they say, he's a prosperous rascal.

MIGUEL: He's a bastard!

*(Mary Gaila drags the cart into the shade of the chestnuts and sits down alongside it. Her eyes and lips sparkle with playful mischief.)*

MARY GAILA: A flea is crawling up my leg and I'm going to try to catch it. Don't look now, Padronés.

MIGUEL: What are you afraid of? That I'll see your imperfections? Everybody knows your legs are bowed.

MARY GAILA: Bowed and wound on a spool!

THE BLINDMAN OF GONDAR: With you around, there's never any sadness. If you and I made the rounds of the fairs and pilgrimages, we'd pack away a pretty penny! But you won't leave this life, anymore.

MARY GAILA: It's the burden of my cursed inheritance.

MIGUEL: Sure—you abandoned the king's palace for it, didn't you?

MARY GAILA: I abandoned *my* house, where I was queen.

THE LEMONADE VENDOR: You may not like this life, ma'am, but your figure is better than ever.

TATULA: And so's your complexion!

MARY GAILA: All my life I've had rose-colored skin, and that's why they accused me of drinking. When all along it was my clean living!

(*The beggars, swarthy and pleasure loving, laugh heartily in the shade of the trees. Along the road comes a little girl in a Nazarene habit; she is leading a lamb adorned with ribbons. She smiles happily between her parents, a pair of old villagers. Girls dressed for the fair sing as they pass by, together with gangs of young men and ashen-faced pilgrims.*)

THE LEMONADE VENDOR: The Viana fair promises to be a good one.

MIGUEL: The best fair this time of year is at Cristo de Bezán.

MARY GAILA: Those far-off places are fine for you, because you're free to move. But how can I cover seven leagues dragging this cart?

THE BLINDMAN OF GONDAR: You find yourself a partner and you make the trip in stages. To make the cart pay, you have to go to the mountains. Those fairs are the richest of them all.

MARY GAILA: The one place I won't miss this year is San Campio de la Arnoya.

THE BLINDMAN OF GONDAR: And you'll see how well you do, if you make an agreement with me.

MARY GAILA: We're already in agreement—but what *you* call an agreement is sleeping together, and don't expect that from me.

TATULA: God Almighty, Satan really has a hard time getting his hands on you!

MARY GAILA: Right—just like this rascal, who's trying to sample my rosy skin. Get your hand out of there, damn it!

THE BLINDMAN OF GONDAR: Don't run away, Mary Gaila.

MARY GAILA: Strike a match and look for me.

THE BLINDMAN OF GONDAR: Do you want to start the pot boiling?

MARY GAILA: Now you've got the idea!

THE BLINDMAN OF GONDAR: I caught a whiff of sardines! How about combining our goodies, Mary Gaila?

MARY GAILA: The only thing I have is four herrings someone donated at their doorway. But you can't eat them without something to drink.

THE BLINDMAN OF GONDAR: Feel my knapsack. There's something good inside.

MARY GAILA: You faker! You take care of yourself as if you were a parish priest.

*(Mary Gaila, her arms uncovered and her curls held in place by a flowered scarf, lights some branches. The flames of the fire sing as they lick upward. The smoke fills the air with the smell of laurel and sardines, the odor of bitter wine and sour cornbread. A venerable old man, who seemed to be sleeping, sits up slowly. His chest is covered with rosaries and he has a pilgrim's cloak over his shoulders.)*

THE PILGRIM: How sorry I am, Christians, not to have anything to offer.

MARY GAILA: Your knapsack looks full to me.

THE PILGRIM: Nothing but my penitence.

THE BLINDMAN OF GONDAR: A ham hock!

THE PILGRIM: The rock where I rest my head at night.

*(He opens the sack and pulls out a river stone with a round, polished depression, the mark of long penitent nights. Mary Gaila feels a joyful compassion at the sight of that prodigy.)*

MARY GAILA: You're in luck. Come over here and we'll divide what we have between the three of us.

THE PILGRIM: Glory be to God!

MARY GAILA: Yea! Glory to him forever!

*(Mary Gaila pulls the cooking sardines from the fire and puts them in a pewter bowl. Then she takes the bread and the wineskin from the Blindman's knapsack and makes a place for the Pilgrim beside the mended cape, which serves as a tablecloth. The Blindman laughs slyly and sniffs his sardine sandwich. While the others talk he cocks his ear.)*

THE BLINDMAN OF GONDAR: His headrest may be solid rock, but his teeth are even harder. Penitence by sleeping badly is one thing, but when it comes to eating badly, to hell with sainthood!

THE PILGRIM: I've gone three days without eating.

THE BLINDMAN OF GONDAR: Indigestion?

THE PILGRIM: Penitence!

THE BLINDMAN OF GONDAR: We're old hands at that little game, my friend.

*(The Pilgrim accepts these remarks with an angelic expression on his face, and the Blindman, after sweetening his gullet with another drink, laughs again. Miguel Padronés, mending an umbrella in the same shady grove, winks maliciously and whistles a tune. A pair of three-cornered hats, black and dusty, penetrates the shade where the gang of vagabonds is taking a siesta. The talking ceases when they see the pair arrive. Two Civil Guards stroll among them, their faces foreshadowing the impending inquisition.)*

A GUARD: Wasn't there a fellow here who just came back from making the rounds of the country fairs with a loose woman? The "Polish Count."

THE BLINDMAN OF GONDAR: Around here we don't have anything to do with such important people.

THE OTHER GUARD: That's the name he's wanted by.

THE BLINDMAN OF GONDAR: Well, he'll change his name easier than his skin.

MIGUEL: In what profession is this individual engaged, officers?

A GUARD: In the worst ones there are! And I'm surprised that you people don't know him.

THE BLINDMAN OF GONDAR: Some travel about the world with honor, and others without it.

MARY GAILA: The officers should be well aware of that.

THE OTHER GUARD: Just to make sure about you people I ought to put you all behind bars for a while. Be careful what you do, because we're on to you.

MARY GAILA: Our lives are an open book, officers.

A GUARD: Well, watch it!

*(The Civil Guards, stern and sullen, their sallow jaws divided by oilcloth chin straps, take their leave, followed by looks of*

*ridicule and trepidation. The leather belts, the rifles and the three-cornered hats gleam nearby in the blinding sunlight of the highway, as:)*

THE BLINDMAN OF GONDAR: Yes, there's no gift like sight! Those two are more blind than we who wander through darkness!

MIGUEL: That could be.

THE BLINDMAN OF GONDAR: I do believe we're both thinking of the same saintly being, aren't we?

MIGUEL: I'm not saying a thing.

THE BLINDMAN OF GONDAR: My lips are sealed.

MARY GAILA: What mysterious language!

THE BLINDMAN OF GONDAR: We understand each other well enough.

MIGUEL: Meow!

*(The young rake, leaning against the trunk of a tree, opens the umbrella to see how well he has mended it, and whistles another song. Mary Gaila, trying to memorize it, listens with a quiet smile, her eyes half-opened. . . .)*

MARY GAILA: A pretty tune! Sounds like it's from Havana.

THE LEMONADE VENDOR: Comrade Meow brought it with him from the other side of the world.

MARY GAILA: It'll be interesting to meet him, all right. I don't even know him—for three nights I've dreamed about him and his dog.

MIGUEL: Soon you'll see if the man in your dreams has Comrade Meow's face.

MARY GAILA: If that happens, Padronés, then I'll admit that he has a pact with the Devil.


SCENE 3

*(Mary Gaila pulls the cart and gives her wit full rein. To attract attention she beats the tambourine. Bursts of sunlight between sudden rainstorms. Fair time in Viana del Prior. Angles formed by*

*the walls of the Seminary. Booths and large signs beneath the*
*arcade. Green and red bunting, dangling packsaddles and harnesses.*
*A sloping field rises gradually at the side of the Seminary. Cattle*
*resting in the shade of large oaks. Near the doors of the tavern,*
*some cattlemen celebrate a deal with a round of drinks. The gaiety*
*of young boys, the proverbs of old men, stories and liturgies recited*
*by beggars. Miguel Padronés, under the watchful eye of the tavern-*
*keeper's wife, clamps together the two halves of a broken platter*
*decorated with blue flowers. Coimbra, bedecked with bright colors,*
*scampers about in the crowd; and the Palace of the Enchanted*
*Bird appears on the shoulder of the drifter, who now wears a green*
*patch on his left eye. Comrade Meow sets up his stand next to the*
*tavern door and Coimbra does her dance to the music of his flute.*
*The magic bird flies in and out of its castle, chirping its prophecies.*
*With the flowered scarf arranged fetchingly on her shoulders, Mary*
*Gaila sings to the Cuban rhythm marked by the flute and hopes*
*that Comrade Meow will notice her.)*

MARY GAILA:

> To Havana I would like to go
> In spite of all the heat!
> To take an evening carriage ride
> And see the people in the street!

MIGUEL: Do you recognize the man in your dreams?

MARY GAILA: The eyepatch changes his appearance.

MIGUEL: Comrade Meow, have the bird tell this woman's fortune.
I'll pay for it.

COMRADE MEOW: It'll be on me. This woman's talent deserves at
least that much. Colorín, tell the lady's fortune. Colorín, consult her star.

MARY GAILA: I'm destined for misfortune.

*(Colorín, in a green hood and yellow pants, appears in the door*
*of his palace with the fortune in his bill. Mary Gaila takes the*
*piece of paper and without unfolding it hands it to the huck-*
*ster. He reads it surrounded by a circle of attentive faces.)*

COMRADE MEOW (*reading*): Venus and Ceres. The mystery of your
destiny will be revealed in this conjunction. Ceres offers you
the fruit of the earth. Venus offers you pleasure. Your destiny
is that of a beautiful woman. Your throne, that of spring.

MARY GAILA: All the predictions match! My destiny is misfortune!

*(Under the wide grape arbor that runs above the doors of the tavern the figures are silhouetted against the greenish, aquatic light. Having mended the platter, Miguel Padronés joins the group. His tongue has found the mole. His smile is twisted, his arms folded, and his hips undulate as he walks.)*

MIGUEL: Why do you cover up that eye, Comrade Meow?

COMRADE MEOW: Because I only need one to see what your intentions are, Miss Queenie.

MARY GAILA: Try again, Padronés.

COMRADE MEOW: Doesn't the covered eye flatter me? Tell me, ma'am.

MARY GAILA: If you uncover it, my friend, I can compare it.

COMRADE MEOW: Then we'll slip away for the comparison, right?

MARY GAILA: What do you mean by that?

COMRADE MEOW: I mean are we in agreement?

MARY GAILA: If you say so.

*(The Blindman of Gondar, his hat at an angle and a glass of wine in his hand, steps out of the doorway of the tavern. He has a merry smile from food and drink.)*

THE BLINDMAN OF GONDAR: Mary Gaila, come have a drink.

MARY GAILA: Delighted to.

THE BLINDMAN OF GONDAR: It will refresh your voice, Mary Gaila. I heard you singing from inside there.

*(Mary Gaila wipes her lips with a corner of the scarf she wears on her head. She takes the red, overflowing cup from the hands of the sly old man and drinks, gurgling the wine in her throat.)*

MARY GAILA: It's delicious!

THE BLINDMAN OF GONDAR: It's from right around here, too.

MARY GAILA: You appreciate it twice as much in all this heat.

THE BLINDMAN OF GONDAR: Now do you want to try some white that they have from Amandi? It tastes like strawberries!

MARY GAILA: You're living like a king!

THE BLINDMAN OF GONDAR: If you want some, come on inside.

MARY GAILA: What if my head starts spinning?

THE BLINDMAN OF GONDAR: We'll go up to the attic to sleep it off.

MARY GAILA: The same old story! What are you doing without a healthy young girl?

THE BLINDMAN OF GONDAR: Girls are too wrapped up in themselves. A blindman needs a real woman.

COMRADE MEOW: It seems like just the opposite! Since he can't see, the only way he can appreciate beauty is to get his hands on some firm flesh.

THE BLINDMAN OF GONDAR: How's your flesh, Mary Gaila?

THE TAVERNKEEPER'S WIFE: After giving birth it's never firm.

MARY GAILA: That depends on what sort of condition the woman's in. After I had my baby, my skin was tight as a drum.

THE BLINDMAN OF GONDAR: Let's see how it is now.

MARY GAILA: If you want me to go with you, you have to keep your hands still.

COMRADE MEOW: If you leave, we can't make our comparison!

MARY GAILA: You mean the comparison of the covered eye?

COMRADE MEOW: Precisely!

MARY GAILA: We'll get together later.

COMRADE MEOW: Will you wait for me in the tavern?

MARY GAILA: I'll wait there with this friend, if it's not too long.

*(Mary Gaila pats the old man on the back and goes into the tavern, pulling the cart behind her. Before disappearing in the darkness of the doorway, she turns and winks good-bye to those remaining outside.)*

COMRADE MEOW: With the talent that woman has, she deserves something better than this. And what a mouth!

THE LEMONADE VENDOR: You can't get your hands on many classy women in these parts! You must have heard of one who's famous all over the world. Carolina Otero! Well, she's the daughter of the road mender in San Juan de Valga. And the very one who sleeps with the King of France!

COMRADE MEOW: The French don't have a king.

THE LEMONADE VENDOR: Well, with whoever it is who rules there, then.

COMRADE MEOW: There it's a republic, as it should be in Spain. In the republics the people rule. You and I, comrade!

THE LEMONADE VENDOR: But who does the road mender's daughter sleep with then? Because the story's true! There's a girl who doesn't forget her mother, either! She took her off the road where she was begging and built her a tavern.

TATULA: Just think, something like that could happen to Mary Gaila!

MIGUEL: Fantasies of our friend, Meow, here!

THE LEMONADE VENDOR: Your friend, after having traveled most of the world, ought to understand it.

COMRADE MEOW: In the hands of someone who knew how to direct her, this woman could go as far as that other one.

THE LEMONADE VENDOR: That's saying a lot!

COMRADE MEOW: I'm not the first to say it. Colorín predicted it too, and the whole science of the future is in his bill. The fortune-telling bird, ladies and gentlemen! The fortune-telling bird, who will unveil your future! Ladies and gentlemen, the fortune-telling bird!

SCENE 4

(San Clemente. Toward the end of evening, the hour of the Angelus. The cemetery is full of birds and violet shadows. Pedro Gailo, the sexton, strolls beneath the portico, jangling his keys. With his sunken cheek bones and gray stubble, his coloring recalls the yellowish flame of the candles. The last of the old women leave the church and Marica Reino prays above the fresh earth of a grave.)

PEDRO GAILO: Good-bye, Marica! When you go, close the gate.

MARICA: Don't leave without talking to me. Just let me finish off this Gloria.

(*The sexton sits on the courtyard wall and jingles his keys. Marica Reino crosses herself. Her brother watches her approach without moving.*)

MARICA: Well, what did we agree to?

PEDRO GAILO: What are you talking about, Marica?

MARICA: Don't you understand? It's quite clear to me!

PEDRO GAILO: If you don't explain . . .

MARICA: What was the agreement about the cart?

PEDRO GAILO: You know everything I know about it.

MARICA: That's how you let your wife run out on you!

PEDRO GAILO: The Lord will guard her honor.

MARICA: How proud you once were, Brother, and now you let them run over you! What did that woman do to you that you don't care about your reputation?

PEDRO GAILO: You come at me like a serpent, Marica.

MARICA: You call me names because I speak the truth!

PEDRO GAILO: You let yourself be carried away by rumors, Marica!

MARICA: Rumors! I wish they were rumors, because that evil woman and her debaucheries are the disgrace of our family!

PEDRO GAILO: This talking, all this talking! It's beginning to wear down my better judgment! Only the tail end of it is left.

MARICA: That's right! Cast aside your patience now and take out the rage of your disgrace on me, your sister!

PEDRO GAILO: My words weren't meant for you, though they might have been. Evil tongues are everywhere!

MARICA: Someday you'll wake up to what's going on, Brother!

PEDRO GAILO: What in hell's name do you expect me to do? Do you want to see your brother in ruins?

MARICA: I'm trying to keep him from giving in!

PEDRO GAILO: You want to ruin him!

MARICA: At least you'll have honor!

PEDRO GAILO: Honor behind bars!

MARICA: I'm not telling you to kill her. Just give her a bit of a good beating.

PEDRO GAILO: She'll get back at me.

MARICA: Not if you hit her hard enough.

PEDRO GAILO: I've got a weak heart! Consider that.

MARICA: That's exactly what I'm thinking about.

PEDRO GAILO: To achieve anything I'd actually have to kill her. A beating isn't enough because she'd find a way to have her revenge. Think about that!

MARICA: Then split up.

PEDRO GAILO: That solves nothing.

MARICA: That evil woman has you enslaved.

PEDRO GAILO: If I kill her some day—then the shackles will be waiting for me.

MARICA: Oh, you're so complacent!

PEDRO GAILO: You want me to destroy myself, and you won't be satisfied until I climb the steps to the gallows! Vicious tongues are spinning my shroud and calling the hangman down upon me! My fate is sealed! Marica, you're going to have a hanged brother! I'll sharpen my knife tonight. And don't worry. I wouldn't want your remorse on my conscience!

MARICA: You keep putting the blame on me! If your honor is disgraced and you try to redeem it, it's your destiny that's involved.

PEDRO GAILO: Yes—a destiny decreed by wagging tongues. May those wicked tongues fry in the flames of hell! Because of them a good man who walked the straight and narrow is damned. Woe is me! Sister Marica, how can you contemplate my fate so calmly?

MARICA: My heart is sheltered in holy sanctuary.

PEDRO GAILO: Ay, but in what a dark dungeon you abandon me!

MARICA: You were born under an ominous star! Never will I take off my mourning clothes if you carry out your evil idea! Ay, Brother, better to see you surrounded by four candles than sharpening your knife! Vicious backdoor jealousy never gave good advice! Ay, my brother, condemned beyond hope! Defending your honor, you bind yourself in chains! Put away your knife, Brother, don't sharpen it! Don't endanger yourself! When I think of it my heart burns with hatred for that evil woman! Think of it! That traitor disappeared with the cart! Ay, Brother! Why is honor so tyrannical that it forces you to wallow in the depths of the earth in search of that woman?

(In the silence of the courtyard, full of purple shadows, the fragrance of dew and the frolicsome flight of birds, the histrionic ravings of the old woman suggest the first sinister thoughts of a child's sacred innocence. The sexton flees along the road to the village. The bare cassock and pointed cap lend his shadow a diabolical air. He stumbles and looks about him. Lost in the darkness, he lifts his long, thin arms above the prayerful murmuring of the cornfields.)

PEDRO GAILO: You're forsaking me to the Devil! You're forsaking me to the Devil!

## SCENE 5

(A starry night. A dilapidated policeman's hut on the beach, leaning to one side. Outlined in silver, the breakers crack apart against the rocks; the shadows of topmasts swing slowly back and forth; buoys glow in the distance. In the tavern, songs and card games. Mary Gaila arrives tugging at the cart and stops to listen, huddled in the shadow of the sentry box. Bells tinkle softly. Coimbra runs along the beach with her nose to the ground. The black figure of Ninth Meow stands in the doorway of the tavern, silhouetted against the lights of the interior. Mary Gaila hisses a whisper, and in the shadow of the sentry box the two meet.)

MARY GAILA: Let's get away from here.

NINTH MEOW: What are you frightened of?

MARY GAILA: I'm thinking about my honor. If they happen to see us together, what an uproar there'll be.

NINTH MEOW: We can hide in the shack.

MARY GAILA: I don't want you so close to me, friend. Take your arm away.

NINTH MEOW: Threatening me with your fingernails, eh?

MARY GAILA: That's the way I am. And how is it you do all this traveling without a female companion?

NINTH MEOW: I haven't been able to win anyone's heart.

MARY GAILA: Who was it you were courting, that they turned you down like that?

NINTH MEOW: I despise all women!

MARY GAILA: You're mad about them.

NINTH MEOW: Only about one, that's you.

MARY GAILA: How passionate! . . . Wasn't my friend traveling with a good-looking woman not long ago?

NINTH MEOW: You met her?

MARY GAILA: I heard some people talking. What became of her?

NINTH MEOW: She committed suicide.

MARY GAILA: What does that word mean?

NINTH MEOW: That she killed herself.

MARY GAILA: Because she was abandoned?

NINTH MEOW: Because of lack of sense.

MARY GAILA: Or because of too much love.

NINTH MEOW: Hasn't a man ever killed himself over you?

MARY GAILA: Ha! What a charmer you are!

NINTH MEOW: I'll be the first, then.

MARY GAILA: My face isn't worth that much fuss.

NINTH MEOW: You can't appreciate it yourself, of course.

MARY GAILA: What a line!

NINTH MEOW: You wouldn't want to see me dead, would you?

MARY GAILA: Neither you nor anybody else. Hey! Don't put your arm around me!

NINTH MEOW: Are you ticklish?

MARY GAILA: Yes, I am. My friend, better be still, because somebody's coming.

NINTH MEOW: No one's out there.

MARY GAILA: Well, there could be somebody. You've got some nerve!

NINTH MEOW: Let's go inside the shack.

MARY GAILA: Persistent, aren't you?

*(The vagabond gently pushes the woman, who resists meekly and affectionately, leaning against the man's chest. The colored lights of the fireworks explode above the water. The tolling of evening vespers. The sudden light from the rockets illuminates the towers of the Seminary. In the door of the sentry box, Mary Gaila bends to pick up a card in the sand.)*

MARY GAILA: The seven of spades! What does it mean?

NINTH MEOW: That tonight you'll compensate for seven misfortunes by sleeping with Ninth Meow.

MARY GAILA: And if I sleep with him all week?

NINTH MEOW: Compensation for a lifetime.

MARY GAILA: You're proclaiming yourself to be God!

NINTH MEOW: I don't believe I've met that particular character.

*(Mary Gaila stops resisting and enters the shack. Her eyes sparkle and she breathes with the joyful laughter of wine and passion. Embracing the hoodlum, she swoons ecstatically.)*

MARY GAILA: Are you the "Polish Count"?

NINTH MEOW: Forget those stories.

MARY GAILA: Well, aren't you?

NINTH MEOW: No, I'm not, but it might be that I know him.

MARY GAILA: Well, if he's your friend, you ought to let him know that the civil guards are after him.

NINTH MEOW: Don't you think he knows it? He's already been alerted!

MARY GAILA: You're not him?

NINTH MEOW: Forget that nonsense.

MARY GAILA: It's forgotten.

NINTH MEOW: Enter.

MARY GAILA: What'll I do with the cart?

NINTH MEOW: Leave it outside. We'll go in, we'll sin, and we'll hit the road again.

MARY GAILA: A cute ditty.

NINTH MEOW: Let's go!

MARY GAILA: Ninth, you don't appreciate me!

*(The rake bites the woman on the mouth and she snuggles up with a sigh, weak with delight. In the door of the abandoned hut they appear bathed in moonlight.)*

NINTH MEOW: I drank your blood!

MARY GAILA: I belong to you.

NINTH MEOW: And who am I?

MARY GAILA: You're my demon!

## SCENE 6

*(The Gailos' house. In the shabby, dirt-floored kitchen, the wick of the oil lamp is smoldering and the hens seek shelter among the darkened stones of the fireplace. Simoniña, her head occasionally popping out from behind a partition made of reeds and branches, takes off her underskirts before going to bed. The sexton descends barefoot from the loft with an old vestment over his shoulders. He has a blackened butcher knife in one hand, a tankard of brandy in the other. Talking with his shadow, he slumps down beside the hearthstone.)*

PEDRO GAILO: Revenge my honor!—it's my duty to do it! Woman is man's ruination! Ave Maria! If it weren't so, we wouldn't need to follow the Scriptures! The Serpent himself is born of woman! And of woman alone! The nine-headed Serpent!

SIMONIÑA: What's my father raving about? Go on to bed!

PEDRO GAILO: Be obedient and shut your mouth.

SIMONIÑA: You had one too many today, drunkard! Go sleep it off!

PEDRO GAILO: I've got to sharpen my knife.

SIMONIÑA: Boozer!

PEDRO GAILO: An all-night job! . . . To avenge my honor! To recover it! Now the blade's getting sharp! Condemned to my fate! You'll find yourself without a mother and father, Simoniña. Think about that! Look at the edge on that blade! See it sparkle? And you, little thing, what will you do in this vale of tears? Ay, Simoniña, the law of honor will leave you with no father!

SIMONIÑA: The brandy got you started on this!

PEDRO GAILO: Without a father! I'll cut off the wench's head with this knife and, holding it up by the hair, I'll present myself to the mayor: Your Honor, have them take me away. This is the head of my lawful wife. In pursuit of my honor I sliced it off. Your Honor's statute books will specify the punishment I deserve.

SIMONIÑA: Quiet, Father, you're turning my blood cold! Your head is spinning with all those wild stories people tell you! Ay, what sinful souls!

PEDRO GAILO: The woman who leaves her husband, what does she expect? And her debauchery, what does it deserve? The knife! The knife! The knife!

SIMONIÑA: Don't let their evil thoughts overcome you, Father!

PEDRO GAILO: It is written! Wife, your libertinism will cost you your head! . . . and you'll be an orphan and you deserve it, you little troublemaker! It doesn't pain me in the least. I've got my own problems. Look at that blade shine!

SIMONIÑA: Criminal! You're not my father. You're the Devil in disguise. A criminal three times over! What's my mother guilty of? Where docs it show?

PEDRO GAILO: You can't see her guilt! You look at it, but you don't see it! Can you see the wind that rips tiles off the roof? Your mother is under a death sentence!

SIMONIÑA: Ay, Father, let God be the one to pass judgment on her! Don't cover your own hands with blood! For the rest of your life they'll be bloody, remember! And who says my mother won't come back?

PEDRO GAILO: The wayward sheep is the first to be butchered! Don't interfere, Simoniña. Stand aside! Let me grab that wicked woman by the hair! I'll drag her through the kitchen! Go ahead, howl, you adulteress! One minute and to quiet you down we'll stick a stone between your teeth, as if you were a pig.

SIMONIÑA: Calm down, Father. Have another drink and go to sleep.

PEDRO GAILO: Shut up, troublemaker! Why did you let word of this scandal get out the door? Buried under the house, it would never have gotten around. . . .

SIMONIÑA: It'll have to be buried in a very deep cave. Have another swig and you'll feel better.

(In her nightshirt, her shoulders uncovered, she takes the pitcher of brandy and holds it over the drunkard's mouth. He pushes it aside with his hand and closes his eyes.)

PEDRO GAILO: You drink first, Simoniña.

SIMONIÑA: It's brandy!

PEDRO GAILO: You drink—just leave me a drop or two. A wife who deserts her home!

SIMONIÑA: Toss down the rest of it and chase off your evil thoughts.

PEDRO GAILO: The wife is joined to the husband, and the husband to the wife. Together their bodies make a Holy Sacrament!

SIMONIÑA: Well, if it's a woman you want, go look for one. You're not too old or feeble. But if you do find a friend, do it away from here, because no one else is going to rule this house.

PEDRO GAILO: And what if some night the Devil excites me, for he's a tempter! And what a tempter, Simoniña!

SIMONIÑA: Scare him off with your Latin.

PEDRO GAILO: And if he entices me to sin with you?

SIMONIÑA: You *are* the Devil!

PEDRO GAILO: Cover up your shoulders. Sin is hidden inside me.

SIMONIÑA: Drink and go to sleep.

PEDRO GAILO: What round legs you have, Simoniña!

SIMONIÑA: When you're as fat as I am all over, your legs are hardly going to be skinny.

PEDRO GAILO: You're so white!

SIMONIÑA: Don't look at things you shouldn't.

PEDRO GAILO: Put on a slip and let's go and explore the cave.

SIMONIÑA: The same old madness all over again?

PEDRO GAILO: My head's killing me!

SIMONIÑA: Go on to bed.

PEDRO GAILO: To what bed, sweetie? I'm not going to bed unless you come with me.

SIMONIÑA: Then put down the knife. That's a good one, our going to bed together!

PEDRO GAILO: Let's go try it.

SIMONIÑA: And you're not thinking about slitting open somebody's throat?

PEDRO GAILO: Shut your mouth.

SIMONIÑA: Stand up and quit pinching my legs.

PEDRO GAILO: You're sweet enough to eat!

*(Simoniña, out of breath, leads the drunkard toward the bed behind the partition and gives him a push. Her nightshirt falls below her shoulder and her braids become undone. She unhooks the lamp and climbs up to the loft to sleep. The confused mumblings of the sexton rise out of the straw mattress.)*

PEDRO GAILO: Come, Simoniña! Come, precious! Since she's putting a crown of horns on my head, you and I will put one just like it on hers. Where are you, that I can't feel you? You're my queen now. If you resist, you won't be my queen any longer. We'll pay her back in kind. How that fiery devil is laughing! He came and straddled my chest! Get him off of me, Simoniña! Scare him away!

*(Simoniña, with the lamp in her hand, listens while crouching on the stairway. The drunk begins to snore, and the indistinct words that mark the beginning of sleep can hardly be heard.)*

## Scene 7

*(Viana del Prior. The tolling of bells. A bright starlit night. A roadhouse outside the town. Stopping there are beggars and peddlers of every sort: grimy fieldhands, common-law farm couples, women from the riverside selling lace, boisterous vagabonds, and sallow-faced invalids who, with blankets over their shoulders and canes in their hand, beg for money to get to the Holy Hospital. Chance has brought them together in that large entranceway, where the only light is from the flames of the fireplace and the melancholy flicker of an oil lamp hanging next to the stable door. Rosa Tatula appears, pulling the cart with the idiot. She arrives at the counter and reaches into her purse, chuckling through her toothless grin.)*

TATULA: Is this *peseta* good, Ludovina?

*(Ludovina—short, red-haired, plump and flushed in the face— makes the coin ring and rubs it between her fingers, examining it by the horn-shaped flame of the lamp. She tosses it once more on the counter top.)*

LUDOVINA: It seems all right. You look at it, Padronés.

MIGUEL: Nothing wrong with it.

TATULA: Give me some change for it, will you, Ludovina? I was afraid it was bad because of the hand that gave it to me. I got it from the Castillian who goes around with the little bird.

MIGUEL: Comrade Meow!

TATULA: That rascal! He's taken up with Mary Gaila. They're watching the fireworks in the plaza like a pair of lovebirds. Since there's such a big crowd around tonight they had me take care of the cart. They're young and they're right to have a good time.

LUDOVINA: They don't have much youth left.

MIGUEL: The tail end of it, that's all. They're birds of a feather.

(*A tall youth steps from the darkness of the patio into the light. He has a half-grown beard and wears a soldier's cape over his shoulders; his discharge papers are displayed on his chest. His arm has been amputated and he begs and plays the accordion with one hand.*)

THE SOLDIER: Mary Gaila is no match for a man like that. The other lady had more class and a better accent!

MIGUEL: The other one carried a baby on her back—but this one has a gold mine in her cart. Comrade Meow will wheel that fat-headed monster all over Spain and make a lot of money.

THE SOLDIER: It's nothing special. Just another freak like all the others you see around.

TATULA: And they're better behaved, too.

MIGUEL: Already Comrade Meow has turned a mangy dog into that horn of plenty, Coimbra.

TATULA: What with the profits from the idiot—or even half the profits—Mary Gaila won't have to do anything.

THE SOLDIER: I tell you it's nothing special.

MIGUEL: It's good enough to show at a festival in Madrid, even! Ludovina, give him a drink on me and bring a piece of paper. I'll make him a hat.

THE SOLDIER: For a head that size, it'll have to be a skullcap.

THE IDIOT: Hoo! Hoo!

THE SOLDIER: You'd make even more money dressed up for a Punch and Judy show.

THE IDIOT: Hoo! Hoo!

MIGUEL: And you'll have it all to yourself, if you ever get out of the clutches of Comrade Meow.

TATULA: Buy him another drink, and watch. With two drinks in him he's a world of fun. Croak like a frog, Laureano.

THE IDIOT: Cua! Cua!

MIGUEL: Want another drink, Laureano?

THE IDIOT: Hoo! Hoo!

MIGUEL: Give him another, Ludovina.

LUDOVINA: That makes three drinks you owe me for.

MIGUEL: Charge it to the soldier there!

LUDOVINA: Long live generosity!

*(Miguel, a sinister smile on his lips and his tongue touching the mole at the corner of his mouth, makes the idiot drink. Half buried by the straw mattress in the cart, he smacks his lips and swivels his eyeballs. His epileptic cries reverberate under the bell-shaped chimney cover.)*

THE IDIOT: Hoo! Hoo!

MIGUEL: Drink, Napoleon Bonaparte!

THE SOLDIER: Paint him a moustache like the Kaiser's.

MIGUEL: I'm going to shave him a crown.

TATULA: What sinful ideas you have.

*(Next to the hearth, an old couple and a pale little girl in a purple habit share their dinner. Potato pancakes, wine, and cherries wrapped in a handkerchief. The girl, dreamy-eyed, looks like a wax figure there between the motionless old couple. The wrinkles are clearly marked on their ochre, honey-colored faces, which resemble those of shepherds in a Nativity scene. Hearing the cry of the idiot, the sad mouth of the little girl blossoms into a smile.)*

THE LITTLE GIRL: Do you want some bread from the party, little Laureano? And a potato pancake?

THE IDIOT: Crap!

TATULA: Look at how his eyes light up when he sees the girl. What a rascal!

*(The idiot thrashes his arms wildly in an epileptic spasm and stares blankly into space. The girl leaves some cherries and pancakes in the cart and sits down again with her parents. She*

*is absorbed and ecstatic. With her purple habit and her waxen hands, she seems a martyred virgin between two old tableau figures.)*

THE MOTHER: Ludovina, don't let them give him so much to drink. They're on the point of killing him!

TATULA: Good Lord!

*(His eyes rolled back, the lifeless tongue protruding from between his blackened teeth, the idiot gasps for breath. The enormous head—ashen, disheveled, slimy—tumbles about the cart as if cut off from the body. Miguel Padronés, stretching open his mouth, curls the tip of his tongue toward the mole and wets the hair on it with saliva. Other silhouettes lean over the cart.)*

LUDOVINA: Give him air.

MIGUEL: Stick him head first in the well, then it'll go away.

LUDOVINA: Tatula, take him outside. I don't want a row in here.

*(With his mouth ever more twisted, he rips at the bedding. Shaking with sudden spasms, his hands snatch at the mended mattress like a couple of claws. The girl and the old couple stand piously, huddled together behind the flames of the hearth.)*

THE FATHER: This would not have happened with the dead woman. She had her faults, but this business of everyone passing him their glass . . .

LUDOVINA: Get the cart out of here, Tatula.

MIGUEL: Stick him in the well, it's nothing.

THE SOLDIER: Nothing more than death!

LUDOVINA: Damn it! I told you I don't want him under my roof!

TATULA: Maybe it's not really death!

LUDOVINA: This will give my place a bad name! And it's all your fault, Queenie!

MIGUEL: After I buy the drinks, I get all the blame.

*(The dwarf has had his last tremor. His baby's hands, the color of dark wax, are clutched together above the ragged blanket.*

*The big bluish head, the tongue between the teeth and the eyes glassy, seems decapitated. The horseflies have swarmed over it. Ludovina has come out from behind the bar.)*

LUDOVINA: I don't want a scandal in this house! Damn it! Now clear out, all of you!

TATULA: I'm going. But everyone had better keep his mouth shut as to how this happened.

LUDOVINA: Nobody saw anything.

*(The old woman begins to tug at the cart; and in the darkened doorway, luminous in the moonlight, appears Mary Gaila. Her shadow, full of elegant rhythms, is outlined against the silvery night.)*

MARY GAILA: To everyone's health!

LUDOVINA: You're just in time.

MARY GAILA: What's going on?

TATULA: Death gives no warning.

MARY GAILA: The idiot?

LUDOVINA: He just croaked.

MARY GAILA: Spades bring bad luck! How could Ninth have known? I'd like to have his powers!

MIGUEL: Where is he?

MARY GAILA: He had to pay a call at the Gentlemen's Casino.

LUDOVINA: My advice is to put him six feet under, without delay.

MARY GAILA: In a churchyard?

LUDOVINA: You're not going to bury him at the foot of a lemon tree, are you!

THE FATHER: Do what's right, and lay him beneath his mother's cross.

MARY GAILA: I'll have to trudge around all night with the corpse in the cart. Damn my luck! Give me a drink, Ludovina. Brandy, lots of brandy! Pour me another—it'll round off my bill. If Ninth Meow comes asking for me . . .

LUDOVINA: I'll know what to tell him. Now get going, Mary Gaila! I don't want the smell of death in my house any longer.

MARY GAILA: Merciful God in Heaven, you've taken away my living and left me with misery. The one who filled my knapsack has left this world! Jesus of Nazareth, you force me to leave the highways, with no other life to turn to! You won't perform your miracles for me! You won't fill *my* oven with bread, Jesus of Nazareth!

<h2 style="text-align:center">SCENE 8</h2>

(*A starry night. Mary Gaila pulls the cart along a moonlit road, through the rustling cornfields. The cuckoo calls. When it stops, the laugh of the Goat Goblin splits the night air. He is sitting atop a craggy pinnacle. A gust of wind ruffles his bushy beard. Mary Gaila recites a charm against him.*)

MARY GAILA:
Moonlight at one o'clock!
Sunlight at two!
Moses' tablets at three o'clock!

THE GOAT GOBLIN: Roo-hoo, roo-hoo!

MARY GAILA: Damn you!

THE GOAT GOBLIN: You really twisted my horns tonight!

MARY GAILA: At four o'clock, the crow of the cock!

THE GOAT GOBLIN: Roo-hoo, roo-hoo! Kiss me on the tail!

(*The scene changes. Mary Gaila follows a causeway which crosses a shimmering estuary. The Goat Goblin, sitting on his haunches in front of her, utters a shrill laugh that makes the tip of his beard quiver.*)

MARY GAILA:
At five o'clock, that which is written!
At six o'clock, the star of the monarchs!
At seven o'clock, tapers of death!

THE GOAT GOBLIN: When you've finished, we'll dance together.

MARY GAILA:
At eight o'clock, the fires of Purgatory!
At nine o'clock, three eyes and three trivets!

At ten o'clock, the sword of Archangel Michael!
At eleven o'clock, the bronze doors swing open!
At twelve, the thunderbolt of the Lord smites the bowels
  of the Devil!

*(Mary Gaila waits for the thunder and hears only the Goblin's
laugh. The scene changes again. A church at a crossroads.
Witches dance around it. A reddish light glows from the door,
and the wind whistles by, full of smoke and the smell of fried
sardines. The Goblin, atop the weather vane on the tower, lets
loose his cry.)*

THE GOAT GOBLIN: Roo-hoo, roo-hoo!

MARY GAILA: Damn you a thousand and one times.

THE GOAT GOBLIN: Why won't you recognize me?

MARY GAILA: You demon, because I never saw you!

THE GOAT GOBLIN: Come with me to the dance!

MARY GAILA: I want none of your celebrations.

THE GOAT GOBLIN: Roo-hoo, roo-hoo. I'll sweep you through the air,
  higher than the sun and the moon. Roo-hoo, roo-hoo!

MARY GAILA: I despise your magic power.

THE GOAT GOBLIN: Do you want me to carry you the rest of the way?
  I can do it with one big puff.

MARY GAILA: I know all about what you can do.

THE GOAT GOBLIN: You've walked all night and you still aren't halfway there.

MARY GAILA: Move aside, Goblin, and let me pass!

*(Mary Gaila pulls on the cart but is unable to move it. It
seems heavy, as if made of stone. The Goblin bellows out his
call.)*

THE GOAT GOBLIN: Roo-hoo, roo-hoo! You'll never reach your door
  tonight. Don't you want my help?

MARY GAILA: What will it cost me?

THE GOAT GOBLIN: Nothing. While we finish the journey we'll do
  a dance.

MARY GAILA: As long as it's only that . . .

THE GOAT GOBLIN: That and nothing else.

MARY GAILA: I've got a better suitor.

THE GOAT GOBLIN: Roo-hoo, roo-hoo! Then trust to your own luck.

(*The Goblin bursts into shrieks of laughter and disappears from the tower, mounted on the rooster of the weathervane. The scene changes once more, returning to the moonlit path bordered by murmuring cornfields. Mary Gaila feels herself swept along by the wind, barely touching the ground. The force of the gusts grows stronger. She is suspended in the air, soaring upward and swooning with sensual delight. Under her dress she feels the jolting of a hairy rump. She puts out her arms not to fall and her hands seize the spiral horn of the Goblin.*)

THE GOAT GOBLIN: Roo-hoo, roo-hoo!

MARY GAILA: Where are you taking me, demon?

THE GOAT GOBLIN: We're on our way to the dance.

MARY GAILA: Which way are we going?

THE GOAT GOBLIN: Over the top of the moon.

MARY GAILA: I'm fainting! I'm afraid I'll fall!

THE GOAT GOBLIN: Wrap your legs around me.

MARY GAILA: You're so hairy!

(*Mary Gaila faints and feels herself carried aloft in the clouds. After a long ride over the moon, she opens her eyes before the door to her house. The full moon, round and bewildered, sheds its light on the cart, where the face of the monster is frozen in the same corpse's grimace.*)

## SCENE 9

(*Simoniña, barefoot and dressed in a nightshirt, descends furtively from the loft. The dark, empty kitchen echoes with the pounding at the door.*)

SIMONIÑA: Someone's knocking, Father!

PEDRO GAILO: Knock, knocking ...

SIMONIÑA: Shall I ask who it is?

PEDRO GAILO: No harm in asking.

THE VOICE OF MARY GAILA: Open up, damn you!

SIMONIÑA: It's my mother, come back home again! She's still loyal!

PEDRO GAILO: I just wonder what misfortune has brought her back to us!

SIMONIÑA: Where are the matches?

PEDRO GAILO: I don't have them.

THE VOICE OF MARY GAILA: Damn you! What are you trying to do, keep me out here all night?

SIMONIÑA: I'm looking for matches.

THE VOICE OF MARY GAILA: I've been out here for ages!

SIMONIÑA: The lamp will be lit in a minute!

*(The shadow of the sexton, long and stark, looms above the reed partition. Beneath the fireplace the lighted lamp swings back and forth, balanced uneasily, and the young girl, her nightshirt falling off her shoulders, slides the bolt on the door. Mary Gaila appears in the moonlight, dusty and beautiful. The cart is leaning to one side, still in the middle of the road.)*

MARY GAILA: You sleep like the dead.

PEDRO GAILO: You can't expect those of us weary from work to sleep with one eye open, like rabbits.

MARY GAILA: What's that you're mumbling, Latin-monger? Why don't you just sleep like that all the time, and never wake up!

PEDRO GAILO: Don't you have anything better to say when you come seeking the forgiveness of your home, sinner?

MARY GAILA: You're giving me a headache!

PEDRO GAILO: I ought to do more than that to your head—slice it off, maybe!

MARY GAILA: Don't play the fool, Latin-monger!

PEDRO GAILO: What's become of my honor?

MARY GAILA: The same old song and dance!

PEDRO GAILO: You've turned into a common tramp!

MARY GAILA: You keep on and I'll thrash your hide!

SIMONIÑA: Don't start fighting!

MARY GAILA: A lot of good your Latin will do us with our bread and butter gone!

SIMONIÑA: The idiot, Mother?

MARY GAILA: Dead and gone.

PEDRO GAILO: So . . . a sudden attack?

MARY GAILA: An epileptic fit. The end of our livelihood!

PEDRO GAILO: His suffering is over, and that's that.

MARY GAILA: I made twenty *pesetas* in the last few days.

> (*Mary Gaila unties the knotted kerchief with her teeth and holds the coins in her hands. When she sees them sparkle, Simoniña begins to wail.*)

SIMONIÑA: The sun no longer warms our doorway! The treasure of our house is gone forever! Ay, he left this life without even a thought for us!

PEDRO GAILO: My sister Marica ought to be notified.

MARY GAILA: Have the girl drop by tomorrow morning. . . .

SIMONIÑA: Good Lord, my aunt's going to have a fit when I tell her! God save us all!

MARY GAILA: You won't say a word to her. You leave the cart at her door and you come straight back.

SIMONIÑA: I have to take the cart?

MARY GAILA: Of course, brat! Of course! The money for the burial isn't coming out of our pockets!

PEDRO GAILO: And we aren't doing any testifying, either!

SIMONIÑA: My aunt will have to agree to that.

MARY GAILA: When she finds the cart in the shadow of her door, she can decide whether she wants to pickle him.

PEDRO GAILO: Since we're all in agreement on this plan, it should be carried out before daybreak!

MARY GAILA: A spark of wisdom at last, Latin-head!

SIMONIÑA: I'm not going near our aunt's house without a handful of rocks in my apron.

PEDRO GAILO: Shut up, you little pipsqueak! She's your aunt, and you're not going to turn against her!

MARY GAILA: If she calls you names, smash the tiles on her roof.

PEDRO GAILO: There's no reason for it to come to that, if you take advantage of the remaining hours of darkness.

MARY GAILA: Correct!

PEDRO GAILO: We have to avoid disputes among relatives. Simoniña, just leave the cart at the door and come back without a word.

SIMONIÑA: My mother could have dropped it off when she passed by, couldn't she?

PEDRO GAILO: These things are for men to decide.

MARY GAILA: Shut up, Latin-head! Don't you think I understand what's going on?

PEDRO GAILO: I didn't say you don't, but men have another way of thinking.

SIMONIÑA: Kill the argument!

MARY GAILA: It's dead and buried. Now get going while it's still dark and take the cart to your aunt's house.

SIMONIÑA: I'm all gooseflesh!

MARY GAILA: Don't be a sissy!

SIMONIÑA: I'm afraid of the corpse!

MARY GAILA: On your way with the cart, now.

SIMONIÑA: I have to walk down that black road!

MARY GAILA: Your mother came that way.

PEDRO GAILO: Do what she says, Simoniña.

SIMONIÑA: Come with me, Father.

PEDRO GAILO: I'll guide you from our doorway, Simoniña.

MARY GAILA: Quit stalling, brat.

(Simoniña hooks her skirt with trembling fingers, throws a scarf over her head like a hood and leaves the house crossing herself and whimpering. She pulls the black cart through the moonlight. The monster's face, ashen and disfigured, has the same contorted grimace. The tiny hands, knotted together on the blanket, give off a waxen glow. Pedro Gailo kneels in the doorway, arms outspread, and escorts his daughter with his words.)

PEDRO GAILO: Do as you're told! . . . You'll be there in no time! . . . Do you hear? . . . Don't be afraid! . . . You have the moon! . . . Hear? . . .

THE FAR-OFF VOICE OF SIMONIÑA: Keep talking to me, Papa!

## SCENE 10

(Daybreak. Rose-colored hues. Singing of birds. From the top of the fig trees the scarecrows reach out with crooked arms. Below, in front of Marica Reino's closed door, two hogs grunt over the cart. The old woman, decrepit and balding, leans out of a window and shouts at the beasts.)

MARICA: Get away! Get away! Get away, you robbers! God save me, the pigs are at the cart! They left it here on the sly! The wretches! Without a word of explanation! (Marica Reino runs from the kitchen, brandishing a broom. Her skirt is unfastened; her breasts, dried up like those of an old she-goat, poke out above her bodice.) Away, you robbers! No mercy! Out, out, out! Poor dear creature, don't be frightened! Don't ever leave me, dear creature! Ay, they ate the face away! Devoured! Devoured by the hogs! Cold from head to toe!

(The neighbors come running at the sound of her cries. They peer out the narrow windows under the eaves of the tile roofs; they gather in the little patios; they step from stables filled

*with the lowing of cattle. With a scream the old witch beats
the meager rumps of her pigs, still grunting and wheeling after
the cart. Serenín Bretal, an old scholar, talks to himself as he
extinguishes a lantern by the stable door.)*

SERENÍN BRETAL: The world is in chaos. Animals turn into savages
and devour Christians.

*(A pregnant woman, surrounded by small children, stands in
the corner of a patio with a sad expression, as of resignation to
a slow death. She crosses herself and spreads her arms out over
her family.)*

THE PREGNANT WOMAN: Holy Mother of God! Holy Mother of God!

SERENÍN BRETAL: You can tell that the creature was out there all
night.

AN OLD WOMAN IN A WINDOW: It would seem so!

MARICA: They brought him back on the sly! Then they sneaked off
without so much as waking me up with a shout or a knock on
the door! This is the horrible result of their wickedness!

THE PREGNANT WOMAN: He answered his mother's call!

MARICA: Look at his body, all cold! Hands and face eaten by the
hogs! It makes a person nauseous, it hurts one's eyes to see this
butchery! You're all witnesses! Devoured by animals!

SERENÍN BRETAL: Animals don't realize what they're doing.

THE OLD WOMAN AT THE WINDOW: He's right about that!

MARICA: It turns your stomach, seeing him ravaged this way! You
were abandoned at my doorstep, little Laureano! Evil souls left
you to die!

THE OLD WOMAN AT THE WINDOW: It's strange he didn't cry out
when they bit him!

A YOUNG GIRL: But maybe he did cry out, Aunt Justa.

MARICA: He would have awakened me.

THE PREGNANT WOMAN: I didn't sleep a wink all night.

THE OLD WOMAN AT THE WINDOW: It's very strange!

SERENÍN BRETAL: But what if he was dead when the pigs started to
eat him? Notice that there hasn't been any bleeding! The cart

would be covered with red! Obviously he died from the hoar frost, always fatal to these so-called prodigies.

THE OLD WOMAN AT THE WINDOW: Find out if he was already dead when they brought him.

SERENÍN BRETAL: You'll all end up having to appear in court.

MARICA: If they're guilty, they won't go free!

THE OLD WOMAN AT THE WINDOW: They came quietly all right!

MARICA: There ought to be a chorus of righteous voices to rise up against this outrage! Who was it deprived you of your life, little Laureano? If you could only talk, dear departed!

SERENÍN BRETAL: Don't make any accusations now, because you might have to prove them later. The child perished of natural causes. No one destroys his own livelihood.

MARICA: Do you mean he died in my custody?

SERENÍN BRETAL: I mean that it was God's will.

MARICA: Then why did they leave it at my door with so much secrecy? He died at their wicked hands!

SERENÍN BRETAL: If that's true, then you should take it back to them. Do as they did.

THE OLD WOMAN AT THE WINDOW: There's a mystery here!

# ACT III

## Scene 1

(*The Gailos' house. In the shabby, smoke-filled kitchen, husband and wife sit huddled, two taciturn shadows. A rock clatters mockingly down the roof tiles. A gang of raucous youths passes by outside, singing this ditty:*)

THE BOYS' SONG:
> Tra-la-la! Mary Gaila,
> Tra-la-la! She made merry!
> Tra-la-la! Mary Gaila,
> Tra-la-la! Did miscarry!

MARY GAILA: Sons-of-bitches!

PEDRO GAILO: Watch what you say!

MARY GAILA: Bastards!

PEDRO GAILO: Don't egg them on.

MARY GAILA: You deserve it!

PEDRO GAILO: Adulteress!

MARY GAILA: Cuckold!

(Again they fall silent. The shadow of an old hag slips along the side of the house and stops to look in the door. It is Rosa Tatula: hunchback, toothless, an empty knapsack and a cane in her hand. Mary Gaila gets up, and in a low voice converses with the old woman. Both step inside. Mary Gaila is singing.)

TATULA: Nothing to say to me, Pedro Gailo?

PEDRO GAILO: We're getting old, Tatula.

TATULA: There's still some life left in you.

MARY GAILA: You bet there is. They say he's furious at me, like an African lion. He even said he'd slit my throat!

TATULA: That's the way men talk.

MARY GAILA: So long as it doesn't go beyond talk! (A deep sigh swells Mary Gaila's bosom. She stretches gracefully for the pitcher and fills a glass, savoring it with eager lips. She steps back and from a distance offers some to her husband.) Have a drink!

PEDRO GAILO: I want to receive the Lord now.

MARY GAILA: Drink out of my glass.

PEDRO GAILO: I want to unburden my conscience.

MARY GAILA: What, you'd drag out all that filth for me to see?

PEDRO GAILO: A dark sin hangs over my soul!

MARY GAILA: Drink, I'm offering it to you.

PEDRO GAILO: My soul doesn't belong to you.

MARY GAILA: Forget your soul! Drink!

PEDRO GAILO: A plague on you!

MARY GAILA: You see how he talks, Tatula!

PEDRO GAILO: Tramp!

MARY GAILA: Drunk!

> (*Black and gawkish, the sexton lurches toward the door. He stops terrified in the threshold, his hairs on end and his arms in the form of a cross. Marica Reino, covered with a shawl, approaches the front of the house pulling the cart.*)

PEDRO GAILO: The world's at an end, sister Marica!

MARICA: I'm returning the gift.

MARY GAILA: You're not going to leave that dead body on my door-step.

> (*Before answering, Marica Reino turns her head: she senses a shadow and a pair of hostile eyes. Simoniña, returning from the well, stands erect in the middle of the road, hands on her hips. At that instant, she is reminiscent of her mother, Mary Gaila.*)

SIMONIÑA: Get that out of here, Aunt.

MARICA: Get out of my way.

SIMONIÑA: Don't try to pass!

MARICA: I'll pass and I'll crack your skull, too.

SIMONIÑA: Help, Father!

PEDRO GAILO: What is this scandal in front of my house?

MARICA: The deceased was your relative, wasn't he?

PEDRO GAILO: Yours too, Marica!

MARICA: He didn't die in my hands.

MARY GAILA: He was delivered to you alive, sister-in-law.

MARICA: Sister-in-law! Damn that word! It makes me gag!

MARY GAILA: Well, spit it out, then! Go ahead! Speak and you'll be answered!

MARICA: Adulteress!

PEDRO GAILO: Seal your lips out of respect for the dead! Banish those evil words in the presence of the corpse!

TATULA: Stop scaring me!

SIMONIÑA: Smooth down your hairs, Father. They're sticking straight up.

PEDRO GAILO: Yes—and it's the one on the doorstep out there who made them stand on end with that look of his! He needs to be buried!

MARICA: And you ought to bury him. But he didn't die with me and the burial isn't my responsibility!

MARY GAILA: Stingy old hag!

MARICA: Adulteress!

PEDRO GAILO: Go on, Marica! Get away from my doorway! Your nephew will have a funeral fit for an angel.

SIMONIÑA: My father is ever so rich!

MARY GAILA: He's a lunatic!

MARICA: Let me by, Simoniña!

SIMONIÑA: You may think you're going to, but you won't get by.

MARICA: This icepick will take care of you!

SIMONIÑA: You witch!

MARICA: I'll rip your liver open!

SIMONIÑA: Help me, Mother!

MARY GAILA: Brat! Let her pass!

PEDRO GAILO: Simoniña, roll the corpse inside. We have to wash him and make him a shroud out of my clean shirt, since he's going to appear in the presence of God.

SIMONIÑA: Did you hear that, Mother?

MARY GAILA: I'm listening, I'm listening—and I'm not saying a word, either.

TATULA: Just don't pick another quarrel. Spend three days in front of church with the cart and you'll make more than enough for the funeral.

MARY GAILA: He won't last three days with this heat.

TATULA: He's been pickled in brandy, hasn't he?

PEDRO GAILO: We'll have to scrub his face, shave off the hairs around his lips and put a crown of lilies on him. As he was still innocent and untouched, he's entitled to the Prayer of the Angels.

MARY GAILA: And what about you, Latin-head—you're going to be the one to say mass, aren't you? Do you think the bells are going to ring themselves?

(Blocking out the light from the doorway in his black, tight-fitting cassock, the sexton gauges the time by the sun, and runs toward the churchyard, his keys clanging. The chorus of youths again encircles the house.)

THE SONG OF THE YOUNG BOYS:
Tra-la-la! Mary Gaila, Mary Gaila!
Tra-la-la! Got in trouble late one night!
Tra-la-la! Mary Gaila, Mary Gaila!
Tra-la-la! An abortion set it right!

## Scene 2

(Mary Gaila and Tatula converse secretly behind the house, beneath the spreading fig tree where the scarecrow opens his arms: a tattered vestment on a cross made of two brooms.)

TATULA: Now we can speak freely.

MARY GAILA: Well, go on.

TATULA: Remember what the cards prophesied for you on a certain occasion?

MARY GAILA: Fortune-telling cards!

TATULA: They predicted offerings of love three times straight.

MARY GAILA: A false prophesy!

TATULA: You read them yourself.

MARY GAILA: My fate won't change.

TATULA: That'll be because you don't want it to. . . . I'm supposed to give you a message.

MARY GAILA: What is it?

TATULA: A message from one who wants an answer.

MARY GAILA: Did Ninth Meow send you?

TATULA: Right the first time. And can you guess how his song goes?

MARY GAILA: I do rather like his music.

TATULA: He wants to talk with you.

MARY GAILA: That devil! How did he react when he learned what happened to the cart?

TATULA: He interrogated everybody there and penetrated to the truth like a judge. You had better know: the idiot died from all the brandy that Queenie poured down him.

MARY GAILA: It would be that thief! And Ninth, what did he say when he found out?

TATULA: All of a sudden he turned quiet, rolling a cigarette.

MARY GAILA: He was faking.

TATULA: You know him, all right! Then he began to drink with everyone, and with Queenie first of all. When he had him good and drunk, he leaped on top of him, shaved off his mole and threw him out onto the road without his shoes. If we didn't have a good laugh!

MARY GAILA: And Ludovina?

TATULA: She died laughing!

MARY GAILA: Doesn't it seem to you that she's played around with Ninth?

TATULA: Yes—she probably has.

MARY GAILA: If she has, she still is.

TATULA: You're jealous!

MARY GAILA: They can do just as they like together!

TATULA: Ninth only has eyes for you!

MARY GAILA: Only *one* of his eyes is for me.

TATULA: His wanting to talk to you proves it.

MARY GAILA: As if one weren't enough! ...

TATULA: Is that your answer?

MARY GAILA: I haven't given you my answer yet.

TATULA: Well, that's what I'm waiting for.

MARY GAILA: I have to think about it.

TATULA: The heart makes up its mind in a hurry.

MARY GAILA: That's what they say. . . .

TATULA: What shall I tell him?

MARY GAILA: Oh, I don't want any of his deals!

TATULA: You're missing a good life!

MARY GAILA: Always on the move.

TATULA: Plenty of money!

MARY GAILA: Burning sun and driving rain!

TATULA: Eating in restaurants!

MARY GAILA: Misfortunes!

TATULA: A queen! Look at these fancy stockings and jeweled earrings I've got here. They're for you. If you'll try on the stockings now I'll take back a description of how they fit on your leg.

MARY GAILA: Do the stockings go up high?

TATULA: Yes—and they're the finest quality. Aristocrats call them cave dwellers.

MARY GAILA: Well, aren't aristocrats witty!

TATULA: What's your answer for Ninth?

MARY GAILA: Tell him thanks.

TATULA: Nothing else, Mary Gaila?

MARY GAILA: If he wants anything else, tell him to come for it.

*(Mary Gaila smiles dreamily, staring at the river, glowing with golden reflections. Along the bank passes a caravan of Hungarians with bears and copper pots. Mary Gaila sings.)*

MARY GAILA'S SONG:
> I'll never acknowledge the message that you send,
> Except to whisper an answer to my messenger, the wind.

TATULA: Ninth wants to talk to you in an out-of-the-way place.

MARY GAILA: So we can say good-bye.

TATULA: To say good-bye, if you don't plan anything else with him. What's your answer?

MARY GAILA: What can a woman in love answer?

TATULA: Will you go where he wants to meet you?

MARY GAILA: I'll go!

TATULA: You swear it?

MARY GAILA: I swear it.

TATULA: Well, give me a drink and I'll be on my way with your reply.

MARY GAILA: Let's go inside for the drink.

TATULA: Wait.

*(The old woman holds Mary Gaila by the arm. The civil guard crosses the road with a man in handcuffs. Watching with amazement from under the fig tree, the two women recognize the Pilgrim with the venerable beard and the stone pillow.)*

MARY GAILA: They always pick on the helpless!

TATULA: Don't kid yourself! That's the "Polish Count"!

MARY GAILA: So that's the one! . . . I took Ninth for him.

TATULA: Ninth's only title is the one he earned making money with his puppets.

MARY GAILA: He's a tricky one!

TATULA: And I'll bet you know his tricks, too!

MARY GAILA: I don't hate him for nothing!

## SCENE 3

(San Clemente. The romanesque church, with golden-hued stone.
The green churchyard. Peace and soft breezes. The sun casts its
youthful, dreamlike tracings on the emerald green of the river.
Ninth Meow appears seated on the wall of the churchyard. Simoniña, kneeling beside the cart in the shadow of the portico, begs
for money to pay for the funeral. The monster's enormous head
stands out against a white pillow, the waxen forehead crowned by
camellias. The deformed profile of the corpse is visible under a
blue cotton shroud, decorated by gold braid. On top of the stomach,
swollen like that of a pregnant woman, a pewter plate full of small
coppers serves as a receptacle for the alms. On the pile of blackish
copper floats a gleaming silver coin.)

NINTH MEOW: How goes it? Making money?

SIMONIÑA: A little.

NINTH MEOW: You people don't realize the fortune you're burying!

SIMONIÑA: You think you're the only one who realizes it?

NINTH MEOW: These freaks are fragile creatures, and they have to
be cared for.

SIMONIÑA: And cared for better than he was!

NINTH MEOW: You're telling me, little girl! Why, even now the cart
doesn't even have a cloth cover or a painting to catch the eye.
And that freak was good enough to take to the festivals in
Madrid!

SIMONIÑA: How they turned my mother's head with all that talk!

NINTH MEOW: Your mother's a resourceful woman.

SIMONIÑA: And not just because you say so, either.

NINTH MEOW: It's no lie, little one. If she had made a deal with me,
she could have left all this misery behind.

SIMONIÑA: My mother cares about her reputation and she doesn't
want to make any deals.

NINTH MEOW: Deals like this one are legal contracts.

SIMONIÑA: Shack-ups!

NINTH MEOW: An understanding between two people who join together in order to make a living: a legal contract. I would have
leased the cart and paid a good return. I could have trained a
pair of dogs to pull it . . . and who knows what else!

SIMONIÑA: Well there's no sense worrying about it now!

*(Simoniña, kneeling at the side of the cart, leans forward over
the stone slabs of the archway and shoos the flies away from
the wax-colored head. Several pious old women leave the
church single file, the aroma of incense clinging to their mantillas.)*

SIMONIÑA: Alms for the burial!

AN OLD WOMAN: What a stench!

ANOTHER OLD WOMAN: It's rotting!

BENITA THE SEAMSTRESS: When are you going to bury him?

SIMONIÑA: When we get enough money.

BENITA THE SEAMSTRESS: Look at the stitching on the shroud! Why,
it's only basting!

SIMONIÑA: It'll do for the maggots.

BENITA THE SEAMSTRESS: Who cut it out?

SIMONIÑA: My mother did everything.

BENITA THE SEAMSTRESS: She doesn't sew very well.

SIMONIÑA: She's not a seamstress, either.

BENITA THE SEAMSTRESS: Doesn't she have better thread than that
to tack on the braid with?

SIMONIÑA: Quit finding fault and shell out a copper or two.

BENITA THE SEAMSTRESS: I don't have any.

SIMONIÑA: Your needle doesn't make much of a living!

BENITA THE SEAMSTRESS: Enough to live decently. Don't you forget
that, to live *decently*.

SIMONIÑA: Not so decent that you avoid gossiping, do you!

BENITA THE SEAMSTRESS: Maybe not, but at least my honor isn't bandied about by wagging tongues.

SIMONIÑA: The rich folks have quite a few things to say about you.

BENITA THE SEAMSTRESS: I may be poorer than you, but I'm respectable.

SIMONIÑA: Oh, you and your respectability!

BENITA THE SEAMSTRESS: That's what I admire most!

SIMONIÑA: Because it's all you've got!

BENITA THE SEAMSTRESS: What do you mean?

SIMONIÑA: That it's easy for you to be respectable. . . .

BENITA THE SEAMSTRESS: In the name of the Father, the Son and the Holy Ghost! Is that the way for a child to talk?

SIMONIÑA: Since I don't hang around with rich people, I don't know how fancy ladies behave.

BENITA THE SEAMSTRESS: I'm going! I don't want to hear any more of your impudence!

SIMONIÑA: You're going without leaving a cent?

BENITA THE SEAMSTRESS: That's right.

SIMONIÑA: It's a good thing everybody isn't as tight as you are!

*(Pedro Gailo, in cassock and surplice, steps from the doorway of the church. The smell from the smoking altar candles pervades the air. In the archway one can see specks of golden sunlight reflected in the shadow.)*

PEDRO GAILO: Damn! What a gossip you are!

SIMONIÑA: They talk to me, I answer.

PEDRO GAILO: You women are all like.

NINTH MEOW: Regardless of how women are, my friend, we couldn't have much fun without them. And don't you complain, because you've got a good woman, there. We happened to meet on the way to a fair, and I saw how well she handled herself and how she took the suckers for their money.

SIMONIÑA: Listen to how they all talk about my mother. And you're too feeble to do anything about it!

PEDRO GAILO: Shut your mouth, Simoniña!

SIMONIÑA: Go on, let the gossips make a fool of you!

*(Coimbra jumps up on her hind legs, wagging her tail and dancing around the sexton, who watches her with a sullen stare. The irreverent Coimbra sniffs at his cassock and sneezes, imitating the cough of an old woman.)*

NINTH MEOW: Spit out that phlegm, Coimbra.

PEDRO GAILO: Damn you!

NINTH MEOW: Shake hands with him, Comrade.

PEDRO GAILO: I'm on to your ways.

NINTH MEOW: Just what are our ways?

PEDRO GAILO: The ways of the Devil!

NINTH MEOW: How they love to gossip, Coimbra!

SIMONIÑA: There must be some reason for that bad eye!

NINTH MEOW: Is that what you believe, young lady?

SIMONIÑA: I believe in God.

*(Ninth Meow spits out his cigar butt, lifts his patch with two fingers, revealing the eye which he keeps covered. Then with a wink he hides it again with the green patch.)*

NINTH MEOW: Now you know there's nothing wrong with my eye!

SIMONIÑA: You must have it hidden for some evil reason.

NINTH MEOW: Only because it's too penetrating. It sees so much that it burns, and I have to keep it covered. It sees through walls and good intentions!

SIMONIÑA: Ave Maria! Only witches can see like that.

PEDRO GAILO: The Devil was expelled because he tried to see too much.

NINTH MEOW: The Devil was expelled because he wanted to understand!

PEDRO GAILO: Seeing and understanding are fruits from the same branch. The Devil tried to keep an eye on eternity, to understand both past and future.

NINTH MEOW: Well, he got what he was after.

PEDRO GAILO: What he wanted was to be like God, and he went blind waiting for the unending hour to pass; the hour that never passes. Had he looked three times he would have become God.

NINTH MEOW: You're full of knowledge, Comrade.

PEDRO GAILO: I study books.

NINTH MEOW: That's what you have to do, all right.

(*Hobbling down the road that runs through the cornfields, the dark form of an old hunchback appears. The vagabond leaves the churchyard, whistling for Coimbra. At the iron gate, he joins the old woman—who is none other than Rosa Tatula.*)

NINTH MEOW: Did you talk with her?

TATULA: And I told her I'd be back.

NINTH MEOW: How did you find her?

TATULA: She's mad for you! She doesn't realize how certain men treat their women!

NINTH MEOW: You mean that one day I'll leave her or she'll leave me? At least she will have seen the world!

TATULA: And plenty of suffering, too!

NINTH MEOW: Are you sure she won't change her mind?

TATULA: Doesn't the Devil keep his flames burning eternally?

NINTH MEOW: She's worth a lot, that woman.

TATULA: Now take the daughter. Twenty years old and she can't hold a candle to her mother.

NINTH MEOW: Her mother's got a way with men.

TATULA: Eating as poorly as she does, who would believe she could keep her flesh so firm, and have the allure of a young girl?

NINTH MEOW: You've got my head spinning, Tatula.

TATULA: You rascal, you!

NINTH MEOW: When did you say you'd see her again?

TATULA: As soon as you send me back and arrange a place to meet.

NINTH MEOW: I don't know these parts very well. Is there a cane-break around here?

TATULA: You're on the right track!

(*The old woman scratches her tangled mop of gray hair, and her toothless gums break into a knowing laugh. The huckster slips off his eyepatch and gazes across the green fields.*)

### SCENE 4

(*The sacred river of Roman times is an emerald that glitters with dreamlike mirages. Bronzed cattle drink along the bank. Young girls as fresh as cherries and decrepit old women—their ochre faces the color of figures in old paintings—are whitening their linen in the sunlight. In the drowsy afternoon, the countryside is covered with a clear, palpitating silence. Miguel Padronés peers over the top of a hedge and, without speaking, winks mysteriously and waves his arm for the people to come forward. Voices in the distance murmur with curiosity.*)

A GIRL: What is it, Padronés?

ANOTHER GIRL: Spill the beans, tell us what's in there.

MIGUEL: Come have a look, it's a sight for sore eyes.

A GIRL: Tell us what it is.

MIGUEL: A nest of lovebirds.

(*Serenín Bretal, like a patriarch, is sowing wheat with his sons and grandsons. The old fellow wears his cap at a rakish angle.*)

SERENÍN BRETAL: Ah, you rascal, now I get it! A couple fornicating!

A YOUNG VOICE: Ho, ho! Let's go see it!

A GIRL: You're a devil, Padronés!

(*At the top of a cliff, covered with yellow heather, looms the black silhouette of a shepherd with his slingshot. Beside him is his greyhound, also silhouetted in black.*)

QUINTÍN PINTADO: If you're lying, Padronés, it won't do you any good to run. I'll whack you one with my sling!

AN OLD WOMAN: Another devil!

QUINTÍN PINTADO: Where's the ceremony?

MIGUEL: In the pasture.

QUINTÍN PINTADO: Ho, ho! Let's go see it!

MIGUEL: Flush them out with the greyhound!

QUINTÍN PINTADO: A royal hunt if there ever was one.

A VOICE: There goes the culprit.

ANOTHER VOICE: After him!

QUINTÍN PINTADO: There's no greyhound fast enough for that one.

A GIRL: Let him go. The man can do what he wants. The women are the ones you have to watch.

YOUNG VOICES: Ho, Ho! Chase the woman!

(*Old men and children leave their work in the fields and come running along the hedgerows. The more daring ones run through the green canefield bordering the river, urging their dogs on ahead. Young girls smile ashamedly; the eyes of the older women burn with rage. Mary Gaila, screaming, runs out into the road, her blouse torn by the dogs' teeth.*)

A VOICE: Who was she with in there?

ANOTHER VOICE: The huckster!

MARY GAILA: You've stolen my honor! Sons-of-bitches!

A VOICE: Bitch in heat!

ANOTHER VOICE: You'll dance in your little undies!

AN OLD WOMAN: Shame of every woman!

CHORUS OF VOICES: Make her dance in her underwear! Dance in her underwear!

MARY GAILA: Too bad the sight can't blind you! Cuckolds! Cuckolds! Cuckolds! (*Pursued by boys and dogs, Mary Gaila runs along the riverbank. She clutches to her waist the shredded*

*skirt, which shows the whiteness of her legs through its tatters.*
*Milón Arnoya, a swarthy giant walking in front of his ox cart,*
*cuts her off and bellows out a howling, orgiastic cry. Mary*
*Gaila stops short and raises a rock above her head.)*

MILÓN ARNOYA: Ho, ho, haaa!

MARY GAILA: I'll smash the head off the first one who comes near
me!

MILÓN ARNOYA: Put down that rock!

MARY GAILA: It's for my own protection!

MILÓN ARNOYA: Put it down!

MARY GAILA: Don't come near me, Milón.

*(With a barbarous laugh, the brute leaps forward and the rock*
*strikes him on the chest. Mary Gaila, her eyes flashing, starts*
*to reach for another; but the ruddy giant grabs her in his arms.)*

MILÓN ARNOYA: Ho, haaa! Now you're mine!

A VOICE: Milón's got hold of her!

MARY GAILA: Let go, Milón! If you ask me for it in private I'll give
it to you. Now let go!

MILÓN ARNOYA: I won't let go.

MARY GAILA: You're a beast! Aren't you afraid your wife might be
shamed someday?

MILÓN ARNOYA: My wife isn't tempted by evil thoughts like yours!

MARY GAILA: Little do you know who you're living with!

MILÓN ARNOYA: Shut up, bitch!

MARY GAILA: Let me go, and some other time, wherever you say, I'll
give you a time you won't forget. Let me go!

MILÓN ARNOYA: To hell with you, since you curse me!

*(Mary Gaila runs from the arms of the giant, her breasts un-*
*covered and her hair undone. The chorus of voices explodes*
*like a skyrocket, with epithets and excited cries.)*

A VOICE: She's getting away!

ANOTHER VOICE: Stop her!

CHORUS OF VOICES: Follow her! Follow her!

QUINTÍN PINTADO: I'll take care of you!

*(He sends his greyhound after her and runs along the bank, swinging his slingshot behind the fugitive. Wooden shoes clatter down the slopes. Mary Gaila wheels to a stop, surrounded.)*

MARY GAILA: You black, black souls! Straight out of hell, all of you!

QUINTÍN PINTADO: You're going to dance in your undies! You're going to show your body!

MARY GAILA: Don't you come near me, Caiaphas!

QUINTÍN PINTADO: I want to see those hidden talents of yours!

A CHORUS OF HOWLS: Hoo, hoo, haaa!

MARY GAILA: Saracens! Devils from hell! If I miscarry because of you, I'll have you in jail!

A VOICE: Don't pull that on us!

ANOTHER VOICE: Dance in your undies!

QUINTÍN PINTADO: Show us your body!

MARY GAILA: Is that what you're after, you sons-of-bitches? I'll dance in my undies and I'll dance naked too!

A CHORUS OF HOWLS: Hoo, haaa!

MARY GAILA: . . . But no one's going to mistreat me! Look till you go blind, but don't lay a finger on me!

A CHORUS OF HOWLS: Hoo, hoo, haaa!

*(Mary Gaila rips off her bodice and steps out of her petticoats, her flesh quivering. A trickle of blood runs down her shoulder. Sullen and determined, full of ancient rhythms, her naked whiteness rises above the golden hues of the water.)*

MARY GAILA: Be satisfied with this!

A CHORUS OF HOWLS: Hoo, haaa!

A VOICE: Have Milón lift her onto his wagon!

OTHER VOICES: Onto Milón's wagon with her!

QUINTÍN PINTADO: Let her dance in her true throne!

A CHORUS OF HOWLS: Hoo, hoo, haaa!

*(The wagon, a mountain of fragrant hay led by bronzed oxen and the red brute, rolls by the verdure of the riverbank, bearing the triumphant bacchanalia.)*

## SCENE 5

*(San Clemente. The silent churchyard, moist and green. The church, with its Romanesque stonework gilded by the afternoon sun. The murmuring of the cornfields. The sexton's cassock swirls along the portico, and near the cart there is a rustle of mantillas. Jostling the sexton as they go by, two irreverent youths run into the church and climb to the bell tower. The bells peal madly. Pedro Gailo jumps with fright and steps on his cassock, his arms held high.)*

PEDRO GAILO: What sacrilege!

MARICA: Worse than sacrilege!

TATULA: It's the brats who just ran up there! Perverted youth!

SIMONIÑA: Crack their skulls together, Father!

PEDRO GAILO: God Almighty, what insubordination!

MARICA: Shameless sinners!

A VOICE IN THE CORNFIELD: Pedro Gailo, they're bringing your wife back in a hay wagon, naked for everyone to see!

*(Pedro Gailo falls to his knees and beats his head against the tombstones. Above, the bells ring on. The clamor of the bacchanal fills the courtyard and the sexton's forehead strikes the stone with a deathly echo.)*

MARICA: Careful! You'll crack your horns!

PEDRO GAILO: Swallow me, earth!

TATULA: What's this all about?

THE VOICE IN THE CORNFIELD: They found her flat on her back with someone on top!

SIMONIÑA: Troublemakers! Liars!

THE VOICE IN THE CORNFIELD: I didn't look at her myself!

PEDRO GAILO: No one looked at her who knows what's proper!

TATULA: That's right! Bad conduct is a private matter.

*(Pedro Gailo stumbles over his cassock and disappears through the door of the church. He climbs to the bell tower, flailing his arms in the narrow stairway like a trapped bird. Once on top, he looks out from between the bells. The ox cart is approaching, encircled by a dancing garland of excited youths. Above, all naked and white, Mary Gaila tries to cover herself with hay. The sexton, black and thin, jumps onto the roof, breaking the tiles.)*

A VOICE: Eunuch!

CHORUS OF BOYS:
Tra-la-la! Mary Gaila,
Tra-la-la! Did her dance.
Tra-la-la! Mary Gaila,
Tra-la-la! Dropped her pants.

PEDRO GAILO: The Blessed Sacrament commands me to await the adulterous woman at the door of the same church where we were married. *(Pedro Gailo, standing on the eaves of the roof, dives off head first. He plummets to the ground and lies flattened by the fall, his arms extended, his cassock ripped open. He appears to be dead. Suddenly he raises himself up and limps through the door of the church.)*

A VOICE: I thought you were dead!

ANOTHER VOICE: He has nine lives!

QUINTÍN PINTADO: Ho, Hoo! Look, he left his horns on the ground!

*(The sexton comes out through the archway with a lighted candle and a missal. He has a crazed and mysterious air about him. With the open book and his cap on crooked, he traverses the churchyard and comes up to the cart of the sensual triumph. As if to receive him, the nude woman jumps down onto the road, covering her sex. The sexton extinguishes the flame over her crossed hands and strikes them with the book.)*

PEDRO GAILO: He that is without sin among you, let him cast the first stone!

VOICES: Complacent cuckold!

OTHER VOICES: No balls!

*(Jeers sail through the air like confetti. Stones fly. A bonfire of waving arms surrounds the couple. Angry, arrogant tongues explode; even the blast of a popular Hebrew swearword passes overhead.)*

AN OLD WOMAN: A disgrace to manhood!

*(The sexton turns with a pious gesture, and squinting at the open missal, recites the radiant prayer in Latin.)*

THE SEXTON'S LATIN PRAYER:
> Qui sine peccato est vestrum,
> primus in illan lapidem mittat.

*(The sexton hands the extinguished candle to the naked woman and leads her by the hand across the courtyard, over the tombstones. . . . The Latin works a miracle! A holy and liturgical spirit stirs their conscience and quells the savage fire in their faces. The old childlike souls breathe an air of eternal life. Some, awed, slip out of sight, while others counsel wisdom. The Latin words, with their enigmatic, sacred reverberations, descend from the heaven of miracles.)*

SERENÍN BRETAL: Let's clear out of here!

QUINTÍN PINTADO: I'm going too. I left the cattle unguarded.

MILÓN ARNOYA: And what if this gets us in trouble with the law?

SERENÍN BRETAL: It won't come to anything.

MILÓN ARNOYA: And what if it should?

SERENÍN BRETAL: Not a word to the police, and don't admit anything!

*(The golden hues of the setting sun float above the churchyard. Mary Gaila, serene and nude, steps barefoot over the tombstones, perceiving the rhythms of life behind the veil of her tears. As she penetrates the shadows of the portico, the idiot's enormous head, crowned with camellias, appears like the head of an angel. Led by her husband's hand, the adulteress takes refuge in the church, a sanctuary wreathed in a resplendent religious prestige which, in that superstitious world of rustic souls, is conjured up by the incomprehensible Latin of the DIVINE WORDS.)*

# THE SHOEMAKER'S PRODIGIOUS WIFE

A Violent Farce in Two Acts and a Prologue

by FEDERICO GARCÍA LORCA

TRANSLATED BY JAMES GRAHAM-LUJAN AND RICHARD L. O'CONNELL

THE EARLIER WORKS of Federico García Lorca (1899–1936) are characterized, almost alternately, by a dual orientation. On the one hand, there is the evocation of the rich vein of traditional Spanish myth and literature; on the other, there is the impact of a much more international style, that of French Surrealism, which seems to have begun to influence the young poet-playwright around the mid-1920's. Side by side with such creations as the *Romancero Gitano* (*Gypsy Ballads*, 1928) appear works such as the poem dedicated to his new friend, and collaborator in stage design, the "Oda a Salvador Dalí" ("Ode to Salvador Dalí," 1929), and the even more purely Surrealistic *Poeta en Nueva York* (*Poet in New York*, 1930). The early works, which almost alternately relate to opposite poles of this dual preoccupation, remind us that the poet was still young; he had not yet managed to mingle inextricably the two streams as successfully as he would only a very few years later.

*The Shoemaker's Prodigious Wife*, begun in 1926, but written largely during Lorca's residence in New York City (1929–30), is, in a sense, the more balanced counterpart of such theatrical works as the tripartite *Teatro Breve* (*Pocket Theatre*, 1926–28)* or the long drama *Así Que Pasen Cinco Años* (*And Thus Five Years Pass*, also 1929–30), with their concentration of Surrealistic wit and nightmare. The play employs the well-known plot of classical comedy, Spanish comedy particularly, in which a young girl is wedded to a crusty, seemingly unappreciative, but certainly fiercely jealous, husband. A plot that appears in Lope de Vega, Alarcón, the short plays of Cervantes, and in a host of lesser dramatists, it anchors the play firmly in traditional realms. At the same time, Lorca incorporates features of dramatic modernism, even Surrealism. The Prologue is one of the most outspoken statements of Lorca's aesthetics in all his works. It warns us that "the poet . . . long ago . . . leapt that barbed fence of fear that authors have of the theatre," but it also notes that: "The author has preferred to set the dramatic example in the live rhythm of an ordinary little shoemaker's wife." Lorca's

---

* It was originally intended that the three short skits of this series also be included here; unfortunately, at the last minute publication rights proved unavailable. A copy of the translation of *Teatro Breve* as *Pocket Theatre* by M.B. is on file with Lorca's American publisher.

fusion of fact and fantasy is echoed in the dilemma of the wife herself, who is ever "fighting with the reality which encircles her and with fantasy when it becomes visible reality." This speech, spoken, as in recently presented works by Pirandello, by "The Author" himself, is ended as the wife insistently shouts "I want to come out!"—thus at the outset placing the wife, however earthly, in the framework of the fantastic. The stagecraft of the play, with its operatic flights into song, its symbolic use of colors, the formalized, choruslike jibes of the wife's neighbors, and other plainly nonrealistic augmentations of the atmosphere, produce a result as rich and engaging as any in Lorca's theatre, and one of his three or four most perfect masterpieces.

M. B.

Let's have ja ~le~o, . ja ~ le ~ o! ~~~~~~~Now that we're

through with the ri ~ ot, let's~~~~have shoot~ing, why be

qui ~et, let's~~~~have shoot ~ing, why be qui~et!~~~~

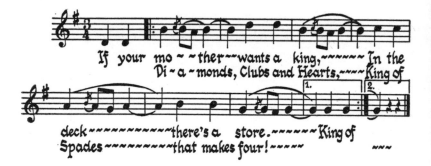

If your mo ~ ~ther~~wants a king,~~~~~~In the
Di ~ a ~monds, Clubs and Hearts,~~~~King of

deck~~~~~~~~~~~~there's a store.~~~~~~King of
Spades ~~~~~~~~~that makes four!~~~~~

### Polka

But-ter ~fly of the breez~es, wind crea-ture so love ~
don't wish to lin~ger, to stay there an in ~

ly; but-ter-fly of the breez~es, wind crea-ture so love ~ly; but-ter-
stant. But you don't wish to lin~ger, to stay there an in~stant. But-ter

fly of the breez~es, so green, so gold~en, a can-dle's flame; but-ter-
fly of the breez~es, so green, so gold~en, a can-dle's flame; but-ter~

1.

fly of the breez~es, I beg you stay there, stay there, stay there! But you
fly of the breez~es, I beg you stay there, stay there, stay

2.

there! I beg you, stay there! But-ter-fly, oh, please, are you there?

Allegretto e ben marcato

Mis~tress Cob ~bler, Mis~tress Cob~bler, since her
Turned her house in~to a tav~ ern where the

hus~band ran a ~ way, since her hus~band ran a ~ way,
men go night and day, where the men go night and day.

# Characters

SHOEMAKER'S WIFE
NEIGHBOR IN RED (Red Neighbor)
NEIGHBOR IN PURPLE (Purple Neighbor)
NEIGHBOR IN GREEN (Green Neighbor)
NEIGHBOR IN BLACK (Black Neighbor)
NEIGHBOR IN YELLOW (Yellow Neighbor)
FIRST OVER-PIOUS WOMAN
SECOND OVER-PIOUS WOMAN
SACRISTAN'S WIFE
THE AUTHOR
THE SHOEMAKER
THE BOY
THE MAYOR
DON BLACKBIRD
YOUTH WITH SASH (Sash Youth)
YOUTH WITH HAT (Hat Youth)
NEIGHBORS, OVER-PIOUS PEOPLE, PRIESTS AND VILLAGERS

(*Gray Curtain.*)

(*The Author appears. He enters rapidly. He carries a letter in his hand.*)

THE AUTHOR: Worthy spectators . . . (*Pause.*) No, not "worthy spectators"; merely "spectators." And not because the author doesn't consider the public worthy—quite the contrary. It's only that behind that word "worthy" there seems to be a slight tremor of fear and a sort of plea that the audience should be generous with the mimicking of the actors and the workmanship of the playwright's genius. The poet does not ask benevolence, but attention, since long ago he leaped that barbed fence of fear that authors have of the theatre. Because of this absurd fear, and because the theatre on many occasions is run for financial reasons, poetry retires from the stage in search of other surroundings where people will not be shocked at the fact that a tree, for example, should become a puff of smoke, or that three fishes through their love for a hand and a word should be changed into three million fishes to feed the hunger of a multitude. The author has preferred to set the dramatic example in the live rhythm of an ordinary little shoemaker's wife. Everywhere walks and breathes the poetic creature that the author has dressed as a shoemaker's wife with the air of a refrain or a simple ballad, and the audience should not be surprised if she appears violent or takes bitter attitudes because she is ever fighting, fighting with the reality which encircles her and with fantasy when it becomes visible reality.

(*Shouts of the Shoemaker's Wife are heard: "I want to come out!"*)

I'm hurrying! Don't be so impatient to come out; you're not going to wear a dress with a long train and matchless plumes; but just a torn dress; do you hear? The dress of a shoemaker's wife.

(*Voice of the Shoemaker's Wife is heard: "I want to come out!"*)

Silence!

(*The curtain is drawn and the darkened stage appears.*)

85

Every day in the cities it dawns like this, and the audience forgets its half-world of dreams to go to market just as you enter your house, prodigious little shoemaker's wife.

(*The light is increasing.*)

Let's start! You come in from the street.

(*Voices arguing are heard. To the audience.*)

Good evening. (*He takes off his tall silk hat and it becomes illuminated with a green light from within. The Author tips it over and a gush of water falls from it. The Author looks at the audience a bit embarrassedly, and retires backward, with great irony.*) I beg your pardon.

(*Exit.*)


## ACT ONE


(*The Shoemaker's house. Shoemaker's bench and tools. A completely white room. Large window and door. The backdrop seen through the large window is a street, also white with some small doors and windows in gray. To the right and left, doors. All this scene shall have an air of optimism and exalted happiness to the smallest details. The soft orange light of afternoon pervades the scene.*

*When the curtain rises the Shoemaker's Wife enters furiously from the street and pauses at the door. She is dressed in angry green, and wears her hair drawn back tight and adorned with two big roses. She has an aggressive and a sweet air at the same time.*)

WIFE: Be quiet, long tongue! Ugly Kate! Because if I've done it . . . if I've done it—it's because I wanted to. If you hadn't run into your house I would have dragged you along, you dusty little snake; and I say this so that all those who are behind the windows may hear me. For it's better to be married to an old man than to a one-eyed one as you are. I don't want any more conversation—not with you nor with you—nor with any one— nor with any one! (*Enters, slamming door.*) I knew that with that kind of people one couldn't talk even for a second . . . but I'm to blame—I and I . . . because I ought to stay in my house with . . . I almost don't want to believe it, with my husband. If anybody had told me, blonde and dark-eyed—and what a good combination that is, with this body and these colors so very very beautiful—that I was going to marry a . . . I would have pulled my hair out. (*She weeps. There is a knock at the door.*) Who is there?

(*Another knock at the door. No answer. Furiously.*) Who's there?

BOY (*fearfully, outside*): A friend.

WIFE (*opening*): Is it you? (*Sweetly and touched.*)

BOY: Yes, Mrs. Shoemaker. Were you crying?

WIFE: No. It's just that one of those mosquitoes that go ping——ng bit me in the eye.

BOY: Do you want me to blow in it?

WIFE: No, my child, it's gone. (*She caresses him.*) And what is it you want?

BOY: I brought these patent-leather shoes, which cost five dollars, for your husband to repair. They are my older sister's, the one who has the nice skin and wears two bow-knots because she's got two—one for one day and the other for the other—at her waist.

WIFE: Leave them here. They'll be repaired sometime.

BOY: My mother says you must be careful not to hammer them too much because patent leather is very delicate—so the patent leather won't be hurt.

WIFE: Tell your mother my husband knows what he's doing. And that she wishes she knew how to season a good dish with pepper and bay the way my husband knows how to repair shoes.

BOY: (*his face puckering*): Don't be angry at me; it's not my fault. And I study my grammar very well every day.

WIFE (*sweetly*): My child! My treasure! I'm not angry at you! (*Kisses him.*) Take this doll. Do you like it. Well, take it.

BOY: I'll take it because, well—since I know you're not going to have any children. . . .

WIFE: Who told you that?

BOY: My mother was talking about it the other day. She was saying: "The shoemaker's wife won't have any children," and her friend Rafaela and my sisters laughed.

WIFE: (*nervously*): Children? Maybe I'll have better-looking ones than all of them—and with more courage and honor—because your mother—I think you ought to know this . . .

BOY: You take the doll. I don't want it!

WIFE (*changing*): No, no—you keep it, son. This has nothing to do with you!

(*The Shoemaker appears at left. He wears a velvet suit with silver buttons, short trousers and a red tie. He goes toward his bench.*)

WIFE: May God help you!

BOY (*frightened*): Good health to you! Till I see you again! Congratulations! *Deo gratias!* (*Goes running to the street.*)

WIFE: Good-bye, child. If I had burst before I was born I wouldn't be suffering these trials and tribulations. Oh, money, money! The one who invented you should have been left without hands or eyes.

SHOEMAKER (*at the bench*): Woman, what are you saying?

WIFE: Something that doesn't concern you!

SHOEMAKER: Nothing concerns me. I know I must control myself.

WIFE: I also have to control myself. . . . Just think of it: I'm only eighteen years old.

SHOEMAKER: And I—fifty-three. That's why I hush up and am not angry with you! I know too much! I work for you, and may God's will be done. . . .

WIFE (*her back is to her husband, but she turns and advances tenderly, moved*): Not that, my child. Don't say that!

SHOEMAKER: But, oh, if I were only forty years old, or forty-five even! (*Hammers the shoe furiously.*)

WIFE (*aroused*): Then I would be your servant; isn't that so? One can't be good. What about me? Am I not worth anything?

SHOEMAKER: Woman, control yourself.

WIFE: Aren't my freshness and my face worth all the money in this world?

SHOEMAKER: Woman—the neighbors will hear you!

WIFE: Cursed be the hour, cursed be the hour, when I listened to my friend Manuel.

SHOEMAKER: Would you like me to make you some lemonade?

WIFE: Oh, fool, fool, fool! (*Strikes her forehead.*) With as good suitors as I've had.

SHOEMAKER (*trying to soften her*): That's what people say.

WIFE: People? It's known everywhere. The best in these parts. But the one I liked best of all of them was Emiliano. You knew him, Emiliano—the one who used to ride a black mare covered with tassels and little mirrors, carrying a willow wand in his hand, with his copper spurs shining. And what a cape he had for winter! What sweeps of blue broadcloth and what trimmings of silk!

SHOEMAKER: I had one like that, too; they're lovely capes.

WIFE: You? What could you have had? Now why do you fool yourself? A shoemaker has never in his life worn such clothes.

SHOEMAKER: But, woman, can't you see? . . .

WIFE (*interrupting him*): And then I had another suitor.

(*The Shoemaker hammers the shoe furiously.*)

He was rather young. . . . He was maybe eighteen years old. That can be said very quickly! Eighteen years!

(*The Shoemaker twists uncomfortably.*)

SHOEMAKER: I was eighteen once, too.

WIFE: You never in your life were eighteen years old! But he was. And such things as he used to say to me. Look. . . .

SHOEMAKER (*hammering furiously*): Will you be quiet? You're my wife whether you like it or not—and I'm your husband. You were perishing without a dress or a home. Why did you love me? Deceiver! Deceiver! Deceiver!

WIFE (*rising*): Shut up! Don't make me speak more than is wise— and get to your duty. I can hardly believe it!

(*Two neighbors wearing mantillas cross the window smiling.*)

Who could have told me, old bag-o'bones, that you would repay me like this? Hit me if you want. Go on, throw the hammer at me!

SHOEMAKER: Oh, woman, don't raise such a row. Look, the people are coming—oh, my God!

(*The two neighbors cross again.*)

WIFE: I've gone below my station. Fool, fool, fool! Cursed be my friend Manuel. Cursed be the neighbors. Fool, fool, fool. (*Leaves, striking her forehead.*)

SHOEMAKER (*looking in a mirror, counting his wrinkles*): One, two, three, four . . . and a thousand. (*Puts up the mirror.*) But it serves me right, yes sir. Because, let's see: why did I marry? I should have known after reading so many novels that men like all women—but women don't like all men. And I was so well off! My sister, my sister is to blame. My sister who kept saying: "You're going to be left alone." You're going to be this and that. And that was my undoing. May lightning strike my sister, may she rest in peace!

(*Outside, voices are heard.*)

What could that be?

NEIGHBOR IN RED (*at the window, accompanied by her two daughters dressed in the same color. With great spirit*): Good afternoon!

SHOEMAKER (*scratching his head*): Good afternoon.

RED NEIGHBOR: Tell your wife to come out here. Girls, will you please stop crying! Tell her to come out here and we'll see if she gossips as much to my face as behind my back!

SHOEMAKER: Oh, neighbor of my soul, don't raise a row, by the little nails of Our Lord! What do you want me to do? Understand my situation; all my life fearing marriage . . . because marriage is a very serious thing, and then, finally, what you can see.

RED NEIGHBOR: You poor man! How much better off you would have been if you had married with people of your own kind, these girls, for example, or others of the village.

SHOEMAKER: My home is not a home, it's a madhouse!

RED NEIGHBOR: You tear my soul! As good a name as you've had all your life.

SHOEMAKER (*looking to see if his wife is coming*): Day before yesterday, she carved up the ham that we had saved for Christmas —and we ate it all. Yesterday we ate nothing but egg soup and parsley; well then, because I protested over that, she made me drink three glasses of unboiled milk one right after the other.

RED NEIGHBOR: How brutal!

SHOEMAKER: And so, little neighbor of my heart, I would be grateful to you with my whole soul, if you would leave.

RED NEIGHBOR: Oh, if your sister still lived! Now there was a . . .

SHOEMAKER: You see . . . and on your way you can take these shoes that are ready.

(*The Shoemaker's Wife looks in at the door on the left where she watches the scene unnoticed from behind the curtain.*)

RED NEIGHBOR (*ingratiatingly*): How much are you going to charge me for these? Times are always getting harder.

SHOEMAKER: Whatever you want. Whatever isn't too hard on either of us . . .

RED NEIGHBOR (*nudging her daughters with her elbow*): Are two pesetas all right?

SHOEMAKER: I leave that to you!

RED NEIGHBOR: Oh, well, I'll give you one then. . . .

WIFE (*entering furiously*): Thief!

(*The women squeal and are frightened.*)

Do you have the face to rob a man this way? (*To her husband.*) And you to let yourself be robbed? Give me those shoes. Until you give me ten pesetas for them, I'll keep them here.

RED NEIGHBOR: Lizard! Lizard!

WIFE: Be very careful what you're saying!

GIRLS: Oh, let's go, let's go! For heaven's sake!

RED NEIGHBOR: It serves you right, having such a wife! Make the most of it!

(*They go out quickly. The Shoemaker shuts the door and the window.*)

SHOEMAKER: Listen to me a moment....

WIFE (*mulling*): Lizard . . . Lizard. What? What? What? . . . What are you going to tell me?

SHOEMAKER: Look, my child: all my life it has been my constant concern to avoid rows. (*The Shoemaker is constantly swallowing.*)

WIFE: Have you got the courage to tell me I cause a row when I come out to defend your interests?

SHOEMAKER: I don't say any more, except that I have fled from rows just as salamanders do from cold water.

WIFE (*quickly*): Salamanders! Oh, how nasty!

SHOEMAKER (*armed with patience*): They have provoked me; they have, at times, even insulted me, and not being even a little bit a coward, I would swallow all that for fear of being the center of attention, and having my name bandied back and forth by gossips and idlers. Therefore, you're warned. Have I spoken clearly? This is my last word.

WIFE: Well, now, let's see. What does all that matter to me? I married you. Isn't your house clean? Aren't you fed? Don't you wear collars and cuffs such as you had never in your life worn before? Don't you carry your watch—so beautiful with its silver chain and charms—which I wind every night? What more do you want? Because I will be everything except a slave. I'll always do just as I want to.

SHOEMAKER: No need to tell me. We've been married three months. I loving you and you mocking me. Can't you see that I can't stand jokes like that?

WIFE (*seriously, as if dreaming*): Loving me, loving me . . . but (*Roughly.*) what is that about loving me? What do you mean, "loving me"?

SHOEMAKER: You may think I'm blind, but I'm not. I know what you do and what you don't do; and now I'm fed up with it—to here!

WIFE (*furiously*): Well, it's all the same to me whether you're fed up or not. Because you don't matter three whistles. Now you know! (*Weeps.*)

SHOEMAKER: Couldn't you speak a little lower?

WIFE: What you deserve—you're such a fool—is for me to fill the street full of shouting.

SHOEMAKER: Fortunately, I think this will end soon; because I don't know how I have the patience.

WIFE: Today we don't eat here—so you can go somewhere else to look for your food. (*The Wife leaves quickly in a fury.*)

SHOEMAKER (*smiling*): Tomorrow, maybe you will have to look too. (*Goes to bench.*)

(*Through the central door the Mayor appears. He is dressed in dark blue, wears a large cape, and carries the long staff of his office with silver decorations. He speaks slowly and with great sluggishness.*)

MAYOR: Working?

SHOEMAKER: Working, Mr. Mayor.

MAYOR: Much money?

SHOEMAKER: Enough.

(*Shoemaker continues working. The Mayor looks everywhere curiously.*)

MAYOR: Everything's not all right with you.

SHOEMAKER (*without raising his head*): No.

MAYOR: Your wife?

SHOEMAKER (*assenting*): My wife.

MAYOR (*sitting*): That comes of marrying at your age. At your age, one should be a widower from at least one wife as a minimum. I'm a widower of four: Rosa, Manuela, Visitación and Enriqueta Gómez, who was the last one—nice-looking girls all of them—fond of flowers and fresh water. All, without exception, have felt this stick time and again. In my house— in my house it is sew and sing.

SHOEMAKER: Well, you can see for yourself what my life is. My wife . . . does not love me. She talks through the window with everyone. Even with Don Blackbird, and it makes my blood boil.

MAYOR (*laughingly*): It's just that she's a merry little girl. It's only natural.

SHOEMAKER: Bah! I'm convinced . . . I believe she does this to torment me, because I'm sure . . . she hates me. First I thought I would tame her with my sweet character and my little presents: coral necklaces, little belts, tortoise-shell combs—even a pair of garters! But she—she's always herself!

MAYOR: And you, always yourself, devil take it! Come now, I see it, and it seems unbelievable how a man who calls himself a man can't dominate not one, but eighty females. If your wife talks through the window with everyone, if she becomes bitter with you, it's because you want her to, because you have no comeback. Women should be squeezed at the waist, stepped upon strongly, and always shouted at. And if with all this they dare to say cock-a-doodle-doo, the stick; there's no other remedy. Rosa, Manuela, Visitación, and Enriqueta Gómez, who was the last one, can tell you that from the other world, if by any chance they happen to be there.

SHOEMAKER: But it so happens that there's one thing I don't dare to tell you. (*Looks about cautiously.*)

MAYOR (*commandingly*): Say it!

SHOEMAKER: I understand it's a beastly thing, but—I'm not in love with my wife.

MAYOR: The devil!

SHOEMAKER: Yes, sir. The devil!

MAYOR: Then, you great rascal, why did you marry?

SHOEMAKER: There you have it. I can't explain it myself. My sister, my sister was to blame. "You're going to be left alone! You're going to this—you're going to I don't know what else!" I had a little money and my health, so I said: "Well, here goes!" But Lord help us. . . . Lightning strike my sister—may she rest in peace!

MAYOR: Well, you've certainly made a fool of yourself!

SHOEMAKER: Yes, sir—I have made a fool of myself. And now I can't stand it any longer. I didn't know what one woman was like. I say! And you . . . four! I'm too old to stand this hullabaloo.

WIFE (*singing within—lustily*):
> Let's have jaleo, jaleo!*
> Now that we're through with the riot,
> Let's have shooting, why be quiet;
> Let's have shooting, why be quiet!

SHOEMAKER: There you are!

MAYOR: And what do you intend to do?

SHOEMAKER: Fly the coop! (*Makes a gesture.*)

MAYOR: Have you lost your senses?

SHOEMAKER (*excitedly*): This business of "shoemaker, stick to your last" is all over for me. I'm a peaceful man. I'm not used to all this shouting—and being talked about by everyone.

MAYOR (*laughing*): Consider what you have said you are going to do; for you're able to do it—so don't be foolish. It's a shame that a man like you should not have the strength of character he ought.

(*Through the door at the left the Shoemaker's Wife appears, powdering herself with a pink powder puff and accentuating her eyebrows with a finger wet in her mouth.*)

WIFE: Good afternoon!

MAYOR: A very good afternoon. (*To the Shoemaker.*) How handsome! She's very handsome!

SHOEMAKER: You think so?

MAYOR: What well-placed roses you wear in your hair—and how delightfully they smell!

WIFE: It's many that you have on the balconies of your house.

MAYOR: Quite so. Do you like flowers?

WIFE: Me? Oh, I love them! I'd have flowerpots on the roof even— at the door—on the walls. But he—that one—doesn't like

---

* Name of an old Spanish dance. "Jaleo" also means trouble, noise, hulla-baloo.

them. Naturally, making boots all day, what would you expect? (*She sits at the window.*) And good afternoon! (*She looks toward the street and flirts.*)

SHOEMAKER: You see that?

MAYOR: A little bit brusque—but she's a very handsome woman. What a pretty waist!

SHOEMAKER: You just don't know her.

MAYOR: Tssch! (*Leaving majestically.*) Until tomorrow! And let's see if that head of yours clears. You, child, get some rest! What a pity! With such a figure! (*Leaves, looking at the Shoemaker's Wife.*) Because, my—those waves in her hair!

SHOEMAKER (*singing*):
If your mother wants a king,
In the deck there's a store.
King of Diamonds, Clubs and Hearts,
King of Spades—that makes four!

(*The Wife takes a chair and seated at the window begins to spin it.*)

SHOEMAKER (*taking another chair—and making it spin in the opposite direction*): You know that's a superstition of mine. You might just as well shoot me. Why do you do it?

WIFE (*letting go the chair*): What have I done? Didn't I tell you you don't even let me move.

SHOEMAKER: I'm tired of explaining to you—it's useless. (*Starts to leave, but the Wife begins once more to spin her chair and the Shoemaker runs back from the door to spin his chair.*) Woman, why don't you let me go?

WIFE: Heavens! Why it's just what I'm hoping—that you'd go.

SHOEMAKER: Then let me!

WIFE (*infuriated*): Well, go on!

(*Outside a flute is heard accompanied by a guitar playing an old polka with the rhythm comically accented. The Wife begins to nod her head in rhythm and the Shoemaker leaves through the left door.*)

WIFE (*singing*): La-ran, la-ran . . . Well, maybe I've just always liked the flute a lot. I've always been crazy about it. It almost makes me cry. What a delight! La-ran, la-ran. Listen. I wish he could hear it. (*She rises and begins to dance as if she were doing it with imaginary suitors.*) Oh, Emiliano! What beautiful ribbons you have! No, no! It would embarrass poor little me. But, José María, don't you see that they're looking at us? Take a handkerchief then, for I don't want you to stain my dress. It's you I love, you. Ah, yes! Tomorrow when you bring the white mare, the one I like. (*Laughs. The music stops.*) Oh, too bad. That's just like leaving one with honey at her lips. How . . .

(*At the window Don Blackbird appears. He is dressed in a black swallowtail coat and short breeches. His voice trembles and he moves his head like a wire doll.*)

DON BLACKBIRD: Ssst!

WIFE (*without looking, her back turned to the window, imitates a bird*): Caw, caw—cheep, cheep!

DON BLACKBIRD (*coming nearer*): Ssst! Little white Mistress Shoemaker, like the heart of an almond—but a little bit bitter, too. Little Mistress Shoemaker—burning golden reed—little Mistress Shoemaker, beautiful temptress of my heart.

WIFE: What a lot of things, Don Blackbird. I didn't know that big buzzards could talk. If there's a black blackbird fluttering around here—black and old—he'd better realize that I can't listen to him sing until later. Tweet, tweet—chirp, chirp.

DON BLACKBIRD: When the crepuscular shadows invade the world with their tenuous veils, and the public walk finds itself free of pedestrians, I shall return. (*Takes snuff and sneezes on the Wife's back.*)

WIFE (*turning in irritation and hitting at Don Blackbird, who trembles*): A-h-h-h!! (*Her face full of loathing.*) And even if you don't return it'll be all right, indecent thing! Wire blackbird! Stove-lamp smudge! Run, now run! Did you ever see such a thing? Look what's sneezing! God go with you! How loathsome!

(*At the window the Youth with Sash stops. His straight-brim hat is down over his face and he shows signs of great sadness.*)

SASH YOUTH: Taking the air, Mistress Shoemaker?

WIFE: Exactly as you are.

SASH YOUTH: And always alone. What a pity!

WIFE (*sourly*): And why a pity?

SASH YOUTH: A woman like you—with that hair and that bosom so very beautiful . . .

WIFE (*more sourly*): But, why a pity?

SASH YOUTH: Because you're worthy of being painted on a picture postcard—and not to be just here—at this little windowsill.

WIFE: Yes? I like postcards very much, especially those of sweethearts about to go on a trip.

SASH YOUTH: Oh, little Shoemaker's Wife, what a fever I have!

(*They continue talking.*)

SHOEMAKER (*entering, then retreating*): With the whole world, and at this hour! What will the people going to rosary at the church say? What will they say at the club? How they must talk about me! In each house they must discuss me—suit, underclothes and all.

(*Shoemaker's Wife laughs.*)

Oh, my lord! I have cause to leave! I'd like to listen to the wife of the sacristan. But the priests; what will the priests say? They are the ones I ought to hear. (*He exits in desperation.*)

SASH YOUTH: How do you want me to say it? I love you, I love *thee* like . . .

WIFE: Really, that about "I love you, I love thee" has a style about it that makes me think someone is tickling me behind the ear with a feather. "I love thee, I love you."

SASH YOUTH: How many seeds has a sunflower?

WIFE: How should I know?

SASH YOUTH (*very near*): Every minute I sigh that many times for you, for *thee*.

WIFE (*brusquely*): Stop that. I can listen to you talk because I like it and it's pretty—but that's all, do you hear? A fine thing that would be!

SASH YOUTH: But that cannot be. Is it that you've given your word elsewhere?

WIFE: Now look here; go away.

SASH YOUTH: I won't move from this spot until you say yes. Oh, my little Shoemaker's Wife, give me your word! (*Starts to embrace her.*)

WIFE (*closing the window violently*): What an impertinent man! What a fool! If I have turned your head you'll just have to bear it! As if I were here just to . . . just to . . . well, can't one talk to anybody in this town? From what I can see there are but two extremes in this town: either a nun or a dishrag. That's all I needed to know! (*Pretending she smells something, running.*) Oh, my dinner's on the stove! Evil woman!

(*It is growing dark. The Shoemaker enters wearing a great cape and with a bundle of clothes in his hand.*)

SHOEMAKER: I'm either another man or I don't know myself! Oh, my little house! Oh, my little bench! Wax nails, calfskins . . . well. (*He goes toward the door and retreats because he runs into the two Over-Pious Women.*)

FIRST OVER-PIOUS WOMAN: Resting, aren't you?

SECOND OVER-PIOUS WOMAN: You do well to rest!

SHOEMAKER (*in a bad humor*): Good night!

FIRST OVER-PIOUS WOMAN: To rest, master.

SECOND OVER-PIOUS WOMAN: To rest, to rest!

(*They leave.*)

SHOEMAKER: Yes, resting—but they weren't looking through the keyhole! Witches! Ugly things! Be careful of that insinuating tone in which you speak to me. Naturally, since in the whole village they talk of nothing else—he this, she that, the servants something else! Ay! May lightning strike my sister, may she rest in peace! But better alone than pointed at by everybody!

(*He goes out rapidly, leaving the door open. Through the left door the Wife appears.*)

WIFE: Supper's ready. Do you hear me? (*Goes toward the door on the right.*) Do you hear me? Well, has he had the courage to go to the café, leaving the door open? And without finishing the boots? Well, when he returns he'll listen to me! He'll have to listen! How like men, men are! How abusive and how . . .

how . . . well! (*Changing.*) Oh, what a nice little breeze. (*She lights the lamp and from the street comes the sound of the bells of the flock returning to the village. The Wife looks out the window.*) What lovely flocks! I'm just crazy about little sheep. Look, look at that little white one that can just barely walk! Ay! But look at that big ugly one that keeps trampling on her and nothing . . . (*Shouts.*) Shepherd, daydreamer! Don't you see that they're stepping on the newborn lamb? (*Pause.*) Certainly it's my business. Why shouldn't it be my business? Big brute! You . . . (*She moves away from the window.*) Well, sir, where could that wandering man have gone? Well, if he delays two minutes more, I'll eat by myself, for I'm self-sufficient and more than that. With such a good supper as I've prepared! My stew with the fresh wild potatoes, two green peppers, white bread, a bit of lean bacon, and squash conserve with lemon peel on top. Because I have to take care of him! I have to take care of him! I take care of him by hand! (*During all this monologue, she gives evidence of great activity, moving from one side to the other, arranging the chairs, taking lint off the curtains, and removing threads from her dress.*)

BOY (*at the door*): Are you still angry?

WIFE: My little darling of a neighbor, where are you going?

BOY (*at the door*): You won't scold me, will you? Because my mother, who sometimes beats me, I love twenty bushelfuls, but I love you thirty-two and a half.

WIFE: Why are you so lovely? (*Seats him on her lap.*)

BOY: I came to tell you something that nobody else wants to tell you. "You go, you go, you go"—and no one wanted to go. And then, "Well, let the child go," they said—because it's some bad news that no one wants to carry.

WIFE: Then, tell me quickly. What has happened?

BOY: Well, don't be frightened—because it's not about dead people.

WIFE: Go on. . . .

BOY: Look, little Shoemaker's Wife! (*Through the window a butterfly enters and the boy, getting down from her lap, begins to run after it.*) A butterfly! A butterfly! Don't you have a hat?

It's yellow with blue and red marks—and I don't know what all!

WIFE: But child, weren't you going to . . .?

BOY: (*sternly*): Be quiet and speak in a low voice. Don't you see it will get frightened if you don't? Oh, give me your handkerchief!

WIFE (*already intrigued by the hunt*): Take it.

BOY: Shh! Don't stamp your feet.

WIFE: You're going to let it get away.

BOY (*in a low voice, as though charming the butterfly, sings*):
> Butterfly of the breezes,
> wind creature so lovely;
> butterfly of the breezes,
> wind creature so lovely;
> butterfly of the breezes,
> so green, so golden,
> a candle's flame;
> butterfly of the breezes,
> I beg you, stay there, stay there, stay there!
> But you don't wish to linger,
> to stay there an instant.
> But you don't wish to linger,
> to stay there an instant.
> Butterfly of the breezes,
> so green so golden,
> a candle's flame;
> butterfly of the breezes,
> I beg you, stay there, stay there, stay there!
> I beg you, stay there!
> Butterfly, oh, please, are you there?

WIFE (*jokingly*): Ye-e-e-s.

BOY: No, now that's not fair.

(*The butterfly flies.*)

WIFE: Now! Now!

BOY (*running happily with the handkerchief*): Won't you light? Won't you quit flying?

WIFE (*also running on the other side*): It'll get away! It'll get away!

(*The Boy runs out the door pursuing the butterfly.*)

WIFE (*sternly*): Where are you going?

BOY (*suspended*): It's true. (*Quickly.*) But it's not my fault!

WIFE: Come now! Are you going to tell me what's happened? Quickly!

BOY: Oh! Well, look—your husband, the Shoemaker, has left never to return.

WIFE (*terrified*): What?

BOY: Yes, yes. He said that at my house before he got on the stagecoach. I saw him myself—and he told us to tell you that —and the whole town knows it.

WIFE (*sitting deflated*): But it isn't possible. It isn't possible! I don't believe it!

BOY: Yes, it's true; don't scold me!

WIFE (*rising in a fury, stamping on the floor*): And this is how he pays me? And this is how he pays me?

(*The Boy finds refuge behind the table.*)

BOY: Your hairpins are falling out!

WIFE: What's going to happen to me all alone in life? Oh! Oh! Oh!

(*The Boy runs out. The windows and the doors are full of Neighbors.*)

Yes, yes—come look at me! Rattlers, gossips! It's your fault. . . .

MAYOR: Look, now, be quiet. If your husband has left you—it was because you didn't love him—because it couldn't be.

WIFE: But, do you think you know more than I do? Yes, I did love him. I should say I loved him. How many good and rich suitors I had—and I never said yes to them. Oh, my poor thing —what things they must have told you!

SACRISTAN'S WIFE (*entering*): Woman, control yourself!

WIFE: I can't resign myself! I can't resign myself! Oh, Oh!

*(Neighbors dressed in various violent colors and carrying large glasses of cooling drinks begin to enter through the door. They turn, run, come and go, with the quickness and rhythm of a dance, around the Wife, who is sitting, shouting. The great skirts open with their turns. All adopt a comic attitude of pain.)*

NEIGHBOR IN YELLOW: A cooling drink?

RED NEIGHBOR: A little refreshment?

NEIGHBOR IN GREEN: For the blood?

NEIGHBOR IN BLACK: Lemon flavor?

NEIGHBOR IN PURPLE: Sarsaparilla?

RED NEIGHBOR: Mint is better.

PURPLE NEIGHBOR: Neighbor.

GREEN NEIGHBOR: Little neighbor.

BLACK NEIGHBOR: Shoemaker's Wife.

RED NEIGHBOR: Little Shoemaker's Wife.

*(The Neighbors create a great excitement. The Wife is crying at the top of her lungs.)*

CURTAIN

## ACT TWO

*(The same set. To the left the abandoned cobbler's bench. To the right a counter with bottles and a pan behind which the Wife washes cups. She wears a burning-red dress with wide skirts. Her arms are bare. On the stage three tables. At one of them Don Blackbird is seated having a soft drink, and at the other the Youth with Hat, with his hat pulled down over his face.*

*The Wife washes glasses and cups with great ardor and places them on the counter. At the right appears the Sash Youth with hat as in Act One. He is sad. His arms hang at his sides and he looks at the Wife tenderly. If an actor exaggerates this character in the slightest he should be hit over the head by the director. No one should exaggerate. Farce always demands naturalness. The author*

*has drawn the character and the tailor has dressed him. Simplicity.*
*The Sash Youth stops at the door. Don Blackbird and the Hat*
*Youth turn their heads to look at him. This is almost a movie*
*scene. The glances and expressions taken together create the effect.*
*The Wife stops washing and looks fixedly at the Sash Youth in the*
*door. Silence.)*

WIFE: Come in.

SASH YOUTH: If you wish it.

WIFE (*amazed*): I? It absolutely does not matter to me one way or
the other, but since I see you at the door . . .

SASH YOUTH: As you wish. (*He leans on the counter. Between his*
*teeth:*) This is another one that I'm going to have to . . .

WIFE: What will you take?

SASH YOUTH: I'll follow your suggestions.

WIFE: Then—take the gate.

SASH YOUTH: Oh, Lord, how times change!

WIFE: Don't think I'm going to start crying. Come now. Are you
going to have a drink? Coffee? A cold drink? What?

SASH YOUTH: A cold drink.

WIFE: Don't look at me so hard—you'll make me spill the syrup.

SASH YOUTH: It's only—I'm dying. Ay!

(*Past the window go two girls with immense fans. They look,*
*cross themselves, scandalized, cover their eyes with their fans,*
*and cross on with tiny steps.*)

WIFE: The drink.

SASH YOUTH (*looking at her*): Ay!

HAT YOUTH (*looking at the floor*): Ay!

DON BLACKBIRD (*looking at the ceiling*): Ay!

WIFE (*turns her head toward each of the three "ays"*): "Ay" some
more! But what is this—a tavern or a hospital? Abusers! If I
didn't have to earn my living with these little wines and sweets
—because I'm alone since the poor little husband of my soul
left me, through the fault of all of you—how would it be

possible for me to bear this? What do you say to that? I'm going to have to throw you out into the nice, wide street.

DON BLACKBIRD: Well said; very well said.

HAT YOUTH: You have opened a tavern and we can stay inside here as long as we want.

WIFE (*fiercely*): What? What?

(*The Sash Youth starts to leave and Don Blackbird rises smiling and acting as if he were in on the secret, and would return.*)

HAT YOUTH: Just what I said!

WIFE: Well whatever you say—I can say more. And you might as well know, and the whole village, that my husband has been gone four months, but that I'll never give in to anybody— never! Because a married woman should keep her place as God commands, and I'm not afraid of anybody; do you hear? For I have the blood of my grandfather, may he be in heaven, who was a horse tamer and what is called a man. Decent I was and decent I will be. I gave my word to my husband. Well, until death.

(*Don Blackbird goes rapidly to the door making motions that indicate a relation between him and the Wife.*)

HAT YOUTH (*rising*): I'm so angry I could take a bull by the horns, bend his head to the ground, eat his brains raw with my teeth, and surely not tire myself with biting.

(*He strides out rapidly and Don Blackbird flees toward the left.*)

WIFE (*with her hands to her head*): Lord, Lord, Lord and Lord! (*She sits.*)

(*Through the door the Boy enters. He goes toward the Wife and covers her eyes.*)

BOY: Who am I?

WIFE: My child, little shepherd of Bethlehem.

BOY: I'm here.

*They kiss.*

WIFE: Did you come for your snack?

BOY: If you want to give me something.

WIFE: I have a piece of chocolate today.

BOY: Yes? I like to be in your house very much.

WIFE (*giving him the chocolate*): Aren't you just a little selfish?

BOY: Selfish? Do you see this black-and-blue spot on my knee?

WIFE: Let me see. (*She sits on a low chair and takes the Boy in her arms.*)

BOY: Well, Cunillo did it because he was singing the couplets they made up about you and I hit him in the face, and then he threw a rock at me that—bang! Look.

WIFE: Does it hurt very much?

BOY: Not now, but I cried.

WIFE: Don't pay any attention to what they say.

BOY: Well, they were saying very indecent things. Indecent things that I know how to say, you understand. But that I don't want to say.

WIFE (*laughing*): Because if you say them I'll take a hot pimiento and make your tongue like a red-hot coal.

(*They laugh.*)

BOY: But—why should they blame you because your husband left?

WIFE: They, they are the ones to blame, and the ones who make me unhappy.

BOY (*sadly*): Don't say that, little cobbler's wife.

WIFE: I used to see myself in his eyes. When I'd see him coming mounted on his white mare . . .

BOY (*interrupting her*): Ha-ha-ha! You're fooling me. Mr. Shoemaker didn't have a mare.

WIFE: Boy, be more respectful. He had a mare; certainly he had one—but you . . . you weren't born yet.

BOY (*stroking his face*): Oh! That was it!

WIFE: You see, when I met him I was washing clothes in the little brook. Through half a yard of water the pebbles on the bottom could be seen laughing—laughing with little tremblings. He wore a tight black suit, a red tie of the finest silk, and four gold rings that shone like four suns.

BOY: How pretty!

WIFE: He looked at me and I looked at him. I lay back on the grass. I think I can still feel on my face that little fresh breeze that came through the trees. He stopped his horse and the horse's tail was white and so long that it reached down to the water in the brook. (*The Wife is almost weeping. A distant song begins to be heard.*) I was so flustered that I let two lovely handkerchiefs, just this tiny, flow down with the current.

BOY: How funny!

WIFE: He then said to me . . . (*The song is heard nearer. Pause.*) Shh!

BOY (*rises*): The couplets.

WIFE: The couplets.

(*Pause. The two listen.*)

Do you know what they say?

BOY (*gesturing with his hand*): Well, sort of.

WIFE: Well, sing them, then, because I want to know.

BOY: What for?

WIFE: So that I can find out once and for all what they're saying.

BOY: (*singing and marking time*): You'll see:
    Mistress Cobbler, Mistress Cobbler,
    since her husband ran away,
    since her husband ran away,
    turned her house into a tavern
    where the men go night and day,
    where the men go night and day.

WIFE: They'll pay for this!

BOY (*beats time on the table with his hand*):
    Who has bought you, Mistress Cobbler,

all those dresses may we guess,
all those dresses may we guess?
Cambrics, batistes, bobbin laces
fit for a proprietress,
fit for a proprietress.

Now she's courted by the Mayor,
now it is Don Blackbird's turn,
now it is Don Blackbird's turn.
Mistress Cobbler, Mistress Cobbler,
Mistress, you have men to burn,
Mistress, you have men to burn!

(*The voices can be heard near and clearly with their accompaniment of tambourines. The Wife takes up a Manila scarf and throws it over her shoulders.*)

Where are you going? (*Frightened.*)

WIFE: They're going to drive me to buying a revolver!

(*The song grows faint. She runs to the door. But she bumps into the Mayor, who comes in majestically, beating on the floor with his staff.*)

MAYOR: Who waits on one here?

WIFE: The devil!

MAYOR: But what's happened?

WIFE: Something you must have known for several days. Something that you as Mayor ought not to allow. The people sing couplets to me, the neighbors laugh at their doors, and since I have no husband to watch out for me I'm going to defend myself—since in this town the authorities are pumpkinheads, good-for-nothings, figureheads!

BOY: Very well said.

MAYOR (*severely*): Child, child! Enough of this shouting. Do you know what I've just done? Well, I put in jail two or three of those who came along singing.

WIFE: I'd like to see that!

VOICE (*outside*): So-n-n-y-y!

BOY: My mother's calling me! (*Runs to the window.*) Wha-a-a-t? Good-bye. If you want, I can bring you my grandfather's big sword—the one who went to war. I can't lift it, you see, but you can.

WIFE (*smiling*): Whatever you want!

VOICE (*outside*): So-n-n-y-y!

BOY (*already in the street*): Wha-a-at?

MAYOR: From what I can see, the precocious and unnatural child is the only person in the village you treat well.

WIFE: You people can't say a single word that isn't an insult. And what is your most illustrious self laughing about?

MAYOR: To see you so beautiful but going to waste!

WIFE: Rather a dog! (*Serves him a glass of wine.*)

MAYOR: What a disillusioning world! I've known many women just like poppies—like fragrant roses—dark women with eyes like inky fire, women whose hair smells of sweet oils and whose hands are always very warm, women whose waists you can encircle with these two fingers; but like you—there's no one like you. Day before yesterday I was sick all morning because I saw laid out on the grass two of your chemises with sky-blue ribbons—and it was like seeing you, Cobbler's Wife of my soul.

WIFE: (*exploding furiously*): Be quiet, old man. Shut up! With grown daughters and a large family you shouldn't come courting in a manner so indecent and so bold-faced.

MAYOR: I'm a widower.

WIFE: And I'm a married woman!

MAYOR: But your husband has left you and will not return, I'm sure.

WIFE: I'll live as if I still had him.

MAYOR: Well then, I can testify, because he told me, that he didn't love you even as much as this.

WIFE: Well, I can testify that your four wives—may lightning strike them—hated you to death.

MAYOR (*striking the floor with his staff*): Now that's enough!

WIFE (*throwing a glass*): Now that's enough!

(*Pause.*)

MAYOR (*under his breath*): If I could have you for my own, I'd show you how I could tame you!

WIFE (*coyly*): What's that you're saying?

MAYOR: Nothing. I was just thinking that if you were as good as you ought to be, you should understand I have the will and the generosity to make out a deed before a notary for a very beautiful house.

WIFE: And what of that?

MAYOR: With a drawing-room suite of furniture that cost five thousand reales, with centerpieces on the tables, brocade curtains, full-length mirrors . . .

WIFE: And what else?

MAYOR (*in the manner of a Don Juan*): The house has a bed with a canopy upheld by copper birds and daisies, a garden with six palms and a leaping fountain, but waits—in order to be happy —for a person I know to want to take possession of those rooms where she would be . . . (*Addressing the Wife directly.*) Look, you'd be like a Queen!

WIFE (*coyly*): I'm not used to such luxury. You sit down in the drawing room, crawl into the bed, look in the mirror, and lie with your mouth open underneath the palm trees waiting for the dates to fall—because I'm not giving up being a shoe-maker's wife.

MAYOR (*in an affected tone of voice*): Nor am I giving up being Mayor. But it's time you knew that daylight won't break any earlier just for our disdaining it.

WIFE: And it's time you knew that I don't like you or anyone in the village. An old man like you!

MAYOR (*indignant*): I'll end by putting you in jail.

WIFE: Just you dare!

(*Outside there is heard a trumpet call—florid and most comical.*)

MAYOR: What could that be?

WIFE (*happy and wide-eyed*): Puppets! (*She beats her knees.*)

(*Two women cross the window.*)

RED NEIGHBOR: Puppets!

PURPLE NEIGHBOR: Puppets!

BOY (*at the window*): Do you think they have any monkeys? Let's go!

WIFE (*to the Mayor*): I'm going to close up.

BOY: They're coming to your house.

WIFE: Yes? (*Goes toward the door.*)

BOY: Look at them!

(*At the door the Shoemaker, disguised, appears. He carries a trumpet and a scroll at his back. The people surround him. The Wife waits with great expectancy and the Boy leaps in through the window and holds on to her skirts.*)

SHOEMAKER: Good afternoon!

WIFE: Good afternoon to you, Mr. Puppeteer.

SHOEMAKER: May a person rest here?

WIFE: And drink if you like.

MAYOR: Enter, my good man. And drink what you like, for I'll pay. (*To the Neighbors.*) And you others, what are you doing here?

RED NEIGHBOR: Since we are out in the broad street, I don't believe we're in your way.

(*The Shoemaker, looking at all with calmness, leaves the scroll on the table.*)

SHOEMAKER: Let them be, Mr. Mayor—for I imagine you are he— I must make my living with these people.

BOY: Where have I heard this man talk before? (*Throughout all this scene the Boy looks at the Shoemaker with a puzzled air.*) Work your puppets!

(*The Neighbors laugh.*)

SHOEMAKER: As soon as I drink a glass of wine.

WIFE (*happily*): But are you going to work them in my house?

SHOEMAKER: If you will permit me.

RED NEIGHBOR: Then, may we come in?

WIFE (*serious*): You can come in. (*Gives a glass to the Shoemaker.*)

RED NEIGHBOR (*seating herself*): Now we shall enjoy ourselves a little.

(*The Mayor sits.*)

MAYOR: Do you come from very far?

SHOEMAKER: From very far.

MAYOR: From Seville?

SHOEMAKER: Leagues farther.

MAYOR: From France?

SHOEMAKER: Leagues farther.

MAYOR: From England?

SHOEMAKER: From the Philippine Islands.

(*The Neighbors give signs of admiration. The Wife is ecstatic.*)

MAYOR: You must have seen the Insurrectionists, then?

SHOEMAKER: Just the same as I am looking at you now.

BOY: And what are they like?

SHOEMAKER: Unbearable. Just imagine, almost all of them are shoemakers.

(*The Neighbors look at the Wife.*)

WIFE (*blushing*): And aren't they in any other profession?

SHOEMAKER: Absolutely not. In the Philippines—shoemakers!

WIFE: Well, perhaps in the Philippines shoemakers are stupid, but in this country there are some who are smart—and very smart at that.

RED NEIGHBOR (*flatteringly*): Very well spoken.

WIFE (*brusquely*): No one asked your opinion.

RED NEIGHBOR: But, child!

SHOEMAKER (*sternly, interrupting*): What rich wine! (*Louder.*) What rich wine indeed! (*Silence.*) Wine from grapes black as the souls of some women I have known.

WIFE: If any of them had souls!

MAYOR: Shh! And of what does your work consist?

SHOEMAKER (*empties the glass, smacks his tongue, looks at his wife*): Ah! It is a work of small show but much science. I present life from within. There are the couplets of the "Henpecked Shoemaker," and "Fierabras of Alexandria," "Life of Don Diego Corrientes," "Adventures of the Handsome Francisco Esteban," and above all, "The Art of Closing the Mouths of Gossipy and Impudent Women."

WIFE: My poor husband knew all those things!

SHOEMAKER: May God forgive him!

WIFE: Now you listen . . .

(*The Neighbors laugh.*)

BOY: Hush!

MAYOR (*imperiously*): Quiet! These are teachings that apply to everybody. (*To the Shoemaker.*) Whenever you wish.

(*The Shoemaker unrolls the scroll on which the story is painted, divided into tiny squares, drawn in red ochre and violent colors. The Neighbors start moving closer, and the Wife takes the Boy upon her knees.*)

SHOEMAKER: Attention.

BOY: Oh, how pretty! (*Embraces the Wife. Murmurs are heard.*)

WIFE: Now pay good attention in case I don't understand everything.

BOY: It's surely not harder than sacred history.

SHOEMAKER: Worthy spectators. Listen to the true and moving ballad of the rubicund wife and the poor, patient little husband, that it may serve as warning and example to all the people of this world. (*In a lugubrious tone.*) Prick up your ears and understanding.

(*The Neighbors crane their necks, and a few of the women take hands.*)

BOY: Doesn't the puppeteer remind you of your husband when he talks?

WIFE: He had a sweeter voice.

SHOEMAKER: Are we ready?

WIFE: I feel a little shiver.

BOY: Me too!

SHOEMAKER (*pointing with a staff*):
    In Cordoba within a cottage
    set about with trees and rosebays,
    once upon a time a tanner
    lived there with the tanner's wife.

(*Expectancy.*)

    She a very stubborn woman—
    he a man of gentle patience;
    though the wife had not turned twenty,
    he was then well over fifty.
    Holy Lord, how they would argue!
    Look now at that beastly woman,
    laughing at the poor weak husband
    with her glances and her speaking.

(*On the scroll is drawn a woman who looks infantile and careworn.*)

WIFE (*murmurs*): What an evil woman!

SHOEMAKER:
    Dark hair worthy of an empress
    had this little tanner's wife,
    and her flesh was like the water
    from Lucena's crystal sources.
    When she moved her skirts and flounces,
    as she walked about in springtime,
    all her clothes gave off the fragrance
    lemon groves and mint exhale.
    Oh what lemons, lemons
    of the lemon grove!

      Oh what a delicious
      little tanner's wife!

(*The Neighbors laugh.*)

      And now look how she was courted
      by young men of striking presence
      riding sleek and shining stallions
      harnessed in fine silken tassels.
      Elegant and charming persons
      would come riding past the doorway,
      flaunting with intent the luster
      of their coin-hung golden watch chains.
      And the tanner's wife was willing
      to converse with all these worthies,
      while the mares they rode went prancing
      on the cobbles of the roadway.
      Mark her how with one she's flirting,
      dressed and combed with fullest grooming,
      while the poor long-suffering tanner
      sticks his awl into the leather.

(*Very dramatically, joining his hands.*)

      Old and decent-acting husband,
      married to a wife too youthful,
      who could be that scoundrel horseman
      come to steal love from your doorway?

(*The Wife, who has been sighing, bursts into tears.*)

SHOEMAKER (*turning*): What's happened to you?

MAYOR: But, child! (*Beats with his staff on the floor.*)

RED NEIGHBOR: A person who has something to shut up about always bawls.

PURPLE NEIGHBOR: Please go on!

(*The Neighbors murmur and shush.*)

WIFE: It's just that I'm filled with pity and can't contain myself. You see? I can't contain myself. (*Weeps, trying to control herself, hiccuping most comically.*)

MAYOR: Quiet!

BOY: You see?

SHOEMAKER: Do me the favor of not interrupting. How well one
   can tell you're not trying to repeat something from memory!

BOY (*sighing*): How true!

SHOEMAKER (*ill-humored*):
         So, upon a Monday morning,
         just about eleven-thirty,
         when the sun left without shadow
         honeysuckle vines and rushes,
         when most happy danced together
         winds and thyme plants on the mountain,
         and the leaves of green were falling
         from the wild strawberry trees,
         there the spoiled wife was watering
         gilliflowers in her garden.
         Just then came her suitor riding,
         riding a Cordovan mare,
         and he told her through his sighing:
         "Sweetheart, if you only wished it,
         we'd have supper this next evening,
         we alone, but at your table."
         "Yes, but what about my husband?"
         "Husband? He won't know about it."
         "Then what will you do?" "I'll kill him."
         "He's a quick one, you might fail.
         Have you a revolver?" "Better!
         I can use a barber's razor."
         "Does it cut much?" "More than cold wind.

(*The Wife covers her eyes and squeezes the Boy. All the
Neighbors are in a high pitch of expectancy which is shown by
their expressions.*)

         And the blade's without a nick yet."
         "You're not lying?" "No, I'll give him
         ten quite well-directed blade thrusts
         in the following distribution,
         which I really think stupendous:
         four upon the lumbar region,
         one just at his left side nipple,
         one more at a place just like it,
         two on each side of his buttocks."
         "Will you kill him right away?"

"This same night when he's returning
with his leather and his horsehair,
where the water ditch starts curving."

(*During this last verse, quickly, there is heard offstage a most loud and anguished shout; the Neighbors rise. Another shout nearer. The scroll and the staff fall from the hands of the Shoemaker. All tremble comically.*)

BLACK NEIGHBOR (*at the window*): They've drawn their knives!

WIFE: Oh, my Lord!

RED NEIGHBOR: Holiest Virgin!

SHOEMAKER: What a row!

BLACK NEIGHBOR: They're killing themselves! They're ripping each other to pieces—all through the fault of that woman! (*Points to the Wife.*)

MAYOR (*nervous*): Let's go see.

BOY: I'm very scared!

GREEN NEIGHBOR: Come on! Come on!

(*They start leaving.*)

VOICE (*outside*): Because of that evil woman!

SHOEMAKER: I can't stand this! I can't stand it! (*Runs around the stage with his hands at his head.*)

(*All are leaving rapidly, exclaiming and casting looks of hate toward the Wife. She quickly closes the window and door.*)

WIFE: Have you ever seen such hatefulness? I swear by the holiest blood of our Father Jesus that I'm innocent. Ay! What could have happened? Look, look how I'm trembling. (*Shows him her hands.*) It seems as if my hands want to fly off by themselves.

SHOEMAKER: Be calm, girl. Is your husband in the street?

WIFE (*bursting into sobs*): My husband? Oh, Mr. Puppeteer!

SHOEMAKER: What's the matter?

WIFE: My husband left me because of these people and now I'm alone—with nobody's warmth.

SHOEMAKER: Poor little thing.

WIFE: And I loved him so much! I adored him!

SHOEMAKER (*starting*): That isn't true!

WIFE (*quickly ceasing her sobs*): What did you say?

SHOEMAKER: I said it's such an incomprehensible thing that . . . it doesn't seem to be true. (*Disturbed.*)

WIFE: You're very right, but since then I haven't been able to eat or sleep, or live; because he was my happiness, my defense.

SHOEMAKER: And, loving him as much as you did, did he abandon you? I can see from that your husband was not very understanding.

WIFE: Please keep your tongue in your pocket. No one has given you permission to voice your opinion.

SHOEMAKER: You must excuse me; I didn't mean to . . .

WIFE: The idea! Why, he was so smart!

SHOEMAKER (*jokingly*): Ye-e-e-s?

WIFE (*sternly*): Yes. You know those ballads and little songs you sing and tell through the villages? Well, that isn't anything to what he knew. He knew—three times as much!

SHOEMAKER (*serious*): That can't be.

WIFE (*sternly*): Four times as much! He used to tell them all to me when we went to bed. Old stories that you probably haven't even heard mentioned (*coyly*), and I would get so frightened. But he would say to me: "Darling of my soul, these are just tiny little white lies!"

SHOEMAKER (*indignant*): That's not true.

WIFE (*surprised*): Eh? Have you lost your mind?

SHOEMAKER: It's a lie!

WIFE (*angry*): What are you saying, you puppeteer of the devil?

SHOEMAKER (*strongly, standing*): That your husband was quite right. Those stories are just lies—fantasy, that's all.

WIFE (*sourly*): Naturally, my good sir. You seem to take me for a complete fool—but you won't deny that these stories make an impression.

SHOEMAKER: Ah, that is flour of another sack, then! They make an impression on impressionable souls.

WIFE: Everyone has feelings.

SHOEMAKER: According to how one looks at it. I've known many people without feelings. And in my town there lived a woman at one time who had a heart so unfeeling that she would talk to her friends through the window while her husband made boots and shoes from morning to night.

WIFE (*rising and taking up a chair*): Are you saying that because of me?

SHOEMAKER: What?

WIFE: If you were going to add anything else, go ahead! Be brave!

SHOEMAKER (*humbly*): Miss, what are you saying? How do I know who you are? I haven't insulted you in any way. Why do you treat me so? But that's my fate! (*Almost weeping.*)

WIFE (*stern, but moved*): Look here, my good man; I spoke like that because I'm on pins and needles. Everybody besieges me —everybody criticizes me. How can I help but be looking for the slightest opportunity to defend myself? Because I'm alone, because I'm young, and yet already live only for my memories. . . . (*Weeps.*)

SHOEMAKER (*weepily*): I understand, you lovely young creature. I understand much better than you can imagine, because—you must know, most confidentially, that your situation is—yes, there's no doubt of it—identical with mine.

WIFE (*intrigued*): Could that be possible?

SHOEMAKER (*lets himself fall across the table*): I—was abandoned by my wife!

WIFE: Death would be too good for her!

SHOEMAKER: She dreamed of a world that was not mine. She was flighty and domineering; she loved conversation, and the sweets I could not buy for her, too much, and on a day that was stormy with a wind like a hurricane, she left me forever.

WIFE: And why do you wander over the world now?

SHOEMAKER: I search for her to forgive her and to live out with her the short time I have left in this world. At my age one is rather insecurely in this world of God's.

WIFE (*quickly*): Take a little hot coffee; it'll be good for you after all this hullabaloo. (*Goes to the counter to pour the coffee and turns her back on the Shoemaker.*)

SHOEMAKER (*crossing himself exaggeratedly and opening his eyes*): May God repay you, my little red carnation.

WIFE (*offers him the cup. She keeps the saucer in her hand. He drinks in gulps*): Is it good?

SHOEMAKER (*flatteringly*): Since it was made by your hands!

WIFE (*smiling*): Thank you!

SHOEMAKER (*with a final swallow*): Oh, how I envy your husband!

WIFE: Why?

SHOEMAKER (*gallantly*): Because he married the most beautiful woman in the world!

WIFE (*softened*): What things you say!

SHOEMAKER: And now I'm almost glad I have to go, because here you are alone, and I'm alone, and you so beautiful and I, having a tongue—it seems to me that I couldn't help making a certain suggestion. . . .

WIFE (*recovering*): My heavens, stop that! What do you think? I keep my whole heart for that wanderer, for the one whom I must, for my husband!

SHOEMAKER (*very pleased—throwing his hat on the ground*): That's fine! Spoken like a real woman—fine!

WIFE (*joking a little, surprised*): It seems to me that you're a little . . . (*Points to her temple.*)

SHOEMAKER: Whatever you say. But understand that I'm not in love with anyone except my wife, my lawfully wedded wife!

WIFE: And I with my husband; and nobody but my husband. How many times I've said it for even the deaf to hear. . . . (*With her hands folded.*) Oh, Shoemaker of my soul!

SHOEMAKER (*aside*): Oh, wife of my soul!

(*There is knocking at the door.*)

WIFE: Heavens! One is in a constant state of excitement. Who is it?

BOY: Open!

WIFE: How's this? How did you get here?

BOY: Oh, I've come running to tell you!

WIFE: What's happened?

BOY: Two or three young men have wounded each other with knives and they're blaming you for it. Wounds that bleed a lot. All the women have gone to see the judge to make you leave town. Oh! And the men wanted the sacristan to ring the bells so they could sing you the couplets. . . . (*The Boy is panting and perspiring.*)

WIFE ( *to the Shoemaker*): Do you see that?

BOY: All the plaza is full of people talking—it's like the fair—and all of them are against you!

SHOEMAKER: Villains! I'm of a mind to go out and defend you.

WIFE: What for? They'd just put you in jail. I'm the one who's going to have to do something drastic.

BOY: From the window in your room you can see the excitement in the plaza.

WIFE (*in a hurry*): Come on, I want to see for myself the hatefulness of those people. (*Runs out quickly.*)

SHOEMAKER: Yes, yes, villains! But I'll soon settle accounts with all of them and they'll have to answer to me. Oh, my little house! What a pleasant warmth comes from your doors and windows! Oh what terrible holes, what bad meals, what dirty sheets out along the world's highways. And how stupid not to realize that my wife was pure gold, the best in the world! It makes me almost want to weep!

RED NEIGHBOR (*entering rapidly*): Good man.

YELLOW NEIGHBOR (*rapidly*): Good man.

RED NEIGHBOR: Leave this house immediately. You are a decent person and ought not to be here.

YELLOW NEIGHBOR: This is the house of a lioness, of a she-hyena.

RED NEIGHBOR: Of an evil-born woman, betrayer of men.

YELLOW NEIGHBOR: But she'll either leave town or we'll put her out. She's driving us crazy.

RED NEIGHBOR: I'd like to see her dead.

YELLOW NEIGHBOR: In her shroud, with flowers on her breast.

SHOEMAKER (*anguished*): That's enough!

RED NEIGHBOR: Blood has been shed.

YELLOW NEIGHBOR: There are no white handkerchiefs left.

RED NEIGHBOR: Two men like two suns.

YELLOW NEIGHBOR: Pierced by knives.

SHOEMAKER (*loudly*): Enough now!

RED NEIGHBOR: All because of her.

YELLOW NEIGHBOR: Her, her, her!

RED NEIGHBOR: We are really looking out for your good.

YELLOW NEIGHBOR: We're letting you know in time.

SHOEMAKER: You big liars! Evil-born women! Hypocrites! I'm going to drag you by the hair. . . .

RED NEIGHBOR (*to the other*): She's captured him too.

YELLOW NEIGHBOR: Her kisses must have done it.

SHOEMAKER: May the devil take you! Basilisks, perjurers!

BLACK NEIGHBOR (*at the window*): Neighbor, run!

(*Leaves running. The two Neighbors do likewise.*)

RED NEIGHBOR: Another one ensnared.

YELLOW NEIGHBOR: Another one!

SHOEMAKER: Harpies! Jewesses! I'll put barber's razors in your shoes. You'll have bad dreams about me.

BOY (*entering rapidly*): A group of men was just going into the Mayor's house. I'm going to hear what they're saying. (*Exits running.*)

WIFE (*entering, courageously*): Well, here I am, if they dare to come. And with the composure of one descended from a family of horsemen who many times crossed the wilds without saddles—bareback on their horses.

SHOEMAKER: And will not your fortitude sometime weaken?

WIFE: Never. A person like me, who is sustained by love and honor, never surrenders. I am able to hold out here until all my hair turns white.

SHOEMAKER (*moved, advancing toward her*): Oh . . .

WIFE: What's the matter with you?

SHOEMAKER: I am overcome. . . .

WIFE: Look, the whole town is after me; they want to come kill me, yet I'm not the least afraid. A knife is answered with a knife, and a club with a club, but at night, when I close this door and go to my bed—I feel such sadness—what sadness! And I suffer such smotherings! The bureau creaks—I start! The windows sound with the rain against them—another start! Without meaning to, I shake the bed hangings myself—double start! And all this is nothing more than fear of loneliness and its phantoms, which I have not seen because I have not wanted to, but which my mother and grandmother and all the women of my family who have had eyes have seen.

SHOEMAKER: And why don't you change your way of living?

WIFE: Are you crazy? What can I do? Where can I go? Here I am and God will say what is to happen.

(*Outside, distantly, murmurs and applause are heard.*)

SHOEMAKER: Well, I'm sorry, but I must be on my way before night falls. How much do I owe you? (*Takes up the scroll.*)

WIFE: Nothing.

SHOEMAKER: I couldn't.

WIFE: It's on the house.

SHOEMAKER: Many thanks. (*Puts the scroll to his back sadly.*) Then, good-bye—forever; because at my age . . . (*He is moved.*)

WIFE (*reacting*): I wouldn't want to say good-bye like this. I am usually very gay. (*In a clear voice.*) Good man, may God will that you find your wife so that you may once more live with the care and decency that you were used to. (*She is moved.*)

SHOEMAKER: I say the same about your husband. But, you know, the world is small: what do you want me to say to him if I meet him by chance in my wanderings?

WIFE: Tell him I adore him.

SHOEMAKER (*coming near*): And what else?

WIFE: That in spite of his fifty and some odd years, his most blessed fifty years, I find him more slender and graceful than all the men in the world.

SHOEMAKER: Child, how wonderful you are! You love him as much as I love my wife!

WIFE: Much more!

SHOEMAKER: That's not possible. I'm like a little puppy, and my wife commands in the castle. But let her command! She has more sense than I have. (*He is near and as though praying to her.*)

WIFE: And don't forget to tell him I'm waiting for him, for the nights are long in winter.

SHOEMAKER: Then, you would receive him well?

WIFE: As if he were the king and queen together.

SHOEMAKER (*trembling*): And if he should by chance come right now?

WIFE: I would go mad with happiness!

SHOEMAKER: Would you forgive him his craziness?

WIFE: How long ago I forgave him!

SHOEMAKER: Do you want him to come back now?

WIFE: Oh, if he would only come!

SHOEMAKER (*shouting*): Well, he's here.

WIFE: What are you saying?

SHOEMAKER (*removing his glasses and the disguise*): I can't bear it any longer! Wife of my heart!

(*The Wife is as though insane, with her arms held away from her body. The Shoemaker embraces her, and she looks at him intently in this critical moment. Outside, the murmuring of the couplets is clearly heard.*)

VOICE (*without*):
> Mistress Cobbler, Mistress Cobbler,
> since her husband ran away,
> since her husband ran away,
> turned her house into a tavern
> where the men go night and day,
> where the men go night and day.

WIFE (*recovering*): Loafer, scoundrel, rascal, villain! Do you hear that? All because of you! (*Begins throwing chairs.*)

SHOEMAKER (*full of emotion, going toward the bench*): Wife of my heart!

WIFE: Vagabond! Oh, how happy I am you've returned! What a life I'm going to lead you! Not even the Inquisition could have been worse. Not even the Templars at Rome!

SHOEMAKER (*at the bench*): House of my happiness!

(*The couplets are heard quite near. The Neighbors appear at the window.*)

VOICES (*outside*):
> Who has bought you, Mistress Cobbler,
> all those dresses may we guess,
> all those dresses may we guess?
> Cambrics, batistes, bobbin laces
> fit for a proprietress,
> fit for a proprietress.
>
> Now she's courted by the Mayor,
> now it is Don Blackbird's turn,
> now it is Don Blackbird's turn.
> Mistress Cobbler, Mistress Cobbler,

> Mistress, you have men to burn,
> Mistress, you have men to burn!

WIFE: How unfortunate I am! With this man God has given me! (*Going to the door.*) Quiet, long tongues, red Jews! And now, come ahead, come ahead if you want to. There are two of us now to defend my house. Two! Two! My husband and I. (*To her husband.*) Oh, this scoundrel, oh, this villain!

(*The noise of the couplets fills the stage. A bell begins to ring distantly and furiously.*)

**CURTAIN**

# THREE TOP HATS

*by* MIGUEL MIHURA

TRANSLATED BY MARCIA COBOURN WELLWARTH

# THREE TOP HATS

MIGUEL MIHURA (b. 1903) has at various times been a painter, a movie scenarist, and an editor of satirical journals as well as a playwright. In this latter capacity he has consistently been one of modern Spain's most prolific and successful writers. *Three Top Hats* was Mihura's first play, originally written in 1932; revised in 1952, it has remained his best-known work. Mihura himself has expressed irritated puzzlement at the singular reputation of this work of his youth, maintaining that many of his later works deserve equal attention. Unhappily, this is not the case, as Mihura since the close of the Civil War has become a dramatist somewhat along the lines of the French *boulevardiers*. Unlike that of many of his gifted contemporaries, his works have remained virtually untouched by the censor's ubiquitous and industrious blue pencil.

*Three Top Hats*, far from being boulevard comedy, is a work of gay, semisurrealistic fantasy. The story of Dionisio, the man who has never known love, condemned to marry the unattractive Margaret with her twelve moles and to be entombed in Don Sacramento's caricature of a staid and respectable family, it abounds in charming and delightfully illogical touches. Dionisio almost comes to know what love is in his thwarted and bittersweet "affair" with the dancer Paula. But he does not really belong to the gay, carefree, amoral theatrical world of Paula and the rest of Buby Barton's Ballet. Surprising apparitions like the Clever Hunter, the Romantic Lover, the Handsome Young Man, and the Happy Explorer are the very stuff of their daily existences. But for Dionisio they are all from a different world which he does not really understand, and so at the end he follows Don Rosario and his bugle tamely out to his fate of boiled eggs and mauve sofas.

Commenting on this play, Eugene Ionesco was moved to note that humor is liberty, and that it gives us a free and clear sense of the tragic or derisory condition of man. *Three Top Hats* is able, he goes on, to unite humor and tragedy, profound truth and drollery. Its "irrational" style can reveal peculiar contradictions, stupidity, and absurdity much better than formal rationalism or mechanical dialectics can. It requires the reader or spectator to dig through the irrational to get at the rational; to shift from one plane of reality to another; to pass from life to dream and from dream to life. In it

128

the atrocious and the gay, the sad and the farcical, the mocking and the grave are inextricably linked. Ionesco describes here the dramatic principles of surrealistic juxtaposition which he himself has practiced so brilliantly. Mihura's work, however, is derived as much from the Spanish literary tradition of life and dream contrast, of retraction from reality, which has come down to him through Valle-Inclán's corroded idylls from Calderón.

G. W.

# CHARACTERS

PAULA
FANNY
MADAME OLGA
SAGRA
TRUDY
CARMELA
DIONISIO
BUBY
DON ROSARIO
DON SACRAMENTO
THE ODIOUS MAN
THE OLD SOLDIER
THE CLEVER HUNTER
THE ROMANTIC LOVER
THE HANDSOME YOUNG MAN
THE HAPPY EXPLORER

# SCENE

(A room in a second-class hotel in a provincial capital. Downstage left, a single closed door, which leads to another room. Another door at the rear leads to a hallway. A bed. A mirrored wardrobe. A folding screen. A sofa. Above the night table, on the wall, a telephone. Next to the wardrobe, a desk. A washstand. At the foot of the bed, on the floor, two suitcases and two high hat boxes for top hats. A balcony, with curtains, and behind, the sky. A lamp hanging from the ceiling. Another small lamp on the night table.)

# ACT ONE

(*As the curtain rises the scene is empty and dark, until, by the door at the back, enter Dionisio and Don Rosario, who lights the center lamp. Dionisio, in street clothes, with hat, overcoat, and scarf, carries in his hand a hat box similar to the ones already on stage. Don Rosario is one of those amiable little old men with a long white beard.*)

DON ROSARIO: Come in, Don Dionisio. We've put your luggage here in this room.

DIONISIO: And it's a very nice room, too, Don Rosario.

DON ROSARIO: It's our best room, Don Dionisio. And the healthiest. The balcony faces the sea. And the view is beautiful. (*Going toward the balcony.*) Come closer. You can't see very well because it's night. But anyway, look over there at the little lights of the beacons in the harbor. It makes a very pretty effect. Everybody says so. Do you see them?

DIONISIO: No. I don't see anything.

DON ROSARIO: You don't seem very bright, Don Dionisio.

DIONISIO: Why do you say that, for heaven's sake?

DON ROSARIO: Because you don't see the little lights. Wait. I'm going to open the doors of the balcony. That way you'll see them better.

DIONISIO: Oh, no. Please don't. It's terribly cold. Leave them. (*Looking again.*) Ah! Now I think I see something. (*Looking through the window.*) You mean the three little lights over there in the distance?

DON ROSARIO: Yes. That's it! That's it!

DIONISIO: It's delightful! One of them is red, isn't it?

DON ROSARIO: No. All three are white. There isn't any red one.

DIONISIO: Well, I think that one of them is red. The one on the left.

DON ROSARIO: No. It can't be red. For fifteen years I have been showing all the guests the beacon lights of the harbor from this balcony, and no one has ever told me that there was a red one.

DIONISIO: But don't you see them?

DON ROSARIO: No. I don't see them. Because of my poor vision I have never seen them. My daddy told me all this. When he was dying, my daddy said to me, "Listen, son, come here. From the balcony of the pink bedroom you can see three little white lights far away in the harbor. Show them to the guests and they'll all be very happy. . . ." And I always show them. . . .

DIONISIO: Well, there's one red one there, I assure you.

DON ROSARIO: Well, then, in that case, from tomorrow on I'll tell my guests they can see three little lights, two white ones and one red one. . . . And they'll be even happier. . . . Isn't it true that it's a charming view? Well, by day it's even prettier! . . .

DIONISIO: Of course! By day there will be more little lights. . . .

DON ROSARIO: No. In the daytime they turn them off.

DIONISIO: That's too bad.

DON ROSARIO: But it doesn't matter, because, instead, you see the mountain, with a very fat cow on top of it, which little by little is eating up the whole mountain.

DIONISIO: Amazing!

DON ROSARIO: Yes, all Nature is amazing, my son.

(*Meanwhile Dionisio has put the hat box next to the others. Now he opens his suitcase and takes out a pair of black silk pajamas with a bird embroidered in white across the chest. He lays them out across the foot of the bed. Afterwards, while Don Rosario is speaking, Dionisio takes off his overcoat, scarf, and hat, which he puts in the wardrobe.*)

DON ROSARIO: This is the prettiest room in the whole house. . . . Now, of course, it is becoming worn out by all the traffic. . . . So many guests keep coming in, in the summer! . . . But even the wooden floor is better here than in the other rooms. . . . Come here. . . . Look. . . . Not this bit here, because it's the passageway and so it's already worn out from so much coming and going. . . . But look under the bed, where it's better preserved. . . . Look at that wood, my boy. . . . Do you have any matches?

DIONISIO (*coming closer to Don Rosario*): Yes. I have a box of matches and some tobacco.

DON ROSARIO: Light a match.

DIONISIO: What for?

DON ROSARIO: So you can see the wood better. Get down on your knees.

DIONISIO: All right.

(*He lights a match and the two of them, on their knees, look under the bed.*)

DON ROSARIO: How does it look to you, Don Dionisio?

DIONISIO: It's magnificent!

DON ROSARIO (*shouting*): Hey!

DIONISIO: What's the matter?

DON ROSARIO (*looking under the bed*): There's a boot under there!

DIONISIO: A man's or a woman's?

DON ROSARIO: I don't know. It's a boot.

DIONISIO: Good heavens!

DON ROSARIO: Some guest must have left it behind. . . . And those maids didn't even see it when they swept! . . . Do you think that's nice?

DIONISIO: I don't know what to tell you. . . .

DON ROSARIO: Please, Don Dionisio. I cannot bend down any farther because of my waistline. . . . Will you go and get the boot?

DIONISIO: Leave it, Don Rosario. . . . It doesn't bother me. . . . I'm going right to bed, and I won't notice it. . . .

DON ROSARIO: I wouldn't be able to sleep in peace if I knew there was a boot under my bed. . . . I'll call the maid right away. (*He takes a little bell out of his pocket and rings it.*)

DIONISIO: No, no, stop ringing. I'll get it. (*Crawls part way under the bed.*) It's OK. I've got it. (*Comes out with the boot.*) Well, it's a very nice boot. It's a man's. . . .

DON ROSARIO: Do you want it, Don Dionisio?

DIONISIO: No, good heavens; thank you very much. Leave it. . . .

DON ROSARIO: Don't be silly. Go on. If you like it, take it. Surely
no one will claim it. . . . Who knows how long it's been there?

DIONISIO: No, no. Really. I don't need it. . . .

DON ROSARIO: Go on. Don't be silly. . . . Would you like me to
wrap it in some paper, my little rosebud?

DIONISIO: All right, whatever you like. . . .

DON ROSARIO: It's not necessary. It's clean. Put it in one of your
pockets. (*He puts the boot in one of his own pockets.*) Like
this. . . .

DIONISIO: Can I get up now?

DON ROSARIO: Yes, Don Dionisio; get up from there. We can't have
you ruining your trousers. . . .

DIONISIO: What's that, there, Don Rosario? A telephone?

DON ROSARIO: Yes, sir. A telephone.

DIONISIO: Is it one of those telephones for calling the fire department?

DON ROSARIO: Yes, sir. And the undertakers. . . .

DIONISIO: But this is just like throwing the house out of the window
piece by piece, Don Rosario! (*While Dionisio speaks, Don Rosario takes from the suitcase a jacket, a pair of pants, and some
boots, and arranges them in the wardrobe.*) I've been coming
to this hotel for seven years, and every year I find a new im-
provement. First you got all the flies out of the kitchen and
moved them into the dining room. Then you moved them
out of the dining room and put them into the lobby. And
the other day you got them out of the lobby and took them
for a walk in the country where, finally, you were able to
shake them off. . . . It was wonderful! Then you put in
heating. . . . Afterwards you got rid of that quince butter that
your daughter used to make. . . . Now, the telephone. . . .
Out of a second-class tavern you have made a comfortable
hotel. . . . And the prices keep on being so economical. . . .
This will ruin you, Don Rosario! . . .

DON ROSARIO: You know me, Don Dionisio. I can't help it. That's the way I am. Nothing is good enough for my darling guests. . . .

DIONISIO: But, still, you go too far. . . . It isn't right that when it's cold you should put hot-water bottles in our beds; or that when we have a cold you should get into bed with us in order to keep us warm and make us sweat; or that you should give us a kiss when we leave on a trip. And it isn't right either that when a guest can't sleep you should have to come into his room with your little bugle and play old ballads so he can drop quietly off to sleep. . . . It's too much kindness! . . . They're taking advantage of you! . . .

DON ROSARIO: The poor little things. . . . Let them. . . . Almost all the people who come here are traveling salesmen or entertainers. . . . Lonely men . . . men without mothers. . . . And I want to be a father to all of them, since I couldn't be one to my own poor little boy. . . . That poor little boy of mine who drowned in a well. . . . (*Becomes emotional.*)

DIONISIO: Come now, Don Rosario. . . . Don't think about that. . . .

DON ROSARIO: You already know the story of that poor little boy who drowned in the well. . . .

DIONISIO: Yes, I know it. Your little boy leaned over the well to catch hold of a branch. . . . And the little boy fell down. He went "Plop!" and that was the end of it.

DON ROSARIO: That's the story, Don Dionisio. He went "Plop!" and that was the end of it. (*Painful pause.*) Are you going to bed?

DIONISIO: Yes, indeed.

DON ROSARIO: I'll help you, my little wallflower bud. (*While they talk, he helps him to get undressed, to put on his beautiful pajamas, and to change his shoes for a pair of slippers.*) I love all my guests, and you, too, Don Dionisio. I liked you from the time you first started coming here; it's going on seven years now! . . .

DIONISIO: Seven years, Don Rosario! Seven years! And ever since they sent me to that wretched, mournful town which, fortunately, is near this one, my only happiness has been to spend a month here every year and see my fiancée and swim in the sea, and buy hazelnuts, and take walks on Sundays around the band-stand, and stroll down the avenue whistling "The Little Dollar Princesses." . . .

DON ROSARIO: But tomorrow you begin a new life!

DIONISIO: From tomorrow it will always be summer for me. . . . What's this? Are you crying? Come, now, Don Rosario! . . .

DON ROSARIO: To think that your parents, may they rest in peace, cannot be with you on a night like this. . . . They would be so happy! . . .

DIONISIO: Yes, they would be happy to see that I am so happy. . . . But let's stop being sad, Don Rosario. . . . Tomorrow I'm getting married! This is the last night that I'll spend alone in a hotel room. It's the end of boardinghouses, cold rooms, the drop of water that leaks out of the washbowl, the napkin with your initial penciled on it, the bottle of wine with your initial penciled on it, the toothpick with your initial penciled on it. . . . It's the end of the smallest egg in the world, always fried. . . . It's the end of chicken croquettes. . . . It's the end of lovely views from the balcony. . . . Tomorrow I'm getting married! All this is over and she begins. . . . She!

DON ROSARIO: You love her a lot?

DIONISIO: I adore her, Don Rosario, I adore her! She's the first fiancée I've had and also the last one. . . . She's a saint. . . .

DON ROSARIO: You must have been there, at her house, all day to-day. . . .

DIONISIO: Yes, I arrived this morning, sent my luggage here, and then I had lunch with them, and supper, too. Her parents like me very much. . . . They're so good. . . .

DON ROSARIO: They're wonderful people. . . . And your fiancée is a virtuous young lady. . . . And, in spite of being from a wealthy family, she's not the least bit conceited. . . . (*Roguishly.*) For she does have a little money, you know, Don Dionisio.

DIONISIO: Yes, she does have a little money, and she knows how to do some very pretty embroidery, and how to make lovely apple tarts, too. . . . She's an angel! . . .

DON ROSARIO (*indicating a hat box*): And what have you got there, Don Dionisio?

DIONISIO: A top hat. For the wedding. (*Takes it out.*) My father-in-law gave it to me today. It's his. From when he was mayor. And I have two others here which I bought myself. (*Takes them out.*) Look at them. They're very pretty. Above all, you can see immediately that they're top hats, and that's what I need. . . . But none of them look right on me. . . . (*He is trying them on in front of the mirror.*) Look. This one doesn't fit. This one makes my head look too big. . . . And this one, my fiancée says, makes me look like a pot-bellied stove with a chimney on top. . . .

DON ROSARIO: Does she mean a domestic stove or a foreign stove?

DIONISIO: She just said a stove. . . . To be sure. . . . She was fed up about it when I left. She's such an innocent young thing. . . . Does the phone work? I'm going to see if she's got over it yet. . . . It will make her so happy. . . . (*He has left the last top hat on his head, and will continue to wear it unless otherwise indicated.*)

DON ROSARIO: Call downstairs and the desk clerk will get you an outside line.

DIONISIO: Yes, sir. (*Into the phone.*) Yes. Would you please get me an outside line? Yes. Thank you.

DON ROSARIO: They have probably gone to bed already. It's late.

DIONISIO: I don't think so. It's not eleven yet. She sleeps next to the room where the telephone is. . . . Here we are. (*Dials.*) One-nine-zero. That's it. Hello. It's me. Dionisio. Call Miss Margaret to the phone. (*To Don Rosario.*) It's the maid. . . . She's coming now. . . . (*Into the phone.*) Hello, my dear little creature! It's me. Yes. I'm calling you from the hotel. . . . I have a phone in my own room. . . . Yes, my little sugar dove . . . No . . . Nothing . . . So you'll see that I'm thinking about you. . . . Listen, I'm not going to wear the hat that makes me look like a stove. . . . I was just kidding. . . . I'll do whatever you say. . . . Yes, my love . . . (*Pause.*) Yes, my love . . . (*All of a sudden he jerks his leg into the air, covers the mouthpiece with his hand, and gives a little cry.*) Don Rosario . . . are there fleas in this room?

DON ROSARIO: I don't know, my boy. . . .

DIONISIO (*into the phone*): Yes, my love. (*Covers the mouthpiece again.*) Your father, when he died, didn't he tell you anything about there being fleas in this room? (*Into the phone.*) Yes, my love . . .

DON ROSARIO: Actually, I think he told me there was one. . . .

DIONISIO (*who continues scratching himself, one calf against the other, getting desperate*): Well, he's devouring my leg. . . . Do me a favor, Don Rosario; scratch me. . . (*Don Rosario scratches him.*) No; lower down. (*Into the phone.*) Yes, my love . . . (*Covers mouthpiece.*) Higher up! Wait a minute. . . . Take this. (*Gives the phone to Don Rosario, who puts it to his ear, while Dionisio nervously searches for the flea.*)

DON ROSARIO (*Listens to the telephone, where one supposes the girl goes on talking; he adopts a very sweet expression*): Yes, my love . . . (*Very tenderly.*) Yes, my love . . .

DIONISIO (*who has finally killed the flea.*): It's all right now. Give it to me. . . . (*Don Rosario gives him the phone.*) Yes . . . I'll sleep with your picture under my pillow, too. . . . If you wake up, you can call me later. (*Scratching himself again.*) Good-bye, my little darling. (*Hangs up.*) She's an angel! . . .

DON ROSARIO: If you like, I'll tell them downstairs to leave you connected with the outside line, so you two can talk whenever you want. . . .

DIONISIO: Yes, Don Rosario. Thanks a lot. Perhaps we will talk some more. . . .

DON ROSARIO: What time is the wedding, Don Dionisio?

DIONISIO: At eight o'clock, but they'll come to get me earlier. Have them call me at seven, so I won't be late. I'm wearing a morning coat, and it's a very difficult thing to wear a morning coat. . . . And then those three top hats . . .

DON ROSARIO: Will you allow me to give you a kiss, my little rose of Pitiminí? It's the kiss your father would give you on a night like this one. It's the kiss that I'll never be able to give to that little boy of mine who fell down the well on me. . . .

DIONISIO: Now, now, Don Rosario.

*(They embrace emotionally.)*

DON ROSARIO: He leaned over the well, went "Plop!" and that was the end of it. . . .

DIONISIO: Don Rosario!

DON ROSARIO: All right. I'm going. You must want to rest. . . . Do you want me to send up a little glass of milk?

DIONISIO: No, no. Thanks very much.

DON ROSARIO: Do you want me to send up a little dried fish?

DIONISIO: No.

DON ROSARIO: Do you want me to stay here until you fall asleep, so you won't be restless? I'll bring up my little bugle and play. . . . I'll play "Carnival in Venice," I'll play Toselli's "Serenade." . . . And you'll sleep and dream. . . .

DIONISIO: No, Don Rosario. Thank you very much.

DON ROSARIO: Tomorrow I'll get up early so I can wake you. We'll all get up early. . . .

DIONISIO: No, good heavens, Don Rosario. Certainly not that. Don't tell anybody I'm getting married. You'll embarrass me terribly. . . .

DON ROSARIO *(already at the door at the rear, ready to leave)*: All right. If you don't want it, we won't all come to the door to say good-bye to you. . . . But it would be so lovely. . . . Well, then, you'll just have to leave all by yourself. Just think, after tomorrow you'll have to make a wonderful girl happy. . . . You should only be thinking about her. . . .

DIONISIO *(has taken a wallet out of his jacket pocket, from which he extracts a photograph, which he looks at in ecstasy. Then he puts the wallet and the photograph under his pillow, and says, very romantically)*: For seven years I have been thinking only of her! Night and day! At all hours . . . In these hours that are left before my happiness is complete, what else should I be thinking about? I'll see you tomorrow, Don Rosario. . . .

DON ROSARIO: Until tomorrow, my little honeysuckle-face. *(He makes a bow. Exit, closing the door.)*

(*Dionisio closes his suitcases, while he whistles an ugly, out-of-date song. Then he lies down on the bed, without taking off his top hat. Looks at his watch.*)

DIONISIO: Eleven-fifteen. Just nine hours left. . . . (*Winds the watch.*) We should have got married this afternoon and not been separated, now, tonight. . . . *Tonight* is too much. . . . It's an empty night tonight. . . . (*He closes his eyes.*) Baby! Baby! Margarita! (*Pause. Afterwards, in the adjoining room, noise of a door slamming and loud conversation, which gradually gets louder. Dionisio sits up.*) Oh, no! An argument now! What a time for a fight! . . . (*His glance catches the mirror, in which he sees that he still has the hat on, and, seated on the bed, he says:*) Yes. Now it seems to give me a face like a steam-roller.

(*He gets up, goes toward the table where he had left the other two hats, and again tries them all on. When he has one on his head and the other two in each hand, the door at the left suddenly opens and Paula enters, a marvelous blonde girl of eighteen who, paying no attention to Dionisio, turns and shuts the door with a bang; and with her face to the closed door, speaks with whoever is left on the other side. Dionisio, who sees her reflected in the mirror, is very startled, but doesn't move.*)

PAULA: Idiot!

BUBY (*outside*): Open up!

PAULA: No!

BUBY: Open up!

PAULA: No!

BUBY: Open up, I say!

PAULA: I say, no!

BUBY (*all very fast*): Imbecile!

PAULA: Fool!

BUBY: Stupid!

PAULA: Cretin!

BUBY: Open up!

PAULA: No!

BUBY: Open up, I say!

PAULA: I say, no!

BUBY: No?

PAULA: No!

BUBY: OK.

PAULA: All right then. (*She turns around and sees Dionisio.*) Oh, pardon me! . . . I thought this room was empty. . . .

DIONISIO: (*in his same position in front of the mirror*): Yes . . .

PAULA: I leaned against the door and it opened. . . . It must not have been latched properly. . . . Not locked . . .

DIONISIO (*terribly upset*): Yes . . .

PAULA: So I came in . . .

DIONISIO: Yes . . .

PAULA: I didn't know . . .

DIONISIO: No . . .

PAULA: I was arguing with my boyfriend. . . .

DIONISIO: Yes . . .

PAULA: He's an idiot. . . .

DIONISIO: Yes . . .

PAULA: Perhaps our shouts annoyed you?

DIONISIO: No . . .

PAULA: He's a boor. . . .

BUBY (*outside*): Open up!

PAULA: No. (*To Dionisio.*) He's very ugly and very stupid. . . . I don't like him. . . . I'm making him mad. . . . I enjoy making him mad. . . . And I don't intend to open up. . . . Let him stew in his own juice. . . . (*Towards the door.*) Oh, go on. Go fly a kite!

BUBY (*beating on the door*): Open up!

PAULA (*doing the same*): No! (*To Dionisio.*) Of course, now that I realize it, I've barged into your room. Excuse me. I'll go. So long.

DIONISIO (*only now turning around and facing her*): So long. Good night.

PAULA (*noticing his strange posture with the hats, which makes him look like a juggler*): Are you an artiste, too?

DIONISIO: Very much so.

PAULA: Just like us. I'm a dancer. I work in Buby Barton's Ballet. We're opening tomorrow in the New Music Hall. Maybe you're opening tomorrow in the New Music Hall, too? I haven't seen the programs yet. What's your name?

DIONISIO: Dionisio Somoza Buscarini.

PAULA: No, I mean your name in the theatre.

DIONISIO: Ah! My name in the theatre! Well, just like everybody else! . . .

PAULA: What?

DIONISIO: Antonini . . .

PAULA: Antonini?

DIONISIO: Yes, Antonini. It's very easy. With two "n" 's . . .

PAULA: I don't know it. Are you a juggler?

DIONISIO: Yes. Of course. I'm a juggler.

BUBY (*outside*): Open up!

PAULA: No! (*She turns to Dionisio.*) Were you rehearsing?

DIONISIO: Yes. I was rehearsing.

PAULA: Is your number a solo?

DIONISIO: Yes, of course. My number's a solo. Well, you see, since my parents died, of course . . .

PAULA: Your parents were artistes, too?

DIONISIO: Yes. Of course. I mean, no—my father was a commander in the infantry.

PAULA: He was a soldier?

DIONISIO: Yes, he was a soldier. But very little. Hardly at all. Only when he was bored. What he did most of the time was swallow swords. He really did enjoy swallowing his sword. But of course, everybody likes to do that. . . .

PAULA: It's true. Everybody likes to do that. Then your whole family were circus artistes?

DIONISIO: Yes. All of them. Except my little old grandmother. Since she was so old, she wasn't any good. She always fell off the horse. . . . And the two of them spent the whole day arguing. . . .

PAULA: The horse and your grandmother?

DIONISIO: Yes. They each had a terrible temper. . . . But the horse did most of the swearing. . . .

PAULA: There are five of us. Five girls. We've been with Buby Barton's Ballet for a year now. And we've got Madame Olga, the bearded lady, with us, too. Her number is very popular. We arrived this afternoon in order to open tomorrow. After supper the rest of them stayed in the café downstairs. . . . This is a miserable little town. . . . There's no place to go, and it's raining all the time. . . . And I'm bored with the idea of the café. . . . I'm not like all the rest of them. . . . I came up to my room to play my record-player a while. . . . I adore record-player music. . . . But my boyfriend came up after me, with a bottle of liquor, and he wanted to make me drink, because he's always drinking. . . . And I fought with him about that . . . and about something else, if you know what I mean. . . . I don't like him to drink so much. . . .

DIONISIO: It's very bad for the liver. . . . A man I used to know . . .

BUBY (outside): Open up!

PAULA: No. And I'm really not going to open up for him either. I'm going to sit down right now and stay put so he'll get mad. (She sits on the bed.) I won't bother you?

DIONISIO: I don't think so.

PAULA: Now that I know you're a fellow artiste, it doesn't bother me, being here. . . . (Buby beats on the door.) He must be furious. . . . He must be blind with fury. . . .

DIONISIO (frightened): Listen, I think we should open up. . . .

PAULA: No. We won't open up for him.

DIONISIO: Well, OK.

PAULA: We're *always* fighting.

DIONISIO: Have you been going together very long?

PAULA: No. I don't know. Two or three days. I don't like him. But a girl gets so bored touring the sticks. . . . The fact is he's really very nice, but when he drinks, or when he's angry about something, he just goes crazy. . . . It's frightening to see him. . . .

DIONISIO (*very timidly*): Listen, I'm going to open up for him now. . . .

PAULA: No. We won't open up for him.

DIONISIO: But he's going to be very angry, and he'll start a fight with me. . . .

PAULA: Let him. It's nothing to me.

DIONISIO: But, just think, your mother will probably scold you because of this. . . .

PAULA: What mother?

DIONISIO: Yours.

PAULA: Mine?

DIONISIO: Yes. Your mother or your father.

PAULA: I haven't got either a mother or a father.

DIONISIO: Your brothers, then.

PAULA: I don't have any brothers.

DIONISIO: Then, who do you travel with? Do you go around by yourself with your boyfriend and all these people?

PAULA: Yes. Of course I go by myself. You mean I can't go around by myself?

DIONISIO: Well, as far as I'm concerned, of course it doesn't matter. . . .

BUBY (*outside, furious now*): Open up, open up, open up!

PAULA: I'm going to open the door for him now. He's getting too angry. . . .

DIONISIO (*even more timid than before*): Listen, I don't think you should open. . . .

PAULA: Yes, I'm going to open the door. (*She opens the door and Buby, a Negro, comes in, with a ukulele in his hand.*) All right now. What's the matter? What's going on? What do you want?

BUBY: Good evening.

DIONISIO: Good evening.

PAULA (*introducing Dionisio*): This gentleman is a juggler.

BUBY: Ah! He's a juggler!

PAULA: He opens tomorrow in the New Music Hall too. . . . His father used to swallow swords. . . .

DIONISIO: Excuse me for not shaking hands with you. . . . (*Indicates the hats, which he still holds, poised in the same position.*) Since I have these, . . . well, I can't.

BUBY (*unpleasantly*): A fellow-artiste—ha! Go inside, Paula!

PAULA: I'm not going, Buby!

BUBY: You're not going, Paula?

PAULA: I'm not going, Buby.

BUBY: Then I'm not going either, Paula.

(*The two of them sit down on the bed, one on each side of Dionisio, who also sits down and is becoming more and more agitated. Buby begins to whistle an American popular song, accompanying himself on his ukulele. Paula joins in. And last of all, Dionisio. The piece ends. Pause.*)

DIONISIO (*in order to break the strained silence, very gallantly*): Have you been black for a long time?

BUBY: I don't know. I have always seen myself like this when I looked in the mirror. . . .

DIONISIO: Good heavens! Troubles never come singly! How did you get this way? Was it a fall?

BUBY: That must have been it, mister.

DIONISIO: From a bicycle?

BUBY: That's right, mister. . . .

DIONISIO: People shouldn't buy bicycles for little children! Isn't that right, miss? A man I used to know . . .

PAULA (*distracted, she isn't paying attention to this dialogue*): This room is better than mine. . . .

DIONISIO: Yes, it's better. If you wish we'll change. I'll go to yours and you two can stay here. It's no trouble for me. . . . I'll gather up my stuff. . . . Besides being bigger, it has a magnificent view. From the balcony you can see the ocean. . . . And in the ocean, three little lights . . . The floor is very nice, too. . . . Would you like to look under the bed? . . .

BUBY (*dryly*): No.

DIONISIO: Go on. Look under the bed. You'll probably find another boot. . . . There must be a lot of them. . . .

PAULA (*who goes on thinking her own thoughts and not paying much attention to what Dionisio is saying; the latter continues to be very embarrassed*): Do some trick with the hats so we'll be entertained. Jugglers fascinate me. . . .

DIONISIO: Me, too. It's wonderful how they throw things in the air and catch them. . . . It looks like they're going to fall, and then they don't fall. . . . It's always a bit of a disappointment!

PAULA: Go on. Do it.

DIONISIO (*wondering*): Me?

PAULA: Yes. You.

DIONISIO (*deciding to risk everything*): I will. (*He gets up. He throws the hats in the air and, naturally, they fall on the floor, where he leaves them. Sits down again.*) There you are.

PAULA (*applauding*): How terrific! Let me try. I've never tried. (*Gathers up the hats from the floor.*) Is it hard? Do you do it like this? (*She throws the hats in the air.*) Whoop! (*And they fall.*)

DIONISIO: That's it! That's it! You've learned it right off the bat! (*Gathers up the hats from the floor and offers them to Buby.*) How about you? Would you like to play a little, too?

BUBY: No. (*The telephone rings.*) A bell?

PAULA: Yes. It's a bell.

DIONISIO (*disconcerted*): It must be a visitor.

PAULA: No. It's here inside. It's the telephone.

DIONISIO (*faking, because he knows it is his fiancée*): The telephone?

PAULA: Yes.

DIONISIO: How strange! It must be some child playing with phone numbers.

PAULA: See who it is.

DIONISIO: No. Let's let him get mad.

PAULA: Do you want me to see?

DIONISIO: No. Don't bother. I'll see. (*Looks into the earpiece.*) Can't see anyone.

PAULA: Speak.

DIONISIO: Oh! That's right. (*Speaks, disguising his voice.*) No! No! (*Hangs up.*)

PAULA: Who was it?

DIONISIO: Nobody. It was a beggar.

PAULA: A beggar?

DIONISIO: Yes. A beggar. He wanted me to give him ten cents. And I told him no.

BUBY (*he gets up, indignant now*): Paula, let's go to our room.

PAULA: Why?

BUBY: Because I want to.

PAULA (*impudently*): And who are you?

BUBY: I'm the one who has the right to say this to you. Get inside right now. This business is all over. We can't go on like this any longer. . . .

PAULA (*on her feet, ranting, facing Buby, and crowding Dionisio, who is very upset, between the two of them*): Yes, you're right! I'm tired of putting up with your rudeness. . . . You're

an intolerable Negro, like all Negroes. And I hate you. Do you
understand me? I hate you. . . . And it's all over. . . . I can't
look at you. . . . I can't stand you.

BUBY: On the other hand, Paula, I adore you. . . . You know I love
you. But you're not going to play around with me. You know
I adore you, my little peach blossom!

PAULA: So what? Do you think I can fall in love with you? Do you
really think I can fall in love with a Negro? No, Buby. I'll
never be able to fall in love with you. . . . We've been going
together for a little while, but now it's enough. I've been your
girl friend out of pity. . . . Because I saw you were sad and
bored. . . . Because you were a Negro. . . . Because you sang
sad songs of the plantation. . . . Because you told me that
when you were a little boy the mosquitoes ate you up, and the
monkeys bit you, and you had to climb up the palm trees and
the coconut trees. . . . But I've never loved you, and I'll never
be able to love you. . . . You ought to understand. . . . Love
*you!* That's why I like this gentleman, who is more good-
looking. . . . This gentleman, who is a well-mannered person.
. . . This gentleman, who is white. . . .

BUBY (*with hatred*): Paula! . . .

PAULA (*to Dionisio*): Do you agree that nobody could fall in love
with a Negro?

DIONISIO: Well, if he is honorable and industrious . . .

BUBY: Get inside!

PAULA: I'm not going in! (*She sits down.*) I'm not going in! Understand? I'm not going in!

BUBY (*sitting down, too*): I'll wait until you get tired of talking to
this paleface. . . . (*Another strained silence.*)

DIONISIO: Would you like it if we whistled something else? I also
know "Santa Lucia." . . .

FANNY (*offstage*): Paula! Where are you? (*She leans through the
door at the left.*) What are you doing here? (*Enters. She is
another happy-go-lucky girl from the ballet.*) What's going
on? (*No one speaks.*) What's the matter with you? What's
going on? Have you two been fighting again? . . . Well, you're
certainly having a great time. . . . On the other hand, we're

having a wonderful time. . . . There are some gentlemen down-stairs, in the café, who want to invite us to have a few bottles of champagne now. . . . The rest of the girls stayed downstairs with them and Madame Olga, and now they're coming up and we're going to sing and dance until dawn. . . . Can't you two talk? Well, you're certainly gloomy. . . (*Indicating Dionisio.*) Who's this guy? . . . (*Pause.*) Don't you hear me? Who is this guy? . . . Don't you hear me? Who is he?

PAULA: I don't know.

FANNY: You don't know?

PAULA (*to Dionisio*): Tell her yourself who you are!

DIONISIO (*getting up*): I am Antonini. . . .

FANNY: How are you?

DIONISIO: Fine. And you?

PAULA: He's a juggler. He opens tomorrow in the New Music Hall, too.

FANNY: Good, . . . but what's the matter with you two?

PAULA: Nothing's the matter with us.

FANNY: Oh, go on. Tell me. What's the matter with you?

PAULA: Let this gentleman tell you.

FANNY: You tell me what's going on. . . .

DIONISIO: Oh, I'd probably explain it very badly. . . .

FANNY: That doesn't matter. . .

DIONISIO: Well, nothing . . . It's just that they're a little bit upset. . . . But it's nothing. It's just that this Negro is an idiot. . . .

BUBY (*threateningly*): You good-for-nothing! . . .

DIONISIO: No. Excuse me. I was mistaken. . . . He's not an idiot. . . . It's just that, since he's a Negro, well, he has his little peculiarities. . . . But the poor fellow isn't to blame. . . . How can *he* help it, if he fell off a bicycle? . . . It would have been much worse if he'd lost a hand. . . . And this young lady told him, . . . and, well! . . . it's got to the point where, where . . .

FANNY: What else?

DIONISIO: No. It's all over now. . . .

FANNY: You've said enough already; anyway, it's always the same thing. . . . Paula, you're a dope.

PAULA (*she gets up; waspishly*): Well, if I'm a dope, so much the better! (*Exit left.*)

FANNY: It's your fault, Buby, for being so bad mannered. . . .

BUBY (*mimicking Paula*): Well, if I'm bad mannered, so much the better! (*Also goes out left.*)

FANNY (*to Dionisio*): Well, then, I'm going to leave, too. . . .

DIONISIO: Well, if you're going to leave, so much the better. . . .

FANNY (*changing her mind, she sits on the bed and takes a cigarette from her purse*): Gotta match?

DIONISIO: Yes.

FANNY: Give it to me.

DIONISIO (*who is distracted and upset, puts his hand in his pocket and, without realizing it, instead of giving her matches, gives her the boot*): Here.

FANNY: What's this?

DIONISIO (*even more upset*): Oh! Excuse me. This is for lighting. I have the matches here. (*Lights a match on the sole of the boot.*) You see? You do it like this. It's very practical. I always carry it for that. . . . Where there's a boot you can do away with those lighters! . . .

FANNY: Sit down here.

DIONISIO (*sitting beside her, on the bed*): Thank you. (*She smokes. Dionisio looks at her in wonder.*) Do you know how to blow it through your nose, too?

FANNY: Yes.

DIONISIO (*elated*): Wow!

FANNY: What do you think of those two?

DIONISIO: They're an attractive couple.

FANNY: Do you really think so, Tonini? (*And, playfully, she pushes him backwards. Dionisio falls back on the bed, with his legs*

*up in the air. This obviously bothers him a bit, but he doesn't
say anything. He sits up again.)* She doesn't love him. . . . But
he, yes . . . He loves her, in his own fashion, and the Negroes
love in a very impassioned fashion. . . . Buby loves her. . . .
And with Buby you can't play around, because when he drinks,
he's bad. . . . Paula was silly to get mixed up in this. . . . *(She
notices a handkerchief that Dionisio has in the breast pocket
of his pajamas.)* This is a pretty handkerchief. *(She takes it.)*
For me, OK?

DIONISIO: Do you have a cold?

FANNY: No. I like it! *(And she gives him another big push, and he
falls into the same ridiculous position as before. This time the
joke bothers him even more, but he still doesn't say anything.)* Paula isn't like me. . . . I'm much more amusing. . . .
If I like a man, I tell him so. . . . When I don't like him anymore, I tell him that, too. . . . I'm most outspoken, dearie. Oh,
how outspoken I am! *(Looks fixedly into Dionisio's eyes.)*
Listen, you have very pretty eyes. . . .

DIONISIO *(still not catching on)*: Where?

FANNY: In your little face, dopey! *(And she gives him another great
push. Dionisio, this time, reacts, angry as a little boy, and says,
now, half crying)*:

DIONISIO: If you push me again, damn you, I'm going to give you
a slap you won't forget in a hurry, damn you.

FANNY: Oh, boy! What a character! And are you opening tomorrow with us, too?

DIONISIO *(angry)*: Yes.

FANNY: And what do you do?

DIONISIO: Nothing.

FANNY: Nothing?

DIONISIO: Very little . . . Since I'm just now beginning, well, of
of course, . . . what am I to do?

FANNY: You must do something. . . . Tell me about it. . . .

DIONISIO: But it's so silly. . . . You'll see. . . . Well, first of all the
music starts up and plays a little. . . . Like this . . . Parapapá,
parapapá, parapapá . . . And then, then, I come, and I come

on stage. . . . And the music stops. . . (*All very fast now, and getting muddled.*) And it doesn't go parapapá or anything. . . . And I, I come, I come on and I go "Hoop!" . . . And I go "Hoop!" And right away I go, I go, and I go off stage . . . and then it's all over. . . .

FANNY: It's very pretty. . . .

DIONISIO: It's not really very much. . . .

FANNY: Do they like your number?

DIONISIO: Oh! That I don't know. . . .

FANNY: But do they applaud?

DIONISIO: Very little. Hardly at all. . . . Since everything is so expensive now. . . .

FANNY: That's true. . . . (*The telephone rings.*) A bell? A telephone?

DIONISIO: Yes, it's just a poor beggar. . . .

FANNY: A beggar? What's his name?

DIONISIO: Nothing. Beggars don't have names. . . .

FANNY: But what does he want?

DIONISIO: He wants me to give him some bread. But I don't have any bread, so I can't give him any. . . . Do you have any bread?

FANNY: I'll see. . . . (*Looks in her purse.*) No. Today I don't have any bread.

DIONISIO: Well then, let him stew in his own juice, and to hell with him!

FANNY: Do you want me to wish him God's blessing?

DIONISIO: No. Don't bother. I'll tell him. (*In a loud voice, from the bed.*) God bless you!

FANNY: Do you think he heard you?

DIONISIO: Yes. Beggars like that hear everything. . . .

(*Through the left-hand door, dressed in street clothes and carrying packages and bottles, enter Trudy, Carmela, and Sagra, three boisterous girls from Buby Barton's Ballet.*)

SAGRA (*still outside*): Fanny! Fanny!

CARMELA (*entering now with the others*): We're here now!

TRUDY: And we've got pastries!

SAGRA: And ham!

CARMELA: And wine!

TRUDY: And even a cake with icing!

ALL THREE (*singing nothing in particular*): La dee da, la dee da!

SAGRA: The man from the café invited us! . . . (*Begins putting the packages and their coats on the sofa.*)

CARMELA: And we're all going to spend some time together here!

TRUDY: He ordered oysters!

SAGRA: And expensive champagne!

CARMELA: And he's even fallen in love with me. . . .

ALL THREE: La dee da, la dee da!

TRUDY (*indicating the room at the left*): We left more things in that room!

SAGRA: We'll get everything ready in the other room!

CARMELA: Take these packages! (*Gives some packages to Fanny.*)

TRUDY: Help us! Come on!

FANNY (*happy, with the packages, exits left*): Won't we have fun?

SAGRA: We'll have fun!

CARMELA: You'll see how we will!

ALL THREE: La dee da, la dee da!

TRUDY (*noticing the top hats, which Dionisio has left on the desk*): Look at those hats!

SAGRA: They belong to this gentleman!

CARMELA: He's the juggler that Paula told us about!

TRUDY: Shall we play with them?

SAGRA (*throwing them up high*): Up! Hurray!

CARMELA: Whoop!

(*The hats fall to the ground, and the three silly girls, laughing all the time, go out through the left-hand door. Dionisio, who is very upset about all this, takes advantage of the opportunity to go and close the door, which the girls have left open. Then he goes and picks up the hats, which are on the floor. He drops them, and, for convenience, he puts one of them on his head. At this moment there is a light knocking on the outside door.*)

DON ROSARIO (*outside*): Don Dionisio! Don Dionisio!

DIONISIO (*hurriedly putting the two hats on the desk*): Who is it?

DON ROSARIO: It's me, Don Rosario.

DIONISIO: Oh! It's you! (*And he gets into bed, very fast, getting between the sheets and keeping his hat on.*)

DON ROSARIO (*entering with his little bugle*): Aren't you sleeping? I was afraid that your next-door neighbors wouldn't let you sleep. They are very bad, and turn everything topsy-turvy. . . .

DIONISIO: I haven't heard anything. . . . Everything is very quiet. . . .

DON ROSARIO: Nevertheless, I can hear their voices from downstairs. And you need your sleep. Tomorrow you're getting married. Tomorrow you have to make a virtuous young lady happy. . . . I'm going to play my little bugle and you'll sleep. . . . I'm going to play Toselli's "Serenade." . . . (*And, standing in front of the bed, facing Dionisio and with his back to the audience, he plays, lost in his art.*)

(*In a little while Fanny opens the door to the left and goes to the right to collect some packages from the sofa. She crosses the scene in the foreground, i.e., in back of Don Rosario, who doesn't see her. She picks up the packages and turns around to go back the same way. But at this moment she notices Don Rosario, and she asks Dionisio, who is looking at her:*)

FANNY: Who's that?

DIONISIO (*very softly, so Don Rosario won't hear*): It's the poor beggar. . . .

FANNY: What a nuisance, don't you think?

DIONISIO: Yes, it's quite a nuisance. . . .

FANNY: See you later. (*Exit left.*)

DIONISIO: So long.

(*In a few minutes, the Odious Man enters and crosses the scene in the same manner as Fanny, and with the same purpose. The Odious Man is wearing a derby hat. When he has picked up a package and is ready to leave, he sees Dionisio and greets him, very politely, taking off his hat.*)

THE ODIOUS MAN: Hello!

DIONISIO (*also taking off his hat in order to greet him*): Hello. Good night.

(*Exit the Odious Man. Immediately enter Madame Olga, the bearded lady, who goes through the same actions.*)

MADAME OLGA (*as she leaves, very sweetly to Dionisio*): I am Madame Olga. . . .

DIONISIO: Ah!

MADAME OLGA: I know that you are an artiste. . . .

DIONISIO: Yes. . . .

MADAME OLGA: Well, I'm glad. . . .

DIONISIO: Thank you very much. . . .

MADAME OLGA: See you in a little while. . . .

DIONISIO: So long . . .

(*Exit Madame Olga, closing the door.*)

(*Dionisio closes his eyes, pretending to sleep. Don Rosario finishes his piece at this moment and stops playing. He looks at Dionisio.*)

DON ROSARIO: He's fallen asleep. . . . He's an angel. . . . He's probably dreaming about her. . . . I'll turn out the light. . . . (*He turns out the light in the center and turns on the lamp on the night table. Then he approaches Dionisio and gives him a kiss on the forehead.*) He sleeps like a little bird! (*On tip-toes he goes out through the door at the rear and closes it.*)

(*But now the telephone rings. Dionisio jumps up and rushes toward it.*)

DIONISIO: It's Margarita! . . . (*But the left-hand door opens again and Paula leans in, remaining leaning against the doorjamb. Dionisio now abandons his dash for the telephone.*)

PAULA: Aren't you coming in?

DIONISIO: No.

PAULA: Come on in. . . . We're inviting you. You'll have fun. . . .

DIONISIO: I'm sleepy. . . . No . . .

PAULA: In any case, we won't let you sleep. . . . (*Indicates noise of revelry going on inside.*)

DIONISIO: I'm tired. . . .

PAULA: Come inside. . . . Please . . . Be nice. . . . Buby's in there and Buby bothers me. If you come in it'll be different. . . . With you there I'll be happy. . . . I'll be happy with you! . . . Won't you?

DIONISIO (*still the same boyish person, lacking all traces of will power*): OK. (*He goes toward the door. They both go in and close the door. The telephone goes on ringing for a few moments, futilely.*)

CURTAIN


ACT TWO

(*The same scene. Two hours have passed and there is a strange atmosphere of carousal. The door at the left is open and inside can be heard the music of a phonograph playing a French java, and also a sailor's accordion. The characters enter and leave comfortably through this door, and one supposes that the banquet is proceeding vigorously in both rooms. The stage is disorderly. Perhaps there are some papers on the floor. Perhaps some liquor bottles. Perhaps some empty tin cans as well. There are many people on the stage. The more we see the happier we'll be. Most of them are strange older people who don't talk. They just dance with each other, or, perhaps with the jolly young girls; we don't know where they've all come from, nor should it bother us much. . . . Among them there is an old sea dog in sailor's clothes. . . . There is an Indian with a turban, or there is an Arab. It is, all in*

*all, an absurd, extraordinary chorus, which will animate the scene
for a few minutes, and then, a few moments after the curtain rises,
it will gradually disappear through the left-hand door. Also among
these people are the principal characters. Buby, stretched out on
the bed, monotonously strums his ukulele. The Odious Man,
leaning against the doorjamb at the left, is looking at Paula
voluptuously. Paula is dancing with Dionisio. Fanny, with the Old
Soldier, who is completely bald and has the whole front of his
uniform covered with decorations and medals. Sagra is dancing
with the Clever Hunter, who, attached to his belt, carries four
rabbits, each one with a price tag attached. Madame Olga, in
dressing gown and slippers, is doing some embroidery, seated on
the divan. At her side, standing, the Handsome Young Man, with
a bottle of cognac in his hand, offers her a drink every once in a
while, staring at her all the while with wide-eyed, bumpkinish
admiration and respect. . . . The curtain has risen. The chorus, all
the while dancing to the music, has slowly been going into the
other room until it has completely disappeared through the left-
hand door.)*

SAGRA (*talking as she dances*): Has it been long since you hunted
   those rabbits?

THE CLEVER HUNTER (*drunk, but always polite*): Yes, miss. I fished
   for them two weeks ago. But I am always so busy that I can't
   find even five minutes free to eat them up. . . . It always
   happens the same way when I fish for rabbits. . . .

SAGRA: For my work, I have a suit like yours. Only instead of having
   those animals attached, I wear bananas. It's prettier that
   way. . . .

THE CLEVER HUNTER: I never get to fish for bananas. I only get to
   fish for rabbits.

SAGRA: But do you hunt rabbits, or fish for them?

THE CLEVER HUNTER (*more polite than ever*): That depends on my
   state of drunkenness, miss. . . .

SAGRA: And don't they bother you when you're dancing?

THE CLEVER HUNTER: Terribly, miss. With your permission, I'm
   going to throw one of them on the floor. . . . (*Detaches a
   rabbit from his belt and drops it on the floor.*)

SAGRA: *Enchantée.*

*(They go on dancing, and the place they occupied is now taken by the Old Soldier and Fanny.)*

THE OLD SOLDIER: I assure you, miss, that I shall never forget this enchanting night. Won't you say anything to me at all?

FANNY: I've already told you that what I want is for you to give me one of those medals. . . .

THE OLD SOLDIER: But the fact of the matter is that I cannot give these medals away, for heaven's sake. . . .

FANNY: Why do you want so many medals? . . .

THE OLD SOLDIER: I need them, for heaven's sake. . . .

FANNY: Well, I want you to give me a medal. . . .

THE OLD SOLDIER: It's impossible, miss. I wouldn't mind giving you a hat, but a medal, no. I can also give you a chandelier for the dining room. . . .

FANNY: Oh go on, stupid. You know, you've got a head that looks like a woman taking a bath. . . .

THE OLD SOLDIER: Oh, how delightfully witty you are, you sweet thing! . . .

*(They have been dancing throughout this entire dialogue; and at this moment the Old Soldier stumbles on the rabbit that the Clever Hunter had thrown on the floor. With a kick, he sends it under the bed.)*

FANNY: Huh? What's that?

THE OLD SOLDIER: Oh, nothing. The cat! *(And they go on dancing, finally going out, left.)*

MADAME OLGA: Oh! I am a great artiste! I have acted in all the circuses in every city. . . . Along with the old bear, along with the sad goat, along with the Siamese twins. . . . Great attraction! I'm a great artiste! . . .

THE HANDSOME YOUNG MAN: Yes, sir . . . But why don't you shave your beard?

MADAME OLGA: My husband, Monsieur Durand, would never have let me. . . . My husband was a very good man, but with old-fashioned ideas. . . . He could never stand those women who plucked their eyebrows and who shaved the napes of their necks! The poor man always used to say, "These women who shave look like men to me!"

THE HANDSOME YOUNG MAN: Yes, sir . . . But, at least you could make it blonde. . . . Oh, boy, a woman with a blonde beard! . . .

MADAME OLGA: My husband, Monsieur Durand, would never have allowed that either. He only liked beautiful women with black beards! . . . A typical Spaniard, no? Andalusian! Gypsy! Hurrray forr yourr fatherrr! Give me another drink. . . .

THE HANDSOME YOUNG MAN: Was your husband an artiste, too?

MADAME OLGA: Oh, he was very lucky! . . . He had the head of a cow and a crocodile's tail. . . . He earned a fortune. . . . But what about that drink?

THE HANDSOME YOUNG MAN (*turning the bottle, which is now empty, upside down*): There isn't anymore. . . .

MADAME OLGA (*getting up*): Then let's go get another bottle. . . .

THE HANDSOME YOUNG MAN (*gallantly*): Will you give me your arm, twinkletoes?

MADAME OLGA: *Enchantée*. (*And, arm in arm, they go out, left.*)

DIONISIO (*dancing with Paula*): Miss . . . I must know why I am drunk. . . .

PAULA: You're not drunk, Tonini. . . . (*They stop dancing.*)

DIONISIO: I must know why you call me Tonini. . . .

PAULA: Didn't we agree that I'd call you Tonini? It's a very cute name, don't you think?

DIONISIO: *Oui.*

PAULA: Why do you say "*Oui*"?

DIONISIO: Miss, I should also like to know why I say "*Oui*." . . . I'm very frightened, miss. . . .

PAULA: You're a marvelous boy!

DIONISIO: There's nothing wrong with you either, miss!

PAULA: You say the sweetest things!

DIONISIO: You're not exactly tongue-tied yourself!

THE ODIOUS MAN (*approaching Dionisio*): Are you tired?

DIONISIO: Me?

THE ODIOUS MAN: Will you allow me to take a turn with this young lady?

PAULA (*rudely*): No!

THE ODIOUS MAN: I'm the richest man in the whole province. . . . My fields are full of wheat! . . .

PAULA: No! No! No! (*And she walks out through the left-hand door.*)

(*Dionisio sits down on the sofa, half asleep. And the Odious Man goes after Paula.*)

THE CLEVER HUNTER (*dancing steadily*): Miss, . . . will you allow me to throw another rabbit on the floor?

SAGRA: *Enchantée*, sir.

THE CLEVER HUNTER (*this time throwing it under the bed*): Thank you very much, miss. (*And they also go dancing out to the left.*)

(*In the room now, only Buby, who is on the bed, and Dionisio are left; the latter talks above the music of the record which keeps on playing in the other room.*)

DIONISIO: I'm drunk. . . . I don't want to drink! . . . My head is buzzing. . . . Everything is going around me in circles. . . . But I'm happy! I've never been so happy! . . . I'm the white horse in the Great Circus! (*He gets up and goes a few steps, imitating the horse.*) But tomorrow . . . tomorrow . . . (*Suddenly noticing Buby.*) Do you have something interesting to do tomorrow? . . . I do. . . . I'm going to a party! To a great party, with flowers, with music, with little girls dressed in white . . . with old ladies dressed in black! . . . With altar boys . . . with lots of altar boys. . . . With a million altar boys!

(*From under the bed comes the voice of a man, singing "Valencia! In my dreams it always seems I hear you softly calling me. . . ." Dionisio bends down, lifts the coverlet, and says:*) Sir, be so good as to come out from there! (*And the Happy Explorer comes out, very serious, with a bottle in his*

*hand, and exits left.*) And then a train . . . And a kiss . . . And
a tear of happiness . . . And a home! And a cat! And a baby!
. . . And then, another cat . . . and another baby . . . And a
baby! And then, another cat . . . and another baby . . . a
million cats, . . . a million babies . . . I don't want to get
drunk! . . . I love her! . . . (*He steps in front of the wardrobe.*
*Listens. He opens it and says to Trudy and the Romantic*
*Lover, who are inside, in a clinch:*) Please come out of there!
(*And the pair of lovers come out, still clutching each other,*
*and go out left, very much in love, pulling the petals off a*
*daisy.*) I must know why there are so many people in my
room! I want someone to tell me why this black man is lying
on my bed! I don't know why this Negro came in here, nor
why the bearded lady came in! . . .

PAULA (*offstage*): Dionisio! (*Enters.*) Tonini! (*Goes toward him.*)
What are you doing?

DIONISIO (*suddenly changed; in a low voice*): I was in here talking
to this friend of mine. . . . I'm not Tonini, nor am I that dead
child. . . . I don't know you. . . . I don't know anybody. . . .
(*Very serious.*) So long. Good night. (*And he goes out, left.*)

PAULA (*trying to stop him*): Come back! Dionisio!

(*But Buby has gotten up and stands in front of the door,*
*blocking Paula's way. He has changed completely and speaks*
*to Paula in an urgent tone.*)

BUBY: You get anything?

PAULA (*disgusted*): Oh, Buby! . . .

BUBY (*more strongly*): You get anything?

PAULA: He's a fellow-artiste. . . . He's going to work with us! . . .

BUBY: And what does that matter? I know that! But even fellow-
artistes sometimes have money. . . . (*In a low voice.*) And we
need money this very night. . . . You know it. . . . We owe
everybody. . . . That money is absolutely necessary, Paula! . . .
If not, everything is lost! . . .

PAULA: But he's a fellow-artiste. . . . It was a stroke of bad luck. . . .
You must understand that, Buby. . . . (*She sits down. So does*
*Buby. Short pause.*)

BUBY: It really was a stroke of bad luck that this room was occupied by a good-looking fellow-artiste. . . . Because he is good looking, isn't he?

PAULA: That doesn't matter to me. . . . And it shouldn't matter to you either! . . .

BUBY (*always ironical, joking, sentimental*): Yes. I know he is good looking. . . . It was a stroke of bad luck! . . . It's not an easy thing to unlock a door from inside and make a big scene, and then find that in the next room there isn't any nice fat traveler with his wallet stuffed, but rather a bad juggler with nothing in his pocket. . . . It certainly was a bad stroke of luck. . . .

PAULA: Buby . . . What we're doing isn't much fun. . . .

BUBY: No. Frankly it isn't much fun, is it? But what shall we do about it? Big Black Buby doesn't know how to dance very well. . . . And you girls dance too badly! . . .

(*At this moment, in the other room, the Chorus of Strange Old People begins to sing, much like a choral society, "The Reliquary." Just for a few seconds. Above the last notes, now very soft, Buby goes on talking.*)

It's hard to dance, isn't it. . . . Your legs always ache, and finally the heart feels tired out. . . . And, nevertheless, pretty young girl dreamers have to devote themselves to something, when they don't want to spend their lives in a sweatshop, or in a factory, or in a clothing store. The theatre is pretty, isn't it? You can do anything you please! You've left your parents at home, a long way away, with their misery and their pains, with their cook-pot on the fire. . . . You don't have to look after your many squalling little brothers and sisters. The sewing machine is left in that corner! But dancing is difficult, isn't it, Paula? . . . And the impresarios don't pay very much to artistes the public doesn't care for enough. . . . There's never enough money for anything! . . . And pretty girls die of misery when their hats go out of style! . . . Death, rather than an outmoded hat! Death, rather than a cheap little dress!! And your whole life, for a fur coat!!!

(*Inside, the Chorus of Strange Old People again sings a few bars of "The Reliquary."*)

Isn't it true, Paula? Yes. Paula already knows about that. . . . And it's so easy for a pretty girl to run away from her boyfriend and enter a room where a man is getting ready for bed. . . . It's very boring to sleep alone in a hotel room! And the fat gentlemen always take pity on girls who are running away from their Negroes, and sometimes they even give them bills of a very nice color when the girls are nice and sweet. . . . And a kiss has no importance. . . . Two don't either, do they? . . . And afterwards . . . Oh, afterwards, if they feel defrauded, it's not easy for them to make a protest! . . . The fat gentlemen don't want a scandal, especially when they know that, besides, a Negro is the girl's boyfriend! . . . A Negro with good strong fists that would knock their ears back if they got too fresh! . . .

PAULA: But he isn't a fat gentleman! He's a fellow-artiste! . . .

BUBY (looking toward the door at left): Shut up!

(Enter Fanny and the Old Soldier, strolling arm in arm. Fanny wears one of the Old Soldier's medals on the front of her dress.)

THE OLD SOLDIER: Miss, I've given you that precious medal. . . . I hope that you will give me some hope. . . . Will you run away with me?

FANNY: I want another medal. . . .

THE OLD SOLDIER: But that's impossible, miss. . . . You must understand the sacrifice I have made already in giving you one of them. . . . It was very difficult for me to earn them. . . . I remember once, fighting against the Sioux Indians . . .

FANNY: Well, I want another medal. . . .

THE OLD SOLDIER: Now, now, miss. Let's drop this subject and you answer me, please. . . . Will you agree to run away with me?

FANNY: I want you to give me another medal. . . .

(They have crossed the scene till they arrived at the balcony; they turn to cross in the opposite direction and now disappear where they came in.)

BUBY: It really has been a stroke of bad luck to find a fellow-artiste in the next room. . . . But, Paula, things can still be arranged. . . . Life is good! What we intended has happened! A little ball in the hotel! Some gentlemen who invite you girls for a drink! . . . Paula, among those gentlemen there are some who have money. . . . Look at Fanny. Fanny is on the ball. . . . Fanny isn't wasting any time. . . . The soldier has medals of gold and even medals with jewels. . . . And there's a rich man who wants to dance with you, too . . . who has asked you a hundred times to dance with him. . . .

PAULA: He is an odious man! . . .

BUBY: Pretty Paula should dance with that gentleman. . . . And Buby will be happier than a little sparrow in the treetop and a monkey in a banana tree!

PAULA (*smiling, amused*): You're a cynic, Buby. . . .

BUBY: Oh, Buby is always a cynic because he gives good advice to the girls who go with him! . . . (*Sarcastically.*) Or perhaps you prefer the juggler?

PAULA: I don't know.

BUBY: It would be sad if you fell in love with him. Girls like you mustn't fall in love with men who don't give them jewels or pretty bracelets for their arms. . . . You'll waste time. . . . We need money, Paula! We're in debt all over the place! And that man is the richest man in the whole province! . . .

PAULA: Tonight I'm not in the mood to talk to rich men. . . . Tonight I want you to leave me in peace. . . . Once in a while these things are amusing to a girl, . . . but at other times, no. . . . .

BUBY: The fact is, that if not, this is all over. . . . We'll all have to go our separate ways. . . . Buby Barton's Ballet will come to an end in the provinces!

(*Inside, the Chorus of Strange Old People now interprets a few bars of "The Volga Boatman."*)

I'm not asking it for myself. . . . A Negro can always get along. . . . But a pretty girl. . . . You can look forward to cheap little dresses and out-of-style hats! . . . The sewing machine that was left in that corner! Or do you have the illusion that you'll find some handsome young man who'll dress you all in white? . . .

PAULA: I don't know, Buby. It doesn't matter to me. . . . I never worried about that. . . .

BUBY: Ah, my dear Paula! . . . Gentlemen love girls like you, but they marry the others. . . . (*Looks toward the left.*) Here comes this gentleman! . . . (*Very close to Paula. Very much the hypocrite.*) You're an affectionate girl, Paula! Long live affectionate girls! . . . Hurrah for affectionate girls! . . .

(*Enter left the Odious Man.*)

THE ODIOUS MAN: It's too hot in the other room! Everybody's in the other room. . . . And they've had so much to drink they're baying like dogs! . . .

BUBY (*very amiable. Very sweet*): Oh, sir! Sit down here! (*Next to Paula, on the sofa.*) Here the air is much more pure. . . . In here the air is so clear that, every once in a while, a bird goes by singing and the butterflies come and go, alighting on the flowers on the curtains. . . .

THE ODIOUS MAN (*sitting down next to Paula*): Are you finally going to open tomorrow?

PAULA: Yes, we open tomorrow. . . .

THE ODIOUS MAN: I'll come to see you, in order to have a few laughs. . . . I have a box reserved. . . . I always have it reserved and I always see the pretty girls who work here. . . . I am the richest man in the whole province. . . .

BUBY: Being rich must be nice, mustn't it? . . .

THE ODIOUS MAN (*proud, odious*): Yes. One does very well. . . . One has ranches. . . . And one has ponds, with fish in them. . . . One eats well. . . . Filet mignons, mostly . . . And lobsters . . . And one also drinks good wines. . . . My fields are full of wheat. . . .

PAULA: But why do you have so much wheat in the field?

THE ODIOUS MAN: You have to have something in the field, miss. That's what they're there for. And one usually has wheat, because to have it in the house is a great nuisance. . . .

BUBY: And, naturally . . . being so rich . . . women must always love you. . . .

THE ODIOUS MAN: Yes. They always love me. . . . All the girls who have played at this music hall have always loved me. . . . I am the richest man in the whole province. . . . It is only natural that they should love me!

BUBY: Of course . . . Poor girls always love a well-mannered man. . . . They're so sad. . . . They need the affection of a man like you. . . . Paula, for example. Pretty Paula is bored. . . . Tonight she can't find any good friend who'll say nice things to her. . . . Sweet little words of love . . . Girls like her are always found among people like us, who don't have fields and who travel constantly, from one place to another, passing through all the tunnels of the world. . . .

THE ODIOUS MAN: And is it from going through so many tunnels that you have turned black? Ha, ha! (*He laughs at his joke exaggeratedly.*)

BUBY (*as if suddenly noticing an imaginary butterfly, and as if he wanted to catch it*): Quiet! Oh! A beautiful butterfly! What pretty colors it has! Quiet! Now it's going out over there! (*Through the door at the left, through which he is already preparing his own exit.*) I'm going to shut the door and I'll catch it inside! I don't want it to get away from me! With your permission, sir!

(*Buby has gone, leaving the door closed. The man comes closer to Paula. There is a short, tense pause, during which the man doesn't know how to start the conversation. Suddenly:*)

THE ODIOUS MAN: What color garters do you wear, miss?

PAULA: Blue.

THE ODIOUS MAN: Light blue or dark blue?

PAULA: Dark blue.

THE ODIOUS MAN (*Taking a pair of garters out of a pocket*): Will you allow me to give you a pair in light blue? The elastic is of the finest quality. . . . (*He stretches them and gives them to her.*)

PAULA (*taking them*): Thank you very much. You really needn't have bothered.

THE ODIOUS MAN: Don't worry. I have more at home. . . .

PAULA: You live in this town?

THE ODIOUS MAN: Yes. But every year I go to Nice. . . .

PAULA: Do you take the wheat with you or leave it here?

THE ODIOUS MAN: Oh, no! The wheat I leave in the field. . . . I pay some men to take care of it, and I go peacefully to Nice. . . . In a sleeping car, naturally!

PAULA: Don't you have a car?

THE ODIOUS MAN: Yes. I have three. . . . But I don't like cars, because it bothers me, this business of the wheels always going around in circles. . . . It's monotonous. . . . (*Suddenly.*) What size stockings do you wear?

PAULA: Size nine.

THE ODIOUS MAN (*takes from his pocket a pair of stockings, without any sort of wrapping, and gives them to her*): Pure silk! Stretch them!

PAULA: No. It's not necessary.

THE ODIOUS MAN: Just so you'll see. (*He takes them and stretches them, so much that the stockings rip in two.*)

PAULA: Oh! They've ripped!

THE ODIOUS MAN: It doesn't matter. I have another pair here. (*Throws the torn ones on the floor. Takes another pair from his pocket and gives them to her.*)

PAULA: Thank you very much.

THE ODIOUS MAN: Don't worry. . . .

PAULA: Then do you go to Nice every year?

THE ODIOUS MAN: Every year, miss. . . . I have a ranch there, and I have a very good time watching them milk the cows. I have one hundred. Do you like cows?

PAULA: I like elephants better.

THE ODIOUS MAN: I have four hundred of them in India. . . . To be sure, now I've put trunks on them and everything, they've cost me a fortune. . . . (*Suddenly.*) Excuse me, miss. I forgot to offer you a bouquet of flowers. (*He takes a bouquet of flowers out of his inside jacket pocket and gives it to her.*)

PAULA (*accepting it*): Enchantée.

THE ODIOUS MAN: Don't worry. . . . They're made out of rags. . . . But, of course, the rags are of the very best. . . . (*And he moves closer to Paula.*)

PAULA: You're married?

THE ODIOUS MAN: Yes. Of course. All we men are married. Men always get married. As a matter of fact, only tomorrow I have to attend a wedding. . . . The daughter of a friend of my wife is getting married and I have no choice but to go......

PAULA: A wedding for love?

THE ODIOUS MAN: Yes. I believe the two are very much in love. I shall go to the wedding, but right after I am leaving for Nice....

PAULA: How I should love to go to Nice, too!

THE ODIOUS MAN: My ranch there is very beautiful. I have a big swimming pool, in which I bathe five or six times a day. . . . Do you bathe frequently, too, miss?

PAULA (*very ingenuous*): Yes. But certainly not as often as you, old boy....

THE ODIOUS MAN (*somewhat disconcerted*): Of course! (*And he takes from his pocket a bag of candy.*) Some candy, miss? For you the whole bag....

PAULA (*accepting it*): Thank you very much.

THE ODIOUS MAN: Good heavens . . . and what do you put in your bath water?

PAULA: Papillons de Printemps. It's a lovely perfume!

THE ODIOUS MAN: I put in seals. I am so used to bathing in Norway that I can't get used to being in the water without having a pair of seals beside me. (*Noticing Paula, who is not eating the candy.*) But don't you eat candy? (*He takes a sandwich out of his pocket.*) Would you like this ham sandwich?

PAULA: I'm not hungry.

THE ODIOUS MAN (*taking another sandwich from another pocket*): Perhaps you'd prefer caviar?

PAULA: No. Really. I don't want anything.

THE ODIOUS MAN (*putting them back*): That's too bad. Well, then, miss. . . . (*Moving closer.*) Will you let me give you a kiss? After this charming conversation anyone can see that we were born for each other....

PAULA (*turning away*): No.

THE ODIOUS MAN (*surprised*): Not yet? (*And then, from another pocket, he takes out a rattle.*) With your permission, I am going to take the liberty of presenting you this. It isn't very valuable, but it *is* entertaining. . . .

PAULA (*taking the rattle and placing it on the sofa*): Many thanks.

THE ODIOUS MAN: And, now, can I give you a kiss?

PAULA: No.

THE ODIOUS MAN: Well, I'm very sorry, but I don't have anymore presents in my pockets. . . . But, if you like, I can run right home and get some more. . . .

PAULA (*suddenly reflecting great melancholy*): No. Don't trouble yourself.

THE ODIOUS MAN: You look sad. . . . What's the matter with you?

PAULA: Yes, I'm sad. I'm terribly sad. . . .

THE ODIOUS MAN: Perhaps I have committed some indiscretion, miss?

PAULA: No. I'm sad because something awful has happened to me. . . . I'm so unlucky!

THE ODIOUS MAN: Everything in life has a solution, my dear. . . .

PAULA: No. There's no solution to this. It can't have any solution!

THE ODIOUS MAN: Have you ruined a pair of shoes, perhaps?

PAULA: Something much worse has happened to me. I'm so unlucky!

THE ODIOUS MAN: Come, now, miss. Tell me what has happened to you. . . .

PAULA: Just imagine!—we arrived here this afternoon, from the journey. . . . And I was carrying a wallet and inside it I had some savings. . . . Quite a few bills. . . . And it must have been in the train. . . . Undoubtedly, while I was sleeping. . . . The fact is, that when I woke up, I couldn't find the wallet anywhere. . . . Just imagine how upset I was. . . . I needed that money to buy myself a . . . a coat. . . . And now I've lost it all. I'm so unlucky!

THE ODIOUS MAN (*now on his guard*): Come, come. . . . And you say you lost it in the train?

PAULA: Yes, in the train.

THE ODIOUS MAN: And did you search the compartment thoroughly?

PAULA: Yes. And the corridors.

THE ODIOUS MAN: Did you also look in the locomotive?

PAULA: Yes. I also looked in the locomotive. . . . (*Pause.*)

THE ODIOUS MAN: And how much money were you carrying in the wallet?

PAULA: Four bills.

THE ODIOUS MAN: Small ones?

PAULA: Middle sized.

THE ODIOUS MAN: Come, come! Four bills!

PAULA: Oh, sir, I'm so upset! . . .

THE ODIOUS MAN (*increasingly agreeable to anything*): And you say there were four bills?

PAULA: Yes. Four bills.

THE ODIOUS MAN: Come, come now. . . . (*Pause.*) Couldn't you manage with just a little less?

PAULA: What do you mean?

THE ODIOUS MAN (*smiling slyly*): Someone who goes to Nice every year knows about these things, miss. . . . What I mean is, if you were a nice girl. . . . Although you have to bear in mind that I've already given you several presents. . . .

PAULA: I don't understand what you mean. . . . Make yourself clear. . . .

THE ODIOUS MAN (*taking a bill from his wallet, very craftily*): Who's going to get this little bill?

PAULA: Don't bother, sir. . . . It's possible I may still find it. . . .

THE ODIOUS MAN (*placing the bill in her hand*): Take it. If you find it you can give this back to me. . . . And, now. . . . Will you allow me to give you a kiss?

PAULA (*still drawing away*): I'm still so upset! Because, just imagine, it wasn't just one bill. . . . There were four. . . .

THE ODIOUS MAN (*taking his wallet out again and taking out three
more bills*): Come, come now. . . . (*Very sweetly.*) Who's
going to get these little bills?

PAULA (*taking them; finally affectionate*): How nice you are!

(*He gives her a kiss. Then he gets up and shoots the bolts on
the doors. Paula gets on her guard.*)

What have you done?

THE ODIOUS MAN: I've closed the doors. . . .

PAULA (*getting up*): What for?

THE ODIOUS MAN: So that neither the birds nor the butterflies can
come in. . . . (*He goes towards her and embraces her. Now he
has abandoned all his artificial manners. Now he simply wants
to collect for his money just as soon as possible.*) You're very
beautiful!

PAULA (*angry*): Open the doors!

THE ODIOUS MAN: We'll open the doors afterwards, won't we?
There's always plenty of time to open the doors! . . .

PAULA (*indignant now, and trying to free herself from the arms of
the Odious Man*): Let go of me! You have no right to do this!
Open the doors!

THE ODIOUS MAN: I don't just throw my money around and get
nothing for it, my dear. . . .

PAULA (*furious*): I didn't ask you for that money! You gave it to
me! Let me alone! Get out of here! Out! I'll scream!

THE ODIOUS MAN: I gave you four bills. . . . You have to be nice to
me. . . . You're too pretty for me to leave you. . . .

PAULA: I didn't ask for them! Let go of me right now! (*Yelling.*)
Buby! Buby!

(*The man, brutishly, insists on embracing her. But Buby has
opened the door at the left and contemplates the scene very
coldly. The man sees him, and, sweating, insolent, and beside
himself, turns menacingly to Paula.*)

THE ODIOUS MAN: Give me back that money! Hurry up! Give me back that money! Scoundrels!

PAULA (*throwing the money at him; he gathers it up*): There's your money!

THE ODIOUS MAN: Give me back my stockings!

PAULA (*throwing the stockings at him*): There are your stockings!

THE ODIOUS MAN: Give me back my flowers!

PAULA (*throwing them at him*): There are your flowers!

THE ODIOUS MAN: Scoundrels! What did you think? (*Goes toward the door to the hall and opens it.*) Did you think you could fool me between the two of you? Me! Me! Scoundrels! (*Exit.*)

BUBY (*cold*): Did you feel scruples?

PAULA: Yes. He thought something that wasn't true. . . . He's a monster, Buby.

BUBY: Maybe you'd like it better if the juggler kissed you. . . .

PAULA (*jittery*): I don't know! Leave me in peace! You get out of here, too! Leave me alone, everybody!

BUBY: Pretty Paula . . . Remember what I said, will you? You're throwing everything away. . . . Everything! It would be better if you didn't go on thinking about that boy, because if you do, I'll kill you or I'll kill him. . . . You understand, Paula? Long live the girls who pay attention to what Buby tells them! (*And he goes out left.*)

(*Paula sits down on the sofa with a look of disgust, and at the left, Fanny and the Old Soldier enter again, as before, strolling arm in arm across the stage from one side to the other. This time Fanny wears all of the medals pinned to the front of her dress. The Old Soldier has only one left, but it's the largest of all.*)

THE OLD SOLDIER: I've given you all my medals. I've only got one left now. The one that cost me the most trouble to earn. . . . I got it fighting the Cossacks. And, now, will you agree to run away with me? Come along with me. We'll go to America and there we'll be happy. We'll buy a big ranch and raise chickens. . . .

FANNY: I want you to give me that other medal. . . .

THE OLD SOLDIER: No. I cannot give you this one, miss. . . .

FANNY: Well, then, I'm not going with you. . . .

THE OLD SOLDIER: Oh, miss! . . . And if I give it to you . . . ?
(*They go off, left. But a few seconds later they come out
again, she wearing the big medal, with a suitcase, her hat and
coat, and he with his cape and plumed hat. And, very lovingly,
they make their way to the door at the rear.*) Oh, Fanny, just
think if we were to have a blonde baby! . . .

FANNY: Good heavens, Alfredo! . . . (*Exit through door at rear.*)

(*Paula remains pensive. And now, left, enter Dionisio, with his
eyes puffy from sleep. He notices Paula, who may have shed a
few tears of pride.*)

DIONISIO: Are you crying?

PAULA: I'm not crying. . . .

DIONISIO: Are you sad because I didn't come? I was in there,
sleeping with some friends. . . . (*Paula says nothing.*) Have
you been fighting with that Negro? We should lynch that
Negro! It is our obligation to lynch the Negro!

PAULA: In order to lynch a Negro it is necessary to assemble a great
many people. . . .

DIONISIO: I'll get up a subscription. . . .

PAULA: No.

DIONISIO: It's no trouble at all for me. . . .

PAULA (*affectionately*): Dionisio . . .

DIONISIO: What?

PAULA: Sit down here . . . with me. . . .

DIONISIO (*sitting down at her side*): All right.

PAULA: I want us to become good friends. . . . If you only knew
how happy I've been since I met you! . . . I was so lonely! . . .
You're not like the others! With the others, sometimes I'm
afraid. With you, no. People are bad. . . . Our fellow-artistes
in the Music Hall don't act the way they should. . . . The gen-

tlemen outside the Music Hall don't act like gentlemen
either....

(*Dionisio, distracted, picks up the rattle, which had been left
there, and begins to play with it, very absorbed and amused.*)

And, nevertheless, one has to live with people, because, otherwise, one never would be able to drink champagne, or wear
pretty bracelets. . . . And champagne is marvelous . . . and
bracelets always weigh down one's arms with happiness! . . .
Besides, you have to amuse yourself. . . . It's very sad to be
alone. . . . Girls like me die of sadness in hotel rooms like this.
. . . You and I must be good friends. Would you like us to
talk about you? . . .

DIONISIO: OK. But just for a moment, no more. . . .

PAULA: No. All the time. We'll talk about you all the time. It's
better. . . . The trouble is . . . the trouble is that you won't be
going on with us when we finish working here. . . . And each
of us will go our own way. . . . It's idiotic that we should have
to separate so soon, don't you think? . . . If only you needed
a partner for your number. . . . Oh! Then we could be together
longer! . . . I could learn to do juggling, couldn't I? Learn to
play with the three top hats, too! . . .

(*Dionisio's rattle has come apart. It no longer rattles. This
makes him sad.*)

DIONISIO: It's come apart. . . .

PAULA (*taking the rattle and fixing it*): Now it works. (*And she
gives it back to Dionisio, who goes on playing with it, very
delightedly.*) It's a shame you don't need a partner for your
number! But never mind! We'll have a wonderful time in
these few days, won't we? . . . Listen . . . tomorrow we'll go
for a walk. We'll go to the beach. . . . By the sea . . . The two
of us alone! Like two little kids, right? You're not like all those
other men! There's no performance until evening! We have
the whole afternoon to ourselves! We'll buy some crabs. . . .
Do you know how to shell the crab's claws properly? I do. I'll
show you how. . . . We'll eat them there, on the sand. . . .
With the sea in front of us. Do you like to play in the sand?
It's marvelous! I know how to make castles and a bridge with
a hole in the middle, for the water to go through. . . . I know
how to make a volcano! You put papers in it and burn them,

and smoke comes out! . . . Don't you know how to make volcanos?

DIONISIO (*by now he has put down the rattle and gradually is becoming more animated*): Yes!

PAULA: And castles?

DIONISIO: Yes!

PAULA: With a garden?

DIONISIO: Yes, with a garden! I put trees in them and a fountain in the middle and a stairway with steps for climbing the castle tower!

PAULA: A stairway out of sand? Oh, you're a wonderful boy! Dionisio, I don't know how to make . . .

DIONISIO: I do. I also know how to make a boat and a train. . . . And figures! I know how to make a lion, too. . . .

PAULA: Oh! How wonderful! Don't you see? Don't you see, Dionisio? None of those other men knows how to make volcanos, or castles, or lions out of sand! Not even Buby! They don't know how to play! I knew you were different. . . . You'll teach me how to make them, won't you? We'll go tomorrow. . . .

(*Pause. Dionisio, on hearing the word "tomorrow," suddenly loses his mood of happiness and his enthusiasm for the games by the seaside.*)

DIONISIO: Tomorrow! . . .

PAULA: Tomorrow! . . .

DIONISIO: No.

PAULA: Why not?

DIONISIO: Because I can't.

PAULA: Do you have to rehearse?

DIONISIO: No.

PAULA: Then . . . then, what do you have to do?

DIONISIO: I have . . . something to do.

PAULA: Save it for another day! There are so many days! What's the difference! Is what you have to do very important?

DIONISIO: Yes.

PAULA: Business?

DIONISIO: Business.

(*Pause.*)

PAULA (*suddenly*): You don't have a fiancée, do you?

DIONISIO: No, a fiancée, no.

PAULA: You musn't have a fiancée! What would you want a fiancée for? You're better off with a very good friend, like me. . . .
You'll have a better time. . . . I don't want to have a fiancé
. . . because I don't ever want to get married. Getting married
is ridiculous! So stiff! So pale! So silly! What a joke! don't you
agree? . . . You don't intend to get married ever, do you?

DIONISIO: Probably . . .

PAULA: Don't ever get married. . . . You're better off as you are. . . .
This way you're handsomer. . . . If you get married you'll be a
wreck. . . . And you'll get fat underneath the dining-room chandelier. . . . And besides, we couldn't be friends any more. . . .
Tomorrow we'll go to the beach to eat crabs! And the day
after tomorrow you'll get up early and I will, too. . . . We'll
meet downstairs and go straight down to the docks and rent a
boat. . . . A boat without a boatman! And we'll wear our bathing suits and go swimming a long way from the beach, where
you can't touch bottom. . . . Do you know how to swim? . . .

DIONISIO: Yes, I swim very well indeed.

PAULA: I can swim even better than that. I can last a long time.
You'll see. . . .

DIONISIO: I can do the dead man's float and dive. . . .

PAULA: I can make like a carp, and from the diving board I can do
a swan dive. . . .

DIONISIO: And I can pick up ten cents from the bottom with my
mouth. . . .

PAULA: Oh! How wonderful! What a wonderful day tomorrow's
going to be! And the day after! You'll see, Dionisio, you'll see!
We'll toast ourselves in the sun! . . .

SAGRA (*from the left, with her hat and coat on*): Paula! Paula! Come on! Guess what we've all decided to do! We've all decided to go down to the harbor and watch the dawn come up! The harbor is nearby and it's almost daylight. We'll take the bottles that are left, and we'll drink them there, where the fishermen are coming out of the sea. We'll have a great time! We're all going down to see the dawn come up! ...

(*From the room at the left people begin coming out. Madame Olga is dressed up now. The Handsome Young Man, Trudy, the Explorer and the Chorus of Strange Old People. The last one, the Clever Hunter, with four dogs tied together—and it would be very nice if they were barking. They all walk in a line, arm in arm. They all carry bottles.*)

THE HANDSOME YOUNG MAN (*almost singing*): We're going down to see the dawn come up!

ALL: We're going down to see the dawn come up!

THE ROMANTIC LOVER: Beside the waters of the bay! ...

ALL: Beside the waters of the bay! ...

THE HAPPY EXPLORER (*almost chanting*): And afterwards we'll throw into the sea—the bottle that's empty, empty, empty!

SEVERAL (*going out through the door at the rear*): We're going down to see the dawn come up!

OTHERS: Beside the waters of the bay!

(*All go out.*)

PAULA (*happy*): Shall we go, Dionisio?

DIONISIO: What time is it?

PAULA: It must be almost six. ...

DIONISIO: Almost six?

PAULA: Yes. Soon the sun will be up. ...

DIONISIO: It can't be. Six o'clock? It's almost six o'clock!

PAULA: But what's the matter, Dionisio? Is something wrong? Let's go with the others! ...

DIONISIO: No. I'm not going.

PAULA: Why not?

DIONISIO: Because I'm sick. . . . I have a terrible headache. . . . I drank too much. . . . No. All this is absurd. I can't do this. . . . It's already almost six o'clock! . . . I want to be alone. . . . I need to be alone. . . .

PAULA: Come on, Dionisio. . . . I want to go with you. . . . If you don't go, I'll stay, too . . . here, by you. . . . I can't be separated from you! (*She comes very close to him, lovingly.*) You're a wonderful boy! (*Leans her head on Dionisio's shoulder, offering him her mouth.*) I like you so much!

(*And they kiss very ardently. But Buby, silently, has come out from the left and has seen this marvelous kiss. Coldly, he approaches them and gives Paula a terrific blow on the nape of the neck; she falls to the ground with a little cry. Then Buby, very rapidly, flees through the door at rear, closing it as he leaves. Paula, on the floor with her eyes closed, doesn't move. One doesn't know if she is unconscious or dead. Dionisio, terrified, goes from one door to the other, sometimes running and other times very slowly. He is more grotesque than ever.*)

DIONISIO: What's all this? What's all this, my God? It's just not possible! . . . (*Suddenly the telephone rings. Dionisio picks up the receiver and speaks.*) Eh? Who? Yes. It's me, Dionisio. . . . No, nothing's the matter with me. . . . I'm fine. You got frightened because I didn't answer when you called? Oh, no! I had a terrible headache and I went out! I went out to the street to breathe the fresh air. Yes. That's why I couldn't answer when you were calling. . . . What did you say? Eh? Your father's coming? What for? But I tell you nothing's wrong with me! It's silly to have him come! . . . Nothing has happened. . . . Nothing's going on. . . . (*And there is a knocking at the door at rear.*) Ah! (*To the phone.*) They're knocking at the door. . . . Yes . . . It must be your father. . . . Yes. (*As he goes, nervously, toward the door, with the receiver in his hand, he breaks the cord. He tries to fix it. He can't. He becomes even more upset.*)

DON SACRAMENTO (*outside*): Dionisio! Dionisio! Dionisio! (*Dionisio, with the receiver in his hand, and all very frantically, runs toward the door. He doesn't know what to do. He goes towards Paula and kneels next to her. He puts his ear to Paula's breast, trying to hear her heart. He makes a gesture of panic. And now he puts the end of the telephone cord, which he is carrying, next to Paula's heart and listens through the receiver, "like the wise doctor.")*

DON SACRAMENTO (*outside, beating on the door*): Dionisio! Dionisio!

DIONISIO (*also answering through the receiver*): Just a minute! I'm coming! (*And grabbing Paula under the arms, comically, ungracefully, ridiculously, he tries to hide her under the bed, as the curtain falls.*)

CURTAIN

## ACT THREE

(*The same scene. The action of the second act continues, a moment later than when it was interrupted. Dionisio has just hidden Paula's body behind the bed and the folding screen, while Don Sacramento continues to call. Finally convinced that Paula is well hidden, Dionisio goes to open the door.*)

DON SACRAMENTO (*outside*): Dionisio! Dionisio! Open the door! It's me! It's Don Sacramento! It's Don Sacramento! It's Don Sacramento!

DIONISIO: Yes . . . I'll be right there. (*He opens the door. Enter Don Sacramento in frock coat and top hat, carrying an umbrella.*) Don Sacramento!

DON SACRAMENTO: Sir! My little girl is unhappy! My little girl—a hundred times she called you on the phone without your answering her calls. My little girl is unhappy and my little girl is crying. My little girl thought you had died. My little girl is pale. . . . Why are you martyring my poor little girl? . . .

DIONISIO: I went out to the street, Don Sacramento. . . . I had a headache. . . . I couldn't sleep. . . . I went out to take a walk in the rain. And I walked around for a while, up and down the same street. . . . That's why I didn't hear her calling. Yes, that's why. . . . Poor Margaret . . . how she must have suffered!

DON SACRAMENTO: My little girl is unhappy. My little girl is unhappy and my little girl is crying. My little girl is pale. Why are you martyring my poor little girl? . . .

DIONISIO: Don Sacramento . . . I have already told you. . . . I went out to the street. . . . I couldn't sleep.

DON SACRAMENTO: My little girl fainted on the mauve sofa in the rose drawing room. . . . She thought you had died! Why did you go walking in the rain?

DIONISIO: I had a headache, Don Sacramento. . . .

DON SACRAMENTO: Decent people don't go out at night to walk in the rain! . . . You are a Bohemian, sir!

DIONISIO: No, sir.

DON SACRAMENTO: Yes! You are a Bohemian, sir! Only Bohemians go out at night to walk the streets!

DIONISIO: But I had a terrible headache!

DON SACRAMENTO: You should have put two slices of potato on your temples. . . .

DIONISIO: I didn't have any potatoes. . . .

DON SACRAMENTO: Decent people should always carry potatoes in their pockets, sir. . . . And they should also carry adhesive tape for wounds. . . . I'd swear you don't carry adhesive tape. . . .

DIONISIO: No, sir.

DON SACRAMENTO: There—you see? You are a Bohemian, sir! . . . After you marry my little girl you'll have to stop being so disorganized in your living. Why is this room like this? Why is there mattress stuffing on the floor? Why are there so many scraps of paper? Why are there empty sardine cans? (*Picking up the rattle which was on the sofa.*) What's this rattle doing here? (*Now he remains, distracted, with it in his hand. And from time to time, while he talks, he gives it a shake.*)

DIONISIO: The rooms in modest hotels are like this. . . . And this is a modest hotel. Surely you understand, Don Sacramento! . . .

DON SACRAMENTO: I don't understand in the least. I have never stayed in any hotel. Only the great playboys of Europe and their international vampires stay in hotels. Decent people stay at home and receive their guests in blue parlors with gilded furniture and old family portraits. . . . Why haven't you hung the pictures of your family in this room, sir?

DIONISIO: I only intend to be here this one night. . . .

DON SACRAMENTO: That doesn't matter, sir! You should have put pictures on the walls. Only murderers and counterfeiters have no pictures on the walls. . . . You should have put up the picture of your grandfather in his cavalry uniform. . . .

DIONISIO: He wasn't in the cavalry. . . . He was a bookkeeper. . . .

DON SACRAMENTO: Well, then, in his bookkeeper's uniform! Honorable people have to be portrayed in uniform, whether they are bookkeepers or whatever they are! You should also have put up a picture of a little boy in his first-communion suit!

DIONISIO: But what little boy was there to put up?

DON SACRAMENTO: That doesn't matter! It's all the same. A little boy. *Any* little boy! There are many little boys! The world is *full* of little boys in their first-communion suits! . . . And you also should have put up some colored lithographs. . . . Why haven't you put up any lithographs? Lithographs are lovely! "Romeo and Juliet speaking over the balcony of the garden," "Jesus praying on the Mount of Olives," "Napoleon Bonaparte in his exile on the Island of Elba." . . . (*In another tone, with great admiration.*) What a great man, that Napoleon, don't you think?

DIONISIO: Yes. He was very military. . . . Wasn't he the one who always held his hand like this? (*He puts his hand on his chest.*)

DON SACRAMENTO (*imitating the posture*): Exactly—that's the way he held it. . . .

DIONISIO: It must have been very difficult, don't you think?

DON SACRAMENTO (*with his eyes rolled to the top of his head*): Only a man like him could have held his hand like that all the time! . . .

DIONISIO (*putting his other hand on his shoulder*): And he held the other one like this. . . .

DON SACRAMENTO (*doing the same*): Exactly—that's the way he held it.

DIONISIO: What a man!

DON SACRAMENTO: Napoleon Bonaparte! . . . (*Admiring pause, both of them imitating Napoleon. Then Don Sacramento goes on talking in the same tone as before.*) You will have to become more organized. You are going to live in my house and my house is an honorable house! You won't be able to go out at night to walk in the rain! Furthermore, you will have to get up at six-fifteen, in order to breakfast at six-thirty on a fried egg and bread. . . .

DIONISIO: I don't like fried eggs. . . .

DON SACRAMENTO: Honorable people have to like fried eggs, my dear sir! My whole family has always eaten fried eggs for breakfast. . . . Only Bohemians have coffee with milk and bread and butter.

DIONISIO: But the fact is that I like them better boiled. . . . Can't you make mine boiled?

DON SACRAMENTO: I don't know. I don't know. That we shall have to take up with my wife. If she permits it, I won't be the one to object. But I warn you that my wife does not tolerate caprices with the food! . . .

DIONISIO (*now almost crying*): But what am I to do if I like them better boiled, for heaven's sake?!

DON SACRAMENTO: No Hollywood stuff, now, eh? . . . No theatrics . . . No Bohemian stuff . . . Supper at seven o'clock . . . And after supper, on Thursdays and Sundays, we'll have a little spree (*roguish*), because we also have to give our spirits room to stretch, what the heck! (*At this moment the rattle he has been playing with comes apart in his hand, and he gets very upset about it.*) It's come apart!

DIONISIO (*like Paula in the previous act, he takes the rattle and fixes it.*) Now it works. (*And he gives it back to Don Sacramento, who, very happily, shakes it from time to time.*)

DON SACRAMENTO: My little girl, on Sundays, will play the piano, Dionisio. . . . She'll play the piano, and perhaps, perhaps, if we're in the mood, we'll have a few visitors. . . . Respectable people, of course . . . For example, I'll have Mr. Smith come. . . . Right away you'll make him a very good friend of yours and you'll have very good times chatting with him. . . . Mr. Smith is a very well-known person. . . . His picture has been in all the newspapers of the world. . . . He is the most famous centenarian in the town! He just celebrated his one hundred

twentieth birthday and he still has five teeth. . . . You'll spend
the whole evening talking with him! . . . And his wife will
come, too. . . .

DIONISIO: And how many teeth does his wife have?!

DON SACRAMENTO: Oh, she doesn't have any! She lost them all when
she fell down that stairway and was paralyzed for life so that
she could never get up from her wheelchair. . . . You'll spend
a lot of time chatting with this charming couple! . . .

DIONISIO: But what if they die when I'm talking with them? What'll
I do, for heaven's sake?

DON SACRAMENTO: Centenarians never die! Then there wouldn't be
anything special about them, young man! . . . (*Pause. Don
Sacramento makes motions as if smelling something.*) But . . .
what smells in this room? . . . Since I've been here I've noticed
a peculiar smell. . . . It's a strange smell. . . . And it's not an
agreeable smell at all! . . .

DIONISIO: They must have left the kitchen door open. . . .

DON SACRAMENTO (*sniffing all the while*): No. It's not that. . . . It's
rather like a human body decomposing. . . .

DIONISIO (*terrified. Apart*): My God! She's dead! . . .

DON SACRAMENTO: What's this smell, young man? There is a
cadaver in this room! Why do you have cadavers in your
room? Do Bohemians keep cadavers in their rooms?

DIONISIO: In modest hotels there are always cadavers. . . .

DON SACRAMENTO (*searching*): It's around here! Here underneath!
(*He lifts the bedspread and discovers the rabbits which the
Hunter had thrown down. He picks them up.*) Oh, here it is!
Two dead rabbits! This is what smelled that way! . . . Why
do you have two dead rabbits under your bed? In my house
you won't be able to keep rabbits in your room. . . . You won't
be able to keep chickens, either. . . . They ruin everything!

DIONISIO: Those aren't rabbits. They're mice. . . .

DON SACRAMENTO: They're mice?

DIONISIO: Yes, sir. They're mice. There are lots of them here. . . .

DON SACRAMENTO: I've never seen such big mice. . . .

DIONISIO: It's because this is a poor hotel that the mice are like this.
. . . In more luxurious hotels the mice are much smaller. . . .
It's just the same in Viennese coffee shops. . . .

DON SACRAMENTO: And did you kill them?

DIONISIO: Yes, I killed them with a shotgun. The owner gives a shotgun to each guest so he can kill the mice. . . .

DON SACRAMENTO (*looking at the ticket on one of the rabbits*): **And**
these numbers that they've got on their necks, what do they
mean? Here it says three-fifty. . . .

DIONISIO: It's not three-fifty. It's three hundred fifty. Since there
are so many of them, the owner has them numbered, in order
to have contests. And to the guest, for example, who kills
number fourteen, he gives a Filipino shawl, or an electric
iron. . . .

DON SACRAMENTO: What a shame you didn't win the shawl! We
could go to the carnival! . . . And what do you intend to do
with these mice? . . .

DIONISIO: I haven't thought about that yet. . . . If you like, I'll give
them to you. . . .

DON SACRAMENTO: You don't need them?

DIONISIO: No. I have a lot of them already. I'll wrap them up for
you. (*He picks up a piece of paper from somewhere and wraps
them. Then he hands them to him.*)

DON SACRAMENTO: Thank you very much, Dionisio. I'll take them
to my little nephews to play with. . . . They'll be so happy!
And now, good-bye, good-bye, Dionisio. I'm going to console
my little girl who is still in a dead faint on the mauve sofa in
the rose drawing room. . . . You know how she is. . . . She
adores you. . . . (*Looks at his watch.*) It's six forty-three. In a
little while the limousine will come to take you to the church.
. . . Be ready. . . . How exciting! Within a few hours you'll be
my Margaret's husband! . . .

DIONISIO: But will you tell your wife I like my eggs better boiled?

DON SACRAMENTO: Yes. I'll tell her. But don't delay me now. Oh,
Dionisio! I can't wait to get home and give these to my little
nephews. . . . How those poor little boys will weep for joy!

DIONISIO: Are you going to give them the rattle, too?

DON SACRAMENTO: Oh, no. The rattle is for me! (*And he goes out the door at rear.*)

(*Paula sticks her head out from behind the bed and looks sadly at Dionisio. Dionisio, who has gone to close the door, sees her as he turns around.*)

PAULA: Oh! Why did you hide this from me? You're getting married, Dionisio! . . .

DIONISIO (*lowering his head*): Yes . . .

PAULA: You weren't even a juggler. . . .

DIONISIO: No.

PAULA (*she gets up. She goes toward the door at the left*): Then I'd better go to my room. . . .

DIONISIO (*stopping her*): But you were hurt . . . What did Buby do to you? . . .

PAULA: He hit me, that's all. . . . He knocked me out. . . . I must have lost my senses for a few minutes! He's very rough, that Buby. . . . He always seems to . . . (*After a pause.*) You're getting married, Dionisio! . . .

DIONISIO: Yes . . .

PAULA (*trying once more to leave*): I'm going to my room.

DIONISIO: No.

PAULA: Why not?

DIONISIO: Because this room is prettier. From the balcony you can see the harbor. . . .

PAULA: You're getting married, Dionisio! . . .

DIONISIO: Yes. I'm getting married, but not much. . . .

PAULA: Why didn't you tell me?

DIONISIO: I don't know. I had a feeling that getting married was ridiculous. . . . That I shouldn't get married! . . . Now I see that I wasn't wrong. . . . I was getting married because I have spent my life stuck in a dreary little town, and I thought that to be happy I had to get married to the first girl who made my heart beat with tenderness when we looked into each other's eyes. . . . I adored my fiancée. . . . But now I see that the happiness I was looking for doesn't have anything to do with my fiancée. . . . My fiancée doesn't like to go eating crabs by the sea, she doesn't enjoy making volcanos in the sand. . . . And she doesn't know how to swim. . . . In the water she just gives a few ridiculous little screams. . . . She goes like this: "Eek! Eek! Eek!" And at the piano she only loves to sing "The Pearl Fishers." And "The Pearl Fishers" is horrible, Paula. She has a voice like a choirboy and she goes like this: (*Sings.*) Tra-la-ra-lá . . . pi-rí, pi-rí, pi-rí, pi-rí! And I hadn't realized that choirboys' voices were full of vanity and that, on the other hand, there were phonograph records called "Love Me in December the Same as You Love Me in May" that make our hearts sing and make us want to turn somersaults. . . . I didn't know that there were women like you, either, who don't just make your heart flutter, when you talk to them, but make your lips flutter in a constant smile. . . . I didn't know anything about anything. I only knew how to stroll and whistle next to the bandstand. . . . I was getting married because everyone always gets married when they're twenty-seven. . . . But now I'm not going to get married, Paula. . . . I can't eat fried eggs at six-thirty in the morning! . . .

PAULA (*now seated on the sofa*): That man with the moustache already told you they'd make them boiled for you. . . .

DIONISIO: The fact is that I don't like them boiled either! I only like coffee with milk, and bread and butter! I am a terrible Bohemian! And the funniest thing is that I didn't know it until tonight when you came . . . and when that Negro came . . . and when the bearded lady came. . . . No, I'm not getting married, Paula. I'm going to go away with you and I'm going to learn how to do juggling with three top hats. . . .

PAULA: Juggling with three top hats is very difficult. . . . They keep falling on the floor . . .

DIONISIO: I'll learn how to dance like you dance and like Buby dances. . . .

PAULA: Dancing is even more difficult. . . . Your legs ache so much, and you scarcely earn enough to live. . . .

DIONISIO: I'll be patient and I'll get to have a cow's head and a crocodile's tail. . . .

PAULA: That's even more trouble. . . . And, afterwards, when you travel by train, the tail is a terrible nuisance. . . .

(*Dionisio goes over and sits down beside her.*)

DIONISIO: I shall do something extraordinary in order to be able to go with you! . . . You always told me that I was a wonderful boy! . . .

PAULA: And you were. You were so wonderful, that in a little while you're getting married, and I didn't even know it. . . .

DIONISIO: There's still time. We'll leave all this and we'll go to London. . . .

PAULA: Do you know how to speak English?

DIONISIO: No. But we'll go to a small town near London. The people of London speak English because they are all very rich and have lots of money for learning such nonsense. But the people in the small towns around London, since they are poorer and don't have money for learning such things, all speak just like you and me. . . . They speak the way they do in every small town in the world! . . . And they are happy! . . .

PAULA: But in England there are too many detectives!

DIONISIO: We'll go to Havana!

PAULA: In Havana there are too many bananas. . . .

DIONISIO: We'll go to the desert!

PAULA: That's where everyone who gets fed up goes—all the deserts are already full of people and swimming pools. . . .

DIONISIO (*sadly*): Then you probably don't want to go away with me. . . .

PAULA: No. Actually I wouldn't like to go away with you, Dionisio. . . .

DIONISIO: Why not?

(*Pause. She doesn't want to talk. She gets up and goes toward the balcony.*)

PAULA: I'm going to open the curtains to the balcony. (*Does it.*) It must be dawn by now. . . . And it's even raining. . . . Dionisio, they've turned off the lights in the harbor! Who do you suppose turns them off?

DIONISIO: The lighthouse keeper.

PAULA: Yes. It must be the lighthouse keeper. . . .

DIONISIO: Paula, . . . don't you love me?

PAULA (*still from the balcony*): And it's cold. . . .

DIONISIO (*taking a cover from the bed*): Come over next to me. . . . We'll wrap ourselves up in this blanket. . . . (*She comes and the two of them sit down together and cover their legs with the blanket.*) Do you love Buby?

PAULA: Buby is my friend. Buby is bad. But poor Buby is never going to get married. . . . And the others always get married. . . . It isn't fair, Dionisio. . . .

DIONISIO: Have you had a lot of boyfriends?

PAULA: A boyfriend in every province and a love in every town! Everywhere there are gentlemen who make love to us. . . . It's all the same whether it's the month of November or the month of April! It's all the same whether there are epidemics or whether there are revolutions! . . . A boyfriend in every province! . . . Really, it's very amusing! . . . The trouble is, Dionisio . . . the trouble is that all the gentlemen were already married, and those who weren't, were already hiding in their wallets the picture of a girl friend they were going to marry. . . . Dionisio, why do all gentlemen get married? And why, if they get married, do they hide it from girls like me? . . . You, too, already had a girl friend's picture in your wallet . . . I hate wallets and I hate the girl friends of my friends, too! . . . Now we can't go down by the sea with the others. . . . Now we can't do anything. . . . Why do all gentlemen get married?

DIONISIO: Because going to football games all the time gets boring.

PAULA: Dionisio, show me your girl friend's picture. . . .

DIONISIO: No.

PAULA: What's the matter with you! Show it to me! In the end they all show it!

DIONISIO (*takes out a wallet. Opens it. Paula looks curious*): Look . . .

PAULA (*pointing at something*): And this? A lock of hair, too? ...

DIONISIO: It's not hers. Madame Olga gave it to me. ... She cut it off her beard, as a little remembrance. ... (*He shows her a photograph.*) This is her picture; look ...

PAULA (*she looks at it slowly, then*): It's horrible, Dionisio!

DIONISIO: Yes.

PAULA: She has too many moles. ...

DIONISIO: Twelve. (*Pointing with one finger.*) There's another one over here. ...

PAULA: And her eyes are so sad. ... She isn't the least bit pretty, Dionisio. ...

DIONISIO: The truth is that this is a very bad picture. ... But she has another one where she's in a Portuguese costume, and if you saw it ... (*Turning his profile to her, with a forced pose.*) She looks like this.

PAULA: In profile?

DIONISIO: Yes. In profile. Like this. (*He repeats the pose.*)

PAULA: And that's better?

DIONISIO: Yes. Because that way you can't see any more than six moles. ...

PAULA: And besides, I'm younger. ...

DIONISIO: Yes. She's twenty-five. ...

PAULA: And as for me ... Well! I must be very young, but I don't know my age for certain. ... No one ever told me. ... It's funny, isn't it? ... A friend of mine who got married lives in the city. ... She used to dance with us, too. When I go to the city I always go to her house. And on the dining-room wall I mark my height with a line. And every time I raise the line a little higher! ... Dionisio, I'm still growing! ... It's wonderful to be growing still! ... But someday when the line stops getting higher it will mean that I've stopped growing and that I've become old. ... How sad that will be, don't you agree? What do girls like me do when they get old? ... (*Looks again at the photo.*) I'm prettier than she is! ...

DIONISIO: You are much, much more beautiful! You're more beautiful than anyone! Paula, I don't want to get married. . . . I'll have horrible children. . . . And eventually I'll get liver trouble! . . .

PAULA: It's daylight already, Dionisio! I want to sleep! . . .

DIONISIO: Put your head on my shoulder. . . . Sleep here. . .

PAULA (*she does it*): Kiss me, Dionisio. (*They kiss.*) Doesn't your fiancée ever kiss you? . . .

DIONISIO: No.

PAULA: Why not?

DIONISIO: She can't until she gets married. . . .

PAULA: Not even once? . . .

DIONISIO: No, no. Not even once. She says she can't. . . .

PAULA: The poor girl! Don't you agree? That's why she has such sad eyes. . . . (*Pause.*) Kiss me again, Dionisio! . . .

DIONISIO (*he kisses her again*): Paula! I don't want to get married! It's silly! Now I could never be happy! Just a few hours have changed me completely. . . . I intended to leave here on the road to happiness, and I really would have been going out on the road to sloppy sentiment and hyperacidity. . . .

PAULA: What's hyperacidity?

DIONISIO: I don't know, but it must be something impressive. . . . Let's run away together! . . . Tell me that you love me, Paula!

PAULA: Please let me sleep! It's so nice like this!

(*Pause. The two of them, heads together, have closed their eyes. There is more and more light on the balcony. Suddenly the sound of a trumpet is heard, playing reveille and getting closer and closer. Then we hear a few knocks on the door.*)

DON ROSARIO (*off*): It's seven o'clock, Don Dionisio! It's time to get ready now! Your limousine won't be late! It's seven o'clock, Don Dionisio!

(*Don Dionisio is upset. There is a silence. She yawns and says:*)

PAULA: It's seven o'clock, Dionisio. You have to get dressed now.

DIONISIO: No.

PAULA (*getting up and throwing the blanket on the floor*): Come on, now! Are you crazy? It's time for you to go now! . . .

DIONISIO: I don't want to. . . . I'm very busy now. . . .

PAULA (*doing as she says*): I'll get everything ready for you. . . . Here you are. . . . The water . . . towels . . . Come on. Come and get washed, Dionisio! . . .

DIONISIO: I'm going to catch a cold. I feel terribly cold. . . . (*He throws himself down on the sofa and sits there, all huddled up.*)

PAULA: It doesn't matter. . . . This way you'll build up your resistance. . . . (*She forces him up.*) And this will clear your head. Come on, hurry up! A good ducking is what you need right now! (*She pushes his head into the water.*) Like this! You can't have a sleepy face. . . . If you do the priest will scold you . . . and the altar boys . . . Everyone will scold you. . . .

DIONISIO: I'm so cold. I'm drowning! . . .

PAULA: That is good. . . . Now, dry yourself off. . . . And you must comb your hair. . . . I'd better comb it for you. . . . Like this. . . . You'll see. . . . You're going to look very handsome, Dionisio. . . . Now you'll probably even find a new fiancée. . . . Wait a minute, though! What about your top hat? (*She picks the three of them up from the floor.*) These are all smashed! . . . None of them will do you any good. . . . But, it's all right! Don't worry! While you're putting on your suit I'll go get one of mine! It's just like new. It's the one I use when I do the Charleston! . . . (*She goes out through the left-hand door.*)

(*Dionisio goes behind the screen and puts on the pants to his morning suit. Immediately enter Don Rosario by the door at the back, absurdly dressed in evening clothes, carrying his bugle in one hand, and in the other a big, white banner. And while he speaks he runs around the room like an imbecile.*)

DON ROSARIO: Don Dionisio! Don Dionisio! . . . I have everything ready! Hurry up and finish! The hallway is decorated with flowers and lace chains! The maids have all put on their Sunday dresses and will throw confetti on you! . . . The waiters will throw bits of bread at you! And the cook, in your honor, will throw whole chickens in the air!

DIONISIO (*leaning over the top of the screen*): But why did you arrange all that? ...

DON ROSARIO: Don't worry, Don Dionisio. I would have done the same thing for that little boy who drowned in the well. ... I've invited the whole neighborhood and they're all waiting for you down by the front door! The women and the children! The young people and the old folks! The cops and the robbers! Hurry up, Don Dionisio! Everything is already prepared! (*And he goes out again by the rear door; from outside he begins to play a lively march on his bugle. Paula comes in now with a top hat in her hand.*)

PAULA: Dionisio! ...

DIONISIO (*he comes out from behind the screen wearing the pants to his morning suit, with the shirttails hanging out*): Here I am! ...

PAULA: I found the hat right away! ... Now you'll see how good you look in it! ... (*She puts it on Dionisio, on whom it looks very bad.*) You see? It's the one that fits you the best! ...

DIONISIO: But you can't be serious, Paula! It's a hat for dancing! ...

PAULA: This way, while you're wearing it, you'll think about happy things! And now, the collar! The tie! (*She begins putting them on him, all wrong.*)

DIONISIO: Paula! I don't want to get married! I'm not going to know what to say to that century-old man! I love you madly. ...

PAULA (*putting in his collar stays*): What, crying already?

DIONISIO: It's just that you're pinching me. ...

PAULA: There, now it's done! (*She finishes. He puts on his morning coat.*) And now, the morning coat ... And the handkerchief in your pocket! (*She studies him, now completely dressed.*) But, this shirt? Do they always wear them like that at weddings? ...

DIONISIO (*hiding behind the screen to tuck in his shirt*): No. It's just that ...

PAULA: What's a wedding like, anyway? Do you know? I've never gone to a wedding. ... Of course, since I go to bed so late I don't have time to go. ... But it must be like this. ... Come out now! (*Dionisio comes out, his shirt in place now.*) I'm the bride and I'm dressed in white, with a veil down to my toes . . . and holding your arm. . . . (*She does so. And they walk around the room.*) And we go into the church . . . like this . . . both of us very serious. . . . And at the end of the church there will be a very nice priest, with white gloves on. . . .

DIONISIO: Paula, priests don't wear white gloves. . . .

PAULA: Be quiet! There will be a very nice priest! And then we will greet him. . . . "Good morning. How are you today? And is your family well? How is the sacristan getting along? And the altar boys, have they all been behaving themselves? . . ." And we'll kiss all the altar boys. . .

DIONISIO: Paula! People don't kiss the altar boys! . . .

PAULA (*annoyed*): Well, I'll kiss all the altar boys, because I'm the bride and I can do whatever I want to! . . .

DIONISIO: It's just that . . . you won't be the bride.

PAULA: It's true! What a shame that I'm not the bride, Dionisio! . . .

DIONISIO: Paula! I don't want to get married! Let's run away together to Chicago! . . .

DON ROSARIO (*outside*): Don Dionisio! Don Dionisio! . . .

DIONISIO: Hide yourself! . . . It's Don Rosario! He mustn't see you in my room!

(*Paula hides behind the screen.*)

DON ROSARIO (*entering*): Now the limousine is here waiting for you! Come down right away, Don Dionisio! It's a white carriage with two dark footmen and two little white horses with light brown spots! What white horses! The maids are already throwing confetti! And the waiters are already throwing bits of bread! Come down right away, Don Dionisio! . . .

DIONISIO (*looking toward the screen, not wanting to leave*): Yes . . . I'm coming right away. . . .

DON ROSARIO: No! No! In front of me . . . I'll follow you waving the flag with one hand and playing my bugle. . . .

DIONISIO: The fact is that I . . . I want to say good-bye. . . .

DON ROSARIO: To the room? Don't think about it! Hotel rooms are all alike! They never leave memories! Come on, come on, Don Dionisio! ...

DIONISIO (*without taking his eyes off the screen*): The fact is ... (*Paula sticks one hand over the top of the screen as if waving good-bye to him.*) Good-bye! ...

DON ROSARIO (*catching him by the coat tails and dragging him after him*): Long live love and flowers, my little white lily bud! (*And he waves the flag. Dionisio waves good-bye again. Paula, too. And Don Rosario and Dionisio disappear to the rear.*)

(*Paula comes out of hiding. She approaches the rear door and looks out. Then she runs toward the balcony and again stares, through the window panes. The sound of Don Rosario's bugle continues, getting fainter all the time, playing a lively military march. Paula salutes, through the window. Then she turns around. She sees the three top hats and picks them up. ... And suddenly, when it looks like she's going to get sentimental, she throws the hats in the air, gives a happy circus-ring cry: "Whoop!" She smiles, salutes, and the curtain falls.*)

FINIS

# NIGHT AND WAR
# IN THE PRADO MUSEUM

*(An Etching, in a Prologue and One Act)*

*by* RAFAEL ALBERTI

TRANSLATED BY LEMUEL JOHNSON

With Lorca, Rafael Alberti (b. 1902), in addition to being a
prolific playwright, is one of the most important modern Spanish-
language poets. Like Lorca also, he was one of the first poets in
Spain to forge from French Surrealism a style of his own. There
are other similarities too: both men wrote elegies on the death of
the great Spanish bullfighter (and their mutual friend), Sanchez
Mejías; both men in their younger days dedicated works to the
movie clown, Buster Keaton; both men—Alberti in his *Trece ban-
das y cuarenta y ocho estrellas* (*Thirteen Stripes and 48 Stars*, 1936)
—wrote poems of their experience of America. Finally, both men,
by the time of the tercentenary of Donne's great contemporary and
Spanish similar, Góngora, in 1927, had woven the metaphorical
extravagances of this poet into the texture of their work. Since the
Civil War Alberti has been living abroad (in Argentina and, at this
writing, in Rome); but gradually, even before that, a divergence in
the course of the two writers had appeared. Whereas Lorca was
moving ever more deeply into Spanish tradition, both literary and
otherwise, in his later writings, Alberti was developing a more international, political perspective. The mythology of even Alberti's
celebrated early volume, *Sobre los angéles* (*About the Angels*, 1927)
is supernatural and placeless. Alberti has written seven plays to
date, mostly dealing with the subject of injustice, both earthly and
divine. *Night and War in the Prado Museum* is the most specifically Spanish of all these plays, harking back not only to Alberti's Civil War days, when he was an ardent Republican, but also
to Spanish history generally.

As does Lorca's *The Shoemaker's Prodigious Wife*, the play
begins with a prologue spoken by "the Author." This prologue is
an especially intimate one. Alberti, like Lorca, was deeply interested in the visual arts, and originally came to Madrid to study to
become a painter; this opening section is Alberti's reminiscence
of the days when he wandered the halls of the Prado, finally coming to be as much an inhabitant of the museum as the paintings
it contained. These thoughts are driven out by the shouts and cries
and finally the actual materialization of the figures who during the
Civil War posted themselves in the Prado to defend it and its
contents. In turn, these forces merge with the defenders of Spain

in past invasions. The Spanish past is evoked through the paintings themselves, which sometimes come alive to serve as sources for the characters of the drama. Alberti's rather Gongoristic metaphor is not only telling but touching, as the fragile old figures of peacetime Spain—some of them of course mythological to begin with—wander the halls of the bombarded Prado, bewildered. Clearly, one of the implications of Alberti's highly original dramatic conceit is that the defenders of freedom in Spain in 1936 and 1808 merge with the proponents of freedom in any place or time.

M. B.

# CHARACTERS

AUTHOR

From the paintings, drawings, and etchings of Goya:

ONE ARM
EXECUTED MAN
KNIFE SHARPENER
WOMAN (MAJA)
STUDENT
BULLFIGHTER
PRIEST
1ST OLD WOMAN
2ND OLD WOMAN
3RD OLD WOMAN
DONKEY
BUCO (Great Horned Goat)
BEHEADED MAN
BLINDMAN

A number of poor persons and the citizens of Madrid.

These characters should be dressed in early nineteenth-century style: some in bright but harmonious colors; others in gray, sepia, white and black—all corresponding to the lights and shades of the drawings and etchings.

From Titian:

VENUS
ADONIS
MARS

Venus should be almost naked, with the whitish color of a statue. Adonis, with a garnet-colored tunic, bare legs and sandals. Mars, at first, with the hide and head of a wild boar. Then, almost naked, with a steel helmet.

From Velasquez:

DWARF
KING

The Dwarf should be dressed as in the portrait titled "Don Sebastian de Morra." The King, as in Goya's Proverb No. 2, titled "Madness of Fear": hideous, dark-colored hood and loose-fitting dress.

Fra. Angelico's ARCHANGEL ST. GABRIEL, in a pale, rose-colored tunic.

From the anonymous altarpiece at Arguis: THE ARCHANGEL ST. MICHAEL, wearing a sword and a bright red tunic.

Contemporary personages:
    1ST SOLDIER
    2ND SOLDIER
    The action takes place in the Prado Museum in November, 1936.

    Many of the words spoken by the characters in this play are the exact words with which Goya captioned his drawings and etchings.

PROLOGUE

(*A large, white curtain, like a cinema screen, is in shadows. On it is sketched in black an outline of the main hall of the Prado Museum. When the Author appears, a spotlight is directed on his face.*)

AUTHOR: Good evening, ladies and gentlemen. Even though it may perhaps be more accurate to say "good afternoon," because on that particular day, the sky was blue and a soft, almost autumnal sun shone warmly against the walls of this building. And so, good afternoon, ladies and gentlemen. But—did I say good? No, not good. The days that followed that particular eighteenth day of July, 1936, were bad days—yes, for this house of paintings even worse than bad. House of paintings, yes. I call it that, a house, because in all the years of my adolescence and my youth, I never found a more beautiful refuge. I'd go in there every morning, losing myself in enchantment in its smallest rooms or in its largest halls—halls and rooms in which I'd suddenly hear the barking of the dogs of Diana—or else, I'd imagine myself in a woodland clearing with the Three Graces: three sprightly, full-bodied goddesses as presented to us by a certain eloquent faun of Flemish landscape. I close my eyes now and even now, ladies and gentlemen, after so many years of exile and misery, they come back to startle me. I was a simple country bumpkin when I first dared to set foot in this house. (*Spotlight on Author's face goes off and Rubens' "The Three Graces" appears on the screen.*)
No, I did not know then that life could bring
Tintoretto-summer, Veronese-spring.
Nor that blonde Graces filled with love went running
Through the halls of the Prado Museum.

(*A short pause.*) Such were the three shining goddesses—and, thanks to the great art and grace of Peter Paul Rubens, they will be living forever, there on those walls of Madrid's museum ... because, ladies and gentlemen, the refuge I considered my home then, as you must have guessed already, was none other than the Prado Museum in Madrid.

(*A loud explosion is heard nearby. "The Three Graces" disappears.*)

VOICE: Hurry! There's no time to lose. Rebel planes have dropped the first bombs on the capital. Any delay could have tragic consequences for our museum. As an emergency measure, until greater security can be arranged, the works of art will be sent for safekeeping to the cellars of the building. . . .

AUTHOR: And so, by decree of the Government of the Republic, the safeguarding of the Prado Museum was started. The first dreams of my life had disappeared in the smoke and the blood of war. (*Goya's "Executions of The Third of May in Moncloa" appears on screen.*) Soldiers of the first days of the war, men of our town, like those whom Goya saw toppling over in their blood under the fire of Napoleon's soldiers, helped save the famous works of art. 1808. 1936. They had the same look, the same convictions and intensity in their veins, the same professions. . . . One of them was probably a mule driver who drove his mules along the roads of Castile. . . . (*"The Third of May" begins to fade out.*) Another, perhaps, a water carrier who went calling out through San Antonio, through Atocha, across the meadows of San Isidro, at the foot of Manzanares. . . . (*Goya's "La Pradera de San Isidro" appears.*) And as also happened in 1808, the girls of Madrid, very much the same as those women and girls conversing there with their lovers by the river, ran to fight beside their men. . . . (*The "San Isidro" disappears.*) Hurriedly, paintings and sketches descended into the cellars. One could almost hear them protest their unexpected condemnation to the walls of cellars. (*A drawing of "La Tauromaquia," which shows a bullfighter preparing for the kill, appears.*) And now the hand reaches out for this bullfighter. . . .

VOICE OF THE BULLFIGHTER: No, No! Let me kill it! It's my last bull! My last bull!

(*Painting disappears and it is replaced by the etching, number 37 of The Disasters of War, entitled "With a Knife."*)

AUTHOR: And this one—he was strangled by Napoleon's invading soldiers. All because of a Knife! Perhaps he was just a knife sharpener. They probably found the knife on him when they searched him and . . . Yes, look at him! One of so many heroes of our war of liberation. (*Painting disappears.*) There were also great patriots among the priests. . . . (*Number 38 of The Disasters of War appears.*) "Savages!" Goya himself exclaims at the bottom of this etching. (*Disappears.*) The painter saw worse horrors. Until he did, no one else ever dared to etch

them in steel. (*Number 39 of The Disasters appears.*) Look.
You almost get the feeling that the severed head of that man
was about to start screaming for justice. (*Number 39 disappears.*) Students, cloaked gallants and rustics, nobles and peas-
ants, everywhere, caught up together in the most terrible disasters of war—they also buried themselves deep in their cellars.
Then the most nightmarish of the great Aragonese painter's
visions began to pass before me. It was the hellish suffering of
the poor, the painful and terrible misery of Spain. It was the
sound of the voices of a dispossessed and hungry people.

CHORUS OF VOICES: Woe, woe, woe, woe, woe! . . .

(*The "Pilgrimage to San Isidro" appears.*)

VOICE OF BLINDMAN (*accompanying himself on the guitar as he
sings*):
    If I could, if I could,
    I would devour
        even the hunger
    gnawing my bowels.

CHORUS: Woe, woe, woe, woe, woe! . . .

(*The painting disappears.*)

AUTHOR: The woe of the crippled, of the sickly, of the blind who
roam through those fairs and highways. And then, "The As-
sembly of the Witches" (*The painting appears*), the gather-
ing of the most ferocious terrors, faces gaping in bewilderment
at the obscure utterances of the great Buco, the bearded and
horned demon-goat.

VOICES OF OLD WOMEN 1, 2 & 3 (*laughing to a screaming, strident
pitch*): Hee, hee, hee! Hee, hee, hee! Hee, hee, hee!

AUTHOR (*as picture disappears*): And the old women laugh, and
laugh and laugh again at the mysterious incantations of their
master. . . .

VOICE OF OLD WOMAN (*as a part of the painting titled "Old Women"
appears*): How do you do?

AUTHOR: How do you do?, Maria Luisa of Parma, a hundred times
ill-treated by Goya, asks the mirror. . . . Maria Luisa of Parma
the featherbrained wife of Don Carlos IV of Bourbon, sovereign Lord of Spain and her Americas.

VOICE OF 3RD OLD WOMAN: How do you do? Well, you can see for yourself. A wrinkled, barren, ugly face with a stench of decay. Ugh! Pray God, your Manolo doesn't see you, pray God your Manolo doesn't see you. Hee, hee! (*Painting disappears.*)

AUTHOR: Her Manolo, Manuel Godoy y Alvarez de Faria, was handsome, an attractive officer (*Portrait of Godoy from the "War of the Oranges" appears*) in the Royal Corps, who, because of his love affair with the queen turned out to be nothing but . . .

VOICE OF ONE ARM: A dictator!

VOICE OF EXECUTED MAN: The ruin of Spain!

VOICE OF PRIEST: He opened our doors to the French. . . .

VOICE OF STUDENT: He brought Napoleon to our country. . . .

VOICE OF KNIFE SHARPENER: Defenseless, he handed us over to Napoleon's barbarous soldiers. . . .

VOICE OF BEHEADED MAN: He tortured us, trampled on us, drowned us in blood. . . .

VOICE OF 3RD OLD WOMAN (*as painting disappears*): Manolo, Manolo, my love, oh, what things they say about us! Oh, protect your love. . . .

(*Voices laugh offstage as Goya's "Donkey Walking on Hind Legs" appears on screen. The laughter changes to braying as the painting disappears.*)

AUTHOR: Still more dangerous hours for our museum. Without rest, the work went on day and night. After the Goyas, the Velazquez went down to the cellars. (*Velazquez' portraits of the dwarf "Don Sebastian De Morra" and "King Philip IV in Hunting Suit" appear together on screen.*) I particularly remember this ugly face of Don Sebastian de Morra, the favorite dwarf of King Philip IV, the king who sacrificed his royal duties to the hunt and the love of an actress. . . . (*The paintings disappear.*) After the Velazquez, came the El Grecos . . . those portraits of nobles in semidarkness, like weak, flickering flames. . . . Virgins and saints with tortured expressions, sculptured and molded as it were in burning clay. . . . And the severe Zurbarans . . . The dark shades of Ribera, the flayed bodies of his martyrs . . . From among the older Castilian masters, it was soon the turn of a warlike Archangel (*The altarpiece of Arguis' showing the Archangel Saint Michael appears*), a brave St. Michael fighting against demons, which I had forgotten. (*Disappears.*) When it was time for the Italian school, among the marvelous works of Raphael, Veronese, Tintoretto, another winged celestial being, one of the resplendent archangelic trinity, passed before me: Saint Gabriel. (*Fra Angelico's "The Annunciation" appears.*) Yes, ladies and gentlemen, it was more than painful to watch the Blessed Fra Angelico's very delicate creature, kneeling in worship before the slender figure of Mary, also thrust down into the gloomy regions of the cellars. (*Disappears.*) And now the strange parade was about to end. . . . Titian was among the last. . . . I was already worn out from so many days of tension and watchfulness. But suddenly a painting passed. . . . Just a minute please! I said to the soldiers who were carrying it. It was a work with whose subject I had become acquainted through the poet Garcilaso; I would invariably recite the poem to myself during my visits to the hall of the Venetian painter. (*"Venus and Adonis" appears.*)

> This clearly was none but Adonis
> as shown by the grief of grief-stricken Venus,
> Venus, who, seeing the wild, open wound,
> lies half-dead upon him.
> Mouth to his mouth, she sucks in
> the fleeting breath which once gave life
> to the body for which, earthbound, she
> once scorned the whole high heavens.

Verses which refer to the end of the legend of Venus and Adonis, to the story of their love destroyed by the jealousy of a god. . . . (*Titian's work disappears and the prolonged howl of a hound is heard.*) When this painting, the very last one, disappeared, I thought I could hear the long howls of the hounds of Adonis as they wandered despondently through the countryside. (*Pause.*) The first phase in the effort to save the Prado had ended. The city proudly kept watch over its treasures. . . . The halls remained empty. Only the rectangles of the paintings remained outlined on the walls. Today, outside, the sky is no longer blue over the roofs of the museum, nor does the sun touch them with its warming hand. I shall end here. But first—forgive my oversight. I neglected to tell you my name. If by any chance you're interested, you'll find it on the poster outside, or in the program giving the title of the play which you'll be watching in a few seconds.

And now, yes: Good evening, ladies and gentlemen.

(CURTAIN RISES.)


## ACT ONE

*(Large, central hall of the Prado Museum, completely empty. The outlines of the paintings, now removed to the cellars, are marked out in different shapes and sizes on the walls. The wooden floor is covered with sand. Sandbags are strewn about. A large sixteenth-century table is half-hidden by the bags. It is nighttime in Madrid during the war's most desperate days: November, 1936. When the curtain rises, nothing can be made out on stage. The distant firing of a cannon is heard. The Executed Man and the Knife Sharpener enter through a dark, upstage door. They carry two bright yellow torches; they set these down on the floor and then they stop beside the table. Each has an old rifle slung across his back. They are accompanied by One Arm who comes in dragging a long sword.)*

ONE ARM *(to Executed Man and Knife Sharpener who move around wearily)*: OK, let's go! These sacks. Here. And those over there, on this side. Make sure there are no gaps between them. From one wall to the other. This is one barricade that's going to hold!

*(Executed Man and Knife Sharpener slowly begin to carry the sandbags.)*

EXECUTED MAN: I hear they've already overrun the fields outside the city.

KNIFE SHARPENER: And that Moors have been seen on the Calle Mayor.

EXECUTED MAN: And that the Emperor is once more at Charmatín.

1ST OLD WOMAN *(as yet invisible)*: Hee, hee, hee! Napoleon! What a laugh!

ONE ARM *(Picking up one of the torches and moving up to the barricade)*: Who could that be moving around behind the sandbags?

(*1st Old Woman appears behind the bags that cover part of the table. She is a terrifying figure, dressed in black; with owlish eyes, moustache, and large, hair-covered wart.*)

1ST OLD WOMAN: Napoleon! Napoacher! Just a poacher! I have a picture of him. . . . At the bottom of my chamber-pot. . . . Hee, hee! And do I bombard that poor man every morning!

ONE ARM: What the devil are you doing here, you old hag?

1ST OLD WOMAN: I'm waiting. I'm a lady-in-waiting to the Queen. Where's your wine jug? (*Teeth chattering loudly.*) Christ, it's a cold night! What a freezing, piercing cold this is!

ONE ARM (*tosses her a small leather bottle of red wine which was hanging from his shoulder*): Here! And keep quiet, you tanked-up drunkard! (*To the men.*) We've got no time to waste. (*1st Old Woman shivering and laughing, takes a long drink; then she tosses the bottle back and hides behind the bags again.*) Good. Now, the ones on that side. (*He points to other bags scattered in the hall. Executed Man and Knife Sharpener move to obey the order; but then the Executed Man leans against the barricade, very much worn out.*) You're all tired out, eh? What's your name?

EXECUTED MAN (*shrugging his shoulders*): Me? They shot me in Moncloa; that's what happened to me. With my hands tied. For what happened on May second at the Puerta del Sol. The goddamned, French sons-of-bitches! I don't know what my name is. I've forgotten. You can just call me one of the executed.

ONE ARM (*picks up the bottle from the floor and gives it to him*): Have some. (*As the other drinks.*) And what were you?

EXECUTED MAN: A water carrier. Between Toledo and Madrid. I arrived the night before. . . . (*After a slight pause.*) There. I feel better. (*To Knife Sharpener.*) Let's go.

KNIFE SHARPENER (*tries to walk but falls to his knees*): First, get this knife out of my body. I can hardly breathe. (*He writhes on floor*).

ONE ARM (*as he tries to remove a knife, almost up to the hilt in the middle of Knife Sharpener's chest*): Let's see! (*To Executed Man.*) You! Help me. It's driven in too deep for one hand to do any good.

EXECUTED MAN (*succeeds in removing knife*): That was really in there! But why did they do it to you?

KNIFE SHARPENER: Because of one of my knives. I was a knife sharpener. I sharpened knives in the streets. They searched my hut. And found that knife buried in a box of geraniums. They strangled me. . . . Then drove in the knife . . . And went away.

VOICE OF 1ST OLD WOMAN: Goddamned Frenchies! Goddamned Frenchies! Hee, hee, hee!

KNIFE SHARPENER (*to One Arm, as he gets up*): And that stump? You weren't born with one arm missing, were you?

ONE ARM: A clay pitcher and a jar . . . That was my profession. . . . I made the rounds, calling out in the Prado, in the Pradera, in San Antonio (*in a somewhat hoarse voice*): Fresh water! Water! From the fountain of Berro! Then I became an artillery man. I was guarding Monteleon Park. . . . A piece of shrapnel tore off my arm.

KNIFE SHARPENER: We'll call you One Arm then—and our captain. There are no generals here—you'll lead us well. I like you.

KNIFE SHARPENER & EXECUTED MAN (*giving him a military salute*): At your command!

1ST OLD WOMAN (*showing her head*): Bravo, bravo, captain of the queen! At your command!

1ST VOICE (*in darkness*): At your command!

(*Student enters.*)

2ND VOICE (*in darkness*): At your command!

(*Woman enters.*)

3RD VOICE (*in darkness*): At your command!

(*Bullfighter appears, sword in hand. These same words—At your command! At your command!—as though repeated by an invisible army, continue to sound offstage, then fade out. A loud explosion sounds nearby.*)

WOMAN: My God! They're practically firing next door.

STUDENT: It's as if Madrid were on fire.

WOMAN: But what's happening? I was out walking with my boyfriend in San Isidro. Suddenly, in the middle of the afternoon bombs began to go off and they rushed us all down to the cellars.

STUDENT: Everybody seemed to be going down in there. The halls of this house were left empty.

BULLFIGHTER: I never got to kill my bull. I've still got my sword.

EXECUTED MAN: Keep a tight hold on it. You'll need it.

1ST OLD WOMAN (*appearing again, with a broom*): Run the Frenchies through with swords? And what if all we've got in Spain is a pack of cowards! I'll beat out, I'll sweep out their insides—all of them! Hee, hee, hee! (*Laughs hoarsely.*)

STUDENT: So you're here too, eh? You old witch!

1ST OLD WOMAN: More respect, my little master student; I'm just as good a patriot as you are. And a lady-in-waiting to the Queen, the one and only Queen of the Spanish Empire.

STUDENT: And the queens of Spain, as we know, are certainly objects of wonder.

1ST OLD WOMAN: Mine was different, sarcastic young man; she was every inch a lady, a most sovereign and majestic lady who'd freeze the blood in the very devil's veins with fear.

ONE ARM: I told you—we don't have any time to waste. Come on!

BULLFIGHTER (*moves admonishingly with sword against 1st Old Woman*): All right, you old owl, let's do as the captain says!

1ST OLD WOMAN: Yes, the captain!—whatever the captain says! But not a little bullfighter with two lizards in his feet. You must be quite a sight running out there in front of those horns!

BULLFIGHTER: I'll run you through and leave you stretched out here on these bags! (*He jumps at 1st Old Woman who laughs and hides.*)

ONE ARM: That's enough! Are you going to obey me or not? We've got to guard this door. It opens out to a pretty wide street out there! Hurry up!

(*They all work in haste to build the barricade. Other nearby explosions are heard.*)

WOMAN (*helped by the Knife Sharpener, she carries a bag*): They're firing again. I've never in my life heard such a din.

KNIFE SHARPENER: Do cannons frighten you?

WOMAN: Not me! Not cannons, not rifles not swords. Look what I've got here. (*She rolls up her sleeve, exposing a large scar.*)

KNIFE SHARPENER: The savages! That's ghastly!

BULLFIGHTER: Lady, that's quite a sword wound you've got there! Even for a bull.

EXECUTED MAN: Women can be pretty brave. And a help too. They shot mine—but she really let them have it first! They had to tie her to a tree. Then, they stripped her naked. Finally they chopped off her arms and nailed them to the branches.

STUDENT ( *in anger and sorrow*): Oh, how truly magnificent—even with corpses!

ONE ARM: We don't distinguish men or women here. We are all the same. Ordinary people from the streets of Spain.

(*Priest emerges from darkness, a bottle of wine hanging from his belt.*)

PRIEST: I've got skirts too, although mine aren't quite as eye-catching as that good woman's. But I'll roll up my sleeves, too.

STUDENT: Hello, Father! Good evening.

PRIEST: Yes, good; it's a good one all right, because things are going to happen here that will be talked about *per in secula seculorum.*

STUDENT & OTHERS (*teasingly*): Amen!

PRIEST: Don't laugh; I'm all set for my beloved Frenchmen.

ONE ARM: We understand, Father; we know you're one of us. Here, give us a hand with the barricade.

PRIEST: Yes, I've still got arms, thank God!

ONE ARM: OK, let's get to work! (*They continue silently piling up the sandbags.*)

KNIFE SHARPENER (*as he carries over a bag to fill up a gap next to the table, he notices a plaque with writing. Turning to Woman*): What does it say?

WOMAN: I can't read.

KNIFE SHARPENER: How about you, Executed One? (*The Executed Man looks from his position and shrugs his shoulders.*) I knew how to read once, myself—but I've forgotten. OK, let's hear it, Student! Let's hear what they've got there.

STUDENT (*brings a light close and reads*): "Gift of Pope Pius V to Don Juan of Austria after the battle of Lepanto."

KNIFE SHARPENER: Who was this Don Juan? I remember hearing something. . . .

STUDENT: A bastard . . .

EXECUTED MAN: What's that?

STUDENT: Well . . . How shall I put it? Someone who's born before his mother and father got married. . . .

EXECUTED MAN: I see; a royal son of a . . .

PRIEST (*excitedly*): No! No! A great hero! A hero who cut down the crescent of Mohammed in the most terrible battle of all times!

ONE ARM: It's always the Moors! Same thing right now.

PRIEST: You mean the Mamelukes—the Emperor's Egyptian guard.

WOMAN: The men who cut up my body with their swords were Moors. Yes, Moors from Morocco! I gouged out the eyes of at least three of their horses.

PRIEST: That's the spirit, beautiful lady! I went around for several days dressed like a Frenchman. And did I let them have it! Until they discovered my tonsure and then I barely escaped being shot or having a stake driven through me.

1ST OLD WOMAN (*appears and sings*):
        Reverend monkey;
        Reverend monk,
        You'll have a stake stuck for sure
        Straight through your tonsure!

PRIEST: Get thee behind me, Satan! Black horror from hell!

1ST OLD WOMAN (*singing*):
        Reverend friar,
        Reverend chicken,
        No wonder you pass up the soup and the nuts:
        Only wine can stir up your guts!

(*They all laugh*).

PRIEST: You're right there, you croaking old bag—but now I'll show what this reverend monkey can still do. (*He is about to throw himself on top of her when the strongest explosion yet brings him to the floor. The explosions continue. Voices in the darkness*):

WOMAN: Savages!

EXECUTED MAN: Murderers!

BULLFIGHTER: The walls are shaking!

PRIEST: The end of the world! The Apocalypse of St. John!

KNIFE SHARPENER: Jesus! What weapons are they using?

PRIEST: The wrath of God! They are the cannons of hell!

1ST OLD WOMAN (*mournfully*): Hee, hee, hee, hee! Hee, hee, hee, hee!

(*Sounds of confusion are heard: falling, breaking glass; piteous screams*).

STUDENT: They're burrowing under the walls!

ONE ARM: Courage! Hang on! Lights! The torches! Light the torches! I've got only one hand! Get some light! Light!

(*Instead of the light of the torches, a dull beam of light penetrates the left side of the room, leaving the barricade in complete darkness. The cannon shots die away. Lying on the floor, half-naked, are Venus and Adonis.*)

VENUS (*as though arousing from sleep, unconscious of her surroundings*): The gods are afraid. Adonis, my love, Adonis! Where are you?

ADONIS (*bending over her*): My love, clearer than clear fountains, riper and sweeter than apples freshly picked at dawn, more delicate and fresher than the rose . . .

VENUS: Adonis, my love, Adonis! Where are we? Are you wounded? I am afraid, my love.

ADONIS: Oh, Venus, white daughter of the foam! Don't tremble so. Get up. We shall escape into the deepest part of the woods. My hounds arc gone. The leashes are broken. I've lost my arrows. We have no defense. The red anger of Mars pursues us. Listen to the thunder of his weapons. He will kill us.

VENUS: Neither his thunder nor his lightning can harm us, Adonis. The weapons of love are stronger than his. You and I are peace, we are the olive branch, the cooing of doves, the flowering of gardens in the spring. Take me, take me away from this place. . . .

ADONIS (*raises her up and embraces her*): Venus, Venus!

VENUS: Adonis, my love, Adonis! (*They remain in embrace. The dull beam of light changes into radiant sunshine.*) Oh! Look! The sun shines again for us. So that I can see you in all your beauty, my Adonis. (*They look at each other.*)

ADONIS: So that I can delight once more in your graceful loveliness, Venus. Like green myrtles are the tresses of your hair. . . .

VENUS: And your hair, the color of ground corn, dried in the sun . . .

ADONIS: White roses, sewn with threads from the honey of bees, such is your skin. . . .

VENUS: And your skin, anemone sown the length of your body by the hands of the air . . .

ADONIS: Two waves of uplifted carnations are your breasts. . . .

VENUS: Your arm is powerful in the hunt, but even more powerful as it presses my body among the mint bushes and the clover of hidden streams. . . . Beech trees and oaks will hang curtains for our lovemaking. . . . Adonis, my love, let us go.

ADONIS (*holds her around the waist and begins to walk*): Oh Venus! Venus! (*A prolonged and strident grunting is heard. Venus and Adonis stop in surprise. From the darkness upstage appears the figure of a man covered in skins and with the head mask of a wild boar.*) The hounds! The hounds! And my arrows! Where are my arrows! Oh, wild beast of the mountains, you come to me when I am without weapons.

VENUS (*shouts in desperation*): Adonis! Adonis! (*The wild boar quickly falls on Adonis who hardly has time to try and struggle with it.*) The anger and jealousy of Mars! The cruel spite of a blinded god! Terrible vengeance which plunges me in the blackest of nights! Adonis! My love, Adonis!

(*Adonis has fallen, mortally wounded by the fangs of the boar. A loud thunderclap reverberates as the light begins to fade.*)

ADONIS (*as, beside the kneeling Venus, he dies*): Venus! Oh Venus!

(*Mars, now without the skin and head of the boar, postures victoriously behind the two lovers.*)

VENUS (*cries as she clings to Adonis' corpse*): The youth of the world is dead; the sweet smell of gardens, springtime in the meadows—all are dead. War! Now comes war! Blood! Death! No escape. Adonis! My Adonis!

(*The light fades out into complete darkness. Silence.*)

VOICE (*in the darkness*): I'm hungry. For so many, many nights now, I've been hungry! Good people, for God's sake, a little song for a few coins to buy a loaf of bread with!

(*Melancholy twanging of a guitar. When the lights come on from the torches, Venus and Adonis have disappeared. A Blindman, in tattered cloak and suit, sings mournfully.*)

BLINDMAN (*accompanying himself on the guitar*):
>    From the twisted fragments
>    Of bombs the blustering braggarts threw
>    The girls of Madrid
>    Make many a corkscrew.

(*Silence.*) The color of hunger is black, they say. For me, everything is black. But I laugh and laugh. As though at the bombs.
(*He begins to laugh alone, bitterly. The laughter infects all in the barricade until it reaches a shrill and almost grotesque level.*)

ONE ARM (*shouting*): Enough! (*They all fall silent at once.*)

BLINDMAN (*after a pause*): I'm hungry.

ONE ARM (*coldly*): We're all hungry.

BLINDMAN: You're all here? Who are you?

ONE ARM: The citizens of the back streets, the denizens of the alleys. That's what they say.

BLINDMAN: I'm one of them too . . . although I'm blind. Give me something.

ONE ARM: Just a sip of wine. There's nothing else.

BLINDMAN: I'll take it. But a bowl of soup would have been better. I'm shaking here. It's a miserable thing to live by begging.

PRIEST (*giving him the bottle he is carrying in his belt*): Patience, brother. It's nighttime and we're in the middle of a battle.

BLINDMAN (*as he drinks*): I suppose that advice comes straight from God?

PRIEST: Yes. Through the mouth of a priest.

BLINDMAN: Liar! You say that and yet you stuff yourself sick and drown yourself in red wine. What a greedy swine you must be! I can just see it! (*Sarcastically.*) Patience! (*He drinks some more.*)

ONE ARM (*taking the bottle away from him*): Come on, let's have it back! There isn't too much of it. The others are thirsty too.

BLINDMAN: The others? Are there many of you? What are you doing here?

ONE ARM (*gestures to the others not to speak*): You ask too many questions.

BLINDMAN: I can't see.

ONE ARM (*quickly*): Where are you from? What sort of people did you hang around with? Where are you going?

BLINDMAN (*in a rising tone*): I can't see! I can't see! I can't see!

ONE ARM (*feeling his clothes*): Answer me! Answer! (*He shouts at him as he takes his guitar away and shakes it.*) What do you have inside the guitar? What did you bring? Tell me!

BLINDMAN (*confidently but furiously*): Nothing! Nothing! Break it, if you want to! I can't see! I can't see! I'm from the Pradera. And you'll find me there with the one-eyed, the crippled, the cross-eyed, the one-armed, with all the maimed and the miserably poor of Madrid. Strip me naked! Rip the rags off my back! Smash the guitar into bits and pieces! But I still can't see! *I can't see!*

ONE ARM (*returning the guitar*): I thought . . . there are people who pass on information to the French.

BLINDMAN: I hate the foreigner. I don't even know what he looks like. But I can hear him; I feel his presence clinging to my flesh—always. He blinded me.

1ST OLD WOMAN (*appearing*): Hee, hee! I know that man. . . .

STUDENT: Then why didn't you say so earlier, you old bat?

1ST OLD WOMAN: I was taking a little nap among the bags. Oh yes, that one over there—he used to be quite a fellow. And the songs he sang me about my beauty! And his hands were always reaching, grabbing! Hee, hee!

BLINDMAN (*laughing*): Are *you* here too, Oh queen's cleaning maid, hell-wrinkle, keeper of the chamber pots, oh excrement from the lowest sewer of the Court? (*He reaches out and gropes around for her.*) Come on, let me see what your dried out chicken-bosom feels like. . . . (*The cannon shots begin again.*) Zambomba!

WOMAN: The cannons again.

BLINDMAN: Girl, do they give you the shivers? My cloak's a nice shelter. Where are you?

WOMAN: Hide your bones in your own rags, foul mouth; I laugh at the bombing and with my body in the open.

BLINDMAN: And the reverend Father from Merced also laughs?

PRIEST: Yes!

WOMAN: And the Executed One also.

EXECUTED MAN: Yes!

WOMAN: And the stabbed Knife Sharpener!

KNIFE SHARPENER: Yes!

WOMAN: And the Student and the Bullfighter.

STUDENT & BULLFIGHTER: Yes!

WOMAN:
> And the garbage collector
> And the barber
> And the terrifying witch
> With the sweeping broom!

And even the teardrops
And all the cobwebs and even the dust
Of all the good people of Spain!

1ST OLD WOMAN (*breaking into a strident laughter*): Hee, hee, hee, hee, hee, hee!

ONE ARM: In this barricade everybody laughs. Those who want to cry can go somewhere else. We're not here to cry; we're here to fight and die, if we have to—and with laughter on our lips. (*The cannon fire intensifies. At a sign from One Arm, they all move up to the barricade and lead the Blindman behind it.*) Fire, fire away, you cowards! We're the same people as the ones on the second of May—yes, the ones stabbed and trampled on at the Puerta del Sol! The ones resurrected from Casa de Campo and the banks of the Manzanares! But now the tears will be yours—our laughter will remain!

BLINDMAN (*from the topmost part of the barricade, he breaks into song with the guitar; the others sing in chorus with him*):
    Madrid, listen to how well you defy
    The bombers;
    As the bombs fall and fly
    Listen to Madrid's laughter!

(*They all laugh until the laughter rises to the highest pitch. Then silence as the barricade remains in darkness. From the back of the room enter Two Soldiers of the Spanish Civil War, quietly humming the song: "Madrid, how well you defy! . . ." They are dressed as in the first months of the struggle (1936). First Soldier has one arm in a sling; 2nd Soldier has a bright flashlight which he directs at the corners, walls and ceiling of the hall, as he continues talking.*)

1ST SOLDIER: It's pretty rough tonight.

2ND SOLDIER: Bombs were falling right next to the museum. Once I thought they'd scored a direct hit. It's going to be close from now on. They'll be removing the most famous works soon. They'll be taken where it's safer. The technicians have been working without any rest. There are some pretty large paintings in there—I saw them down in the cellars; I don't know how they're going to get them out through the doors. The Goyas are hanging down there: "La carga de los Mamelucos en la Puerta del Sol" and "The Third of May." And, inside, the Titians, the Velazquez . . .

1ST SOLDIER: Yes, comrade, Madrid's burning! We're not going to forget this November, 1936.

2ND SOLDIER: They're fighting in Useras, in Casa de Campo, in the Manzanares, at the Puente de los Franceses, in Moncloa, at the University . . . and it's pretty rough fighting, comrade!

1ST SOLDIER: What's rough is being shut up down here! I was wounded in the mountains. . . .

2ND SOLDIER: They thought they were going to get through! There are dazed Moors wandering all over the place out there, even as far as the Gran Via.

1ST SOLDIER: The girls from the south side fought like wild cats at the Toledo Bridge.

2ND SOLDIER: Everybody's fighting. Young and old. With rocks, homemade bombs—with weapons so obsolete, heaven knows where they must have dug them up. (*They walk upstage left.*)

1ST SOLDIER: They'll never get through! Not even with the help of all the Germans, Moors, Italians and Portuguese in the world. . . . (*As they exit.*) They'll never get through!

(*A bearded and miserable-looking Dwarf, Velazquez' Don Sebastian de Morra, emerges from the darkness upstage.*)

DWARF: The truth is, I don't know where I am. I've lost my king. (*Looks around.*) Hey, you! Big nose! Are you here? You've been leaving quite a lot of fuss behind you, you know. You've got the palace all shaken up. The queen, my poor mistress! (*Shouts.*) Philip! Philip! Where the hell are you? And stop all that thundering; I've just about had it, Philip! (*Weeps; but with a certain amount of pretext.*) Shove a cork into your —you-know-where. Come on, don't make an ass of yourself! It's downright rude for a great king like you to try to scare your best friend by firing out all these smelly blasts. (*A burst of machine-gun firing sounds nearby. After a terror-filled pause, he continues.*) Eh? What new one is that, my Lord? First, boom!—One big explosion—And then sharp, little ones like the rattling of a crane! (*Imitates a machine gun.*) Ra-ta-ta-ta-ta-ta-ta-ta-ta! It's amazing the number of things kings can do! The number of things they've got stored up in their heads —I mean, the majestic pots they've got behind them where they compose and fire off their royal decrees! (*Sound of a strong and loud slamming of a door.*) I'm afraid. I'm shaking all over, Philip. Don't be unkind to your faithful servant, your poor, dear little Sebastian de Morra. (*He weeps. A trapdoor opens through which there appears first a long, trailing sleeve, like that of a shroud. It holds up the tiny flame of a candle. The Dwarf crosses himself and falls down on his knees.*) Regina angelorum! Refugium pecatorum! Auxilium cristianorum! Consolatrix aflictorum! (*In the meantime, a tall, frightful figure, completely covered by a loose, black shroud, has emerged from the trapdoor. It stands for a moment then lets the hand holding the candle drop and crumples onto the floor. The Dwarf screams. Then he approaches timidly and walks around the fallen figure. Finally he decides to remove the candle from the hand of the figure; he pulls down the cape and holds up the light to the face. In great surprise*) What the hell! It's the King! (*He kneels down and takes the King's head between his hands.*) What a scare you gave me! What a silly fellow you are, Philip! I'll never forgive you. I ought to tear off your moustache right now so nobody'd recognize you again. Christ! What a horribly grotesque scarecrow!

(*The King tries to get up but the terrified Dwarf gives such a jump that he is knocked over again.*)

KING: Lord! Who would believe that I, I am King Philip IV!

DWARF (*softly*): Nobody.

KING: Are you here, Don Sebastian de Morra?

DWARF (*firmly, bravely*): I'm here. What's the matter?

KING (*raising his head slowly*): I had such a fright looking for you!

DWARF (*with ironic incredulity*): Fear, Your Majesty? Forgive me, but I don't believe you, Philip.

KING (*panting*): It was horrible! And you, my son?

DWARF (*boastingly*): Me? The firing gave me courage. I saw myself as the Duke of Olivares, complete with horsemen and all the rest of it.

KING: As for me, dear Sebastian, now that you alone can hear, I confess: even a simple rifleshot upsets me.

DWARF: Now, really! Does Your Majesty mean to say that you feel inclined to take your kingly body and . . .

KING: Almost, almost.

DWARF: That's a military secret that would be unwise to spread around at Court, isn't it?

KING: I'd be much obliged to you, dear Sebastian.

DWARF: Well, neither bullets nor swords nor guns will force it out of me. You should have appointed me your prime minister. Appoint me this very minute. I command you to do so. Do as I say, Philip.

(*Again the sounds of the machine gun.*)

KING (*as he falls down, fainting*): Aie! Aie! Aie!

DWARF (*terrified, he jumps about and speaks at the same time*): The sons of bitches! (*He kneels down once more beside the King, holding the King's corpselike face between his hands.*) You're not going to die, are you? Are you going to leave me all alone, my lord? For some other master to aim kicks on my already black and blue backside? For someone else, my King, to make me the confidant of his loves? What a great misfortune, Don Sebastianillo de Morra! (*Changes the plaintive tone.*) But—come on, big nose, get up! Quit fooling around! You aren't dead yet! You'll see! (*He spits on his hands and rubs the King's face.*)

KING (*regaining consciousness*): I can't figure out what this battle's all about. Are we at war, my son?

DWARF: Did your royal ancestors ever stop being at war?

KING: All right, but still . . .

DWARF: Come on now—to your feet, Your Majesty, let's find a safer place to be.

KING (*as the Dwarf helps him to his feet*): I wonder, could this perhaps be a punishment from God for all my sins?

DWARF: More likely it's the devil celebrating the fact that you committed them.

KING: Do you really think so, Sebastian?

DWARF: You committed adultery with the actress. . . . You squandered taxes on vain luxuries and trifles. . . . You've always lived with the idea that all decent people need to live on is air. . . .

KING: Quiet! Keep quiet!

DWARF (*recites in a lugubrious and deep voice*):
> Any decent poor man, any decent gentleman
> Without bread and the butcher's help, will sicken.
> From depending on cabbages for their only sustenance
> Spanish hearts and hands do weaken.

KING: I order you to keep quiet!

DWARF:
> See how the miserable poor, lonely and hidden,
> Silently call to you with a thousand screams.

KING: Sebastianillo, I order you to and I insist that you shut up: I, the King!

DWARF:
> The rich signify, with each and every plan
> Life is short, let's steal all we can!

KING: I'll have you hanged Don Sebastian. I'll kill you myself! Quiet! (*He turns angrily to fall upon the Dwarf who has already disappeared behind the barricade. The King stands motionless, surprised and silent.*) Sebastian! (*Pause. He calls out in terror.*) Sebastianillo! Where are you? I forgive you. Do not leave your King alone. (*After a pause. Almost crying.*) Don't torture me, son. Come to me. You can go ahead and say whatever you want, if that's all you want. . . . (*After another pause.*) I wonder, could I be already dead and waiting at the gates of hell?

DWARF (*reappearing, mocking and unperturbed*): Your Majesty may be right, considering the yellowish tinge of your face, and the infernal clothes you've got on tonight. . . .

KING (*embracing him*): You mustn't make fun of your good father. I disguised myself because of you. It was a pity they recognized me.

DWARF: You've got good reason to be afraid, my lord. With a "fear overmastering"—the kind of fear a monarch should have. But I'm not afraid. Observe how calm I am.

KING: You've always been brave.

(*The sounds of the cannon are heard again.*)

DWARF (*babbling with fear*): D . . . d . . . damn . . ed th . . . th . . . ings!

KING: I am damned, oh Lord! And now it's too late to be saved! (*He grabs hold of the Dwarf by the hair when he tries to run away.*) Don't leave me, Sebastianillo! Don't desert the king, your most unfortunate King Philip!

DWARF: King, royalty, my foot! If, as you say, your Majesty is dead, I'm getting out of here so I don't get killed, too!

KING (*moving with him toward the trapdoor*): You're coming with me! Whether you want to or not, I'm taking you along! I'm sure we'll find a place that's absolutely safe! The queen's bedroom! Let's go! (*He pushes the Dwarf down the trapdoor and disappears down it after him. When the noise dies down, the barricade is seen once more*).

STUDENT: It's all right to laugh, One Arm. But, what weapons do we have? Two old rifles, one blunted sword, the bullfighter's sword; a knife; a guitar and—tonight's cold weather.

WOMAN: A knife? Two knives! I've got another here, hidden in my garter. (*She raises her skirts and pulls out the knife.*)

PRIEST: And a hunting knife which I've got hidden in my robes. (*He shows his knife.*)

1ST OLD WOMAN: And a broom that's as good as ten cannons. And something else which I'm not showing.

BLINDMAN: I've got nothing—But a swipe at their heads with this guitar might help.

ONE ARM: What other weapons did we have on May second? Now, let's see: Knife Sharpener!—You take the rifle. Give the Student your knife.

STUDENT (*taking the knife*): But things are different now. Those must be new kinds of cannon they're firing.

ONE ARM: That's the way it is. We're simple people and fight simply. We'll have weapons enough. They're hidden all over the place. And if that's not enough, then we'll use fingernails and teeth! They'll leave a few marks on the necks of the invaders anyway!

EXECUTED MAN: You're right, captain. And if they kill us—if they kill us—we'll rise up again!

STUDENT: It's true what they say: the people never die. And they have dreams of weapons so powerful that they can destroy all those who tonight or any night wish to destroy Madrid.

KNIFE SHARPENER: We're not going to fail because they're not going to get past us. I'm sure of it. There are people everywhere who will help us.

PRIEST: It's a night for heroes, my sons. Even the stones are singing. I see the ghost of a villain covering his ears, wrapped up in smoke and fire. He wants to come in but cannot. He tries to find a path among the flames, but a barricade of invincible hearts prevents him from coming out of his hiding place.

1ST OLD WOMAN (*as if seeing a vision*): Yes! Yes! I see him there! Look at him! A fat, messy toad, drooling spittle all over his stomach. Hey there, you criminal! How much blood have you drunk today? You're swelling up, eh? I'll soon flatten you with my broom. Hee, hee!

BLINDMAN: I see him! I can see him! You're the very one who blinded me, you son of a bitch! You!

EXECUTED MAN: You brought those who shot me. You!

KNIFE SHARPENER: You drove the knife into my chest. You!

WOMAN: You! You ripped open my side with your sword. You!

ONE ARM: Do you see this arm? Look at it. It's gone. You tore it away with your blind shrapnel. You!

BULLFIGHTER: Traitor! Murderer! Robber of our land! You!

ALL (*pointing accusing fingers at the ghost*): You! You! You!

(*A loud cry is heard upstage. A man, carrying his blood-covered head in his hand, comes toward the barricade.*)

BEHEADED MAN: Justice, justice for me! They've chopped off my head with an axe! It's still talking and will continue to talk till the end of the world!

ONE ARM: A terrible tragedy.

BEHEADED MAN: That's how they treated us. We're a different race, they said. But I'm not dead. I'll never die. I beg for punishment, I plead for vengeance against those who do this. Justice! Justice!

ONE ARM: You've come to the right place. All of us here are shouting out the very same words. The executed, the crippled, the murdered, the blind: all of us miserably betrayed, but with the fires of a volcano burning in our hearts; the fires we'll roast them with!

PRIEST: War! War!

1ST OLD WOMAN: Show no mercy!

STUDENT: There won't be holes enough to bury them in.

(*Firing is heard nearby, sounding almost as if inside the museum.*)

BULLFIGHTER: War!

ONE ARM: Everyone to his post! Protect the barricade! Fire those rifles!

(*Executed Man and Knife Sharpener pull several times at the triggers.*)

EXECUTED MAN (*angrily*): They're old—rusty! They won't fire.

KNIFE SHARPENER: They can still be of use. The butts are still hard!

BEHEADED MAN (*at the top of the barricade and holding out his head by the hair*): It'll make a perfect shell. The best! It's filled with a deep and undying hatred. No one can stand up against it! (*He throws the head violently toward the main entrance of the museum. The trunk falls from the top of the barricade, lifeless.*)

ONE ARM (*from above*): He's not dead. He can't die. None of us can die. (*The firing has stopped. There is a short pause. From their battle stations they look down at the Beheaded Man, lying on the floor.*)

EXECUTED MAN: There you are, fallen, shrouded in your clothes. At least they won't be able to strip them from you the way they've done with so many others.

KNIFE SHARPENER: Naked, naked! They take advantage even of the dead.

WOMAN: I saw soldiers, in the middle of the night, tear at and steal the clothes of the wounded.

BULLFIGHTER: I saw worse: I saw them buried alive.

PRIEST: Sacred passion of our city! Still more naked—thirstier and bleeding more—than Jesus at Golgotha!

STUDENT: More humiliated and bound than the meanest of slaves.

ONE ARM: Raped and starved . . .

STUDENT: Sold to the foreigner by those who claimed to be our protectors, the great protectors of our country.

PRIEST: Monstrous cowards!

1ST OLD WOMAN (*loudly and comically*): Aie! Aie! Aie!

EXECUTED MAN: What's the matter with you, you old witch?

1ST OLD WOMAN: I'm giving birth—but through a different part than you might think. Not from the front. Aie!

ONE ARM: What a coarse swine! Get away from here, filthy pig! And far away too!

1ST OLD WOMAN: No, no! Every time I see things which that damned —aie!—does to us, my insides explode and bam! I've got to lift my skirts.

ONE ARM: You can lift them anyplace you want to—but not here!

1ST OLD WOMAN (*descending*): Of course, of course. I have his picture. That's what I use it for, you fools, you stupid fools. What did you think I got it for? I never let him miss any of these occasions.

(*Second Old Woman, also with broom but very lame, advances from the darkness upstage.*)

2ND OLD WOMAN: Hey! Hey! Hubilibrorda! I was looking for you.

1ST OLD WOMAN: I just stepped out for a couple of seconds, Genuflexa.

2ND OLD WOMAN: I hear the Frenchmen can't get inside. You must have heard them all buzzing around in rage.

1ST OLD WOMAN (*clutching at her stomach*): Aie! Aie! As if they wanted to empty themselves of happiness!

2ND OLD WOMAN: What a laugh! Come on, try and control those desires of yours a little, Hubilibrorda! This calls for a celebration!

1ST OLD WOMAN: Fine—step right over here! Let's go!

(*They dance and sing the following seguidillas from La Mancha, using the brooms in their movements. The Blindman accompanies them on the guitar.*)

1ST OLD WOMAN:
>If by morning the toad
>has not been exploded on its log
>it's because the poor thing
>has really been changed into a frog.
>On with the playing!
>Whenever I shit on toads, also
>I take a piss in passing.

2ND OLD WOMAN (*croakingly and dancing lamely*):
>Big muskets and cartridges
>with cartridge cases, whole,
>will fit, so they say, in a toad's
>arsehole.
>What a laugh! That's
>Why nobody picks up the toad
>Near its pick-up spot.

BULLFIGHTER (*joins the dance waving his sword*):
>Such skill I have
>At the toad-killing art;
>There's no part of him I can't
>Skewer apart.
>Keep up the rhythm!
>While I burn my sword
>Through his bottom.

WOMAN (*joins in the dance waving her knife*):
>And if ever the toad
>Should spit on my coat,
>I'll rip out his insides
>With my knife.
>On with the dance!
>There never was a toady
>Could hide from a woman like me!

1ST OLD WOMAN: Open out the circle!

2ND OLD WOMAN: Let's go!

1ST OLD WOMAN: Fat, big-bellied toad!

2ND OLD WOMAN: Shitheaded toad!

(*The Woman, Bullfighter and Blindman return to the barricade. Lights fade out on the barricade and a spotlight envelops 1st and 2nd Old Women in a strange light*).

2ND OLD WOMAN: Bravo, bravo, Hubilibrorda! You can still do some pretty fancy steps!

1ST OLD WOMAN (*mockingly*): Not quite as fancy as yours, Genuflexa. Nobody'd believe you're just a year older than me!

2ND OLD WOMAN: I'm one hundred already! (*As though telling her a secret.*) The truth is, Hubilibrorda, I haven't managed to grow as many corns and bunions on my feet as you have!

1ST OLD WOMAN: Stop fooling yourself, Genuflexa. Do you think I haven't seen those feet of yours? You seem to forget how your nails go curving around and burying themselves in your feet. And that you've always limped . . .

2ND OLD WOMAN: The things I have to listen to! We'll see!

1ST OLD WOMAN: The truth. And with the terror and noise that's around these days, it doesn't help any to have such long claws. Sit down here with me. You usually carry a pair of scissors, don't you—?

2ND OLD WOMAN: Yes . . . But they're used for other things—

1ST OLD WOMAN: What?

2ND OLD WOMAN: Guess!

1ST OLD WOMAN: Let's have them.

2ND OLD WOMAN: No.

1ST OLD WOMAN: Let me have them! (*Second Old Woman takes out scissors so large they look like garden shears.*) What in heaven's name could you possibly do with these? Maybe you think the fat toad's going to get through to us?

2ND OLD WOMAN: I'd beat it to death with my broom. . . . Or I'd drive the scissors in its eyes.

1ST OLD WOMAN: Yes, I know, I know. . . . But just suppose he appears suddenly, just like that, with a whole regiment!

2ND OLD WOMAN: I'll fly off. That's why I've got my broom here with me too.

1ST OLD WOMAN: Yes, yes . . . But sometimes you've got to run a bit before you can take off—and you'd not be able to. It's one thing to dance and quite another to fly off. Let me have the scissors.

2ND OLD WOMAN: No, no! I'll sacrifice anything but my nails! Are you drunk, Hubilibrorda? Would you like to see me cut off that moustache of yours or the hairs on that wart?

1ST OLD WOMAN: That would be terrible, all right. But it's not the same thing, Genuflexa. This mole and its curly hairs makes my face beautiful. That's why, like you, I am lady-in-waiting to the Queen.

2ND OLD WOMAN: The Queen, the Queen! When is that royal puppet going to appear anyway? Where could she be prowling around tonight?

1ST OLD WOMAN (*flapping her hands, like wings*): She's off on a trip. She must be cooking up something good. (*Angrily.*) But you're not going to get off, you fox—I want those scissors right now! (*She falls on her and tries to take away the scissors.*)

2ND OLD WOMAN (*struggling*): No! No!

1ST OLD WOMAN: I'll clip your nails or else tear them out—as the Holy Inquisition does. . . .

(*Loud braying sounds are heard upstage.*)

2ND OLD WOMAN (*shouting*): Perico! Perico! You've come in time! Save me!

1ST OLD WOMAN (*throws her to the ground and pummels her*): The scissors! The scissors! I'll kill you! I'll rip out your insides! I'll gouge out your eyes!

2ND OLD WOMAN: Madwoman! Madwoman! Drunkard! You screw for goats! Made pregnant by a goat!

(*A figure dressed as a donkey walks in on two legs.*)

DONKEY (*in a braying, slow, cavernous voice*): What's going on
here? What's happening? May I ask why you're screaming
and scratching at each other's faces?
>Tonight is not a night for delighting in a fight
>although, indeed, there is fighting tonight.

(*The Old Women separate.*)

2ND OLD WOMAN (*tearfully*): Perico! Oh, Perico! This drunken old
sot here, she wanted to cut off my nails! But I wouldn't let her!
Nobody's ever touched them! Not even me.

DONKEY:
>The French must be killed
>With toenails.
>And for those without nails
>Cloven hoofs are their flails.
>Thus is zoology
>Fighting with bravery.
>Let the donkey fight
>And the cock, the hen, even the horse!

1ST OLD WOMAN: But what if she can't fight? Her nails are buried
halfway into her feet!

DONKEY:
>Have no anger or fear,
>Just find a good knife sharpener
>To straighten them for her.
>Ten nails are ten knives,
>Ten knives are ten graves.

1ST OLD WOMAN: The Frenchies will get her. She can't fly away.

DONKEY:
>Silence you old bat,
>Or I'll tear out your wart.
>If she can't fly, for a start
>I'll carry her on my back.

(*Second Old Woman jumps with her broom onto the Donkey's back. Both exit upstage, laughing and braying. First Old
Woman laughs too, softly, as she disappears into the darkness
of the barricade. A bright light appears upstage. The Archangel, St. Gabriel, in pale pink tunic, enters from the right,
crying. One of his wings is broken.*)

GABRIEL: I lost her, I lost her. . . . She disappeared when I was about to deliver my message. Hail, Mary! I began. But a great storm and a thick darkness which blackened over everything left me with unspoken words. . . . Hail, Mary! Our Lady, where are you? Where shall I look for you . . . me, a poor, lost dove, broken-winged, and songless, yes, songless—I've lost my memory. What was the rest of the divine message? (*He spells, trying to remember.*) H-a-i-l, M-a-r-y! . . . Oh! How wretched the messenger for whom light turns into darkness— a messenger who, bringing the message of sunlight and hope, is left holding a blackened crystal in the night! Hail, Mary! . . .

(*He weeps, his hands covering his face. The Archangel Saint Michael enters, right. He wears a bright red tunic and holds a sword.*)

MICHAEL (*stopping*): Gabriel. (*He moves toward him and lays his hand on his head.*) Lift up your face, friend. Why these tears? Answer me.

GABRIEL: Because now I have no one to deliver my message to.

MICHAEL: Archangels do not cry. Could any one stand seeing the face of the most beautiful and resplendent of beings covered by tears?

GABRIEL: The most beautiful was Lucifer. . . .

MICHAEL: Was . . . yes, that's true. But once, at the head of my hosts, I beat him down into hell with this very sword. Now he is the most hideous of angels.

GABRIEL: But not half as wretched as I am at this very moment, Michael.

MICHAEL: You're delirious. My poor friend!

GABRIEL: He's serving his sentence now as he burns there in hell. My punishment, on the other hand, is just about to begin. And I'm afraid.

MICHAEL: Your punishment? What are you talking about? Tell me —I'm your brother.

GABRIEL: Hail, Mary! What greater punishment could there be than to lose track of the girl to whom I was going to bring the news that she was to become the mother of God, the most blessed among women? (*Unhappily and raising his hand to his broken wing.*) Oh!

MICHAEL: Are you in pain, Gabriel?

GABRIEL: The pain of perhaps never being able to fly again, and of having to remain forever a prisoner in this world of demons. (*He shows him a blood-covered hand.*) Look.

MICHAEL: Blood!

GABRIEL: I'm fallen for all time. My wing is broken at the very joint. I was flying down to bring joy but hatred crossed my path. I don't understand what's happened tonight.

MICHAEL: Once more, the forces of evil are speeding through the world. They've brought destruction even to this peaceful land. But don't be afraid. My sword will protect you. Come.

GABRIEL: Hail, Mary!—but first, will you help me find her? (*He leans against Michael's shoulder as Michael holds him around the waist and they begin to exit.*)

MICHAEL: I know we'll find her. Come now.

GABRIEL: Perhaps she's been wounded, too. She may be dead. Oh, black night of murder! Where am I, Michael?

MICHAEL: Come along now. Lean your head firmly against my shoulder. Let me lead you.

GABRIEL: Hail, Mary! . . .

(*They disappear. The stage is in darkness. There follows a gradual fade-in and loudening of an air raid siren. First and 2nd Soldier pass through; the darkness is illuminated by the lantern.*)

1ST SOLDIER: Aircraft, comrade. Everything's happening tonight.

2ND SOLDIER: I wonder which section of the city they'll be bombing.

1ST SOLDIER: It doesn't make any difference to them.

2ND SOLDIER: The cellars are still filled with paintings, all ready to be moved away.

1ST SOLDIER: It would be a crime if . . .

(*They disappear. When the lights come on again, the warning signal is sounding loudly once more. To this sound is*

*added an infernal din caused by strident, ear-splitting trum-
pets, rattles, tympany, guitars, drums, and pipes, accompanying a large procession—very similar to that which Goya titled
"The Burial Of The Sardine." The procession enters upstage.
Leading the march is a masked figure holding a flag on which
a hideous bird—half eagle, half vulture—spreads its wings beneath the words "Death to the savage vulture!" Behind him,
two other masked figures enter, dancing to the music of the
discordant instruments and the following song:*

Hit it, yes, hit it,
Hit it, yes, hit!
Pound it, pound it,
Yes, pound it!
Hit it, yes, pound it,
Beat the drum!
On with the dance!
Death to the traitors!

*It is a procession of the crippled, of misery; of the gnawing
hunger of Spain. Some, in addition to their assorted musical
instruments, carry twigs; while others crown themselves with
broken chairs and chamber pots. Bringing up the rear and riding on the back of a figure all in black, representing a goat
with large, twisted horns, is something or someone completely
covered by rags. Beside this, 2nd and 3rd Old Women carry
someone, also completely swathed, on an old chair. The
brooms of the old women are tied to their backs. The face
of the 3rd Old Woman is hidden by a half mask. The air raid
siren has fallen silent.)*

ONE ARM: Thunder and lightning! What's all this?

3RD OLD WOMAN: Don't worry, my dear One Arm. All this noise is
nothing compared to what's going to happen when you find
out just who I am and just what we've brought you.

ONE ARM: Why have you come with all these pipes and rattles on
a night like this?

3RD OLD WOMAN: You'll positively piss all over yourself when I tell
you.

PRIEST: You've come from the sewers of hell, from the gutters of
the devil. Indecent masked woman!

3RD OLD WOMAN: Quiet, Reverend! You'll dance on your head with your skirts hanging down and your private parts hanging out when you find out who you're talking to!

1ST OLD WOMAN: Hubilibrorda, Hubilibrorda! I'm bursting, my wart's popping to find out who she is!

2ND OLD WOMAN: Just a minute, Genuflexa. It'd be a crime to lose such a fine, hairy little chickpea.

KNIFE SHARPENER: Come on! The toad's starting to snort now.

BLINDMAN: Let her speak!

WOMAN: Take off her mask!

ALL: Let's see! Let's see!

STUDENT: That's enough! Let One Arm alone do the talking!

BULLFIGHTER: First, I want to say something. . . .

EXECUTED MAN: Go stick a sword in your tongue. . . .

1ST OLD WOMAN: Hee, hee! It'd be the first good thing you ever did in your life!

(*They all laugh between the shrill sounds of pipes and trumpet blasts.*)

ONE ARM: Let me speak! Quiet! This is no night for fooling around!

3RD OLD WOMAN: I agree with you. At your command!

ONE ARM (*firmly*): Take off the mask!

3RD OLD WOMAN: I obey, sir captain. (*She removes the mask to show the hideous face of a witch. Pause.*) Well? Don't you recognize me? I'm the Queen!

1ST OLD WOMAN: Engurdegunda! Engurdegunda! I knew it! My, aren't you beautiful! Stand at attention, Captain, before your true sovereign!

ONE ARM: Cut out the jokes! At once! Engundegarda or whatever the hell your name is, and you, Hubilibrorda, tell us: what have you been keeping covered up in that old chair over there?

3RD OLD WOMAN: Captain, you have our permission to take off the covering. Forward! Courage!

(*Silence. One Arm jumps down from the barricade, tears off the covering and exposes a stuffed figure with yellow face and disheveled hair, wearing a long black lace dress.*)

ONE ARM (*stupefied*): The wife of King Charles IV! Queen Maria Luisa!

ALL (*whispering*): The great whore herself!

(*In the silence that follows, One Arm to Buco who, with a bellow, takes a step back.*)

ONE ARM: What's the matter with you, goat? You're feeling brave, eh? Quiet! (*He grabs Buco's twisted horns and forces it to its knees. Then he uncovers the face of the figure riding on its back: an enormous toad with bulging eyes and human features, in military uniform, with a sword at the waist, a big sash across the chest and medals.*) It couldn't be Napoleon Bonaparte, could it? (*After a slight pause.*) No, it's Don Manuel Godoy! (*With irony.*) The Generalissimo! The Prince of Peace! Butcher!

ALL (*quietly*): The queen's great, open fly!

A VOICE: Death to the traitors!

ANOTHER: To the gallows with them!

ALL: Kill them! Kill them!

ONE ARM: People of Madrid! Volunteers at this barricade! Soon it will be daybreak. We've got no time to waste. They'll both be judged and sentenced as quickly as possible. But first, to confirm the charge against them, each one of you will face this pair of criminals, who until recently were crowned with the blood and hunger of Spain and tell them what you feel you must.

STUDENT (*from the top of the barricade. Somewhat pedantically and grandiloquently*): Queen of the most miserable King in all our history! Prince of Peace! Generalissimo of the kingdom, so deservingly reincarnated now by the miserable fat belly of a toad: the gallows are hardly enough for the discredit you brought on our country before all the nations of the earth. You, execrable and hypocritical sir, you are at one and the same time the invader and the invaded, the conqueror and

the conquered, the evil Frenchman and the still worse Spaniard, both conspiring to bring the infamy of slavery to one of
the strongest, one of the most virile, one of the most dedicated of all people in its love for liberty and independence.
Remember Numantia, the treachery of Rome, the traitor Wi-
tiza and the great Don Pelayo, the glory of Covadonga. . . .

A VOICE: Fine, fine! Bravo! Let's hear somebody else! This is no
time for long speeches!

STUDENT (*drowned by the shouting*): I ask for the gallows, yes;
But I also ask that first, they should be dragged through the
streets!

VOICES: Somebody else! Somebody else!

KNIFE SHARPENER: Citizens! A murder victim speaks to you now.
And he tells you: the people have sharp noses. Yes, they have
a dog's sharp nose. They know they're betrayed and nothing
else. They don't understand a lot of speeches. But they're not
wrong now in asking for a rope to throw around the necks of
these two traitors. . . .

VOICES: To the gallows! To the gallows!

EXECUTED MAN: One morning we got up to find ourselves without
a king, sold out, surrounded by foreign invaders, thrown back
on our strength. These two, and others like them, who suck
our blood from their palaces and swear to make themselves our
faithful protectors, ran to kneel down at the feet of our execu-
tioner. I also ask for the gallows as their punishment. I speak
as one who was shot by Marshal Murat.

VOICES: Death! Death!

WOMAN (*with mocking dignity as she bows before the stuffed figure
of the queen*): Most worthy lady: Bon voyage to you! The
people are not the only ones that die. Now death reaches out
for you even in your lover's arms. And you're not going to die
from a nice simple knife wound or gun shot. That kind of
death is for us, the down and out. You, Your Majesty, and
you, Highness, will be hanged high—as high up as befits your
very high ancestry.

VOICES: Hang them! Let's hang them!

1ST OLD WOMAN (*reverently to 3rd Old Woman*): Engurdegunda!
You deserve it. Now you're really queen of the Spanish Em-

pire. Quite a few merry pranks you pulled on us! I humbly kiss your feet. Maybe that'll help your chilblains.

BULLFIGHTER (*pushing himself forward*): Leave me alone! Everybody out of the ring! (*A trumpet call, like the trumpet flourish at a bullfight is heard. The Bullfighter, sword in hand and jacket on arm, turns to the figure of Queen Maria Luisa and toasts her, his cap held high.*)
Queen on the junkyard throne
Mistress of the Butcher,
May my bullfighting days be forever done
If I don't defeat your champion.

(*Silence; he challenges Buco:*) Eh, toro! Eh, eh! Come on! Straight and quiet! Look up! If you throw me to the toad, you'll get the sword.

(*Buco lets out a bellow, charges at him and passes under the jacket.*)

ALL: Olé!

BULLFIGHTER (*as he makes the passes*): Come on! This one, quick and oblique, for the whoring idler! This one, aimed straight at the snout, for his Crime! This one, curving, natural, for the traitor and criminal! And this other one, flashing out, for the Generalissimo and all those he hanged!

ALL: Bravo!

(*The Bullfighter gets into position for the kill. Silence.*)

3RD OLD WOMAN (*mockingly*): Hubilibrorda, Genuflexa: help support the queen. Courage, my dear. Don't faint. Many have died this way. For loving a she-ass.

BULLFIGHTER: Toro! Eeeep!

(*He aims the sword at the toad's head; Buco rolls on the floor, with the toad still on its back, all to the applause and shouts of the others.*)

3RD OLD WOMAN (*to the figure of the Queen*): Well, sweetie? Your dear Manolo has fallen like a brave man. Come on, give him a kiss. . . . In these last moments he'll find them much sweeter

than those you used to fire him up with, there on the royal
bed. (*Buco gets up. First and 2nd Old Women pick up the
figure and set it down on Buco's back beside the toad. The Old
Women join them in a tight embrace.*) There—now it's more
than mere gossip. All cuddled up, as always, but now before
the whole town.

ONE OF THE PARADERS (*taking the chamber pot from his head and
crowning the Toad*): You were longing for the crown, weren't
you? There; now you've got it. You can also use it whenever
your insides act up on you.

1ST, 2ND, 3RD OLD WOMEN (*bowing*): We bow to Your Sovereign
Majesties!

A VOICE: Death to the new monarch of the Spanish Kingdom!

ANOTHER: To the gallows with them!

(*The Blindman steps from behind the barricade amid the din
of shouts and strident noise of the musicians.*)

BLINDMAN (*accompanying himself on the guitar, while the two
masked figures dressed in rags dance beside him.*)
> Sovereign lady,
> With bouncing belly,
> You'll reign hanged
> By the neck.
> Off with that hand!
> For the people of the land
> Are my only majesty.

A CRIPPLE FROM THE PROCESSION (*also accompanied by the guitar*):
> Minister of the devil,
> Damned bulging toad!
> Now your open fly
> Has no one to ply!
> Off with that sword!
> On a minister who is dangling
> It doesn't mean a thing!

VOICES: Yes! Off with it!

PRIEST (*as though preaching*): Miserable adulterers! Don't expect
any absolution from us. Confessionless, you go now to wallow
forever among the hotbeds of hell.

ONE ARM: Quiet! Quiet! Now it's my turn. Defenders of this great barricade of Madrid! Poor, trampled people! You have all listened to the charges. Do you all agree with the verdict?

ALL: Yes!

ONE ARM: Well, there they are! That's all that's left of them: two hideous, rag-covered puppets; but behind them is Spain's humiliating subjection to the ravages of a foreign power and the destruction of our lands and of our crops and cattle; the enslavement of our women and children; the prisons, the executions. Who was the man who laid claim to the crowns of our kings and gave himself the high-sounding titles of Generalissimo and Prince of Peace? A violator of that same peace, an ambitious accomplice to the most hated destroyer of cities, a bloodthirsty murderer. And what do we see happening today? Once more we have his hypocritical friend, his insatiable master, the real toad—that carnivorous vulture—bringing death to the heroic walls of our capital city. It's almost daybreak. We must hurry. Let's put away these putrid symbols of shamelessness and tyranny as quickly as we can. They'll never return, they'll never set foot on this soil again if, working together, we make sure that our barricade can never be broken.

(*Slow roll of drums. The masked figure carrying the flag leads the way to the barricade. Behind him comes Buco with the two puppets, surrounded by the three Witches and their brooms. One Arm, the Priest and all the other characters of this etching follow them. In the silence, broken only by the roll of the drums, antiaircraft fire and the explosions of the first bombs can be heard. The procession does not stop. At the top of the barricade, 1st, 2nd and 3rd Old Women hand their brooms to One Arm. The noise of aircraft sounds directly over the museum. 2nd Old Woman cuts the disheveled hair of the queen with her scissors. One Arm, with the help of the Executed Man and Knife Sharpener, passes a noose around the necks of the puppets. And hanging from the brooms now fixed upright in the sandbags, the bodies of Queen Maria Luisa and the Generalissimo, her lover, are flung into the air. They swing back and forth like mute bell clappers. A muffled shout, a mixture of shock and joy, comes from the company as incendiary bombs drop into the other rooms of the Prado Museum and in a rain of broken glass, daylight penetrates onstage from the high skylight of the central hall. The Beheaded Man, who*

*stood up beside the barricade when the bombing began, recites*
*in a loud voice as the curtain slowly descends):*

BEHEADED MAN:
Madrid! Madrid! How lovely your name sounds!
The bulwark of all Spain today.
The earth trembles, the sky thunders.
You smile with bullets in your body.[1]

[1] Antonio Machado.—Author

# SUICIDE PROHIBITED
# IN SPRINGTIME

*by* ALEJANDRO CASONA

TRANSLATED BY ADAM D. HORVATH

Alejandro Casona (1903–65) was yet another member of that generation which began to leave its imprint on Spanish literature in the 1930's, working in a mode which created a peculiarly Spanish, ultimately native version of Surrealism—if Surrealism it is at all. The work of Casona is shot through with a gentle, wistful feeling for the improbable and the imaginative; however, it is a feeling which is also characterized by a particularly calculated and deliberate relation to reality. *Suicide Prohibited in Springtime* was written in 1936–37, just before Casona's self-imposed exile in Argentina (where he lived until just before his death), yet it sets forth in no uncertain terms and with delightful wit and fancifulness the concerns which were to occupy him throughout his later life. (Indeed, Casona's earliest writings, including poetry and his thesis, *The Devil in Literature and Art*, reflected this tradition-oriented concern for the place of the imagination.)

The play is the story of a Utopia of sorts, a home for suicides founded by a pupil of a certain mysterious Doctor Ariel, the figure who is also the absent patron saint of several other Casona plays. It is the apparent intention of Doctor Ariel's pupil that this establishment should encourage suicides by facilitating them. Every convenience for the pleasurable consummation of self-immolations is provided: a Gallery of Silence, Werther Gardens, perfumed gasses, poisoned flowers, and a whole series of places and devices apparently designed to make suicide irresistible. Actually, the purpose of all this is, by showing would-be victims the most alluring things they might think of, reconciliation with life. The Utopia is actually a kind of laboratory for the study of the relationship of the fantastic to reality. It is by learning to love something in life, even something odd, at the very end of life, that patients grow stronger, more willing to confront their difficulties. The outlandish and charming case histories presented during the play all seem to be on the road to survival at its close. Not all their lessons are based —as in the case of the Imaginary Lover who meets his great love in the flesh and is thereby cured—on the confrontation of reality; there is also a journalist, who understands that the factual side of life is only one side of it, and that fantasies, too, have their place. All these conversions relate not only to Surrealist championing of the real role of the imagination, and to Surrealism's official interest in the theories of Dr. Freud-Ariel, but also to the cultivation of connections between the ideal and the real which occurs throughout Spanish literature from its beginnings. Although Casona teaches a lesson of wisdom, the instruction is not grim, being as light and crystalline as that given in the tragicomedies of the seventeenth century. It is noteworthy that even during the grimmest days of 1950's-style Socialist Realism, Casona could be performed in most of the countries of East Europe, as well as widely in the West.

M. B.

# Characters

DOCTOR RODA
HANS
THE UNHAPPY WOMAN
THE IMAGINARY LOVER
ALICE
CHOLE
FERNANDO
JOHN
FATHER
CORA YAKO

# ACT ONE

(*In the Home for Suicides, Dr. Ariel's spiritual sanatorium. A vestibule as in some mountain inn, reminiscent of all the tourist inns built on the ruins of old monasteries and artistically rejuvenated to suit new taste. Everything here is strange, suggestive, and comfortable: the furniture, the molding, the rows of arches, indirect lighting. On the walls, in conspicuous positions, are oil paintings depicting the death scenes of famous suicide cases: Socrates, Cleopatra, Seneca, Larra. Over an arch, carved into the stone, are St. Theresa's verses: "Come, Death, so secretly—that I know not when you are nigh—for my pleasure thus to die—will not renew the life in me." Through an iron grillwork in the background may be seen a garden of willows and rose bushes. The garden has a lake, only partly visible, and recedes into a distant blue sky and jagged snow-covered mountains. In the right-hand corner of the stage a dark enclosure appears, with its arched entrance, heavy iron doors and, over the entrance, this inscription: "Gallery of Silence." In the foreground, also to the right, is a similar enclosure, but bright and doorless, with the inscription: "Garden of Meditation."*)

*On stage are Dr. Roda and Hans, his assistant, in a male nurse's uniform. The doctor seems intelligent and congenial; his assistant, deadly serious both in expression and in speech. Dr. Roda, beside a table piled high with his work, reviews his files.*)

DOCTOR: Disillusioned lovers, eight. Skin diseases, two. Aimless lives, four. Economic disaster . . . dope addict. . . . Don't we have any new cases?

HANS: The young man who arrived last night. He is wandering in the willow park, talking to himself.

DOCTOR: Diagnosis?

HANS: Uncertain. A love problem. He seems to be one of those whose curiosity is aroused by death, but who become afraid when they are confronted at close range.

DOCTOR: Have you spoken with him?

HANS: I have, but he wouldn't answer me. He wants just to be left alone.

DOCTOR: Has he made up his mind to go through with it?

HANS: I don't think so: he's very pale, his hands tremble so. On leaving him in the garden I stepped on a dry twig and he started nervously, a look of fear on his face.

DOCTOR: Nervous fear . . . very well. Then there's no danger yet. His file?

HANS: Here it is.

DOCTOR (*reading*): "No name given. Bank employee. Twenty-five years old. Moderate income. Disillusion in love. Has a book of unpublished poems." Ah, a romantic . . . I don't think he could be dangerous. In any event, watch him without his being aware of it. And instruct the violinists to play some Chopin in the woods around sunset. That will be good for him. Have you seen anything of the woman from the green pavillion?

HANS: The Unhappy Woman? She's out in the Werther garden.

DOCTOR: Being watched?

HANS: What for? I've been observing her for some days now. She's visited all of our facilities: the lake of the drowned, the forest of the hanged, the perfumed gas chamber. . . . Everything seems excellent to her in principle, but she cannot bring herself to decide on anything specific. She only likes to cry.

DOCTOR: Leave her, then. Crying it out is as healthful as sweating it out, and more poetic besides. It should be applied as often as possible, just as the ancients applied bloodletting.

HANS: But the same thing is happening to the Philosophy Professor. He's already thrown himself into the lake three times, and each time he's come out swimming. Excuse me, Doctor, but I am convinced that none of our current guests has a serious intention to die. I am afraid that we are failing.

DOCTOR: Patience, Hans. Undue haste accomplishes nothing. The Home for Suicide is based on an absolute respect for its inmates, and on the philosophic and aesthetic cult of death. Let's wait and see.

HANS: Let's wait and see. (*Pointing.*) The Unhappy Woman.

(*The Unhappy Woman arrives from the Garden of Meditation.*)

WOMAN: Excuse me, Doctor. . . .

DOCTOR: Madam. . . .

WOMAN: I have followed your advice with the best of intentions: I've cried all morning, I sat underneath a willow staring fixedly at the water. . . . And all for nothing. I keep feeling more and more cowardly.

HANS (*encouragingly*): Have you seen our splendid showroom of poisons?

WOMAN: Yes, the colors are charming, but the taste must be awful.

HANS: We might add a little mint, some lavender. . . .

WOMAN: I don't know . . . I would like the lake, too, but it's so cold. I don't know, I just don't know what to do. . . . What must you think of me, Doctor?

DOCTOR: Good Heavens, Madam. I assure you we're in no hurry.

WOMAN: Thank you. Oh, it is so beautiful to die, but . . . to kill oneself! Tell me, Doctor, while walking through the garden I felt a strange dizziness—those plants, aren't they poisoned perhaps?

DOCTOR: Ah, no. We have not discovered any method of poisoning the scent of a flower yet.

WOMAN: A pity—it would be so nice! Why don't you try?

DOCTOR: It's difficult.

WOMAN: Try to do it. I'm not in much of a hurry. I can wait.

DOCTOR: If that's the case, we'll try it.

WOMAN: Thank you, Doctor. You are very good to me.

(*She starts to leave, but stops on seeing the Imaginary Lover arrive. A young man with a romantic and sickly look, he is engrossed in himself. When a bell tolls behind him somewhere, he starts nervously. Recovering himself, he speaks uneasily.*)

LOVER: Good morning . . .

DOCTOR: Have you selected your . . . method?

LOVER: No, not yet. I've been thinking about it.

HANS (*advertising the merchandise in the best bazaar fashion*): We have a special willow for lovers, a lake steeped in legend. . . .

If you prefer the classical conventions, we can offer you a rose branch with asps, Cleopatra model, lukewarm bath, Socratic hemlock. . . .

LOVER: Why so much fuss? When life weighs heavily any old tree will serve.

HANS (*hastily making a note in his book*): Ah! Very good. "Hanging" it is. Perfect. Your neck size?

LOVER: Seventeen, large.

HANS: Seventeen. Did you have any particular tree in mind?

LOVER (*reacting brusquely*): Oh, be quiet! I can't stand listening to you! You're as cold as a civil servant. It's disgusting to hear Death discussed that way! (*Modulating.*) Forgive me. . . . (*He starts to go into the Gallery of Silence.*)

DOCTOR: Just a moment. If you still have not decided . . . that gallery should not be entered except at the crucial hour. The garden for meditation is over this way.

LOVER: Thanks.

DOCTOR: Is there anything you require? Books, liquor, music?

LOVER: Nothing, thank you. (*He leaves, nodding a greeting to the Unhappy Woman.*)

WOMAN: Another desperate one? How awful, so young! Some sort of disenchantment in love?

DOCTOR: It seems so.

WOMAN: But he's a child! In any case, he is fortunate. If only *I* had a love story to remember! (*She goes out.*)

HANS: And that's the way they all are. Lots of crying, lots of poetic sadness. But none of them ever gets around to killing himself.

DOCTOR: Let's wait and see, Hans.

HANS (*without much conviction*): Yes, let's wait and see. Any orders for today?

DOCTOR: Yes, please check over the electrical apparatus. The last time the Philosophy Professor threw himself in the lake the alarm bells didn't seem to be in perfect working order.

(*Hans leaves. The Doctor turns to his note-taking. Suddenly a woman's shout is heard. Alice runs from the Gallery of Silence. More girl than woman, sweet-looking, she is dressed with tasteful simplicity and neatness. She appears frightened, as though fleeing some imminent danger.*)

ALICE: No! I don't want to die, I don't want to die! (*She sees the Doctor, who hurries toward her.*) Let me pass! Let me out of here!

DOCTOR: Calm down, girl. Where are you going?

ALICE: I don't know. Out in the fresh air! Back to life again! Let me alone! Let go! (*Turning suddenly.*) What was that?

DOCTOR: Nothing.

ALICE: I saw a shadow. I heard it laugh. . . .

DOCTOR: Come, come now—hallucinations.

ALICE (*she begins to feel relieved; wipes her forehead with one hand*): Who are you?

DOCTOR: Dr. Roda, director of the Home. Relax.

ALICE: Why do you do this? Those queer trees, with nooses dangling from them, that music from out of nowhere, that gloomy gallery that goes this way and that! It's horrible!

DOCTOR: Don't think that, please. You're being overcome by childish fears; I assure you that you're being unduly upset. Do you want to go back there with me?

ALICE: No! I'm not going back there! I just want to get away from here.

DOCTOR: Nobody's stopping you. I don't know who you are, or how you got in, or why you came here. But that's unimportant. Our grounds end over there. Going along the lake, you'll come to the highway. On the other side of the mountains, in the distance, you can see the city. You're absolutely free.

ALICE (*with profound bitterness*): The city . . . The city again . . .

(*She falls into a chair, crying. The doctor watches compassionately. There is a pause.*)

DOCTOR: Why did you come here? Do you know where you are?

ALICE: Yes, it was in a moment of desperation. I had heard some talk about a Home for Suicides, and I couldn't go on any longer. Hunger ... loneliness ...

DOCTOR: Have you always lived alone?

ALICE: Always. I never had friends, brothers, or love.

DOCTOR: Did you ever work?

ALICE: More than I could stand. And at so many things! First I was a nurse. But I wasn't any good. I showed too much affection for my patients, I gave them all my soul. And it was so bitter afterward to see them die . . . , or to see them get well, and go away, also forever.

DOCTOR: Didn't you see any of them again?

ALICE: None. Health is too egoistical. Only one of them wrote to me once, but from so far away! He had gone to Canada, to chop down trees to make himself a house—and to move into it with another woman.

DOCTOR: What made you decide to come here?

ALICE: It was last night. I couldn't go on. I hadn't been working for almost two weeks. I was hungry. It was dirty, painful hunger. Hunger so cruel it made me vomit. In a dark street a man accosted me—said something disgusting and waved money at me. . . . And it was all so brutal that I began laughing like a lunatic, until I fell in a heap on the pavement, crying in disgust, in shame, humiliated by hunger.

DOCTOR: I understand.

ALICE: No, you don't understand. Here, among trees and mountains, you cannot understand those things. True hunger and loneliness exist only in the cities. There you are able to feel what it is to be alone among millions of indifferent beings and lighted windows! There you can understand what hunger is, standing in front of the shop windows and restaurants for the rich! I was a fashion model for a while. I didn't know then how sad it is to sleep afterward in a cold house, stripped of a hundred outfits, with your fingers still tingling with the touch of furs.

DOCTOR: I hope it wasn't envy of luxury that brought about your desperation.

ALICE: Oh, no! I never asked too much from life. But life didn't want to give me anything! Hunger can be conquered—I had already conquered it on other occasions. But . . . what about solitude? Do you know why I came here?

DOCTOR: That's what I still don't understand.

ALICE: It's simple. In a desperate moment, you kill yourself anywhere. But I, who have lived alone always, I didn't want to die alone too! Now do you understand? I thought that in this refuge I would find other castoffs resolved to die, and that some one, *any* one of them would give me his hand. . . . And I began to dream of this madness—of dying embraced by someone—as if it were perfect bliss. I dreamed of entering upon a new life at last, with a traveling companion. It's a ridiculous idea, isn't it?

DOCTOR (*showing interest*): Not at all. Did you try to find this companion?

ALICE: What for? When I arrived here I couldn't feel anything but fear. I lost myself in those galleries, I seemed to see a strange shadow searching for me . . . and I began to run, screaming, toward the light. It was as though my blood were crying out. Then I understood my tremendous mistake: I was running from solitude—and death is the absolute solitude.

DOCTOR: That's magnificent, my girl. Your youth has saved you. You don't need me any more, although perhaps I need you. Tell me, are you really interested in going back to the city where no one awaits you?

ALICE: Where am I to go?

DOCTOR: Would you like to remain here?

ALICE (*still frightened*): Here!

DOCTOR: Don't be afraid. It appears that this is no more than an extravagant club for suicides. But, behind all that, it is trying to be a sanatorium. You, who ask life only for a friendly hand and a warm corner, have much to teach others, who have good fortune and love, and think themselves unfortunate. Help me to save them.

ALICE: But, what can I do?

DOCTOR: You've taken care of sick people, now be our spiritual
nurse. We'll talk it over. For the moment, forget about last
night's panic. There'll always be a place for you at my table.
Will you take my hand as a friend?

ALICE (*reaching out, greatly moved*): Thank you . . .

DOCTOR: This way. And don't lose faith. Never ask for anything
from life. Wait . . . and someday life will present you with a
marvelous surprise. (*He leaves with her.*)

(*The stage is empty for a moment. Offstage, a woman's happy
laugh is heard. Chole enters running. She is an impulsive, vigorous young woman. Appearing at the gate in the background,
she utters the jubilant cry of a mountaineer.*)

CHOLE: Ohohooooho! (*She pushes the grillework gate wide open
and enters. Looks about her with a pleasant air of surprise, and
calls offstage again.*) Ohohooooho!

(*Fernando's powerful voice answers from offstage.*)

VOICE: Ohohooooho! (*Fernando enters, young, happy, and determined, just as she is. He is dressed for travel, with a valise, and
a camera case slung over one shoulder.*)

FERNANDO: Solid ground?

CHOLE: And what ground! Mountains with sun and snow, a lake, a
comfortable hotel, and us! Look—what pretty names. "Gallery
of Silence" . . . "Garden of Meditation" . . . and there in the
park—have you seen it?—"Lovers' Willow," with ropes dangling from it . . . for the swings. Thank me now, Fernando.

FERNANDO: Thank you, Chole . . . What an odd feeling there is
about all this!

CHOLE: Enchanting!

FERNANDO: Enchanting, but odd. It's probably one of those tourist
inns for English eccentrics and lovers.

CHOLE: Just what we needed. Ah, what a holiday, Fernando! See?
You ought always to let me lead the way. You toss the maps
aside, get out on the highways where nobody else goes, close
your eyes when you come to an intersection and put your foot
on the gas . . . and you always wind up someplace undreamed
of and wonderful. The first time you left things up to me we
discovered some Gothic ruins, remember? The second time . . .

FERNANDO: The second time we ran into a horse chestnut tree.

CHOLE: But the only thing that got hurt by it was the car. And what about that fisherman's cottage where we took shelter? And the absolutely stunning cut you got on the shoulder? How becoming that sorrowful expression was to you, Fernando! I had never seen you that way. Where was it . . . ?

FERNANDO: Some coast—Cantabria . . . the Baltic . . . I don't remember now.

CHOLE: I don't either. But it was an authentic sea spot: without beach crowds, without casinos. With a few big, fair-haired men chanting in a chorus! And now, what do you say to me now? Have I been a good helmsman?

FERNANDO: Magnificent!

CHOLE: You said to me, "We have one week's vacation from the newspaper; let's go snuggle our love in some quiet, happy corner. . . ." And here it is.

FERNANDO: Then once and for all, are we staying here?

CHOLE: What could be better? Besides, we couldn't go on even if we wanted to. Everything about this trip has been so providential! I took this road because it wasn't on the map. Just as we arrived here, we ran out of gas. And as soon as we got out a lark hopped off to the right. A good omen!

FERNANDO: So be it. But isn't there anybody in this hotel? (*Shouting to one side.*) Ohooooho!

CHOLE (*shouting the other way*): Ohooooho! (*Pause.*)

FERNANDO: Nobody.

CHOLE: Even better. The mountain and us! What more do we need? (*Solemnly.*) In the name of Spain, we take possession of this desert island. Hurray, Captain!

FERNANDO: Hurray, helmsman!

CHOLE (*opening her arms*): What shall we christen this happy spot?

FERNANDO: How do we christen all the corners of the earth where you and I are?

CHOLE: Paradise!

FERNANDO: Paradise . . . (*They kiss, laughing, happily young and in love. The Unhappy Woman enters and contemplates them with a tenderness tinged with pity. Fernando steps to one side on seeing her.*) Aha! The Serpent!

WOMAN: Poor things . . . you too?

FERNANDO: Madam . . .

WOMAN: How awful! So young, with a whole life ahead, and loving each other so . . . you're sweethearts, aren't you? Oh Lord, how awful, how awful! . . . (*She crosses the stage and leaves.*)

FERNANDO: Why does it upset this lady that we're so young?

CHOLE (*gaily*): Because she herself seems never to have had the honor. Did you observe that melancholy air?

FERNANDO: Must be liver disease. I'm sorry for your sake, Chole—here you promised to take me to Paradise, but I think you've plopped me down at a spa.

CHOLE (*who has been looking in amazement at the paintings*): Well, it's certainly *not* a spa.

FERNANDO: No?

CHOLE: Look . . .

FERNANDO (*reading the inscriptions she is pointing to under the paintings*): "Socrates. Fifth-century Greece. Hemlock . . ." "Seneca. First-century Rome. Blood-letting . . ."

CHOLE: "Larra. Romantic Era in Spain. Pistol . . ."

FERNANDO (*growing uneasy*): Ah . . . , ah . . . , ah . . .

CHOLE: And here? Over the arch: (*She reads*)
Come, Death, so secretly
That I know not when you are nigh,
For my pleasure thus to die
Will not renew the life in me.

ST. THERESA

(*A pause. They look at each other disconcertedly.*)

FERNANDO: So we've run smack into a convent!

CHOLE: A convent! You don't mean it: a cloister with myrtle trees, a fountain, lines of white habits in the corridors, the matins services . . . It would be magnificent!

FERNANDO: For tourists. But it doesn't exactly seem to me the ideal place for two lovers on vacation.

CHOLE: Two lovers, two lovers . . . When you put it that way, we seem to be two lovers just like the rest. No! (*Fiercely.*) *The* lovers! The *only* ones! Who has loved in this world before us?

FERNANDO: No one!

CHOLE: Who would dare to love afterward?

FERNANDO: No one!

CHOLE (*spreading her arms again*): Captain!

FERNANDO: Helmsman!

(*Their embrace is interrupted as Hans passes through the arch in the back of the garden. He is ringing a little bell. He enters the scene and shouts.*)

HANS: Hemlock room . . . . vacant!

(*He goes on ringing the bell. There is a pause. Chole and Fernando look at each other, paralyzed.*)

CHOLE (*terrified*): Did he say "hemlock room"?

FERNANDO: Wow! (*He picks up a book from the Doctor's table.*) What the hell?

CHOLE: What?

FERNANDO: This book! . . . *Suicide Considered as One of the Fine Arts.* (*He thumbs through the book.*) I think, Chole, that we'd best not let you lead the way any more.

CHOLE (*preparing to flee*): Where did you put the bag?

FERNANDO: Hey, wait. We're not running away! We're newspapermen, Chole. When a newspaperman comes up against something sensational, he doesn't back down, even if what he's up against is a rhinoceros. He'd sooner die. Put that bag down.

(*The Doctor enters. He goes toward his table; stops on seeing them.*)

DOCTOR: Is someone taking care of you?

CHOLE: No, thanks. We just came by to take a peek. Very interesting, very interesting . . . Fernando!

FERNANDO: Chole! Calm down! (*She rallies herself, puts down the little suitcase, advances bravely.*) Let me introduce myself,

stranger. Fernando Zara, newspaperman. Specialist in sensational stories.

DOCTOR: My pleasure.

FERNANDO: Thank you. This is Chole, my companion, sweetheart,
Egerian nymph and polar star. We're the happiest couple in
the land.

DOCTOR: I congratulate you. Dr. Roda, director of the Home. But
. . . if you are a happy couple, what the devil are you doing
here? Have you come here . . . voluntarily?

CHOLE: We came here unavoidably. I was driving.

DOCTOR: And do you realize where you are?

FERNANDO: Not yet. But we'll know soon—it's our profession.

DOCTOR: Unless I stand in your way.

FERNANDO: Useless to stand in our way. We're newspapermen: if
you throw us out the door, we'll come back through a window.
Disguised as gardeners, telephone inspectors, fruit vendors—
you'll have us around here irremediably. There's nothing you
can do, Doctor.

CHOLE (*advancing toward him*): We don't back down even if we're
up against a rhinoceros. . . . Oh, excuse me!

FERNANDO: Your reply?

DOCTOR (*he looks at them with mingled severity and amusement*):
You will excuse me if I advise you that like all happy beings,
and like all newspapermen, you are somewhat impertinent?

FERNANDO: Excused. But listen to us, Doctor: sensationalism is
difficult to cultivate. Fewer and fewer interesting things are
going on in the world, and the public, on the other hand, is
hungrier and hungrier for them. You cannot imagine the explorer's fervor we feel in snooping out the extraordinary; our
professional pride when we come up against a band of kid-
napers, or a nice adultery case. . . .

CHOLE: Oh, the tyranny of the public! And then, there's the tyranny of the editor. To him everything is nothing. For the
coming month he's assigned us a shipwreck, a prison break,
a birth of quintuplets, and an aurora borealis. It's no easy
work, believe me.

FERNANDO: You don't know what it's like to plow through a world of exhausted themes to make that one sensational find the public waits for eternally. What we in the newspaper field call the "Sea Serpent Story."

DOCTOR: And do you think you've found your "sea serpent" here?

FERNANDO: We've spotted his tail, anyway.

CHOLE: Don't shut the door on us. Help us, Doctor!

DOCTOR (*smiling sympathetically*): All right. Let's see. You two are, in fact, a happy couple?

FERNANDO (*putting his arm around Chole*): Unequaled anywhere!

DOCTOR: Illnesses?

CHOLE: None.

DOCTOR: Spiritual problems?

FERNANDO: They don't exist.

DOCTOR: Love?

CHOLE: Torrential!

DOCTOR: Material difficulties?

FERNANDO: Us? Put us in the middle of an African jungle tonight, and tomorrow morning we'll be sipping coffee with cream.

DOCTOR: Enviable. In that case, I will be able to help your work. But you, on the other hand, can perform a great service for me.

BOTH: We're at your command.

DOCTOR: For the success of this place, I have found it necessary to find the two extremes of fortune: a life of defeat, loveless, without a past and without a future. And a life of plenty, bold, loving, filled with hopes and new horizons. The first one I found a moment ago. Would you two like to be the happy life here?

CHOLE: We're at your service, Doctor. We're on vacation.

DOCTOR: Well, if that's the case, listen to what I've got to say, as collaborators and friends.

(*They sit down.*)

FERNANDO: Chole! (*She readies her pencil and notebook.*)

DOCTOR: No. Promise me you won't write a single line until you know the institution inside out.

FERNANDO: Chole . . . (*She puts away the pencil and notebook.*)

DOCTOR: Did you know Dr. Ariel?

FERNANDO: Dr. Ariel . . . , yes . . .

CHOLE: Sure, sure . . . Dr. Ariel . . .

DOCTOR: Fine. You did not know him. Dr. Ariel was my mentor. His family, for several generations, was the victim of a strange ill fortune: his father, grandfather, and great-grandfather all died by suicide in the ripeness of manhood, when they had just begun to shed their youth. Dr. Ariel lived tormented by this knowledge. He dedicated all his studies to the biology and psychology of suicide, penetrating to the deepest regions of this disturbing area of the soul. When he believed that his own fatal hour was nearing, he retired to these mountains. Here he changed his friends, his food, and his books. Here he read the poets, showered under cold waterfalls, hiked several miles each day, and listened to Beethoven in the evenings. And here, having conquered his fate, he died a noble, quiet death, at the happy age of seventy.

CHOLE (*enthusiastically*): That's absolutely marvelous!

FERNANDO: Very journalistic. A terrific opener for the ladies.

DOCTOR: The doctor left behind a marvelous book, his own. (*He takes it from the table.*)

FERNANDO: Yes. *Suicide Considered as One of the Fine Arts.*

DOCTOR: Oh! You've heard of it before?

FERNANDO: Well, let's say I've recently become acquainted with it.

DOCTOR: This book is full of science—but of human understanding and tenderness too. Look at this dedication: "To my poor friends the suicides." (*Fernando takes the book, thumbs through it from time to time, interested in its charts and statistics.*) To those poor friends Dr. Ariel also left his fortune. With it, the Home for Suicides was established, and I was entrusted by the master to its operation . . . and you are both welcome here.

FERNANDO: Thank you.

CHOLE: So far, I follow you. But if Dr. Ariel finally died happy, why the founding of this home?

DOCTOR: That's where the secret begins. Dr. Ariel did not confine himself to an extravagant goal. He founded, wisely, a Sanatorium for Souls. On the surface, this house is no more than a club for perfect suicide. Everything in it is designed with a voluntary, aesthetic, and comfortable death in mind. The best poisons, rose baths and music . . . We have a legendary lake, cells for individuals and groups, parties in the Borgia family tradition, harpists—and the most beautiful countryside in the world. A desperate man's first reaction on arriving here is postponement. His heroic sense of death is frustrated. Everything is so naturally supplied, so naturally gratified here. It gives the moral effect of a cold shower. Even the first night some accept food; others go to sleep; and invariably they all burst out crying. That's the first step.

CHOLE (reaching for her pencil): Magnificent. Second step. (Fernando stops her with a gesture.)

DOCTOR: The meditative phase. The patient spends long hours in silence and solitude. Afterward he asks for books. Then he seeks company. He gets interested in the cases of his companions. He comes to feel a pious sympathy for the brotherhood of pain. And he ends up by going outdoors. Fresh air and the countryside begin to work at him. One day he catches himself caressing a rose. . . .

FERNANDO: And the third phase begins.

DOCTOR: The final one. The soul tones up in time with the muscles. The past goes on losing its shadows and its strength. A hundred little roads open up in front of him, to the future, spreading and flowering. One day he sees the new apples ripening on a branch, a farmhand singing while he perspires in the sun, lovers kissing while laughter nibbles at them . . . and a warm desire for life takes hold of him inside with the abruptness of a shout. On that day the patient strolls out the door, and as soon as he crosses the garden, breaks into a run without looking back. He is saved!

CHOLE: Delightful. It's like a Scotch ballad.

FERNANDO: Not bad. Journalistically, it would be more interesting if he'd kill himself. But tell me, isn't that system grounded excessively on the client's favorable attitude? Haven't you ever come up against the authentic suicide, against the hopelessly desperate individual?

DOCTOR: Only the hesitant ones ever arrive here. Unfortunately, the profoundly desperate kill themselves wherever they might be, without the least consideration for clinical procedures or for Dr. Ariel. (*Rising.*) May I count on you?

CHOLE: You may, from this moment on.

DOCTOR: I'll go now, and have them arrange your rooms.

FERNANDO: Thank you. Will you permit us, meanwhile, to interview some of your patients?

DOCTOR: All right—but gently. They're usually mistrustful—they don't readily expose their hearts to strangers.

CHOLE: That young fellow coming by now—is he a patient?

DOCTOR: Oh, yes! A romantic lad. We call him the Imaginary Lover. Take a look at his file. . . . He arrived last night.

FERNANDO: Then he's in the cold shower phase, right?

DOCTOR: Precisely. Don't push him the other way too much. And, above all, be natural. (*He leaves.*)

CHOLE: Be natural, Fernando.

(*The Imaginary Lover, always engrossed in himself, enters, draws near on seeing them, with a ray of hope.*)

LOVER: Excuse me . . . You're one of us?

CHOLE: Staff members.

LOVER: Oh! Staff members . . . (*He starts to leave, disillusioned.*)

FERNANDO: Stay a moment. Why don't you sit down! You look very tired.

CHOLE: Would you like something to drink?

LOVER: No, thanks. I just want to end it all as soon as possible. (*Motioning solemnly toward the Gallery of Silence.*) This very day I shall traverse that final doorway.

FERNANDO: Have you selected your method yet?

CHOLE: Don't make up your mind without consulting us. We have the best poisons, a legendary lake, individual cells and . . .

LOVER (*sharply*): Oh, you too! Be quiet! Everything is cold here . . . hatefully cold. I hoped to find a companion spirit.

CHOLE: Then you may count on us. We have seen your file: "Disillusion in love." We would like so much to know your background. . . .

LOVER: Really? (*Eager to tell his story.*) You'll listen to it? I'm not sure it's worth the bother. . . .

CHOLE: Of course. Do you want to tell us?

LOVER: Thank you . . . (*Pauses.*) I was a banking employee. I worked with numbers by day and verses at night. I had always dreamed of travels and adventures, but none of them had ever come true. One night I went to the opera. Cora Yako sang the role of Marguerite. A splendid woman!

FERNANDO: I know her, all right. She gave us quite a bit to get into the magazine section.

LOVER: Cora Yako sang all night for me. No, it was no illusion. Her eyes were locked on mine, up there in the highest balcony. She sang, and cried, and died for me alone! I could not sleep that night. The following day I got everything fouled up at the bank. And I went back again to the theatre, trembling, two hours before the performance began.

CHOLE: Did they do *Faust* again?

LOVER: No, it was *Madame Butterfly*. But the same phenomenon occurred. The night before it had been two blue eyes and some blonde locks; now it was two dark, almond eyes, and a spangled kimono. But the same embrace of glances united us. . . . In the bank, all the money passed through my hands. I took a fair amount—two months' salary. And I sent her an orchid corsage and a card. Afterward . . . (*He hesitates, and falls silent.*)

CHOLE: Afterward, what then? Tell us.

LOVER: Afterward . . . Afterward, all was happiness! . . . Ocean liners and luxury hotels. Vienna, Cairo, Shanghai. We kissed each other one day in the desert, among the sycamores, and the following day in a lotus garden. I, a miserable employee of a Spanish bank, have embraced Marguerite, Madame Butterfly, Brunhilde, Scheherezade, and in all languages!

FERNANDO: Congratulations. And what else?

LOVER (*drily*): Nothing more.

CHOLE: Nothing more? Then . . . ?

LOVER: What? Why do you look at me that way? Don't you believe me? I swear it's the truth! I've been Cora Yako's great love! It's true, it's true!

FERNANDO (*exchanging a glance with Chole*): It isn't true.

LOVER: I swear it is! Why shouldn't it be? What's wrong with me, that a woman shouldn't love me?

FERNANDO: It's got nothing to do with you. You're a fine fellow, certainly. But you've told your story in such an odd fashion. . . .

CHOLE: Why did you lie? Please talk with us openly, as you would to two friends.

LOVER (*won over by Chole's cordiality*): You're right. Why lie, if nobody believes me. . . . And, nonetheless, I've only partly lied. It's true that I've destroyed my youth over a bank clerk's desk. It's true that Cora Yako looked at me as she sang. And it's true that I stole for her. But the love and the travels . . . those I've only dreamed. The following day, when I returned to the theatre with my new necktie on, the lobby was filled with trunks and tangles of stage equipment. My corsage was lying in a corner, the card unopened. The only thing left from my dream was the miserable reality of the embezzlement—and a trampled corsage. But no one need know about that! Let me tell the world the story my way. Everyone must believe it. I must believe it too . . . and afterward, die happy. (*He turns suddenly.*) The doctor is coming. Don't tell him anything. He's too old to understand things like this. . . . Don't tell him anything. (*He tiptoes out. The Doctor enters.*)

DOCTOR: Your rooms are ready. Do you want to come to see them?

CHOLE: I'm coming. You get the suitcases from the car, Fernando. Whenever you're ready, Doctor. (*She goes out with the Doctor, carrying the small bag. Fernando, alone, takes a few steps*

*in the direction toward which the Imaginary Lover had gone.
He turns around on seeing the Unhappy Woman enter.*)

FERNANDO: Madam . . .

WOMAN: Are you new here?

FERNANDO: I am . . . the Doctor's new assistant.

WOMAN: I thought I saw you here a moment ago, kissing a young
lady.

FERNANDO: Ah, yes! . . . She had painted her lips with arsenic, and
wanted to conduct an experiment.

WOMAN: How fascinating, to die by a kiss! I was looking for something like that.

FERNANDO: You still haven't found your method?

WOMAN: They're all too brutal.

FERNANDO: Nonetheless, one can always find subtle variations.

WOMAN: I have asked the Doctor to undertake to poison a rose. I
would love to die sniffing a flower's scent.

FERNANDO: I congratulate you—your inclination to expire through
the nostrils is a most delicate example of romanticism. But it's
no easy matter.

WOMAN: I read once that Leonardo da Vinci did an experiment in
poisoning trees.

FERNANDO: Yes, it seems that he tried to envenom the fruit of a
peach tree by means of its sap. But that summer the peaches
ripened more healthy than ever. I, on the other hand, when I
was a child, had a sick apple tree in my orchard. To revive it,
it occurred to me to give it an injection of cod liver oil through
the roots—and it dropped dead right away! Trees have strange
reactions.

WOMAN: A pity . . .

FERNANDO: You'll be able to find some other way. Are you familiar
with Dr. Ariel's book? No? Ah! It's the ideal manual. Look
at this appendix showing the geographic distribution of suicides. (*He draws out a large folding map from the book.*) Each
people has its predilections and its destinies. In the orange

tree area—Spain, Italy, Rumania—death for love predomi-
nates. In the walnut tree zone—France, England, Germany—
political and economic suicide. In the evergreen region—Switzerland, Norway, Denmark—voluntary deaths decrease, in pro-
portion to the rising level of salaries and democracy. That's
civilized Europe for you!

WOMAN: Where does it show passionate suicide?

FERNANDO: Here—in the flesh-colored strip. Take a look at the sta-
tistical graph in the margin. "Annual index of love suicides:
England, fourteen; France, twenty-eight; Germany, forty-one;
Italy, sixty-three; Spain, four hundred and eighty . . . United
States, two."

WOMAN: Only two?

FERNANDO: Two. They were two Mexicans who became naturalized
citizens. (*He puts down the book.*)

WOMAN: Ah! How good it is of you to read me these figures. Those
statistics show me the road of my own people. I would love so
much to die for love! Unfortunately, one will isn't enough to
make it possible—two are necessary . . . Would you help me?

FERNANDO: I am truly honored, madam, but . . . I am already spoken
for. I must do myself in tomorrow morning with a Polish
pianist.

WOMAN: I always just miss the boat.

FERNANDO: Forgive me.

WOMAN: And how often have I dreamed of it! Those Japanese
couples who leap—hands locked together, and crowned with
chrysanthemums—into Fujiyama's crater!

FERNANDO: A beautiful death, indeed. Unfortunately, Spain is in a
ruinous state: there isn't even a tiny volcano left for such cases.
(*The Unhappy Woman sits. She sighs sadly.*) And now, if you
will honor me with a confidence: why do you wish to die?

WOMAN: For so many reasons!

FERNANDO: Do you suppose you could tell me one of them?

WOMAN: Well, absolute disenchantment, for one. This world of
material things is not mine. I hate everything coarse: flesh, the
tyranny of muscle and blood. If only I had been born a plant,

a stream of water—or just a soul! I grieve for this poor body of mine, which has never provided me with anything but pain.

FERNANDO: And in compassion for your body you've decided to get rid of it right in the middle of life? That seems to me a bit like overdoing it! That's what the Germans call throwing out the baby with the bath water.

WOMAN: Why preserve something that's no use to anyone? My flesh doesn't exist. Only my soul has lived.

FERNANDO: Are you sure? Will you permit me a simple experiment? (*He takes out a pencil and notebook.*) Tell me, what do you have for breakfast?

WOMAN: What's that got to do with it?

FERNANDO: I ask you to tell me—it's for your own peace of mind. What do you have for breakfast?

WOMAN: A glass of milk. Sometimes some fruit . . .

FERNANDO: Lunch?

WOMAN: Nothing much: a little veal, vegetables . . . usually peas.

FERNANDO: And more fruit, right? How about supper?

WOMAN: The same. Why do you ask?

FERNANDO: I'll tell you in a minute. What interesting things can you remember from your life? Have you traveled?

WOMAN: A little. I know Paris, London, Florence.

FERNANDO: Have you cultivated any artistic interests?

WOMAN: I play the piano.

FERNANDO: Read much?

WOMAN: Almost always the romantics. I know everything Victor Hugo ever wrote.

FERNANDO: Ever been in love?

WOMAN: Love . . . only once. When I was still almost a child. He was a Navy lieutenant. We kissed on the ship's bridge, and he sailed for the Philippines. I didn't see him again.

FERNANDO (*who has been taking notes and computing figures rapidly.*): Magnificent. Well then, madam, figuring on only

half a life, and assuming modest portions, it comes out that
in order to take three short trips, learn to play the piano, read
the complete works of Victor Hugo and kiss a Navy lieutenant
... you've had to consume eighteen hundred gallons of milk,
three carloads of fruit, two and a half acres of peas, and seventeen calves! The body, madam, is an incontrovertible reality.

WOMAN (*horrified*): No! It isn't possible!

FERNANDO: Arithmetically exact.

WOMAN: How embarrassing!

FERNANDO: But don't be unduly disturbed over it. When all is said
and done, the body's source is as divine as the soul's. And one
must render unto Caesar what is Caesar's. (*Consolingly.*)
Don't make yourself unhappy. Reconcile yourself to yourself.
Would you like me to accompany you on a stroll around the
park? The sun is delightful today.

WOMAN: Thank you ... (*She accepts his arm. She rationalizes.*)
You may think what you like of me. I won't ever be a great
spirit; I know I'm just a poor, vulgar woman. ... But I swear
to you that I haven't eaten those seventeen calves!

(*Their departure leaves the stage empty. Suddenly one, two,
and then various alarm buzzers and bells are heard. Alice enters
running—she shouts tearfully.*)

ALICE: Doctor! Doctor! (*He hurries in.*)

DOCTOR: What's happened?

ALICE: There! (*She points to the Gallery of Silence.*)

DOCTOR: Quick ... Hans! Stop it before it's too late!

(*From within the Gallery of Silence a single gunshot is heard.
The alarms fall silent. Alice covers her face with her hands.
Hans comes in scuffling with John, who is struggling desper-
ately to free himself and recover his weapon.*)

JOHN: Unhand me! Let go! ...

DOCTOR: What happened?

HANS: Nothing yet. I succeeded in disarming him in time. Here's
his weapon.

DOCTOR: Let's have it.

JOHN: Let me go! (*He frees himself violently.*)

DOCTOR: Hurry, Hans, calm down the others. Don't let anyone get in here. (*Hans leaves. Alice remains in the background and listens throughout the whole scene. John tries to grab the pistol from the Doctor.*)

JOHN: Let me alone! That's mine!

DOCTOR: Quiet!

JOHN: It's mine!

DOCTOR: No! (*The Doctor pushes John back. He falls into an armchair; hides his head between his arms, sobbing convulsively. The Doctor goes slowly over to a desk. He locks up the pistol.*) What were you going to do?

JOHN: Die. I need to die. Tomorrow may be too late!

DOCTOR: And why?

JOHN: If I don't die, I'll end up killing. I know it. . . . And I don't want to kill!

DOCTOR: Come on, pull yourself together. Why should you have to kill anyone?

JOHN: I just know I will. I've already felt the temptation once. I feel it moving my blood right now. And it's horrible, because the man is good. He loves me . . . and doesn't even realize the pain he causes me!

DOCTOR: Who is he?

JOHN: My brother. Everything that I might have wanted, he has taken from me without knowing it. First he robbed me of my mother's tenderness. He robbed me of the intelligence and the health that I would have wanted to have. He robbed me of the only woman who could have made me happy. He has accomplished effortlessly, laughing, everything that I have longed for painfully, in silence, laboring. He has always trampled over me, without realizing it—always while smiling at me! But it isn't his fault. He is good. What's more, he's my brother! Free me from this nightmare, Doctor. I don't want to kill him . . . I do not want to kill him!

(*Chole and Fernando enter excitedly.*)

CHOLE: Has something happened, Doctor? (*Surprised to see the other.*) John!

JOHN: You two!

DOCTOR: Do you know each other?

FERNANDO: He's my brother . . . (*Fernando advances toward John, arms held out.*)

CURTAIN

ACT TWO

(*The action takes place in the same spot, three days later. Late afternoon light. The paintings of death scenes have disappeared, and in their place Chole has just hung a single new canvas: Botticelli's "Springtime."*)

(*Alice wears the white uniform of a nurse, a red cross on her sleeve.*)

CHOLE: Does that look all right?

ALICE: Yes, very good. The other paintings were so sad. . . .

CHOLE (*arranging a vase of flowers*): And these flowers—do you like them?

ALICE: Very much. They smell as if they came from far away. Where are they from?

CHOLE: From the south.

ALICE: Ours here haven't blossomed yet.

CHOLE: It won't be long now. Tomorrow is the first day of spring. When they blossom we'll have to put them in all the rooms, too.

ALICE: Thank you.

CHOLE: Why do you thank me?

ALICE: Because that's a lovely idea. Even though I may not be here to see them . . . What did you do with the other pictures?

CHOLE: I put them in the cellar. With all due respect, I put them in the cellar. (*They stand looking at each other.*) You're very gay today, Alice.

ALICE: I'm happy.

CHOLE: Why?

ALICE: I don't know. . . . You've been laughing all morning. There's never been anyone who laughed around me.

CHOLE (*laughing*): That's charming—you're happy because I'm laughing!

ALICE: It's so good to hear laughter. I never had a girl friend, either. And you gave me your hand, looking into my eyes, your eyes so deep and clear. . . . Would you like to give me your hand again?

CHOLE (*stretching her hand out tenderly*): Are we friends forever?

ALICE: Forever!

CHOLE: And don't say "thank you." Let me say it to myself. You always say it, for everything. You'd say it to any little bird who happened onto your windowsill.

ALICE: Why are you laughing now? You're laughing at me!

CHOLE: Yes. You're such a child!

ALICE (*listening happily. She also smiles*): Thank you . . . (*She leaves.*) (*The Doctor comes in.*)

DOCTOR: Miss Chole . . .

CHOLE: Good afternoon, Doctor. Notice anything new around here?

DOCTOR: I don't know . . . Those flowers? (*Turning around.*) The pictures! You've taken them down.

CHOLE: They were too gloomy. They weren't doing these poor people any good.

DOCTOR: Nonetheless, they had a certain solemn dignity. So . . . (*He contemplates the picture.*) Botticelli's "Springtime."

CHOLE: Did I make a good selection?

DOCTOR: Yes, it's luminous, tranquil. . . . I see you're really becoming interested in my patients.

CHOLE: Very much so. I had never imagined such a disconcerting human spectacle. So comic and tragic at the same time.

DOCTOR: It's curious. And you're going through the same phases they are. That first day you arrived here like a gust of wind, eager to pounce on something original to thrust into the public eye. Since then, you've been getting inside these souls, searching for your truth in the silence. You're smack in the middle of the Meditation and Tenderness phase.

CHOLE: Some of these intimate tales have affected me, I guess.

DOCTOR: But what about that sensational news story?

CHOLE: I won't write it now.

DOCTOR: Fernando will do it, then.

CHOLE: Maybe. He's a man, and he's tough. As for myself, today, I wouldn't dream anymore of putting these agonies on public display—just to satisfy an already overfed curiosity.

DOCTOR: It's the woman in you coming out.

CHOLE: That little child! Always alone, but giving thanks for everything that is beautiful, as if it were a gift. And that poor bank teller, who has never stepped out of his office or his boarding-house, and who dreams himself the hero of extraordinary loves and travels . . .

DOCTOR: What's more, you're working seriously. Last night I know you locked yourself up in my library until dawn.

CHOLE: Your books, and your statistics, fascinate me. I've discovered in them things I never would have imagined.

DOCTOR: For example?

CHOLE: The constant juxtaposition of suicide with the logic of life. Why do the triumphant kill themselves more often than those who fail? Why do more men kill themselves in youth than in old age? Why do lovers kill themselves more readily than those who have never known love? And why do they kill themselves in the morning rather than at night, and in spring more than in winter?

DOCTOR: For a happy woman, these are difficult things to account for. But the observations are scientifically accurate.

CHOLE: Killing oneself is always a brutal negation. But killing oneself in the ripeness of youth, at the moment of love and springtime, is an insult to Nature.

DOCTOR: Perhaps.

CHOLE: Besides, it runs contrary to every instinct! Animals don't commit suicide.

DOCTOR: Sometimes they do. The scorpion, when he senses that he is surrounded by fire, pricks himself with his own poisonous tail.

CHOLE: But that is not to seek death freely. That's to advance it an instant, to elude the pain.

DOCTOR: Pain—there's the supreme motive. It appears to me that, without realizing it, you have just given the answer to all the doubts you expressed before. Don't you believe that pain is a hundred times more intolerable when love and triumph surround us, when one's blood is young, when everything around us seems rose-colored?

CHOLE: No, Doctor, don't force me to doubt. Life is not merely a right. It is, above all, an obligation.

DOCTOR: God grant that you may always think that.

(*During the pause, the Other Alice's Father appears in the shadows in the garden. His is a noble white head, distorted by an expression of pain. He hesitates, then moves forward, and speaks with a humble, broken voice.*)

FATHER: Excuse me ... Dr. Roda? ...

DOCTOR: At your service.

FATHER: I have something to ask of you. . . . Something very personal, very hard . . . , but necessary.

CHOLE: Shall I go?

DOCTOR: By no means. The young lady is thoroughly within my confidence.

FATHER: Doctor ...

DOCTOR: Go ahead.

FATHER: Doctor—make me die!

DOCTOR: Me?

FATHER: Yes . . . I understand that this is a strange request. But you don't know. . . . I'm a doctor, too. I've asked this same thing of other colleagues. All of them sympathized with me, but none wanted to help me. You can do it! Out of compassion, Doctor. I did it once myself. I swear to you that it is absolutely necessary!

DOCTOR: Why?

FATHER: Because it is monstrous to continue living this way. I've never had overwhelming motives for desiring life. But before, I had her. I had an obligation: eyes and a voice that needed me.

DOCTOR: Who was she?

FATHER: She was my child . . . she was a paralytic almost from birth. Lying in a hammock, day after day. Nothing in her body moved. Only the eyes . . . and that musical voice, that in itself was an entire life. I read Tennyson's poems to her. She listened to me, watching. And we talked sometimes . . . very little, very softly, but enough for both of us. Until, one day, I began to sense myself growing ill. I could not deceive myself about it; it was one of those slow and certain diseases, the kind that never relent. Alone then, I felt the terror of leaving her alone. Poor motionless flesh! What was to become of her life without me? I couldn't resign myself to that prospect. I had morphine at my fingertips . . . and administered it to her in her sleep, softly—without pain—until she awoke no more. Do you understand? She was my daughter and my life. I killed her myself. And I am still here! I am learning with horror that my disease is withdrawing, that I will end up curing myself . . . and I have no strength to finish myself off. . . . Coward! . . . Coward! (*Overcome by emotion, he falls weakly into a chair. There is a pause. The Doctor takes Chole's hands and holds them with anguish.*)

DOCTOR: Yes, life is an obligation. But it is, at times, a painful obligation.

CHOLE (*calling in a loud voice*): Alice!

FATHER (*agitated*): Alice! Who here is called Alice?

CHOLE: She is our nurse.

FATHER: . . . She too was named Alice. (*Alice enters. She carries a book under her arm. The Other Alice's Father approaches her slowly, staring at her intensely.*) It is extraordinary . . . how they look alike . . . the same eyes. But hers were sadder. Permit me to . . . the same hands. (*Bitterly, as though it were an injustice.*) But these are healthy, warm. . . . And the voice? Would you mind saying something, miss?

ALICE: (*Not knowing what to say, smiling*): Thank you . . .

FATHER: Ah . . . no . . . the voice, no. Forgive me. You have a very pleasant voice. But she . . . , when she said "thank you," everything fell silent. What were you reading? Poetry—do you know Tennyson's poems? If it won't disturb you, I shall read them to you aloud. May I, Doctor? . . . In the garden, does that suit you? You, stretched out in a hammock, quiet. I, at your side . . . May I call you by your first name?

ALICE: I'd be grateful to you if you would. . . .

FATHER: No . . . Look at me, if you want to—but do not speak. . . . Don't say anything . . . Alice. Alice! (*He goes out with her.*)

DOCTOR: Do you think we can save him?

CHOLE: It seems to me he's already saved.

(*A pause. From outside, Fernando's mountaineering cry is heard.*)

VOICE: Ohooooho!

CHOLE: Ohooooho! (*Running to him, on seeing him enter.*) Captain!

FERNANDO: Helmsman! Excuse us, Doctor. (*He kisses her.*)

CHOLE: You've been away all day!

FERNANDO: Up on the mountain, since dawn. The doctor insisted on making me suffer all the enchantments of Nature.

CHOLE: And you went off without saying good-bye.

FERNANDO: You were asleep like a log . . . like a slow-burning, sandalwood log.

CHOLE: You've been thinking about me?

FERNANDO: All day long.

CHOLE: Why didn't you write to me?

FERNANDO: I shall write to you tonight.

CHOLE: Did you see the sun come up?

FERNANDO: Sure—a very elegant event. The poor thing comes up with such a sleepy face! And as soon as he looks around, it gets even colder than it was before.

CHOLE: And is there really frost . . . and shepherds wearing thick coats, and flocks of sheep?

FERNANDO: Sure, there are sheep. And some very hardy shepherds, with heavy coats, who throw rocks at the sheep.

CHOLE: Marie Antoinette always liked to dress up like a shepherdess.

FERNANDO: And they chopped off her head. With your permission, Doctor. (*He flops into a chair.*) I'm simply dripping with health.

CHOLE: Didn't you bring me anything?

FERNANDO: Oh, yes! A rose from the Alps—a white one. The kind that grows up in the snow, up beyond the cliffs. I left it up in your room.

CHOLE: Why did you do that? They say that they wilt when they come down to the valley. Poor rose . . . (*She leaves.*)

FERNANDO: Ah, women. I might have killed myself getting it for her, and all for nothing. But the rose wilts—Poor rose!

DOCTOR: You don't seem very happy after your day in the country.

FERNANDO: There's no doubt about it, I'm an urban savage.

DOCTOR: That air charged with the scents of apple blossoms, the forest of hemlocks, those snowcapped peaks—haven't they said anything to you?

FERNANDO: Nothing. The very same things happened to this mountain last year, and the year before, and for the last forty centuries. Not a bit of daring, no originality. Twilight, springtime, the falling of the leaves . . . The same stunts over and over again!

DOCTOR: You would like an anarchic nature, full of surprises.

FERNANDO: With imagination! Ah, if we weren't here to assist her . . . Yes, she produces all the foods. But all quite crude, really.

Not to mention that it never occurred to her to invent the elevator, the typewriter, even the simple wood screw. She's been in charge of the trees since the world began, and it hasn't even occurred to her to think up grafting! I'd like to see that mentally impoverished Nature working for a newspaper.

DOCTOR: And nonetheless, Nature is more than half of art.

FERNANDO: That's true: literarily I have no complaints about her. The rustic countryside is the natural habitat for goats and poets. But journalistically, she's pretty flat. Only man is interesting!

(*Hans enters.*)

DOCTOR: Some news for us, Hans?

HANS: None. The Philosophy Professor threw himself into the pond, as he does every morning. And he came back out swimming, as is also his custom. He's drying off.

DOCTOR: The bank teller?

HANS: In the Werther grove. He keeps on telling the whole world the Cora Yako story. Nobody believes it. And late in the afternoon, he cries.

DOCTOR: And the woman from the green pavillion?

HANS: The Unhappy Woman? I don't know what's going on with her. For the last three days she has steadfastly refused to eat.

(*Fernando laughs, remembering.*)

DOCTOR: We must prevent that at all cost.

HANS: I have already attempted to do so. I have been insistent with her: Madam, this cannot continue. For the sake of the Home . . . a glass of milk, perhaps a veal cutlet—and as soon as I say that, she begins to cry like a crocodile. I don't understand her.

FERNANDO: I do.

HANS: It seems as though she would like to kill herself by starvation. And she said she was looking for an original method! I just don't understand her. (*Sternly, to Fernando.*) You can laugh? Well, I can't!

DOCTOR: You're not in a very good mood today, Hans.

HANS: If the doctor will forgive me for saying so, there are certain things which run against my character. I am a serious man. I have come to a serious place. In order to carry out a serious function. And for the past few days this has not been the case.

FERNANDO: Since we arrived?

HANS: Exactly. Why are you laughing? Nobody used to laugh here. Miss Chole too has been laughing all morning long. And it seems to be contagious: last night I caught the Philosophy Professor whistling the "Blue Danube." Where will all this end?

DOCTOR: Calm down, Hans. It will all work out.

HANS (*without much faith*): We shall see. (*He starts to leave, but stops, horrified.*) Oh, Doctor ... the pictures!

DOCTOR: It was Miss Chole's idea. The others seemed too gloomy to her.

HANS: But they were appropriate here. The one of Seneca bleeding himself had an elevating serenity. That one of Larra, disheveled and romantic! (*He remains, contemplating the Botticelli with profound disdain.*) Springtime! What business has springtime got here? This is not serious. This is not serious. It just isn't serious. ... (*He leaves.*)

FERNANDO: Your assistant is a funny fellow.

DOCTOR: He was mutilated in the World War.

FERNANDO: Mutilated?

DOCTOR: Yes, in the soul. War leaves everyone scarred—those who fall and those who are saved. That fellow owned a tavern in a small town. He was a happy lad, sang the old songs, had friends, wife and children. During the war he served four years in a field hospital. Four years seeing and handling death around the clock! After the armistice, when he went back to his country, his friends, his wife and their children had disappeared. And his tavern, too. And the place where the tavern once stood. Hans was a finished man. He was only good for hovering over death. He went around to sanatoriums and hospitals, looking for work. And that's how he came to be here. And now I don't know whether he's here as an assistant or as a patient.

FERNANDO (*enthusiastic, reaching for his notebook*): But that's terrific! Why didn't you tell me that before?

DOCTOR: Journalistic appeal, right? Write. And when you're done, come to see me in my office. For you, you happy man, I have another story to tell. A story about two brothers . . . perhaps that will interest you more. Write on, write on. (*The Doctor leaves. Fernando, alone, makes his notes.*)

FERNANDO: "The Death Lover" . . . small town . . . tavern . . . 1914 . . .

(*Cora Yako enters, a splendid woman, of no particular age, at once spectacular and banal. She looks around her curiously. Finally she approaches Fernando.*)

FERNANDO: Madam . . . (*He slips on his jacket, which he had slung over one arm, hurriedly.*)

CORA: Are you one of the employees?

FERNANDO: Secretary and chronicler.

CORA: I hope that I will not have been mistaken. Is this the . . . ?

FERNANDO: Dr. Ariel's establishment.

CORA: Exactly. So it's true then? Stupendous! I was afraid it might have been a joke. Do you have a vacancy?

FERNANDO: Always. Here we do not ask anyone where he comes from or where he is going. You may look forward to a stay in the Blue Pavillion. Is yours an urgent case?

CORA: To tell you the truth, no. I must admit at once to you that I haven't the slightest intention of killing myself.

FERNANDO: You don't?

CORA: I am an artist, you see. Successful in a hundred countries. Unfortunately the years go by, one's faculties wear out. . . . And when one's talents wear out, there isn't much one can do but increase the advertising. I don't know if you follow.

FERNANDO: I think I do. What you need is some suicide propaganda in the headlines and three-color photos in the magazines. And naturally, without any risk.

CORA: That's it, that's it. You're very bright.

FERNANDO: Oh, well—I do my best.

CORA: It appears that we're going to understand each other perfectly. As for the cost, it makes no difference to me.

FERNANDO: Nor to me. We'll make it really juicy. May I take down some information to begin your record with? (*He takes a file card and notes.*) Profession: artist.

CORA: Opera singer.

FERNANDO: Singer. Spanish?

CORA: International. I was born on the high seas.

FERNANDO: Age—how does twenty-four sound to you?

CORA: Thanks . . .

FERNANDO: Twenty-four. Your name?

CORA: Cora Yako.

FERNANDO: Cora Yako. (*Remembering suddenly.*) Cora Yako! But . . . are you really Cora Yako in person? Oh, let me shake your hand!

CORA: You've heard me sing?

FERNANDO: Never! But it's just as well. What a great idea you had to come here!

CORA: Well, why not? It's one of the few things I've never tried. My career is filled with duels, scandals, a shipwreck. . . .

FERNANDO: You were married to an Indian raja. The divorce took place in California.

CORA: Ah—you knew him?

FERNANDO: I'm a newspaperman. We newspapermen find out everything—we're always reading the newspapers, you know. (*Contemplating her enchantedly.*) Cora Yako! Will you excuse me if I leave you alone for a moment? There's someone here who would be so pleased to meet you. I'm going to get him. Cora Yako, Cora Yako! (*He goes out.*)

CORA (*Watching him go*): Nice fellow. (*She looks around, curiously. She notices the Imaginary Lover, who arrives from the opposite side of the stage like a romantic shadow that has lost*

*its way. He comes in plucking petals from a daisy. He sits*
*down. He sighs.*)

CORA: Excuse me. . . . Are you an employee of this establishment?
(*He looks at her vaguely. Shakes his head in the negative.*)
Ah, then you are a . . . a . . . (*He affirms in the same way.*)
How interesting! It makes me shiver all over. But why?

LOVER: Love! I have loved greatly, deeply. I have been as happy as
a man can be. Why live on? In my arms I have held Marguerite, Brunhilde, Scheherazade. . . .

CORA (*looks at him uneasily*): So . . .

LOVER: Why do you look at me that way? You think I'm crazy,
don't you? Like all the rest. Ah, it is not easy to understand
me. You have to have seen her once! I saw her for the first
time in *Faust.*

CORA: Was she a singer?

LOVER: She was a silvered voice linked to a soul. I was just a poor
boy. But I was youthful, I wrote verses . . . and Cora needed
no more than that.

CORA: Her name was Cora?

LOVER: Cora Yako.

CORA: Oh, Cora Yako. How interesting!

LOVER: I was in the highest part of the highest balcony. But all that
evening she sang for me.

CORA: Just for you?

LOVER: Her eyes—which never left me for an instant—told me so.
I went back the following day. I sent her an orchid corsage.
Those flowers cost me more than I had even to buy myself
food. But I could not refuse them to her . . . So I stole the
money.

CORA (*interested*): You stole?

LOVER: What would I not have done for her?

CORA: You came to love her so much in one night?

LOVER: Sometimes an entire life is contained in an hour.

CORA: And she?

LOVER: She understood. She kissed the flowers slowly, slowly, looking at me. . . . And thus the love began. A week in Vienna . . . the Danube, the ship. . . . We left for Cairo.

CORA: Cairo . . . ah yes, I remember. Isn't that the big, dirty city with the hotel right across the street from the theatre?

LOVER: I don't remember the hotel.

CORA: Yes. And where they water the streets with leather skins.

LOVER: I don't know. I only remember one afternoon on camel-back over the red sand; the banks of the Nile, the drums in the desert! . . . and afterward, the pyramids!

CORA: You mean to say that there are pyramids right around there?

LOVER: Don't you know Egypt?

CORA: Yes, I've been there three times. But always in the theatre, in the casino.

LOVER: Cora went with me to explore the countryside. The songs, the gestures of the people! And one night, in Athens . . .

CORA: Athens! I remember Athens too. It's on the way back from Montevideo, no?

LOVER: Sometimes, yes.

CORA: Sure, a terraced town right on the sea . . . with a bunch of hotels with no baths, some pretty spicy meals. . . . (*Hitting on the key memory at last.*) There was a blond theatre manager who spoke Spanish!

LOVER: That might be. What I remember is that night in the Parthenon. Cora wanted to sing Massenet's *Thais*, in the nude, on the steps of Phidias. . . . And afterward, India: the jungle gods, with seven arms, like candelabra. Japan of the dragons and samurai. . . . Do you know the Orient?

CORA: I don't know. I've been there, but I don't think I've followed you exactly. Tell me—you've really been there? Truly? Truly? (*During the preceding dialogue she has been drawing nearer and nearer to him, attracted by curiosity that is half amused and half sentimental, until they end up beside one another.*)

LOVER: Why do you ask?

CORA: Because now I realize what I missed. I would like us to go back, together. I too know how to sing . . . and how to dress myself up as Brunhilde, as Scheherazade. . . .

LOVER (*With a violent emotion, almost fearful, grasping her hands.*) Why do you look at me like that? Those eyes . . . , those eyes . . . Who are you?

CORA (*tranquilly*): Cora Yako.

LOVER: No! It isn't possible!

CORA: Don't squeeze so hard. You have to tell me slowly about all those trips we've made together. I'm staying in the Blue Pavillion. It will truly be my pleasure to receive your flowers there . . . even if they're not orchids.

LOVER: Cora! . . . Cora! (*He follows her out, dazzled, his voice choked.*)

(*John wanders in aimlessly, flops into a chair. Silence. Chole returns. Her glance slips past John as though she had entered an empty room.*)

CHOLE: He's not in here. Have you seen Fernando?

JOHN (*with a vaguely reproachful tone*): Good afternoon, Chole.

CHOLE: Good afternoon . . . Have you seen him?

JOHN: No.

CHOLE: I left him here just a minute ago.

JOHN (*harshly*): I don't think he'll get lost.

CHOLE (*surprised*): Why are you speaking to me that way? I ask you about your brother and you answer me as if I had hurt you.

JOHN: I'm the one who *is* here.

CHOLE: Yes, but I was looking for him.

JOHN: I know, I know. For him, always for him. You run after him with your eyes shut, as if no one else existed around you. And if on passing by you run into me and dash off without looking at me, and I say "Good afternoon, Chole," I'm still the rough one, the nettlesome one. That's admirable egoism you've got there!

CHOLE: Forgive me. . . .

JOHN: It's nothing. I'm used to it by now. (*He starts to leave, but Chole stops him imperatively.*)

CHOLE: John! . . . I'll never learn to understand you. We've grown up almost as brother and sister, I love you as something of my very own, and yet I've never succeeded in really understanding what you are inside. What do you carry around inside you that's always gnawing at you?

JOHN: Nothing.

CHOLE: Why do you hide from your brother? Since we've been here he hasn't managed to see you once. If I speak to you about him . . .

JOHN: Enough, Chole! Talk about yourself, or the world . . . or be quiet. No more about Fernando!

CHOLE: He's your brother.

JOHN: And why has he bothered to be my brother? So that my misery could stand out in contrast! He was born healthy and strong—I was born sick. He was the pride of the house— I, the dull and useless one, the eternal second-born. He never studied—why should he?—he had grace and talent. I had to knock myself out over books in order to accomplish painfully half of what he succeeded in learning without any work. I copied out his maps and solved his mathematics problems while he played in the gardens—and his grades were always better than mine!

CHOLE: But that doesn't mean anything, John. Fernando can't be guilty of something that isn't within his control.

JOHN: You're right: while it was a matter of child's play and silly trifles it meant nothing. But this anguish has been growing with me until it has come to poison my whole life. You know how I loved my mother—I adored her on my knees. I spent my childhood contemplating her in silence, as though she were a sacred thing. But she couldn't really return my love. Fernando was there between us, and wherever he was everything was for him. . . . When she became critically ill and the doctors asked for a blood transfusion, I offered mine first. But the doctors rejected it. It wouldn't do. . . . I've never been good enough!

CHOLE: But, John . . .

JOHN: But you can bet Fernando's was good enough. Why? Weren't we brothers? Why should the blood from one have been better than the blood from the other? . . . And afterward . . . I watched over her week after week. He went on playing happily in the gardens. He didn't arrive until the last minute. And nonetheless . . . my mother died facing him!

CHOLE: Don't remember those things now. You're unfair.

JOHN: I? I'm the one who's unfair! But life has been fair, right? And Fernando too. And you!

CHOLE: I?

JOHN: You! . . . But, do you mean to say you haven't noticed? Is it possible that you are unaware that, after my mother, there hasn't been any other woman in my world except you?

CHOLE: John!

JOHN: Is it possible that you don't know you've been as blind to me as all the others have? That I have loved you as I loved her, contemplating you on my knees as I did her . . . and haven't known how to tell you?

CHOLE: Oh, good heavens, John . . .

JOHN: If you liked tulips and found a bunch on your table one day, it would only occur to you to think, "How much Fernando loves me!" But it was I who had cut them. If you fell asleep over your work and found it finished the next day, it would only occur to you to think, "poor Fernando!" But Fernando had slept through the night. Fernando has always been my undoing. He isn't to blame, I know that. If only he were! If he were, then this drama of mine could be played out to its conclusion.

CHOLE: What are you saying? John!

JOHN: But he isn't. The bitterest part of it is that he is good. He is hatefully good! And therefore I must swallow my tears, and see how happy he is, robbing me of everything that is mine. While I—the one deprived—continue being to everyone the egoist, the miserable and wicked brother.

CHOLE (*with a desperate cry*): Quiet! For the sake of your mother's memory!

JOHN: I won't be quiet anymore! I've been quiet all my life. Now I want you to know me completely. To know how desperately I love you. Everything that you've been to me—everything that you're helping to cheat me of without knowing it, when you laugh with him, when you kiss him.

CHOLE (*supplicatingly*): For the sake of what means most to you, listen! Can't you see that what you're saying is hateful? That you're destroying yourself and making our happiness an impossibility?

JOHN (*bitterly*): *Your* happiness . . . How well you guard it! And let me give you my advice, Chole: if you *are* happy, hide yourself even better. You can't just stroll around in your finest jewels through a beggars' district. You can't just promenade a happiness like yours through a world peopled with wretches! (*He pauses. Chole, distraught, cries silently. John, refreshed by his confession, attends to her sadness.*) Forgive me, Chole. This is all very bitter, I know. But I swear to you that I'm not wicked. I love Fernando, too. If only he weren't so happy!

CHOLE: If Fernando were not so happy . . . then what?

JOHN: If one day I were to see him miserable, I would go running to him with all my heart. Then we'd really be brothers! . . . Chole, I made you suffer, but I had to say that to you. I was rotting away, here, inside. He won't ever know. Forgive me.

CHOLE: You forgive us, John. Forgive us both . . . but leave me alone, now.

JOHN: Good-bye, Chole. (*John leaves.*)

(*It has been darkening and the stage is now in shadows. Lights along the lake glimmer in the background. Chole debates with herself in an interior battle between cruel silences.*)

CHOLE: Impossible, impossible . . . "If one day Fernando were miserable, then surely we'd be brothers. . . ." You will be, my poor John. I stood between you two without knowing it . . . but I'm not going to be there anymore. Run away?—that wouldn't be enough. But the path through the Gallery goes straight down to the lake . . . and they say that death in the water is sweet, like forgetting. You remember your whole life in an instant, and after that, nothing—a cold cloth laid over

SUICIDE PROHIBITED IN SPRINGTIME

the soul. (*She stares fixedly toward the lake which, illuminated in the night, now assumes a kind of stage presence, as another "character" in the drama. Chole approaches the Gallery of Silence.*) To die . . . to forget . . . (*She stops suddenly. From the depths of the pathway Grieg's melancholy violin in "Aase's Death" begins to be heard. Chole, as if drawn by the music, finally advances, as one who offers herself.*)

(*As she disappears, the scene is empty for a moment. Hans tiptoes in. He peers down the Gallery, genuinely excited.*)

HANS: At last we've got one! And it's her, best of all—the laughter and springtime girl. Good girl!

(*The sound of the violin dims. Fernando and the Doctor enter.*)

DOCTOR: Hans! Those lights . . . (*Hans lights them and goes to place himself in the entrance to the Gallery of Silence, his arms ritualistically crossed.*) Are you waiting for something?

HANS: I am waiting.

DOCTOR (*goes to the table*): And you, Fernando? Do you plan to work tonight?

FERNANDO: No.

DOCTOR: Cigarette?

FERNANDO: No.

DOCTOR: You seem preoccupied.

FERNANDO: Yes, Doctor, I am. That story you told me just now, about the two brothers—what does it mean?

DOCTOR: Oh, nothing. A trite story: the healthy and successful brother, and the sickly and unsuccessful . . .

FERNANDO: Yes, but—why did you tell that to me without once looking at me?

DOCTOR: All I did was to explain to you clinically a case that we've had here. And to this morbid distortion in the spirit of the weak, in the hated children, in the physically insufficient, science has given a stupid enough label: "inferiority complex." The title is relatively modern, but the drama is as old as the world. If you apply the term historically, the first inferiority complex in the history of mankind must have been the case of Cain.

FERNANDO: Fine. But why did you tell it to me without looking at me? Who are those brothers?

DOCTOR: Anyone.

FERNANDO: No, they're not just anyone. One of them is me!

DOCTOR: Maybe.

ALICE (*she enters terrified, screaming*): Doctor, Doctor . . . Fernando!

DOCTOR: What's going on?

ALICE: Miss Chole—she's in the lake!

FERNANDO: Chole?

DOCTOR: What? What do you mean? What's this all about, Hans?

(*Offstage John's voice can be heard, anguished.*)

JOHN: Chole! . . . Chole! . . . (*He enters, carrying Chole in his arms; his clothes and hers are both soaked with water. He carries her in her miserable condition to a chair. Hans remains in the shadows.*) Quickly, Doctor . . . Quickly!

DOCTOR: What happened?

JOHN: She hasn't a pulse beat. I can't hear her breathing. . . . Doctor!

(*The Doctor examines her.*)

FERNANDO: But, what happened?

JOHN: I saw her fall in. I don't know if I got to her in time.

FERNANDO (*to the doctor*): Is she alive?

DOCTOR: Silence . . . (*A pause. Chole's lips half part in a moan.*) She's saved.

FERNANDO: Chole! . . . Chole, look at me!

(*She comes to, slowly. She smiles on seeing Fernando at her side. She reaches for his hands, and clasps them emotionally.*)

CHOLE: . . . Was it . . . you . . . ? Thank you, Fernando . . .

JOHN (*he has stood apart. He repeats as a bitter echo*): Fernando
. . . Always Fernando!

CURTAIN

ACT THREE

(*The same place, on the following day. It is the first day of spring.
Strong morning light. Beethoven's "Hymn to Nature" is heard
from the garden, as the curtain is slowly raised.*

*Alice, motionless in the shade at the back of the stage, listens.
Chole enters, fatigued and weakened. Alice starts, as if to hasten
over to her; but Chole motions her to remain still. And both of
them listen until the music ends.*)

CHOLE! What was that music, Alice? Beethoven?

ALICE: The "Hymn to Nature."

CHOLE: How solemn it is! And what a feeling of consolation, of
serenity. It's almost like a religious chant.

ALICE: Yes, the doctor explained it to me. Beethoven wanted to
sing the world's very first springtime in those chords. Man's
pious emotion at the awakening of Nature. A song of life and
fertility.

CHOLE: And of hope.

ALICE: That too. Dr. Ariel always had it played when he was
tormented by the idea of his fate. And always, as if it were
an obligation to fulfill, on this day, too.

CHOLE: Today! Why, what's today?

ALICE: It's the first day of spring! (*She pauses.*) Are you feeling
better?

CHOLE: Oh, it was nothing. And you, Alice? Is something bothering
you? Your eyes look tired.

ALICE: I couldn't sleep all night.

CHOLE: For my sake?

ALICE: For your sake. You are laughter itself, and love, and youth.
. . . To think that it could all vanish so swiftly. When I saw

you with your eyes and hands clenched tight, so cold and white . . .

CHOLE (*upset by the memory*): Please, stop.

ALICE: I couldn't believe it. I felt my heart sink; I ached as if someone had struck me.

CHOLE: Why did they tell you?

ALICE: Nobody told me. I saw it. I was hunting for four-leaf clovers by the lakeside when you fell in.

CHOLE: But why do you say "when you fell in?"

ALICE: Because that's how it was. It couldn't have happened any other way, Chole! You came walking along the shore, with your eyes turned upward. I thought that you were coming to look for me. And, suddenly, you screamed . . . you slipped on the plants underfoot. That's the way it happened, isn't it Chole?

CHOLE (*gratefully squeezing her hand*): Yes . . . that's the way it happened.

ALICE: When I heard that scream, I felt my blood pulsing wildly— but I stood there, motionless, as if I were tied down. You were there beside me, struggling against death, and I couldn't move! That's when he arrived.

CHOLE: He? You saw him?

ALICE: Yes.

CHOLE: Tell me, Alice, there's something I've got to know . . .

ALICE: What?

CHOLE: I wanted to know . . . (*She stops herself fearfully.*) No, don't tell me anything. I am afraid it might not be.

ALICE: What?

CHOLE: Nothing. (*She changes her tone and asks.*) What's that book you've got there?

ALICE: Tennyson's poems. They're for the old man, you remember? For the other Alice's father. He's waiting for me.

CHOLE: Is he calmer now?

ALICE: He is, when we read.

CHOLE: Do you talk to each other?

ALICE: Sometimes. Very little, and very softly . . . He's getting accustomed to my voice now.

CHOLE: Go to him. Don't make him wait any longer.

ALICE: You don't need me?

CHOLE: He needs you.

(*The Doctor comes in, bringing a bunch of flowers. Alice leaves.*)

DOCTOR: How's it going?

CHOLE: Everything's all right now.

DOCTOR: I've been up to your room looking for you. I thought you'd be staying in bed today. I brought you some flowers.

CHOLE: They're lovely. Thanks, Doctor.

DOCTOR: You're welcome. They're not from me.

CHOLE: From Fernando?

DOCTOR (*hesitates*): Not from him either.

CHOLE: Now . . . now I know. From John.

DOCTOR: He didn't have nerve enough to bring them up himself. Poor boy. He spent the whole night outside your door, trembling like a child, listening for your breath. Are you breathing easily now?

CHOLE: It's still a bit tiring. The air seems heavy.

DOCTOR: Yes, almost weighted down. It's the arrival of spring. Down there, in the cities, one doesn't sense it. They notice it bit by bit—they find out from the calendar, or when the girls buy new hats. But here, what strength it has! It arrives suddenly. It climbs up the hillsides, shouting, laden down with mint and resins, resounding throughout the mountains. . . . It is as though a cry sounded from the inside of the earth and the whole countryside leaped up! Don't you feel a little giddy?

CHOLE: Yes, a little.

DOCTOR: It's the earth that's calling to us from within. Civilization goes on cutting off our feeling for these things. But when the sap runs white in the almond trees, when the seeds grow warm, when we breathe in the aroma of moist earth . . . How we realize then that we're made of this same clay! You're smiling?

CHOLE: I admire you, Doctor. You have unlimited faith in Nature.

DOCTOR: And you haven't?

CHOLE: I did have, once. Do you remember our conversation, right here, yesterday? I said that to kill oneself in the ripeness of youth, in the moment of love and springtime, was an insult. I had youth, I had love, springtime was at the threshold. . . . But nevertheless, that very same evening . . .

DOCTOR: And why, Chole, why?

CHOLE: What does it matter now? It happened in a fit of thought-lessness. I suddenly saw myself situated as an obstacle between two brothers who love each other and who run from each other. And I thought that, if it weren't for me, they would come together. What nonsense!

DOCTOR: Everything will work out by itself. Life is filled with roads of possibility.

CHOLE: For some. There are others who find them dead ends.

DOCTOR: Then, are you still thinking . . . ?

CHOLE: No, don't be afraid for my sake. I've been close to death and I've seen that it doesn't resolve anything. That all the problems have to be resolved standing upright, and facing them.

DOCTOR: Do you feel stronger now?

CHOLE: I will attempt to be stronger now. Life has suddenly opened up rather a bitter question for me. And there's nothing to do but provide an answer. I don't know when or how. But I know for sure that it won't be here.

DOCTOR: You aren't comfortable among us?

CHOLE: No, and I mean that sincerely. Forgive me, Doctor. You're a great spirit and a great friend. But it seems to me that Dr. Ariel and you, with the best of intentions, have gone astray.

You've conceived of a refuge for undecided spirits, but you never imagined that such an atmosphere could be contagious for others. The two of you flirted with the notion of death, making an ingenious joke of it. But death is more cunning than you, and there are moments when it presents itself so beautifully, so simply. . . . It's a dangerous game.

DOCTOR: Perhaps—

CHOLE: Believe me: in my home, surrounded by friendly objects, I would never have felt last night's dark temptation. Why did I feel it here? Think about it, Doctor: if I had killed myself yesterday, I would have done something evil, it's true; and neither Dr. Ariel nor you would be free to rest perfectly easily.

DOCTOR: Excuse me—

CHOLE: Close down this place, my friend. Send your talents and Dr. Ariel's fortune to work out there where men live and work. And today, when the world's life is beginning anew, bolt the door to this Gallery for good. Will you do that?

DOCTOR: Perhaps.

CHOLE: Do it for me, for us all. . . . Today is the first day of spring. Today it's a sin to die! (*She leaves.*)

(*The Doctor remains, lost in himself. He repeats almost unconsciously.*)

DOCTOR: Maybe, maybe . . .

(*Hans comes in.*)

DOCTOR: What's going on, Hans? Why have you taken off your uniform?

HANS: I've thought it all over very carefully. The Doctor cannot doubt my loyalty. But I'm no good for certain things. I've come to say good-bye.

DOCTOR: You're leaving us?

HANS: Yes, Doctor. I'm sorry. I had become fond of our establishment, had high hopes for it. But it's not working out.

DOCTOR: You aren't satisfied?

HANS: And how could I be? I came to your staff filled with lofty illusions. You know that. I've carried out my role as well as I might, I have complied with all of my obligations faithfully. And for what! Since I've been in the house, only the gardener's dog has made up his mind to die! And he died of old age. No —there's no future here.

DOCTOR: Have you found another position?

HANS: They spoke with me at the General Hospital yesterday. That's a well-organized place! There people die every day as God wills, without any help from esthetics. Pardon me, Doctor, but every man has his destiny.

DOCTOR: I understand, Hans. And I won't be the one to stand in your way.

HANS: I've hesitated a good deal, I assure you. I've waited day after day. Last night, with Miss Chole, I experienced a ray of hope. Illusions! Today, you will already have noticed, she's more eager to live than ever. And let's not even *talk* about the others. As of this morning, even the Philosophy Professor isn't throwing himself into the water any more! The opera singer wanders around among the willows, madly kissing that poor boy. The Unhappy Woman herself, as you know, isn't sad any more. That, too, fell through. . . .

DOCTOR: All right, Hans, all right. Stop by my office anytime you want to put your account in order.

HANS: Oh, that's not worth bothering about. One doesn't do these things for the money. I am an idealist. Good-bye, Dr. Roda.

DOCTOR (*extending his hand*): Good-bye, Hans . . . Good luck.

HANS (*leaving*): And believe me, Doctor, if this doesn't take a turn for the better, you might as well close down the whole place. There's just nothing else to be done. (*Leaves.*)

DOCTOR: Close down . . . Perhaps they're right. (*He calls.*) Alice . . . Alice! (*Goes out looking for her.*)

(*The Imaginary Lover comes in from the garden. He looks around the doorway, as though he suspects he is being followed. He falls wearily into an armchair with a sigh of relief. Immediately, Cora arrives.*)

CORA: Where has my little pussy-cat hidden himself?

LOVER (*Startled*): You!

CORA: My hero, my young wolf! Cheer up, sweet thing. Jump, shout, howl. Now you have me right here!

LOVER: I was waiting for you.

CORA: Nobody would know it, to look at that face. . . . You seem pained at the sight of me.

LOVER: Me! I've been looking for you all morning.

CORA: Where, my little birdie? I arose singing, ran across the mountains shouting your name, bathed in the stream. . . . Afterward I threw pebbles at your window. Were you so sound asleep?

LOVER: But I've been up since the crack of dawn!

CORA: And you didn't hear me? At first I threw little stones, until I broke the windowpanes. Then I threw bouquets of violets. Didn't the violets even reach you?

LOVER: Hardly.

CORA: How cruel! You were asleep! And Cora was there at your door, waiting like a little lark. Cora, who searched for you. Cora, who needs you. Cora Yako, my little wolf, Cora Yako! (*She sits down on the arm of his chair. She courts him with caresses and words.*) Are you happy? Have you been thinking about me? Am I just as you'd dreamed I'd be? . . . (*He answers with some guttural exclamations in the superlative. She imitates him.*) Hmmmm, aha! Hmmmm, aha! Don't you know how to talk?

LOVER: You won't let me!

CORA: What is it that you like in me? No, not everything. There's always something special! My hands? The neck?

LOVER: Your eyes. Your eyes more than anything. They are the eyes of that night!

CORA: That night when I was singing for you alone without knowing it! Look at those eyes, my little wolflet. Here they are, yours . . . don't I get a kiss?

LOVER: Yes.

CORA: Why are you trembling? Are you afraid of me? Ah, what a poor boy, what a poor thing, you are, my hero, my poet, . . .

my poor tiny poet. Are you sad? I imagined you vibrant, passionate. . . . Climbing over walls to see me, uprooting the
underbrush as you ran, throwing me over your shoulders . . . !

LOVER: You must have imagined a cross between a wild boar and
an orangutan.

CORA: Something of the sort. But that doesn't matter. Don't be
sad, my little wet linnet, my pocket poet. I love you the way
you are: small, cowardly, a dreamer. . . . Why did you read so
much, my poor little thing? Don't you know how it weakens
a person? You aren't going to do that anymore, are you? (*Vol-
uble, following her own words across the stage.*) Now we will
live! Run around the world together! In an embrace!

LOVER (*with anticipation*): Cora!

CORA: Now you'll share with me everything you dreamed of: Egypt,
and the desert, and the jungles, and the lush islands—

LOVER: The lotuses and the white elephants! The Buddhist pago-
das with their roofs like wooden shoes, hung with bells!

CORA: And so many other things that you don't even know about,
that aren't in books. But you must make yourself strong, my
little wolfboy—as soon as you get away from Europe, there's
nothing but mosquitos.

LOVER: Mosquitos?

CORA: Lots of green mosquitos, tiny poisonous ones, that work
their way inside everything. And that bring fever, and deep
sleep—and, sometimes, even madness. But don't be frightened,
my hero! There are also insecticides, and special skin lotions.
Oh, modern science! For every mosquito God produces, the
Germans produce an injection.

LOVER: I feel better already.

CORA: Can you visualize going to India with me?

LOVER: Oh, yes! Yes! The gods of the Ramayana, the secred Ganges
with its three sources!

CORA: Look—you're better off without the Ganges. There are snakes
you know?—and crocodiles. And then, intestinal fevers that
turn you yellower and yellower. . . . (*Abruptly.*) You love me?
Do you love me? Do you love me?

LOVER (*drawing himself up gallantly*): I love you like a Cossack!

CORA: Are you ready for anything!

LOVER: For anything!

CORA: Why don't we go right now?

LOVER (*terrified on seeing it all so near*): Now? . . .

CORA: Now, now . . . What are we waiting for? (*She consults her watch.*) The car can be ready in a minute. You know how to drive?

LOVER: No.

CORA: All right, I'll drive. But I'll warn you, I don't know how to drive at anything under ninety. It's quarter to eleven. We'll leave at eleven on the dot, and by four at the latest we'll be in Valencia—where we can still catch the afternoon plane. That's fine. Tonight we have supper in Marseilles. How's that? Just a moment. I'll go get the car ready.

LOVER: But, Cora dear. Wait one minute.

CORA: What?

LOVER: We're leaving just like that—without even saying good-bye?

CORA: To whom? I never say good-bye.

LOVER: To the Doctor, to our comrades . . . And then, too, you have to consider everything: we need money.

CORA: Phoo! To get us started—haven't you got thirty thousand pesetas on you?

LOVER: I?

CORA: Fifteen thousand . . . ten thousand, however many . . .

LOVER: I don't even have *one!*

CORA: But—the bank robbery?

LOVER: I only took enough for the orchids.

CORA: No more! . . . Well, all right, it's all the same. We'll find what they call a "white charger" for ourselves.

LOVER: And just where are we going to find a white charger? Anyway, we'll need at least two.

CORA: Two! (*Laughing in amusement.*) You *are* a hero! Do you realize how undone you're becoming? (*Stops laughing.*) Listen, you really don't know what we mean by "a white charger"?

LOVER: No, I really don't know—when I was studying, a white horse was a white horse.

CORA: Ah, child, child . . . , but, what did they teach you at the University? How much there is for you to learn. Go on! Get your things ready.

LOVER (*indecisive*): So—we're going?

CORA: We're going.

LOVER: It's just that . . . I haven't got a passport.

CORA: Forget it. That can be taken care of on the way. All of the consuls in the world are my friends. The English are the worst, but when you know just how to smile, they give in, too. You know English?

LOVER: No.

CORA: Makes no difference. They all speak French.

LOVER: But I don't speak French either.

CORA: So you keep quiet, then—you keep quiet in every language. Let's go, what are you waiting for?

LOVER: I'm going. . . . I'm going. . . . (*Vacillating.*) To Marseilles, huh?

CORA: To Marseilles.

LOVER: In an airplane?

CORA: In an airplane. Why?

LOVER: It's just that . . . this is the first time I'm to take a plane. I think those things make you seasick. . . .

CORA: Old wives' tales. Smoother than a ship!

LOVER: Yes, but I haven't gone by ship either.

CORA (*impatient*): They give you pills!

LOVER: Ah . . . there are pills! Then, it's all set?

CORA: All set. How much longer are you going to dilly-dally about getting your things together?

LOVER (*on the verge of tears*): Cora, Cora . . .

CORA: What?

LOVER: It's just that I haven't any luggage either!

CORA: Nothing? Not even a dinner jacket?

LOVER: I have two shirts . . . and a book.

CORA: Well, get a move on, grab the shirts.

LOVER: The book is a manuscript of mine . . . unpublished. Poems.

CORA: I don't care if it is yours. Any more books, and we're lost. If you hadn't read so much you wouldn't be going through all this now. At eleven on the dot?

LOVER: At eleven.

CORA: Ten minutes to go. Do you have a watch at least?

LOVER (*nervously, he pokes his hands into his pockets. He smiles happily on finding it*): Yes, a watch, yes. Silver, too. It's a memory of my father. (*He holds it up to his ear, alarmed.*) Stopped!

CORA: Well, set your father's watch. And you're not going to keep me waiting, either! That's one thing I've never let any man get away with. If you're not here at eleven I'll honk three times. But on the third honk I'm off.

LOVER: I'll be there.

CORA: Until a few minutes from now, my hero, my handsome wolf-boy. (*She drives him across the room with kisses. The Lover exits.*)

(*Fernando has come in in time to witness the end of the scene.*)

FERNANDO: You two are leaving?

CORA: Within ten minutes. For Marseilles. And if there's a ship in the morning, to India. Say good-bye to Chole for me. I haven't time. We'll cable her from Cairo. So long, Fernando!

FERNANDO: Bon voyage. (*She leaves. Fernando wriggles his fingers, recovering from her handshake, and casts a look of pity in the direction in which the Imaginary Lover exited.*) Poor boy . . .

(*Hans enters with light luggage: a bundle and his umbrella.*)

FERNANDO: You're leaving too?

HANS: Yes, me too.

FERNANDO (*staring at his luggage*): For Cairo?

HANS: For the city—they've offered me a post at the General Hospital.

FERNANDO: Ah, congratulations.

HANS: That's another place entirely: it's got atmosphere. I've just read an account in the *Medical Gazette*—in just one week, twenty-five cases!

FERNANDO: Splendid.

HANS: Here, on the other hand, you see how it is. The thing had some promise at the start. People hurried out here; there were several attempts. In sum, it wasn't a bad beginning. But now! That Cora Yako has just driven me crazy, already. Have you seen her laugh? It's insulting! And kiss?

FERNANDO: She's got plenty of life in her.

HANS: Too much. (*Confidentially.*) Do you know that she's attempted to seduce me?

FERNANDO: You!

HANS: Me. This morning. I was peacefully shaving myself by the window and, in a playful way, she began tossing pebbles at me. I was forced to take shelter inside. Four stones the size of nuts flew through the windowpanes. And next, a bunch of violets. That business about the stones, OK, but a bouquet of violets for *me* . . . Oh, keep your distance, madam! And the case of the Unhappy Woman? It's frightful. Try to envision how last night, on that very lawn, among the acacias. . . . (*Seeing her arrive.*) Her!

(*The Unhappy Woman comes in, softly singing the "Blue Danube." She is smiling, dressed in bright colors; graciously rejuvenated, but without anything to suggest ludicrousness.*)

WOMAN: Good morning, Hans. Good morning, Fernando.

FERNANDO: Madam . . .

WOMAN: Have you seen what a lovely morning it is? Everything is narcissus white. The scent of the countryside is everywhere. Ah, the echoes of this wild springtime! How do you like this outfit?

FERNANDO: It's very gay.

WOMAN: Nice, isn't it? But believe me, that's only the start. A bit of pretty organdy . . . a silver pin . . . you haven't seen anything yet. Excuse me for dashing off, but they're waiting for me. Why this sad look, Fernando? On a day like today! Do you feel ill? Cheer up, my friend. Why don't you come to eat with us?

FERNANDO (*astounded*): To eat?

WOMAN: We're eating up there, beside the fountain. There'll be everything: venison from the mountain, trout from the stream, fresh fruits, and red Andalusian wines, the kind that startle the soul. Shall we wait for you? Cheer up, Fernando. See you later. Good morning, Hans! (*She waves good-bye delightfully, twiddling her fingers, and goes out humming happily, unconsciously making the movements of a waltz step.*)

(*Fernando looks at Hans distractedly.*)

FERNANDO: Well, has the woman gone out of her mind?

HANS: Worse yet. Didn't you notice her humming the "Blue Danube"?

FERNANDO: Yes, that's what it sounded like.

HANS: And doesn't that bring anything to mind?

FERNANDO: The Philosophy Professor!

HANS: The very same. Last night I surprised the two of them, in bright moonlight, out among the acacias. (*Philosophically.*) Have you ever noticed the sort of eyes cows have?

FERNANDO: Yes. The very image of a damp tenderness.

HANS: Well then: last night the Professor had cow's eyes. They were seated on a little hill. He looked at the moon; afterward, he looked at her. And sighed. When a philosophy professor hazards a sigh, he is lost.

FERNANDO: You saw them?

HANS: What haven't I seen in this lifetime? They were very close together, holding hands. He leaned against her shoulder, and recited into her ear softly and intimately.

FERNANDO: Verses?

HANS: Of course. I couldn't hear more than one stanza. But it went this way: (*He recites lyrically.*) "The weight of any body submerged in water will be diminished by an amount equal to the weight of the liquid it displaces." Judge for yourself!

FERNANDO: But that's amazing!

HANS: Amazing. That's spring for you. There's nothing to be done about it. They've already said good-bye to the Doctor. They'll go off this afternoon—together! (*He pauses. In a confidential tone.*) Only one hope remains—a remote one. Do you remember the Professor's fondness for throwing himself into lakes? (*He draws nearer, emphasizing the secret.*) They're going to Switzerland. . . . (*Like a pair of accomplices, they both indicate silence by putting a finger to the lips.*) To Switzerland! (*Hans leaves.*)

(*Fernando remains alone, wrapped up in himself, with a sad gesture indicating the struggle to pull himself together. He lights a cigarette. The Lover returns, peering furtively about him.*)

LOVER: She's not here?

FERNANDO: Cora?—In the garden, getting the car ready.

LOVER: What a woman, Fernando . . . awful. Why did she ever have to come? She's beautiful as I had imagined her, but—

FERNANDO: And, nonetheless, she's the same one. The same one who sang for you the night they did *Faust.*

LOVER: Ah, no. My Cora was something else again: an illusion, a wordless poem. The eyes, yes. They are the same as they were that night.

FERNANDO: It could be a great adventure for you.

LOVER: A dangerous adventure. You don't know her. That woman will kill me within two weeks.

FERNANDO: It's love!

LOVER: But such a love! I had dreamed of this woman's kisses as a soft smooth caress, like a tingling of petals on the skin. But that's not Cora.

FERNANDO: A strong kisser, eh?

LOVER: She bites! She vibrates—she explodes! By now I'm getting a little bit used to it. But yesterday . . . her first kiss floored me! And the clutches! She wraps herself around you, squeaks, and sobs some throaty things that make your hair stand on end. She's an earthquake, Fernando, an earthquake!

FERNANDO: You're scared of her.

LOVER: Scared, no, not scared. I love her, I want to see her always. But from a little way off.

FERNANDO: From the highest balcony.

LOVER: Yes, that's it—from up high.

FERNANDO: Weren't you two going away together?

LOVER: Well, she's here, so . . . Yes, I have no alternative but to go off with her. Oh! The minutes are flying by, but I just don't know what to do!

FERNANDO: The great adventure only comes once in a lifetime. You have it in your grasp now. Think it over carefully.

LOVER: If only I could just keep her eyes!

FERNANDO: But wasn't this the moment you've been dreaming of?

LOVER: Ah, dreaming is something else again.

FERNANDO: Cora Yako is love! ships! faraway countries!

LOVER: But such countries, Fernando. Filled with horrible dangers: green mosquitos—intestinal diseases—consuls!

FERNANDO: She's the India of the gods! The Japan of the heroes and lovers!

LOVER: I can't. . . . I can't. . . . (He sits down, weakly.)

FERNANDO: In that case, there's another solution. Renounce the authentic Cora Yako. Remain with the one you've dreamed about. And dedicate yourself to writing.

LOVER: To writing?

FERNANDO: Sure—after all, it's just another form of heroism. Novels are always written by those who are incapable of living them. What was your salary in the bank?

LOVER: Nothing to speak of. A couple of hundred.

FERNANDO: I am prepared to offer you three times as much for working on our newspaper, with paid vacations. How would you like to take over the travel and adventures page?

LOVER (*excitedly*): Do you really think I'll do?

FERNANDO: Why not?

LOVER: It's just that I've never really been out of my hotel room.

FERNANDO: And what difference does that make? Art isn't a matter of experience—it's an affair of the imagination. Xavier de Maistre made some marvelous journeys around his room; Beethoven was deaf; Milton, when he wrote his song of light, was blind.

LOVER: For what it's worth . . . I have a book of verses.

FERNANDO: Tear them up right away. And don't dare to admit that to any of your colleagues—you'll lose their respect for good.

(*The first honk is heard from the garden.*)

LOVER: Here she is already! (*Without looking at his watch.*) What time is it?

FERNANDO: Eleven on the dot!

LOVER: At the third honk, she's off. What do I do, Fernando, what do I do?

FERNANDO: One down! Don't think any longer. (*Waving alternately toward the garden and toward the interior.*) Either you go there to live adventures . . . or you go in here to write them.

LOVER: It's just that I haven't a cent . . . I'm certain I'll be sick on the plane. . . .

FERNANDO: But it's a woman that's calling to you!

LOVER: I only have two shirts. . . .

FERNANDO: It's Cora Yako!

LOVER: Those green mosquitos . . .

FERNANDO: It's love!

LOVER: The crocodiles . . .

(*Another honk is heard.*)

FERNANDO: Two!

LOVER (*shouting*): I'm coming. (*He turns toward the garden. He stops in the shadow. He turns, nervous and urgent.*) Fernando —what is a white charger?

FERNANDO: Now he asks! Scientifically, it is a simple four-footed equine monodactyl with light pigmentation.

LOVER: And aesthetically?

FERNANDO: Ah! aesthetically . . . it's the old donkey who pays in the end.

LOVER (*reduced to nothing*): The old donkey . . . who pays . . . (*Reacting violently.*) And that's what she proposed to me. . . . To me! (*Shouting again.*) I'm not coming!

(*The third call sounds.*)

FERNANDO: And three! (*He goes to look out into the garden. He is seen waving good-bye.*)

LOVER (*looking melancholically at his watch*): Eleven o'clock. In Valencia at four . . . in Marseilles at dusk . . . , the sea . . . (*With a repentant impulse.*) Cora . . . Cora!

FERNANDO: She's already gone.

LOVER: I'm a ruined man. . . .

FERNANDO: You're a hero! Let her go in peace, and remember her. It's better this way. Yours and hers are two lives that could never become one. And now, let's write the columns for the coming week! Title of the first one: "A Night with Cora Yako in Japan."

LOVER: In Japan?

FERNANDO: Sure. We'll make up the photographs in the lab, as always.

LOVER: Will you let me put in something about geishas?

FERNANDO: And about robins—and about cherry blossoms. But carefully, eh? Realistically!

LOVER: Something like this? "We'd taken the morning plane from Yokohama ..."?

FERNANDO: That's it, very good.

LOVER: "Cora laughed at my side, three thousand feet above the islands white with chrysanthemums. ..." (*Going out.*)

FERNANDO: That's it. That's it ...

(*Chole enters.*)

FERNANDO (*when he sees her, he hurries over*): Chole! Are you better? Do you still feel weak?

CHOLE: That's all over with now.

FERNANDO: Completely?

CHOLE: The pain, the danger ... The rest will have had to work itself out, sooner or later. (*She pauses. Gently reproachful.*) Why are you hiding yourself, Fernando? I haven't seen you since yesterday. Do you think hiding is going to accomplish anything? There is a cruel truth before us that we can't erase by shutting our eyes.

FERNANDO: Don't think of that now. The reason why I haven't seen you is because the doctor forbade me to. You were feverish. You needed rest and quiet.

CHOLE: Didn't you see me last night?

FERNANDO: Sure. You still weren't breathing. When you fell into the lake ...

CHOLE: You too? You also say "when you fell"? Why do you want to fool yourself? I didn't fall: I wanted to do it. I went looking for death.

FERNANDO: No. Chole, that isn't possible!

CHOLE: It seems that way to me now, too. But yesterday ... Tell me, Fernando: there's something I must know, that I haven't asked anyone about because I'm afraid of the truth. But I can't keep quiet about it any more. Tell me—last night ... when I fell ... there was a man who risked his life for me. I saw him as though in a dream. ... It was you, wasn't it? (*She watches him, anguished, hoping.*)

FERNANDO: I would have wanted it to be. But it was John. He saw you fall. I didn't know about it until afterward, when they brought you here.

CHOLE: It wasn't you? . . .

FERNANDO: No.

CHOLE (*she fondles the brother's flowers, unconsciously*): Poor John . . . He spent a sleepless night, with his ear to my door, listening to me breathe. He has suffered more than I myself. You don't know, Fernando, how good—how good and how unlucky your brother is.

FERNANDO: I know all about it.

CHOLE: All? . . . Have you talked with him?

FERNANDO: With the doctor. *He* would never tell me. I wouldn't dare to speak with him, either. We've been running away from each other like two bitten dogs, afraid of one another.

CHOLE: And how long are you going to go on that way?

FERNANDO: It's over now! I can't keep it up. You've got to understand this, Chole: even to be miserable there must be some sort of predisposition. I cannot, I do not resist. But I don't know how to suffer!

CHOLE: Have you thought of a solution?

FERNANDO: To get away from here . . . run away!

CHOLE: And where? Where would we be able to hide, that John's memory wouldn't be with us? No. Fernando . . . Happiness is no longer possible. The shadow of your brother would intervene in our kisses, freezing us both.

FERNANDO: And what can we do? Was what you thought last night the solution? Did you think that because of your disappearance we'd come together, he and I? Your death would have separated us even more, changing to hate what has only been pain until now.

CHOLE: Possibly. But I haven't stopped thinking about it since last night.

FERNANDO: And what are you thinking?

CHOLE: John has never had anything for himself. He has always been alone among us, watching our happiness with his hungry eyes, like a wretched child outside a store window. He can't go on alone. See if you can. I'm staying.

FERNANDO: With him?

CHOLE: I will be the mother who didn't know how to understand him, the sister he never had. So that there will be at least the illusion of a woman in his world.

FERNANDO: But that just can't be, Chole. That's not the way John loves you.

CHOLE: I know that. I heard him proclaim that yesterday. And even yesterday I was unjust to him, once again. I had beside me a heart aching desperately and I felt only fear, almost repugnance . . . as if a beggar had stopped me in the street.

FERNANDO: It won't work, Chole. You're blind, tormented by guilt for sins that don't exist.

CHOLE: No. We were blind before, when our happiness was the only thing on earth. It never once occurred to us to look around. And there was John, always, scratching like a dog at our door!

FERNANDO: But don't you think I feel it too? Do you think my brother's heart doesn't ache in me also? I would do anything for him to make him happy. But the fact is that we can't do anything for him that wouldn't be just fooling him. Don't torment yourself anymore. Let's just leave. You'll never be happy with him.

CHOLE: It's got nothing to do with whether or not I'm happy now. I *have* been! Now what matters is him.

FERNANDO (*obviously upset, taking her by the arms*): No, Chole, don't try to play with your sentiments. You must see that the heart contains dangerous surprises. . . . You must see that tomorrow can be too late!

CHOLE: This isn't the time to worry about that. My post is here now, at his side.

FERNANDO: Because he saved your life?

CHOLE: Because he has given his own over to me entirely.

FERNANDO: But then . . . (*He holds her chin up.*) Take a good look at me! What's beginning to start inside you? Answer me!

CHOLE (*she becomes suppliant, but is resolved*): For the sake of what you love most—leave me!

FERNANDO: No, it's not possible. . . . It's your woman's sense of pity laying a trap for you. And John himself must prevent you from falling into it. Let him forgive us, or let him kill us together. But to deceive him—not that! (*He goes inside shouting.*) John! John! . . .

(*John appears in the background shadows. Chole, pale when she sees him, casts a pleading look in Fernando's direction, then turns to John.*)

CHOLE: Don't listen to him, John! Don't listen to him!

(*John, his eyes riveted on his brother, comes forward ignoring Chole. Without looking at her, with quiet energy:*)

JOHN: What's all the shouting for me about? Is something of yours in danger? And do you need me, as always, to save you?

FERNANDO: No. All I want is that, whatever the cost, there be nothing standing in shadows between us. Now I've got to have the whole truth.

JOHN: Haven't you heard it yet? Or do you think that Chole, in gratitude, was going to act out that cruel old farce? She, so loyal, so unblemished . . . can you really imagine her trying to pay for a true love with some scraps of the happiness that overflows the two of you?

FERNANDO (*retreating dumbfounded when he realizes that John had heard them talking*): John. . . .

JOHN: No, Fernando, I won't accept charity, and she will not fall into the sin of a compassionate lie. You want proof? I'll give it to you right now . . . eye to eye. Right, Chole? (*Chole, between the two, backs off also.*) Let's go. What are you waiting for? Here's your Fernando. The happy man. The one who's never had to fight for anything because life gave him everything. The one who went out into the garden to play while his mother died. . . . You've got him here. He never knew there was any pain in the world. With him come happiness, health, all the graces of life. Here there is only poor

John, with his misery and his love. Choose, Chole. For once and for all!

(*She hesitates. She pleads with Fernando in a gesture, and advances painfully toward John.*)

CHOLE: John ...

JOHN (*takes her in his arms with sudden, superabundant emotion. His words waver with emotion*): Do you see her, Fernando? In my arms! Now you're not the only one. John also can triumph, once! (*He raises her tear-filled face with his hand.*) But also ... for once ... I am to have the pride of being stronger than you, more generous than you! Take her away—far away from here. Now you can both be happy without any guilt. But I also, even if only once, have been good like you, and happy like you ... and have seen you cry.

FERNANDO (*fraternally*): John!

JOHN: Brother! (*All of their suppressed tenderness breaks out in an embrace.*) Thank you, Chole ... I knew before that it couldn't be, that you were just trying to fool yourself. But thank you for what you wanted to do. Take her, Fernando. I ask only that you go far away to live. Leave me just the one happy day I've had in my lifetime....

(*Chole, unable to find the words to say good-bye, squeezes John's hands. She picks up her flowers and holds them close to her; goes out with her head pressed against Fernando's shoulder. Now, John shows signs of the effort he has made; sways momentarily; regains control of himself. He wears a look of fatal indifference. He goes to the desk, unlocks it and takes out his pistol. Alice passes by. On seeing her he hides the weapon, turns around.*)

ALICE: Good morning, John ... (*She clanks shut the bolt on the gate to the Gallery of Silence, and places in a conspicuous spot a sign that reads: "Suicide Prohibited in Springtime." In the garden, very softly, one can begin to hear Beethoven's hymn again, played by string instruments only.*) This finale is by Chole's order.... Is something wrong with you, John?

JOHN: No, nothing ...

ALICE: You're trembling.

JOHN: Just a little temperature, maybe.

ALICE: It's the weather. . . . Do you hear that music?

JOHN: What is it?

ALICE: Beethoven—a hymn of thanks to spring. He too was alone and in turmoil when he wrote it. But he knew that spring always brings with it a flower and a promise for everyone.

JOHN: You believe that?

ALICE: The doctor told me once: "Don't ask anything of life. And one day life will give you a marvelous surprise."

JOHN: And you wait?

ALICE: Always . . . Would you like to do something for me, John? Today is a day of life and hope. Everything that reminds one of death must disappear from this place. . . . Would you like to give me what you're hiding there?

JOHN (*upset, handing over the gun*): Sorry . . .

ALICE: I'm going to throw it in the pond. In the same place where Chole slipped yesterday. (*Starts to leave.*)

JOHN: Alice . . . Wait . . . I'm afraid to be alone. Will you let me come along with you?

ALICE: Thank you . . . (*She offers him her arm. They go off together toward the garden.*)

(*Beethoven's hymn—strings and wind instruments now— powerful and solemn. The curtain falls slowly.*)

# FIRST COMMUNION

*A Play in One Act*

*by* FERNANDO ARRABAL

TRANSLATED BY MICHAEL BENEDIKT

# First Communion

Fernando Arrabal (b. 1932) has lived in France since 1954. In the late 1950's he became a French playwright—thanks in part to the exigencies of Spanish censorship, as well as, no doubt, to the relatively liberal atmosphere in French theatre circles, which had just seen the birth of the post-Surrealist or "absurdist" school of Ionesco, Genet, and their colleagues. He has virtually ceased to write in Spanish. Arrabal's Spanishness is nevertheless plain, even painfully so. His central theme is the uncomfortable relationship between established reality and the desires of the individual imagination. Arrabal conceives of a particularly fierce conflict of forces. Humans are like the little boy at the mercy of the morality-ridden and sex-crazed Aunt in his autobiographical novel *Baal Babylon* (1959). In the name of reality and morality they are confronted by forces so sinister and twisted as to render the misdeeds of obvious evildoers, however monstrous, relative peccadilloes.

In *First Communion* Arrabal returns to a landscape of evil similar to the one he imagined in his early play, *Oraison (Funeral Oration,* 1957). Here, two individuals sit discussing morality at the brink of the coffin of their own child, whom they have killed. The coffin of *First Communion,* with its attendant necrophiliac, would at first appear to be a scene of utmost criminality; yet it soon becomes apparent that it is the traditional morality dispensed during the inanely ritualistic conversation of the grandmother and child, who discuss the Good Life beside the coffin, that represents real viciousness. The final transformation of the innocent child into a lethal weapon of vengeance is pictured as a natural result of the "pious" advice she has accepted. It is interesting that although Arrabal's plays are without direct reference to politics, and are deeply concerned with the question of a true morality, they are forbidden in his native land for "moral" reasons.

M. B.

## Characters

TWO MEN, DEAD WOMAN, NECROPHILIAC, non-speaking
LITTLE GIRL
GRANDMOTHER

(*It is night.*

*On stage, at the left, an empty coffin, two candelabras and an iron crucifix.*

*To the right, a set of communicant's vestments, laid out for the little girl. An incredibly baroque dress.*

*Enter the Two Men. They carry a lady, deceased, and completely nude. They place her in the coffin. They kneel down and begin to pray.*

*A distant rustling is heard.*

*Suddenly one of the two men stops praying and looks to the right; the other follows suit. They seem horrified.*

*They hastily close the coffin and hoist it to their shoulders. They leave hurriedly, to the left, carrying the coffin.*

*Silence.*

*The necrophiliac enters from the right and follows the two men. He wears a costume reflecting his propensities.*

*He crosses the stage and goes off to the left.*

*Silence.*

*Enter the Little Girl (wearing only panties) and the Grandmother. They walk over to a pew.*

*The old lady will dress the communicant item by item, with great care, throughout the act.*)

GRANDMOTHER: Today is the day, my little dear, the most important day of your life. God himself is going to deign to descend to you.

LITTLE GIRL: Yes, Grandmother dear.

GRANDMOTHER: You will become a little woman. Beginning today you must set an example for the entire world by your conduct. I have already taught you all that a woman ought to know. Someday you will marry. . . .

LITTLE GIRL: Really?

GRANDMOTHER: Yes, my child, some day you are going to marry and become the pride of your husband. There is nothing that a man appreciates more than a good housekeeper, just like you are. You will be a true jewel for some lucky man. For you must remember that when men get up in the morning they love to put on gleaming white, ironed shirts, socks without holes, and trousers which have been perfectly pressed. You will be a true pearl to your husband. You already know how to press, darn socks, and even cook. Now, since you are going to receive communion, you are going to become a perfect Christian. I'm quite certain that you're going to become an exemplary hostess, isn't that right, my child?

LITTLE GIRL: Yes, Grandmother dear.

GRANDMOTHER: The most important thing of all is the kitchen. A dirty kitchen transforms the cleanest household into a pigpen. I have already taught you to keep everything in perfect order: plates always in the sideboard, utensils in the cupboard, every dishrag in its proper place, for disorder is the first step toward filthiness. And above all wash the table and dishes after every meal. Nothing gives rise to a more disagreeable impression than entering a kitchen and discovering dirty plates heaped all over the sink and every available table. How much trouble is it to do a sinkful of dishes? It takes just a few minutes. As for the result—you see what a place of beauty my home is. And still, alas, I am old now and am unable to keep things as clean as I would like to. I'm sure you understand what I'm getting at, don't you?

LITTLE GIRL: Yes, Grandmother dear.

GRANDMOTHER: Men are very exacting; some people might say that these things are of no interest to them, but how many times haven't household quarrels arisen because of a woman's lack of cleanliness?!

(*From the right enter the Two Men who carry the coffin. The Grandmother and the Little Girl fall silent and watch. The Two Men cross the stage from right to left. They exit.*

*Silence.*

*Enter from the right the Necrophiliac, following them. One can clearly make out a certain disturbance arising around his groin.*

*The Necrophiliac crosses the stage and exits, left.*)

GRANDMOTHER: And that is why, my child, you ought always to be very neat and very orderly. Just as I say, the first thing is the kitchen, but meanwhile the other rooms also must not be neglected. Vacuuming in the morning takes but a moment. You see how, even at my age, it's something I never fail to do. Besides, these days because of the housing shortage homes are so tiny that it is not in the least difficult to keep them quite clean. To enter a house with dust on the cupboard and dusty glass everywhere is to suffer disaster. But I know that you know how to keep your house. Isn't that right, my child?

LITTLE GIRL: Yes, Grandmother dear. (*Pause. Coldly:*) What is that puffed up part under the stomach of that man who just passed through here?

GRANDMOTHER (*icily*): That's his sex! (*Pause.*) Windowpanes when dirty create a deplorable impression. It is so easy to wash them! You ought to do them two or three times a week at least. It will only take you a few minutes, and the time could not be better spent. You just rub on the panes with some old newspaper soaked in water and you will see . . . it works like magic. It will be a pleasure to gaze into the street, then. A husband will never forget that. Believe me when I tell you that men, despite all appearances, take a deep interest in these little details. You are still too little a girl to be able to understand of just how much a man is actually capable. Most of the time when a husband leaves his wife it is simply because he does not find his hearth and home as neat and clean as he expected on his way home from work. But I know that you will be just like me.

LITTLE GIRL: Yes, Grandmother dear.

GRANDMOTHER: You ought never forget the daily dusting, either. It hardly takes any time at all. It's quite easy to run a rag over all the furniture once a day. Only lazy, slovenly women have furniture covered with dust. I remember that once, when I was very little, my mother took me to visit a very dirty neighbor. I amused myself by drawing a cat on a sideboard door, there was so much dust on it! What shame for that woman!

(*The little girl laughs.*)

GRANDMOTHER: I know very well that you won't turn out to be like that. At your house the beds will always be made, **the** sheets clean, the closets won't smell bad, the floor will gleam, the utensils will always be in order, the dishpan scoured, fresh linen always ready, the windowpanes clean and clear, the furniture without an atom of dust and the sweepings swept into a box. But a good housekeeper like yourself ought not forget, despite all that, that in order to keep a husband you must cook well for him. A man who finds a tasty meal waiting for him when he comes home will do anything his wife wants. These days food is so expensive that, it is true, one cannot prepare special treats all the time, as one could formerly, but a good housekeeper can work miracles if she really knows how to cook. You are just a little girl and already you know how to cook; when you get married you will be worth your weight in gold.

LITTLE GIRL: Yes, Grandmother dear.

GRANDMOTHER: A woman who knows how to cook properly can rest assured that her husband won't ever abandon her. You ought never forget that.

(*Enter from the right the Two Men with the coffin. They cross the stage and exit, left.*

*Silence.*

*Enter from the right the Necrophiliac. A sort of snake has appeared between his legs. He crosses the stage from right to left. He exits, left.*)

GRANDMOTHER: So you see, my child, it is not difficult to be a good housekeeper. Especially if you put my advice to good use. You can see that, although I am old, and can hardly walk, I keep my house bright as a new penny. Believe me, my child, these sloppy women have no excuse. I admit that we may not have the most luxurious furniture, because prices keep going up these days, but I am unable to condone dirty or dusty furniture. Cleanliness doesn't cost anything at all. And still some women are lazy and filthy! How do they keep from blushing for shame! In their position I wouldn't dare ever let anyone even enter my house. Do you understand?

LITTLE GIRL: Oh yes, Grandmother dear. (*Pause; then coldly, but with mild curiosity in her voice*): Why does that man have such a big sex organ now?

GRANDMOTHER: Because now it's getting stiff! (*Pause.*) But there is one thing that you absolutely ought not tolerate: that your husband smoke. Nothing ruins nice, white curtains more quickly; it soon turns them pure yellow. Finally the walls and the whole house end up smelling bad. Besides, it's an unnecessary expense. My husband, your grandfather, God rest his soul (*she makes the sign of the cross*) had this habit, but I succeeded in getting him to give it up. Every time I caught him in the middle of smoking I would open all the windows wide to air out the house and blow away every last trace of smoke from the rooms, rain or shine, snow or storm. He would get so cold that, little by little, he decided to abandon it. Now and then, at first, he would go down into the cellar to have a cigarette, but finally he had to give that up too. What do you say to that?

LITTLE GIRL: You did the right thing, Grandmother.

GRANDMOTHER: In order to keep your floor bright and shiny you will always put a certain number of throw-rugs at the disposition of your visitors; you will never let any enter the dining room without them. The best idea is to stay in the kitchen: you will eat there, and there you will listen to the radio while doing the sewing. The dining room must be kept impeccable so you can receive visitors there on Sundays. You will cover the armchairs with slipcovers during the week. And you will watch out for the sun; it absolutely must not get on the furniture. When you receive guests you will place flowers in the center of the table. Now will you follow my advice to the letter?

LITTLE GIRL: Yes, Grandmother dear.

GRANDMOTHER: If you never forgot the modest suggestions given you by this poor old lady you're certain to end up by creating a happy home atmosphere, just as I have. And you and your future husband will be thankful to me for the rest of your lives.

(*The Two Men enter from the right with the coffin.*

*At once the Necrophiliac enters, following them. The snake which had appeared between his legs is still longer now.*

*The Two Men place the casket on the ground and exit, running.*

*The Necrophiliac throws himself on it. He lifts the cover.*

*He ecstatically contemplates the dead woman.*

*He slowly starts undressing himself, in a manner suggesting some kind of ritual.*

*One by one, he hands his garments to the Grandmother.*

*Finally he penetrates the casket.*

*The Little Girl and the Grandmother watch attentively. The Little Girl is now dressed completely as a communicant.*

*After having contemplated at length what is going on in the casket the Grandmother and the Little Girl walk slowly off toward the left hand side of the stage.)*

LITTLE GIRL (*coldly*): What is he doing to the dead lady?

GRANDMOTHER: He is sleeping with her.

*(The Little Girl and the Grandmother exit, left. In the distance the voice of the Grandmother is heard.)*

VOICE OF GRANDMOTHER: Today, when you receive your first communion, you will become a true little woman. God is going to descend into your heart and remove all your faults. . . .

*(Long silence.*

*The lights dim.*

*The Little Girl dressed for her first communion comes onto the stage, carrying a knife. She approaches the coffin, contemplates at great length what is going on there. Finally she thrusts several times into the casket and into the body of the Necrophiliac.*

*The blood spatters on her communion dress.*

*She laughs.*

*Several red balloons, released from the coffin, rise to the skies.)*

CURTAIN

# THE NEWS ITEM

*by* LAURO OLMO

TRANSLATED BY MARCIA COBOURN WELLWARTH

# THE NEWS ITEM

Lauro Olmo first achieved prominence with *La Camisa* (*The Shirt*), which won the National Literature Prize for 1961–62. The heightened slice-of-life commentary *The News Item* was written in 1963 as part of a group he has planned under the general title *El Cuarto Poder* (*The Fourth Estate*), dealing with the state of the Spanish press today. He could hardly have picked a subject which probes closer to the crux of the mechanics of totalitarianism, for it is clear that those who control the means of communication (which become propaganda in a totalitarian society) control people. One acts on what one knows; and one knows what one is told. We never learn what the news item is which so upsets the readers in this play. For them it is one more straw added to the growing pile; for the news vendor it is the backbreaker. But there is nothing he can do about it: he is alone in the extremity of his indignation. Like the others, he has a family, an institution assiduously fostered by authoritarian societies. Habitual bachelors are considered a danger to society by dictators as much as they are by Puritans. And so the insulting news item is swallowed: another pill to gall the entrails while the face falls back into its uneasy, acquiescent mask. For the readers the vendor's final cry announcing the scores of the football games, opiates of the masses in their own right, is a tremendous relief; for the vendor himself it is the epitome of ironic despair.

G. W.

## CHARACTERS

NEWS VENDOR
FIRST MAN
SECOND MAN
READERS

TIME    the Present

(*At the left, not too far back, a board fence stretches horizontally almost out to the center of the set. It is a fence on which, in large letters, can be read, "Long live the," and no more because the rest is illegible; crossed out with broad streaks of black paint. To the right of the fence is a newsstand, just a step from the side of the stage. The background is clear sky.*

*Leaning against the fence, two men are reading a newspaper, looking very serious. Alongside the newsstand the vendor, also serious, is reading another copy of the same newspaper. From the right another man comes in and stops in front of the newsstand as if requesting a copy of the paper from the vendor. The latter looks at him, and, without stopping what he is doing, indicates by a gesture that the man should help himself. This done he resumes his reading, very intently. The client takes his copy, leaves his money, and, leafing through his paper, walks toward center stage. On arriving there he stops and seems to begin to devote his attention to the same article the others are reading. Suddenly he crushes his paper between his hands and, with a gesture of indignation, throws it on the floor. Quickly he goes on his way and exits. The others look at him. As soon as he is offstage the three of them come together in the center of the stage, exclaiming almost simultaneously:*)

FIRST MAN: It's an outrage!

NEWS VENDOR: There's no explanation for it!

SECOND MAN: This is too much! We've been screwed!

NEWS VENDOR: *You* figure it out.

SECOND MAN: And it happened here. Just think about it! Here!

FIRST MAN: It makes you feel betrayed. How can anyone talk of dignity or honor now?

NEWS VENDOR: I ought to shout it out! I have to shout the news out! (*He brings his hand up to his mouth as if to shout.*)

SECOND MAN (*putting his hand over the vendor's mouth*): Shhh! Have you gone crazy?

NEWS VENDOR: I'm fed up! One of these days I'm going to shout out all the things I've been keeping quiet about ever since . . . (*Seriously, to the First Man.*) Who're you?

SECOND MAN (*forcefully*): Yes! Who are you?

FIRST MAN (*in the same tone*): And you two? Who are you?

NEWS VENDOR: I . . .

SECOND MAN: I . . .

FIRST MAN: Relax. I . . .

NEWS VENDOR: Does it really matter who we are? We're men, aren't we?

SECOND MAN: Frightened men.

NEWS VENDOR: Frightened or not, we're *men!* And things have a limit. And I myself am going to shout, whatever happens. I'll shout, yes! The news is "ta-raa!" like that: so "ta-raa!" I'll shout it out. It's my job to shout it out. That's how I make my living, isn't it? And how I support my family. And I'm not going to go on shirking my job. No! I won't stand for it! The other day I risked everything and shouted out the news. Sure, I know I did it sort of on the sly. I suppose you think it doesn't bother me, eh? But I did it! And my long-lost youth smiled back at me, when I was nineteen and life was bubbling up inside me and pushing me forward.

FIRST MAN: Are you . . . one of those who. . . ?

NEWS VENDOR: No. (*Firmly.*) The opposite.

FIRST MAN: Well, *I'm* one of them. (*Observing the frightened appearance of the other two.*) No, no, don't get upset. I'm just as fed up as you are. And besides . . . too many years have gone by! I have five children, and two little grandchildren. My oldest son is a doctor. The other is a lawyer. The third one died. The lawyer is a socialist. And one of my daughters—there are two of them—one of them is a member of the board of directors of the Young Workers for Catholic Action. The only thing the little one cares about is dancing the twist.

NEWS VENDOR: I am . . . Well, I was a member . . . Actually, I threw away a few years in school and I just avoided flunking out by the skin of my teeth. I tell you again: I was nineteen years old, and life was bubbling up within me.

SECOND MAN: For me politics never . . .

NEWS VENDOR: Politics? Okay, call it that if you like. As I see it, it was just a very messy situation and there was no other way out. And you know what? If things keep on like this we'll be taking up arms all over again. (*To First Man.*) And that will be the end of peace around your little hearth. And as for me . . . Well, back to the scuffle again! (*To Second Man.*) So go ahead and call it politics if you want. They're going to catch you asleep. Are you married?

SECOND MAN: Yes and no.

NEWS VENDOR: Gotta mistress?

SECOND MAN: If you *don't* mind . . .

NEWS VENDOR: Don't get mad. What I wanted to tell you . . . (*He stops talking as he notices the other is holding out some papers of identification.*)

SECOND MAN (*shows the papers and exclaims*): Inspector!

FIRST MAN (*taking a sudden step backwards*): What?

NEWS VENDOR (*same action*): How's that?

SECOND MAN (*serious and justifying himself*): Insurance inspector! You guys didn't let me finish. And you even . . . You even got me scared, too!

NEWS VENDOR (*with enthusiasm*): Life is a funny thing, my friends! Life! It's so . . . So . . . Nuts, I can't think of the right word! (*To First Man.*) And you (*slyly*), you've got a little mistress, eh? Chicks! Women! Even the little birds chirp about them! (*He imitates, whistling, the warble of a bird.*) It's a funny thing, my friends, yes indeed! The other afternoon I picked a lettuce, a nice fresh, firm one, and I ate up the whole thing myself. How good it tasted! I swear to you that it made the tears come to my eyes. (*In an intimate tone.*) And I looked, I looked all over for someone I could thank! Any living creature! Believe me, there are moments when hate is not possible. (*To the Second Man.*) And these moments are worth defending with tooth and nail!

FIRST MAN: Yes—there are moments when everything seems to be made right.

NEWS VENDOR: Yes indeed. Moments in which you open your arms so wide they get dislocated—"pop"—so that everybody will fit in his embrace! Everybody: the tall, the short, the fat, and the skinny! (*Losing his enthusiasm; suddenly hard, serious; he exclaims pointing to the newspaper.*) But then this—news like this!

FIRST MAN (*same as before*): It's an outrage!

NEWS VENDOR: There's no explanation for it!

SECOND MAN: Slander! They've added insult to injury!

NEWS VENDOR (*determined*): Damn it, I'm going to shout it out! (*Lifts his hand to his mouth, like a megaphone.*) *The Daily Wind*—hot off the presses!! Buy *The Daily Wind* with the terrifying news of . . . (*The two men leap on him and clap their hands over his mouth!*)

SECOND MAN: Shut up!

FIRST MAN: Do you want them to . . . ?

NEWS VENDOR (*twisting away from them*): I'm fed up, fed up! (*Facing First Man.*) I've got children, too, do you hear? Two strong lads who shout out whatever they think. And I have to set an example for them. I have to risk shouting my lungs out in the street again. If I don't do it someday something could happen to them: Two shots! Two grotesque flip-flops to the ground! And I'm all alone! I'm left all alone! Alone and rotting away forever! (*Grabbing Second Man by the lapels.*) And you're so calm! You stand peacefully in front of the mirror repeating: "No, for me politics doesn't . . . !" (*Letting go of him.*) If you've got any blood, you've got to realize one thing: that the fact of reading this news item (*Points to it in the paper.*) is a political fact. You've been moved! You've shouted: "This is too much. They've screwed us!" (*To the other.*) You're a witness. (*Turning back to Second Man.*) And your shout has returned my strength to me, it has given me courage. And I know that I am going to shout out the news. Because you, too, said, "It happened here, don't you realize, here!" (*To First Man.*) And you stressed the point: "One feels betrayed. Who can talk now of dignity, of honor? It's an outrage." (*To both.*) I heard you. And you've set something going inside me. (*Again confronting Second Man.*) And I'm not going to let you get away with it if you try to leave me alone with my sons. Actors belong on the stage, sir! Over there the curtain's going up, yes indeed. But no one goes away until it comes down again. Just look how respectable the thing is! But an actor in the street? Raise the curtain and do a pirouette? No! You shouted: "This is too much! They've screwed us!" And since I listened to you and got all excited, you, whether you like it or not, are a politician. Or would you prefer it if I called you a citizen? I'm going to give you some advice: If you really want to keep the cat in the bag, go cut your tongue out! (*Turning around and shouting again.*) *The Daily Wind!* Buy *The Daily Wind* with the terrifying news of ... !

(*Just as before, the two men again succeed in clapping their hands over his mouth. The News Vendor twists around. They struggle a minute. Finally the News Vendor breaks loose, exclaiming:*)

NEWS VENDOR: That's enough!

FIRST MAN: You've got no right to give us away!

SECOND MAN: Go ahead and commit suicide, but do it alone!

(*The two men return to their original position, alongside the fence, looking very serious, and they become involved again in reading the news item. The News Vendor looks at them. Suddenly, going toward them, he exclaims:*)

NEWS VENDOR: And furthermore ... !

BOTH MEN (*cutting him off*): And furthermore, what?

NEWS VENDOR (*pointing out the newspapers to them*): It's published in them. Or didn't you realize that?

SECOND MAN: You think we're stupid?

NEWS VENDOR (*surprised*): Think *we're*?

FIRST MAN: Exactly: think *we're*!

NEWS VENDOR (*to First Man*): Hasn't your son ever said things to you like: No, it's not true that a real union exists among us. The truth is that what we're really united by is fear. A fear that has been growing in us and which makes us nervous every time we go around any corner of the city. The words of my son, do you understand? Nineteen years old, a lathe operator. (*Half begging, half commanding, pointing out the paper to them.*) Read, read it. Out loud, if you please! (*To First Man.*) Our sons are young. And at the age of nineteen it's not easy to sit still and keep quiet. Please, read it out loud! Comment on it out loud! Let's set an example! (*To Second Man.*) You, what's your opinion? Don't back down! Keep saying that this news item is just too much! That we've been screwed! (*To*

*First Man.*) You feel betrayed, yes. Say it! Now, you have to say it now! I'm going to shout it out. I'll shout it out, yes! Read it, read it out loud! Each one of you read a little bit, okay? Or, if you prefer, we'll all read it together. That's an idea, a good idea! Okay? You'll see with what pride, with what enthusiasm I'll shout it out, then! (*To Second Man.*) Life is a funny thing, sir! Chicks! Women! (*To both.*) I told you that business about the lettuce, didn't I? (*To First Man.*) And you spoke about "Moments when everything seems to be made right." It used to be like that, right? So shout, shout it out with me: *The Daily Wind!* Buy *The Daily Wind* with the terrifying . . . !

FIRST MAN (*authoritative*): Shut up!

SECOND MAN (*the same*): Everything has a limit!

NEWS VENDOR (*restrained*): I . . . I thought . . .

SECOND MAN: What did you think?

NEWS VENDOR: I thought . . .

FIRST MAN: Shut up!

SECOND MAN (*almost simultaneously*): Shut up!

(*A man enters and picks up a newspaper. The vendor goes up to his stand and collects the money which the new customer hands out to him. Everything in complete silence. Opening the paper, the buyer goes and takes up his stand with his back to the fence, alongside the First and Second Man. Another man comes in and does the same thing after buying his paper. And another. And another. The more the better. Until they take up the whole fence, always reading in silence.*

*The News Vendor, nervous, takes two or three steps. Finally he decides and shouts out:*)

NEWS VENDOR: *The Daily Wind!* (*Instantly the readers along the fence lower their papers and shoot glances at him. The News Vendor stares back at them a moment. Finally, decided, he shouts:*) Buy *The Daily Wind* with the results of the football games!

ALL THE READERS (*with relief and enthusiasm*): On what page?

NEWS VENDOR (*with disgust*): Look it up!

CURTAIN

# FOOTBALL

*by* JOSÉ-MARÍA BELLIDO

TRANSLATED BY DAVID TURNER

NOTE TO THE READER: It has not been possible for the publishers to include in this volume the musical score that should accompany the following special sections in *Football* by José-María Bellido: "The Song of the Blind Man," "The March of the Slaves," "The Debutantes' Twist," and "The Dance of the Man in the Vest." Those interested in having this music for performances of the play should write to the author c/o Kurt Hellmer, 52 Vanderbilt Avenue, New York, N.Y. 10017.

Contemporary Spanish drama has divided itself into two principal categories: light comedy of the Broadway-West End-Boulevard variety and political allegory. Both these forms are directly attributable to the censorship system which is in force in Spain. Under this system only these two types of drama are possible. The former is designed to keep the populace entertained while avoiding all topical issues, unless it be for the purpose of making an obligatory obeisance to the Establishment. The latter attempts to criticize by indirection, partially for artistic reasons and partially because of a desire to get past the censor, if possible (subtle intellect, as Shaw long ago pointed out, never being a censor's strong suit). The political allegory being written in Spain today usually takes one of two forms: either historical allegory, in which parallels to the present political situation in Spain are sought in her past history, as in Alberti's *Night and War in the Prado Museum*; or fantastic allegories, in which imaginary situations and countries are created to reflect contemporary Spain. *Football* by José-María Bellido (b. 1922) is perhaps the most elaborate and carefully worked out example of the latter type.

Bellido sets his play in an imaginary village curiously similar to Spain: a sort of down-at-the-heels microcosm. Thirty years before, civil war in the form of a football (i.e., soccer) match had taken place in this village. And now the winners lord it over the losers with their gleaming new uniforms and their shiny, bright soccer balls, symbols of a strutting, cock-of-the-walk *machismo*, the Latin mystique of virility. The losers—crushed, poverty-stricken, dressed in threadbare uniforms and bouncing degrading, Yo-Yo-like rubber balls—nurse their grievances and hope for better days. Whenever they try to forget their loss and bolster their egos by carrying soccer balls, these are quickly and contemptuously deflated by the awls of the police. All their hopes are pinned on a mystical prophecy that a divine referee will come and save them by reversing the disputed result of the fatal match. And they have one material hope, too. From the second generation of the team has come Zapatoni, the super-star, symbol of the latent strength and material potential of their village. And just as the tremendous industrial potential smoldering beneath the surface of Spain (where it has been kept untouched by the smugly complacent "Athletic Club" members, who have been too busy preening and strutting and crowing over their fallen opponents for thirty years) is coveted by the two great opposing world powers, so in the play Nestor and Fani, caricatured Russian and American respectively, try to buy Zapatoni for their teams. Salvador, the ridiculous little Christ figure, the "referee from the sky," tries vainly to bring peace with his ineffectual bible reading and humanitarian pleading. The leaders of the two clubs combine to sell out their people; and Salvador is killed by a shot which could only have come from the church tower. Bellido deliberately leaves the origin of the shot ambiguous: it came from the direction of the church tower, but Fani enters with a rifle at the end. The members of the two clubs unite to fight for their freedom together, for they cannot trust their leaders; or the outside powers represented by Fani and Nestor; or the Church, which has blessed their football games for so long.

G. W.

# CHARACTERS

SALVADOR, A bit-part actor in a traveling company, aged between forty-five and sixty

BARTO, Manager of the Athletic Club, 30–35 years

LONDEQUE, Manager of the one-time United Club, 40–48 years

TICHOMI, Bar owner

NESTOR, Tiger hunter

FANI, Oil prospector

ROBERT, Bus driver, 25–30 years

ZAPATONI, Talented young footballer, 16–20 years

LOSING OPTIMIST, 16–20 years

UNITED CLUB MEMBER

ATHLETIC CLUB MEMBER

YOUTH A

YOUTH B

BLIND MAN, 40–50 years

KOPAS, President of the Athletic

RABIT, Former president of the United

BRAD 1, Local police chief

BRAD 2, Police chief's assistant

Company of actors, referees who carry placards, slaves.

The action takes place in a small town in the South of Europe. Time: the present. A rainy afternoon in May.

# ACT ONE

## Scene 1

(*House lights out. Suddenly the left of the proscenium is lit by a spotlight. A march is played. Moving to the rhythm of the march, a man dressed as a football referee enters from the left and moves across the forestage to the right; he holds above his head a placard which reads: "The teams are coming out of the tunnel." He is followed by another man dressed in an identical manner carrying a board which reads: "Warming-up routine." Similarly, a third enters with a sign which reads: "Football Derby. The teams pose for the Press."*

*As soon as the third placard has disappeared, the first man re-enters, this time from the right and moving to the left; he holds a board which reads: "Line up." The second man follows with a sign reading: "Toss up." Finally the third man re-enters with the notice: "Can you spot the winner?"*

*These men carrying placards march off in time to the music, and put on the masks of "happy, smiling people." The last of the three, before making his exit, right, will remain absolutely still before the audience, displaying his sign. A referee's whistle is heard and the actor swiftly turns the board. On the other side appears in large letters the directive: "Spot the winner!" Offstage a male voice shouts, "This side will win." The actor points with his right arm towards the left. The male voice shouts again, ". . . Or this side will win." The actor points with his left arm toward the right. He follows this movement with a gesture which indicates: "Who the hell can tell?"*

*The follow spot which up till now has been on the actor suddenly widens its diameter. The curtain will rise, revealing a drop gauze, in the center of which is painted a map. A referee's whistle is heard and the actor leaves, left.*

*At the foot of the map are the phrases: "Guide to our Town. Scale: 0 = 1,000." The map is trapezoidal in shape. Admitting that there can be a certain similarity between the shape of the map and that of Spain, I indicate below possible locations of the monuments and places of interest in our town which are printed on the map.*

*Football Stadium = Caspe*
*Bull Ring = Seville*

333

Recreation Club = Malaga
Sports' Club = Asturias
Orange Grove = Valencia
Olive Grove = Jaen
Town Hall = Madrid
Church of St. Anne = Bilbao
Banderillas Co., Inc. = Cordoba
Wicker Work Co., Inc. = Barcelona
Straw Hats Co., Inc. = Alicante
Mineral Oil Co., Inc. = Zaragoza
Garbage Dump, Wild Beasts = Galicia

*After some fifteen seconds one of the three referees appears again on the left. He carries a placard reading: "Up the Athletic!" Below this inscription is an arrow pointing to the other side of the stage. A rock-'n-roll group launches into a number. The Group is behind the drop with the map, on stage right. The drop rises slowly.)*

## SCENE 2

*(Played before drapes which are hung as near as possible to the front of the stage. Using a rhythm of two beats to the bar and miming with their bodies and limbs, the following characters are positioned in a line to the right of the stage. According to the resources of the company, the following characters from the ranks of the "Athletic," in order of importance, are presented.*

THE GROUP. *Dressed in purple dinner jackets. They continuously play percussion instruments.*

THE GREEN BULLFIGHTERS. *Dressed in green—and headgear. They remain stolidly next to the Group.*

THE MAN WITH THE SILK HAT. *Dressed in tails, blue football shorts, football boots and blue stockings and pompoms. He has a pointed handlebar moustache and a small pointed beard.*

THE DIGNIFIED LADIES. *Wearing evening dress. Bejewelled, refined, low necklines, fat, dyed hair, heavily made up.*

MIDDLE-AGED LADIES. *Similar to the previous ones, only younger.*

THE YOUNG BULLFIGHTER. *Dressed in a splendiferous silk sheen costume. He carries a cape.*

THE SHAREHOLDERS. *Middle aged and very elegant. They push the Young Bullfighter toward the public.*

THE MAN WITH THE BULL'S HEAD. *He is elegant and holds a bull's head made of cardboard.*

THE SAD GIRL FROM CORDOBA. *A gypsy dancer dressed in butter muslin. She poses as if to begin dancing a Sevillana. Body stretched upwards, hands above her head, she is next to the Young Bullfighter.*

THE EXCEEDINGLY FRUITFUL MOTHER. *Young, attractive, pushing a fancy baby carriage.*

THE WONDERFUL BOYS. *Short blue trousers, blue socks and boots. They carry phonograph records. White shirts and bow ties.*

THE NICE YOUNG LADIES. *Blue bikinis. High heels.*

*Masks are not absolutely necessary but they can be used as long as they help to define the exact characteristics of each type. Six or seven steering wheels can be distributed among the group (Boys, Girls and Shareholders). Each actor would then mime steering a car.*

*The whole group gives out plenty of merriment, smiles are exchanged and now and again there are peals of laughter.*

*After a few moments, the referee's whistle is heard, but nobody takes any notice of it. On the contrary, they suggest it has no significance for them. Eventually, the Shareholders indicate to the Group that it should stop playing and The Man in the Silk Hat comes downstage. He opens his arms as a preliminary to singing. At this moment, the Man with the Bull's Head puts on the cardboard disguise and begins to attack the Young Bullfighter. The Sad Girl from Cordoba now dances with great dignity to the rhythm of the seguidilla.)*

THE MAN WITH THE SILK HAT (*singing with plenty of flamenco flourish*):
> Can any town in the whole wide world
> Offer you so much as our town, days or nights?
> Flamenco dancing and magnificent womanhood,
> Permanent sunshine . . . and don't forget the bullfights!

(*On to the refrain. The Whole Group choruses "Oles" at the end of each rhythmical phrase.*)

THE MAN WITH THE SILK HAT:
> There is no town in the world like my town,

A perfectly organized municipality,
Golden beaches, delicate wines,
Haute cuisine . . . but we've got no money.

(*On to the chorus. The Whole Group intersperses "Oles" as
before.*)

THE SHAREHOLDERS:
                    Come and invest, come and invest,
                    Friends from foreign lands
        Repeat { We assure you that your money
               { Is safe when in our hands.

THE WHOLE GROUP (*in unison*):
        We assure you that your money
        Is safe when in our hands.

(*The above song of the Man in the Silk Hat has been accompanied by a guitar which blares out through the loudspeakers
of the auditorium. As the Chorus enters with, "We assure
you . . . ," the Group strikes up on its cymbals, drums, etc., in
such a way that the song of the Wonderful Boys and the Nice
Young Ladies blends with the foregoing.*)

THE WONDERFUL BOYS AND THE NICE YOUNG LADIES (*singing shrilly*):
        Patronage,
        We want your patronage.
        Tourists,
        Please give us patronage
        For the sake of our standard of living.

THE FROGMAN (*entering from the left in underwater gear. He carries a number of black scarves*): One moment! Seemliness, if
you don't mind! No stark reality, please!

(*The Group stops playing, the Boys and Young Ladies freeze
in their actions and are silent. The Frogman covers the girls'
limbs with the black pieces of material.*)

THE FROGMAN: Let there be rhythm and melody, the harmony of
God's chosen. (*He blows on a toy trumpet which is hanging
round his neck. The Group starts playing again.*)

THE WONDERFUL BOYS: OK, Daddyo! (*They sing in unison with the
Young Ladies.*)
        Your sins, your sins,
        Can always be forgiven.
        But we must have sins—

And patrons, too—
For the sake of our standard of living.

(*As the Chorus begins to sing the last line, there is heard far off the opening bars of the March of the Slaves. It is sung by a male chorus. While this tune swells in intensity, the members of the Athletic Club start leaving the stage. The Wonderful Boys and the Nice Young Ladies offer some opposition by singing in a low voice the last line of their song for a second time. Eventually the Frogman is alone on the stage, staring with bulging eyes at those who are about to appear from the left. Now and again he blows his trumpet and makes gestures to them that they should stop in their tracks. But the torrent of male voices pours across the stage.*

*Darkness. A spotlight illuminates the desperate gestures of the Frogman. Eventually he too leaves, following in the direction of the last of the Athletic Club Members.*)

## Scene 3

(*After a few moments of almost complete darkness, the stage is illuminated very slowly. The drop curtain of bright, cheerful, springlike tones which served as a background to the previous scene has now been exchanged for one which is sad, murky, and lugubrious. The slaves appear from the left, dragging themselves along the ground in time to the music.*

*During the scene the slaves rise, first onto their knees and then onto their feet. When they leave, right, they should be upright, valiant, chests expanded, and have confident, threatening gestures. Their precise moment of departure is when the chorus of male voices intones the doh-me-soh of the final bars.*

*The group of slaves is made up of: The Wrinkled Old Woman in Rags; all her clothing is black; a black handkerchief covers her head; yellowish skin; thin, sad; she has a walking staff. The Donkey Man; a middle-aged farm laborer; he pulls on the halter of an ass which has a heavy load of firewood. The Children Without Handkerchiefs; dirty, beggars' apprentices, faces smeared with snot; patched clothing, five or six years old; they hold the hands of the Defenseless Being. The Defenseless Being; he stares upwards to the heavens; he feels himself to be powerless, defeated; he has lost faith in everything. The Man With a Bike; he appears among the rear of the crowd when the slaves move forward on their knees; an old bicycle is slung on his shoulder.*

*The Miner, The Man with the Yellow Skin, The Hindustani, The Negroes, The Barge Lad, who carries a monkey wrench, A Solderer whose blowlamp is lit, The Shivering Girls who wear threadbare coats, collars turned up, rubbing their hands, going to or coming from work.*

*The Intellectuals; books underneath their arm, parchment skin, several days' growth of beard, cigarette butts in their lips, the lapels of their jackets drawn across their chests to protect them from the cold of the great storm. The Industrious Women; burdened with baskets of recently laundered clothing or with baskets of green vegetables and seven-pound loaves; babies at their breasts.*

*Just as the characters who appeared in the second scene were dressed in clothing of bright, gay tones (Green, pink, yellow, blue —particularly blue) the actors who interpret this scene are dressed in black which slowly turns to red. The last to appear will be dressed entirely in red. This effect can be produced by means of the filters in the spotlights.*

*As the last of the slaves disappears stage right, the backdrop of this scene is hoisted rapidly and at the same time the lighting goes up to its maximum. There appears another curtain on which is written:*

*Joe Bloggs (here we see the full name of the director) presents:*

FOOTBALL
*A Musical Farce in two acts by*
*José María Bellido*
*Words and music by the author*

*The musical background is once again the march which was played previously. The inscribed curtain is held for a few seconds for the audience to read.)*

SCENE 4

*(The scene presents the one and only bar of a small town in the south of Europe. For the moment it is in darkness. We can scarcely make out the outlines of the actors who are motionless.*

*The march stops playing and there are a few moments of silence.
Then simultaneously a single spotlight comes up and a Toccata of
Bach's is heard. The spotlight picks out the roof of the auditorium
and then the boxes. Next the beam glides slowly over the stage
decor. It comes to rest on a group consisting of: Barto, Londeque
and Tichomi. A moment later the spotlight moves to Nestor and
Fani, then to The Members of the United Sportsclub, and finally
to The Members of the Athletic Club. This central spotlight goes
out, the music stops and a fresh spotlight shines diagonally across
the stage from proscenium right. It is centered on the Blind Man
who has come on stage a few moments before from the left. He has
a white stick.)*

THE BLIND MAN *(singing)*:
          He'll arrive with his face half-hidden,
          On a rainy afternoon in May.
          He'll come down from the heavens, the Savior
          Who'll bring peace to my people and my town.
          Referee . . .

*(The spotlight cuts in and out as if it were lightning. At the
same time thunder is heard.)*

          Referee,
          Referee, Mediator, Referee,
          Referee we have dreamt of,
          Referee long-awaited,
          Referee, Mediator, Referee!

*(The spotlight centers on the face of the Blind Man. It goes
out and the Blind Man leaves. The scene is then lit, giving the
impression of late afternoon.)*

VOICE OFFSTAGE: An afternoon in May. A small town, off the beaten
          track, in an underdeveloped country.

*(There's nothing modern about this bar. Sporting calendars
and yellowing photographs of footballers hang on the walls.
There is also a bull's head. The walls are a dingy ochre. Plaster
is peeling off here and there. There are blotches of faded paint.
A thick brush has been used to daub on the walls phrases
which allude to the problem at the heart of all the characters:
"Long Live the Athletic!" . . . "Down with the United!" . . .
"Zapatoni, Get Cracking!" . . . "Who Swindled us out of the
Cup?" . . . "The hell with Barto!")*

*The bar counter, downstage left, is crude and old fashioned.
Behind it stands Tichomi, bordering on 60, fat, high com-
plexioned. He is dressed in a sleeveless shirt with red and
white horizontal stripes. It is crumpled, shrunken, patched and
darned. He wears white shorts hidden behind an apron which
covers the front of his legs.*

*Barto and Londeque are seated on stools on the other side of
the bar. Barto is dressed in a blue jersey, closed at the neck,
and has blue shorts. Everything about him is brand new and
brash, including his specially styled football boots and white
stockings. He exudes decision, arrogance and strength. He carries under his arm a brand new football which he now and
again bounces and tosses about.*

*Londeque is 40 years old, worn out, bald and with glasses. We
guess that he was interested in sports when young. He wears
an old red jersey, similar in shape to Barto's, white shorts and
red socks. His football boots are hacked to pieces. Hanging
from the middle finger of his left hand is a small rubber ball
which he nervously bounces against the floor. He is introspec-
tive and defeated. Barto helps himself from a bottle of champagne. Londeque drinks cheap red wine. There are a variety
of bottles on the shelves behind the bar.*

*Youth A and Youth B are playing bar-football. Around the
bar-football table which is up right, are a number of comfortable armchairs. In one of them is seated another young Member of the Athletic Club. These three youths are dressed in
red and white shirts with vertical stripes, blue shorts and white
socks. Their clothes are brand new.*

*Downstage left, drinking wine from a jug, are seated the Los-
ing Optimist, the Member of the United Club, and Zapatoni.
All three are dressed in short-sleeved shirts with red and yellow
horizontal stripes, white shorts, red socks and track boots. All
their clothing is well worn. They are excited, arguing and gesticulating. Near the bar-football machine taken over by the
members of the Athletic Club are three large, new footballs.*

*The members of the United Club play about with the same
kind of rubber ball as Londeque.*

*Downstage right are Nestor and Fani. Their faces are lit in such
a way that the features have strong highlights and deep shad-*

*ows. They are seated on either side of a table full of empty beer bottles. They make gestures which indicate that they feel the heat. They drink and argue. Nestor, aged 50, is dressed in a dark jumper, covered with medals and decorations, black rubber boots which cover his calves, a cossack hat and wide trousers with the legs tucked into the boots.*

*Fani, the same age as Nestor, wears an exotic shirt, dark glasses, cowboy trousers, and a camera hanging from his shoulder.*

*To the rear, a wooden door provided with a wooden bar to secure it from the inside. The door gives on to the street. To the right, a door which leads to the stables and to the yard. Beyond the bar, two doors labeled "Ladies" and "Gents" and above them the phrase, "If you want me, I'm here."*

*Fani and Nestor fan themselves.*

*At the beginning of the action, Tichomi is talking to Barto and Londeque.*

*The action begins.*

*Youth A claps his hands for service and looks toward Tichomi.)*

TICHOMI (*responding*): What is it? (*In reply, Youth A waves an empty bottle.*) Right you are . . . right! (*Tichomi gets another bottle of champagne from behind the bar and starts peeling off the wire and silver paper.*) They're going at it a bit, aren't they, Señor Barto?

BARTO: Eh?

TICHOMI: Your lads.

BARTO: Bah! Let 'em be. Give 'em what they ask for. They played like marvels this afternoon. (*To Londeque.*) You hear that, Londeque? They played like marvels! (*He claps his hand on Londeque's shoulder.*)

LONDEQUE: Leave me alone, can't you?

(*Tichomi moves from the bar with the bottle of champagne.*)

YOUTH A (*to Youth B*): Come on . . . help yourself! It's the last one. Get it down!

LOSING OPTIMIST: Not another spot! Not another spot will pass my lips. Why do you want me to drink? I ask you, why do you want me to drink? So that I'm happy, is that it? . . . There's no cause to be happy. So that I forget? That's what you want me to do, isn't it? Forget!

TICHOMI (*uncorking the bottle near the Losing Optimist*): Shhh!

LOSING OPTIMIST: I don't want to go home through the streets, singing at the top of my voice, laughing like an idiot. I'm not going to let that Barto think I can be happy. So no more drink. (*He throws the jug on the ground.*)

BARTO: What's wrong with him?

TICHOMI (*rapidly picking up the jug while the Losing Optimist becomes calmer and sits down. Tichomi continues to bounce his rubber ball all the time*): Nothing, Señor Barto. It was me. I knocked it over by mistake.

YOUTH B (*to Tichomi*): Come on, then, hurry up! We're dying of thirst here!

BARTO (*to Losing Optimist*): So you'd like to play football once more, is that it? (*He smiles sarcastically.*) You poor old wreck!

FANI (*foreign accent*): The midday temperature was eighty-five degrees . . . not a degree under.

NESTOR: Eighty-five? You're out of your mind! It couldn't be eighty-five!

FANI: Fahrenheit.

NESTOR: Ah, Fahrenheit. (*Tichomi serves the two youths, A and B.*) Yes, of course, you've still got those ridiculous thermometers.

FANI: Traditional.

NESTOR: Traditional . . . ridiculous . . . same thing.

FANI: And what about your alphabet? It isn't like anybody else's alphabet.

TICHOMI (*referring to new footballs*): Very nice cover . . . lovely paneling.

YOUTH A: They were given as first prize in the Intermediate Examination for Religious Knowledge. The Inspector came to see our college, you see . . . and he put this problem to us. A man has got nine children. Suddenly he learns that his wife is going

to have yet another. So he buys a candle three feet high, strikes a match and lights it, simply to show how overjoyed he is. Now then, what is his name? Bill Loaf or Bill Laugh?

TICHOMI (*after thinking about it*): Bill Loaf.

MEMBER OF UNITED: Bill Laugh.

YOUTH B: Sorry, neither. Bill Leaf. (*Pronounced "Belief."*)

YOUTH A: That's it . . . Belief! I gave the answer and as a reward, the Inspector presented our class with these footballs. As soon as he'd gone, the teacher gave us the rest of the day off so we could practice.

BARTO: He knows how to use his heels, this one. (*Miming.*) You move forward, don't you, lad, then suddenly—back with your heel, still on the trot. Oh yes, they've got very pretty footwork. Nice to see it, lads! Mmm? (*Seeing that Londeque is taking no notice.*) Well, what's up with you today? (*Offering him the bottle of champagne.*) Here you are . . . have a swig.

LONDEQUE (*shakes his head*): No, I'd rather stay with the wine. (*Raising his glass.*) Wine, red wine! It burns out your guts, but all the same, red wine forever!

BARTO: Off he goes . . . tut-tut-tut . . . off he goes!

TICHOMI (*to group of United supporters in a low voice*): Have you been to work today?

ZAPATONI: No.

UNITED MEMBER: We're not turning up tomorrow, either.

LOSING OPTIMIST (*indicating Zapatoni*): Not till they let him play football.

TICHOMI: I should look out if I were you. They've told me that the Brads . . .

LOSING OPTIMIST: I know. We're being watched. (*He shrugs his shoulders.*) Yesterday we pinched an old football from that pack of madmen. (*Indicating the Athletic Group.*) We met Zapatoni, went down to an empty lot and practiced cornering. Anyway, the Brads turned up. They didn't catch us, though.

FANI: For God's sake, man, to some extent . . . yes.

NESTOR: What's the difficulty, then?

FANI: After every match, we've always destroyed the footballs, haven't we? My firm, Metacarpis Limited, makes the finest footballs in the world. There's years and years of wear in a Metacarpis football. But, I ask you, if we allow footballs to be used over and over again, what would happen to all the Metacarpis football factories?

(*Tichomi moves behind bar and speaks to Barto and Londeque*)

NESTOR: Train your workers to make leather jackets and footwear instead.

FANI: OK . . . where's your market? Who'll buy 'em?

NESTOR: If there's nobody to buy 'em, give 'em away. There are plenty of people in this world going about ill clad and ill shod.

FANI (*solemnly*): Very well. Let 'em first learn how to play football and we'll supply 'em with boots and shirts as part of our program.

(*The Losing Optimist stands on his seat and waves his arm in an aggressive manner at Barto.*)

UNITED MEMBER (*trying to pull him down*): Sit down! Don't be a damn fool!

LOSING OPTIMIST: Let go of me!

ZAPATONI: Don't start anything! There's no point to it. Take it easy. Remember the Blind Man . . . remember his words. There's truth in those words!

LOSING OPTIMIST: Let go of me, I tell you.

ZAPATONI: He's coming . . . got it? He's coming with his face half hidden . . . on a May afternoon when it's pouring cats and dogs. He's coming from up there and he's bringing peace to this town. That's what the Blind Man says.

LOSING OPTIMIST: Upstairs? Nothing comes from upstairs . . . nothing any good, anyway. So let go of me.

TICHOMI: No, Señor Barto. Give people a fair hearing. It was a good match . . . a brilliant match.

LOSING OPTIMIST: If I could get that Barto by himself, without any Brads to come to his aid . . .

ZAPATONI: Shut up, will you?

BARTO: Shut your trap, for Chrissake . . . don't make me laugh.

TICHOMI: That's how it was, I tell you. Celestino wasn't offside.

UNITED MEMBER (*to Zapatoni*): Listen! They're talking about your Dad.

TICHOMI: Pinocho wasn't up with the forwards. He was outside the penalty area, tying up his boot.

FANI: Only one boot, you say?

NESTOR: Exactly. You'd make the right boot and we'd make the left.

FANI (*smiles*): Oh, yes . . . and what would your good friend Chou-en-Fung say to all this?

BARTO: All right, then, he was tying up his boot! What of it?

TICHOMI: And when Voldova returned the ball to him . . . bang! Onto his toe . . . and into the net.

LONDEQUE (*becoming interested*): No, he stopped it with his chest . . . then he kicked it. I was five yards away from him.

TICHOMI: Oh no, it wasn't, Londeque. It was a straight shot . . . onto his toe and into the net.

BARTO (*angrily*): He stopped it with his hand.

LONDEQUE: Ah well, here we go . . . here we go again.

TICHOMI: It was a straight shot.

BARTO (*taking his football and kicking it in fury*): He stopped it with his hand, I tell you! He stopped it with his hand. I saw him!

TICHOMI: How old were you? You must have been in the cradle.

BARTO: With his hand . . . It was a foul. Got it?

LONDEQUE: I saw him stop it with his chest.

TICHOMI: Onto his toe and into the net.

BARTO: I tell you he stopped it with his hand!

TICHOMI: Oh no, he didn't. It was a straight shot. All the same . . .

BARTO (*moving with his football through the bar. The Athletic Club Members stop playing bar-football and stare at Londeque and the United Members. A moment of extreme tension*): It was a foul, a dirty, filthy foul! He stopped it with his hand!

ATHLETIC CLUB MEMBERS (*as a chorus*): He stopped it with his hand!

YOUTH B: Long live the Athletic!

BARTO, YOUTH B AND OTHER ATHLETIC CLUB MEMBERS (*as a chorus*): Hooray!

YOUTH B: Down with the United!

CHORUS (*as before*): Boo!

LONDEQUE: Well, p'raps you're right. It all took place a long time ago. (*The Losing Optimist moves in a threatening manner from the table towards the bar.*) All the same, it seemed to me he stopped it with his chest.

LOSING OPTIMIST: You're right, Londeque. He stopped it with his chest. It was my father and he stopped that ball with his chest. He told me so himself. Take no notice of what Barto says. Take no notice of these liars.

(*Barto throws himself on the Losing Optimist. He knocks him down and then moves off in the direction of the street door, shouting:*)

BARTO: Brads! . . . Brads!

LOSING OPTIMIST (*with a bottle in his hand, moving after Barto, shouting*): My father was not a liar!

(*The Athletic Club Members launch themselves upon him, take the bottle from him, beat him and knock him to the ground. He tries to get up. Tichomi has moved from behind the bar and is at his side.*)

TICHOMI: Take it easy, will you, for God's sake!

LOSING OPTIMIST: Why do they have to insult my father?

ZAPATONI: I'd get out of here if I were you.

BARTO (*on the threshold, shouting*): Come on, get over here! Brads!

LOSING OPTIMIST: He stopped it with his chest, Señor Tichomi. You've told me so yourself many a time.

TICHOMI: He might have stopped it with his hand, inadvertent-like. He probably *did* stop it with his hand. (*Looking at Londeque.*) No?

(*Londeque moves from the bar and drinks from the jug.*)

TICHOMI: You'd better sit down and keep quiet.

BARTO (*entering in a threatening manner. He stands in the center of the stage, his feet apart, erect*): This town will not permit insubordination. You will now see how the rebellious are punished.

LOSING OPTIMIST (*sitting at his table but struggling to get up*): Why, Señor Tichomi, why? Señor Londeque . . . why? You played in that match with my father, side by side, shoulder to shoulder. Why won't you speak out?

TICHOMI: Best forget. Let sleeping dogs lie.

LOSING OPTIMIST: And why must *I* forget, and not *they?*

(*The Brads enter by the street door, advancing with the goose step. The two of them are dressed in light green shorts and large, soft, flat hats. Each carries in his right hand a bradawl. They halt and come to attention, making a salute with their fists holding the bradawl. Instead of the flat hats, they can wear a fireman's helmet.*)

BRAD 1: Your orders, sir?

THE UNITED (*low murmur*): The Brads!

BARTO (*singing the "ee" sound as a sergeant major would*): Dee-ee-flate!

BRAD 1: Sah!

BARTO: Bradawls at the ready!

BRAD 1 (*menacingly*): Which one, sir?

BARTO (*pointing at Losing Optimist*): Him!

(*They turn with puppetlike military movements and goose step toward the table where the Losing Optimist is seated.*)

BRAD 1: Hand it over!

LOSING OPTIMIST (*standing and turning his back*): I don't want to.

LONDEQUE: Give it him. . . . For God's sake give it him!

ZAPATONI: Go on!

(*The Losing Optimist reluctantly hands over his small rubber ball to the Brad 1. He and his companion turn in a semicircle and approach the audience. Then they turn inward, face to face. Brad 1, very stiff, gives the ball to Brad 2 who blows it up a little and holds it in the air. Brad 1 stabs it with his bradawl. The ball hisses. The United Members chorus "Oooh!" The Brads turn their backs to the audience and advance with the miserable bit of rubber to the table. The Brads are now facing Barto, who laughs, as do the other Athletic Members. He rubs his hands with glee. The Losing Optimist weeps and his club companions console him.*)

BARTO: No more, Brad. You can go now. (*The Brads repeat their fist salute.*) Wait! Any news?

BRAD 1: Yes, sir. On guard duty at sixteen hours today . . . young persons from the United were discovered with balls blown up beyond regulation limits. They were near the straw hat factory, sir.

BARTO: Playing football?

BRAD 1: Difficult to ascertain, sir. Immediately routed.

BARTO: Be vigilant . . . ever vigilant.

BRAD 1: As always, sir.

(*Click of heels, salute, halt, turn. They leave.*)

BARTO (*moving toward the bar, rubbing his hands*): Mission accomplished.

TICHOMI (*to Barto*): Whose round is it? What's everyone having?

LONDEQUE: I'm not drinking this time. (*He pushes the glass away from him.*)

BARTO (*moving to the United Members*): You know now, don't you? He stopped it with his hand. Why? Because that Celestino was a dirty player and a filthy bastard. Got it? (*He makes a threatening gesture to the Losing Optimist.*)

YOUTH A: He's a real tough guy, isn't he?

YOUTH B: He's got 'em where he wants 'em.

ATHLETIC MEMBER: You won't find a better trainer than him!

YOUTH A: He's got 'em by the short hairs.

YOUTH B: And what about their trainer, eh? Him over there . . . Londeque?

YOUTH A (*jeering*): Bah . . . that poor old wreck! They haven't got a hope in hell, have they? Not a hope in hell.

ATHLETIC MEMBER: He was all right in his day, you know. Dad used to tell me he could set up a match box, shoot the ball from twenty yards and knock it down.

FANI (*refusing Nestor's matches*): Matches? No, thanks. I've got my lighter. . . . We've got the same trouble back home, you know. Every football we make is deemed obsolescent after its first match. We gather them in and burn them. However, there are a lot of pirate clubs not on our agency list. They try to practice the game with footballs made out of newspaper.

NESTOR: I follow.

BARTO (*at the bar with Londeque*): I do not follow nor do I give a damn. The goal was disallowed and that's that.

LONDEQUE: Oh well, there's no talking to you, is there?

FANI: It's talking for talking's sake. The proposition is so unheard of it would arouse suspicion.

YOUTH A: Who do you suspect then?

YOUTH B: This here draftsman.

YOUTH A: And he works for your father, does he?

BARTO: My father was certain of it. It was a penalty, if ever there was one—a penalty.

LONDEQUE: Can I say something?

BARTO (*scornfully*): Say what?

LONDEQUE: If your father told you that . . . all respects due . . . it points to one thing: he knew nothing about football.

TICHOMI (*moving toward Barto to avoid a possible reaction*): Calm now, Señor Barto . . . calm!

BARTO (*without any reaction*): Nothing to worry about, Tichomi. It's quite obvious our friend here is talking through his wounds, as you might say . . . and is trying to make the best show he can. They lost and they still haven't accepted the fact.

LONDEQUE (*wildly*): We lost because of that penalty!

BARTO (*joking*): Oh, so now you're going to tell me you lost because the referee was on our side?

LONDEQUE: Exactly. And I shall go on repeating it. We lost because that Sampson . . . or Sholson . . . or—

TICHOMI: Simpson.

LONDEQUE: Simpson, that's it!

BARTO: The finest referee in Europe! The one and only!

LONDEQUE: Simpson . . . that's his name, the swine!

NESTOR: Pork? Oh, you mean swine meat? And only once a week, you say?

FANI: On Tuesdays.

(*They speak quickly.*)

NESTOR: For dinner?

FANI: I prefer it for lunch.

NESTOR: Or perhaps breakfast?

FANI: Or before breakfast?

NESTOR: So you have it for dinner, then?

FANI: Dinner? How do you mean, dinner?

NESTOR: Before breakfast is the same as saying after dinner of the previous day and before breakfast on the following day.

FANI: Which following day?

NESTOR: The day which follows the day of the dinner on the day previous to the day you have your breakfast.

FANI: What breakfast?

NESTOR: You are not in favor of the center forward eating pork, are you?

FANI: No, because it's harmful.

YOUTH B: Harmful. Bernard Harmful, that's his name. Not a bad draftsman, either. He's invented a safety match for courting couples ... with two heads.

ATHLETIC MEMBER (*surprised*): I see.

YOUTH B: Anyway, he's written to the Football Association.

YOUTH A: What ... with a safety match?

YOUTH B: No, with a typewriter. He tells the lot of them he's going to try to get that Cup Final disallowed.

YOUTH A: You're joking!

BARTO: You're joking! You actually think you can buy up a referee?

LONDEQUE: If you've got enough money ... yes.

(*The street door opens suddenly. The two sections bang against the wall. Wind howls. Lightning flashes, followed by thunder. Robert enters with a dripping umbrella. His face is almost concealed behind a thick muffler, which he unties as he enters. He shakes his umbrella to get rid of the water. Everyone stares at him, fascinated, except for Fani and Nestor, who continue their conversation, gesticulating. Robert meets the silent stares by studying the faces and garments of those in the bar. He has an irresistible desire to laugh.*)

ROBERT (*after closing the door*): Good afternoon, gentlemen.

ALL (*in sepulchral tones*): Good afternoon.

ROBERT (*after looking at them*): People like football round here ... is that it? (*No one replies. Pause. He tries to break the ice.*) I see what's happened. The match has been canceled, the weather being what it is. (*Pause. Indecisive.*) Are you the boss?

TICHOMI (*without moving from behind the bar*): Yes, I am. What do you want?

ROBERT: Could we go outside for a minute? I'd like to have a word with you.

TICHOMI (*about to leave*): Very well.

BARTO (*to himself*): He wants to have a word with him.

LONDEQUE (*to himself*): He wants to have a word with him. (*He grabs Tichomi by the arm.*) Be careful!

(*Tichomi grunts.*)

BARTO (*grabbing his other arm aggressively*): Who is he?

TICHOMI: I don't know.

BARTO: Liar!

TICHOMI: It's the truth! I haven't got the faintest!

BARTO: He's a footballer, isn't he? I've seen him play somewhere.

LONDEQUE: Didn't he play for the Anthropophagi? Or was he with the Politbury Wanderers?

TICHOMI (*attempting to move toward Robert*): How should I know? Ever since that Cup Final, I haven't seen a single match.

BARTO: I've seen him on the field, I swear it.

LONDEQUE: Barto, he's the goalie for the Independent, isn't he?

BARTO: You mean Poposki? No, Poposki's taller than him. He looks a bit like Guripa . . . inside left for the Krapena Killers. Don't you think so?

LONDEQUE: No, it isn't him.

ROBERT: Are you coming? I'm in a hurry.

TICHOMI: Righto. (*To Barto.*) Let go of me, will you?

BARTO (*still hanging on to him*): Wait a minute . . . he's a University player. Gurupena University . . . that's who he plays for.

LONDEQUE: You're thinking of Campoyes.

UNITED MEMBER: No, it can't be him. . . . The blind man said he'd be coming down from heaven.

ZAPATONI: There was lightning, wasn't there, when he came in?

LOSING OPTIMIST: It was the flash of lightning . . . that's what he came down on . . . the flash of lightning!

BARTO (*shouting*): I have no wish to see that type of person in my town! I don't want strangers. He's not dressed like us—

therefore, why should we have anything to do with him? I stand for the Athletic. And the Athletic won. D'you hear me, everybody? Then mark it—you mark it as well.

ROBERT (*perplexed*): Sorry . . .

BARTO: I told you to mark it . . . mark what I'm saying.

ROBERT: Excuse me, but I'm not quite with you.

ZAPATONI: Here, wait a minute. Can you remember, everybody? When he came in, he had a muffler covering his face.

LOSING OPTIMIST (*declaiming*):
"He'll arrive with his face half-hidden,
On a rainy afternoon in May."

MEMBER OF UNITED: It's him . . . it's him!

BARTO (*to Robert*): You play for Gurupena, don't you? In defense. You're one of the backs.

YOUTH A: I bet you he's from the Football Association.

ROBERT: I'm afraid you're mistaken. I'm a bus driver.

BARTO (*anxiously*): Bus driver? Who are you a bus driver for? It's the Rangers. . . . It's the Rangers, isn't it?

ROBERT: Rangers? What are you talking about? I'm the driver of this bus outside.

BARTO (*terrified*): Are you telling me there's a bus out there? A bus?

(*We hear the horn being sounded.*)

ROBERT: See? They're getting impatient out there.

LONDEQUE: A busload of 'em!

TICHOMI: A busload!

LOSING OPTIMIST: Four busloads of 'em come down from heaven!

ATHLETIC MEMBER: Hear what they say? Ten busloads have come to disallow the match!

ROBERT: What match are you talking about? All I know is I've got a busload of people out there.

BARTO: What kind of people?

ROBERT (*at the peak of exasperation*): Who is this man? I've come in here to speak to the owner . . . nobody else. I've got nothing whatsoever to do with football! I'm a stranger . . . all right! But I'm not having you take me for a fool! (*He moves to go.*)

TICHOMI (*stopping Robert after getting a glance of approval from Barto*): No, wait! Look, let me explain. (*He takes Robert by the arm and they move toward the audience.*) In this town, quite a few years back, two football teams, the Athletic and the United, met for a Cup Final. The winners were the Athletic . . . or rather, the United lost. Anyway, the Athletic received the Cup trophy. Ever since that afternoon, people's feelings in this place have run high.

ROBERT: Yes, but . . .

TICHOMI (*silencing him with a gesture*): These two gentlemen . . . (*indicating Barto and Londeque.*) are regulars here. Señor Barto is the manager of the Athletic . . . (*Then whispers to him.*) . . . the town boss. . . . (*He continues out loud.*) This other gentleman, Señor Londeque, played for the United as left half during the famous match. If they were suspicious of you and started questioning you, it's because they have nothing else but football on their minds and in particular the result of that memorable Cup Final which, in spite of all the years that have passed, is still on everybody's mind. That's true, isn't it?

BARTO: Yes . . . as if it had been played only an hour ago.

LONDEQUE (*violently*): And me.

ALL: And all of us.

TICHOMI: Whether we're mad or sane, that's something that history will judge.

BARTO: Balls to history!

TICHOMI: Football is our only vice—football, football and more football—and we're addicts. Got it . . . Am I right?

ALL: Football, football and more football!

TICHOMI: Now if it so happens that you have no interest in football . . . (*Pause. He looks at Barto and Londeque who have calmed down.*) . . . I believe we can safely say we will hold nothing against you.

BARTO: What Señor Tichomi is saying is this: we thought at first that you had come here to discuss something related to the Cup Final and naturally ...

ROBERT: For heaven's sake, you're barking up the wrong tree! I'm a bus driver. I've got a load of passengers who want to use your rest room out there. I pulled up here, just as I might have pulled up anywhere else! Pure chance! But as for football ... I've got other things to think about.

TICHOMI: Well, that being the case, I think we might ... (*He makes a gesture to Barto, asking permission.*)

BARTO: Certainly ... go ahead. Talk to him if you want to.

LOSING OPTIMIST: It's not the one we were waiting for.

ZAPATONI: No ... no, it isn't.

TICHOMI: I'm at your service.

ROBERT (*offering his hand*): The name's Robert ... Robert Yuqui.

TICHOMI: Pleasure.

ROBERT: The people I've got outside are a company of actors. They're on tour ... doing the provinces. Tonight they're opening in Catirinada.

TICHOMI: Catirinada?

ROBERT: Yes. (*Looks at his watch.*) We've got to be there by nine. D'you know where we've come from?

TICHOMI: No idea.

ROBERT: Sunton.

TICHOMI: Sunton? That's about five hundred miles, isn't it?

ROBERT: It's far enough! You can imagine what they feel like out there, We finished the second show at two in the morning. Curtain down . . . everybody into the bus . . . and off we go! They didn't even have time to take off their costumes. Poor slobs—it's no kind of a life, you know. Anyway, how's the toilet situation around here?

TOCHOMI: Right over there. Not exactly spotless—still, they'll do. Go and have a look at them if you like.

ROBERT: There's no need for that. You got a separate ladies' room?

TICHOMI: We don't get a great many women in here. Anyway, there's two toilets, and if your boys are a little pressed for time, they can always dash out into the yard.

ROBERT: No, no, two toilets should be plenty. I'll tell them to come on in. Oh, and I'll tell them to have a drink—make it worth your while.

TICHOMI: Just as you wish.

ROBERT: Yeah—and you'll take care of me, won't you?

TICHOMI: You want a commission?

ROBERT: Well, that's the usual thing, isn't it? I usually stop in Boce-junillas, but what with this rain . . .

TICHOMI: OK, OK—what do you get?

ROBERT: Ten percent.

TICHOMI: OK—ten percent it is!

ROBERT (*shaking hands*): You're on. Be right back.

(*He leaves. Tichomi moves over to Barto and Londeque, who are chatting. There is a growing noise from the street.*)

LONDEQUE: Are you thinking of having a word with them?

BARTO: You're not in favor of tourists mixing with our townspeople, are you?

TICHOMI: They're not tourists—they're actors.

LONDEQUE: Nothing good can come from outside.

TICHOMI: That's true—but this lot is pretty harmless.

LONDEQUE: Well, as long as they just use the toilets and have a drink and keep their noses out of our affairs, I suppose it's all right.

BARTO: Sure, why not?

TICHOMI: It would be a pretty good thing for the town if busses stopped here.

LONDEQUE: You mean it would be a pretty good thing for you since you own a bar. Anyway, you do what you like, Barto; I'm getting my people out of here.

BARTO: Well, if you're going to take that attitude . . . (*To Tichomi.*) Go and tell them to wait outside for a minute.

TICHOMI: Anything you say, Barto. (*He leaves.*)

BARTO (*taking up a position in the middle of the bar*): Listen to me, everybody! Silence! . . . We've got a group of visitors outside who just want to take a piss in the corner here. . . .

VOICE: Corner? Did he say "corner?"

OTHER VOICE: Penalty!

OTHER VOICE: Foul!

OTHER VOICE: Offside!

TICHOMI (*coming from bolting the door*): Quiet!

LONDEQUE: Shut up!

BARTO: Thank you. (*Solemn and mysterious.*) These strangers who are about to enter the sacred precincts of this bar are as yet unknown to us. But in order to avoid . . . (*He grabs a fly in the air.*) . . . so much for flies. . . . In order to prevent any single one of us from forgetting what he is and what he has always been, a staunch supporter of either the Athletic or the United, sworn to his club, never deviating, even in the face of death, I believe it is the solemn duty of all of us to get out of here.

A VOICE: Well said.

ANOTHER VOICE: He's talking sense. . . . That's sense, that is.

BARTO: We do not return until they are back in their bus and out of this town. No word, no single word, will be exchanged with them. Agreed?

(*Voices of agreement. The voices are lowered in tone so that the audience can clearly hear Nestor and Fani:*)

NESTOR: That young chap Zapatoni . . . we're buying him up for our Works' team.

FANI: You think so? Sorry, we intend to buy him up for our Works' team.

ALL: Agreed.

BARTO: Very well. Look lively. Get outside.

(*They all leave, running, by the door that leads to the yard.*)

BARTO: Let 'em in, then. (*He leaves, too.*)

(*Only Tichomi, Nestor and Fani remain on the stage. Tichomi puts the chairs and tables in order and carries a supply of newspapers to the lavatories. Someone bangs on the street door.*)

TICHOMI: Let 'em hold it for a bit. Let's see now: the bus driver gets ten percent, so my prices go up twenty percent . . . or perhaps thirty . . . why not make it forty?

FANI: This is the greatest town in the whole wide world.

NESTOR (*laughing*): You think so?

FANI (*laughing*): That's what they tell you.

NESTOR: And it's best not to contradict. Right?

FANI: Exactly.

NESTOR: You're a very dangerous rival, Fani.

FANI: Prices are low here. I've come to buy cheap, like you.

NESTOR: Don't count on buying up Zapatoni. He's going to sign with us.

FANI: I'm afraid your firm hasn't got the money . . . not our kind of money.

NESTOR: There are some things in this world that can't be bought.

FANI: You think so? In this town, everything's up for sale. The whole damn shooting match.

NESTOR: And you pay for your captives . . . mmm?

FANI: You might hand out the philosophy and all this hokum about fair play, but I tell you, money never fails. What's more, we never deceive anybody. We simply judge the right moment, put the money on the table and simply ask the question, yes or no.

NESTOR: Zapatoni will sign for us. The best players in the football world end up signing for us. In a few years your much-vaunted Metacarpis will look like a fourth division side in comparison with Estrépitos.

FANI: In that case, we'll get all the supporters.

NESTOR: You'll what?

FANI: People always side with the weaker.

NESTOR: How much do you want for Phimpson?

FANI: You're interested in Phimpson?

NESTOR: Yes.

FANI: All right, we'll let you have him for a couple of seasons. It'll cost you three million.

NESTOR: His boots included?

FANI: Yes . . . three pairs.

NESTOR: Phimpson's left-footed, isn't he?

FANI: All right. We'll let you have him with three right boots and five left. How's that?

NESTOR: How about exchanging him for Caspo?

FANI: Caspo's the one with the beard, isn't he?

NESTOR: He's also left-footed.

FANI: Well, naturally. We know as well as anybody that the best forwards are left-footed. (*Meditates.*) No, sorry . . . I'm not interested.

## SCENE 5

(*Tichomi has unbolted the door. Robert appears with the actors, who are highly excited. This scene must be produced as a ballet. A general desire to get to the lavatories. The forming of queues. Pushing and shoving. A few go to the bar for a drink, others look at the bull's head. All the actors have cameras hanging from their shoulders. Their clothing should include two or three Cardinals, Joan of Arc, Don Juan, Don Luis Mejia, Celestina, Romeo, a Nun, Juliet. About fifteen characters altogether. There follow a number of phrases which the director can distribute among the actors. He may, if he wishes, make alterations and cuts.*)

PHRASES FOR THE ACTORS:

God, it's cold!

I'm frozen stiff!

Has that bus given me the backache!

I'm packing it in after this tour, I tell you!

What a hole!

God-forsaken dump!

Toilet paper? Are you mad? Newspapers! . . . And they're a month out of date!

My costume's absolutely ruined!

The forecast was "Clear skies and sun all day."

Bob, do they serve coffee?

Bob . . . Bob, love!

Bob, she wants you!

Robert, get me a coffee, will you?

Did we *have* to stop here?

The flats will be ruined, you know.

ROBERT: Don't worry, the prices are very reasonable.

If they overcharge us, it'll be the last straw.

Darling, you're in the wrong queue!

How much further is it, Robert?

Poor old Robert—tired out, are you?

ROBERT: The road being what it is . . . three hours.

Another three hours!

You can do it faster than that!

We don't want him to take risks. Take it steady, Robert.

Summer storm! It's a bloody cyclone!

(*Indicating Fani and Nestor.*) Hey, look! They've got tourists here.

What's up, then?

We ought to have had this set for *Point of Departure!*

(*Knocking on door.*) Come on ... time's up!

(*To Tichomi.*) Glass of beer.

TICHOMI: And you, sir?

Something to eat.

You haven't quarreled with her again, have you?

There's been nothing but rows ever since we got married.

(*Woman coming out of lavatory*): Well, dear, that was better out than in.

I'm not drinking, thanks.

Bob, have you locked the bus?

ROBERT: You can get in through the back.

Are you back on the hard stuff?

It's only a single.

Any tonic?

TICHOMI: Sorry, sir.

What a life! I ask you, what a bloody life!

Will we get the scenery up in time?

Don't worry ... they write plays without scenery these days. What's more, they like 'em without actors.

Eh? You've heard about that show in London, haven't you? Curtain goes up and a huge mirror comes down. Two-hour show with the audience just looking at themselves. They say it's a smash hit.

FANI (*stage now silent*): Officially, I am here as a leopard hunter. (*He can pick up air rifle.*)

NESTOR: There are leopards round here, then?

FANI: Of course not. But I let them think that if I were to go away, there'd be leopards coming down from the mountain. Consequently, they hang on to me.

ACTRESS: I haven't been to Catirinada since I was a girl. We did *Doll's House*. Not a bad town. We stayed in the Station Hotel. It was while the war was on.

I was too young. I can't remember the war.

I've got three altogether . . . my mother looks after them. Well, you can't drag 'em round with you, can you, not in this trade!

What's happening to the coffees I ordered?

Give me a double brandy—see if I can get rid of this cold.

ROBERT: Hurry up, everybody. Hurry up. If you haven't had a drink, make haste and get one.

Here, let go of me!

TICHOMI: One at a time, if you don't mind, one at a time or I'll get in a mess.

Just give me a drink—I don't care what it is.

Let go of me, I tell you!

TICHOMI: Let's see now . . . five . . . seven . . . altogether it's eight-twenty. And yours is six-fifty, sir.

Hey, don't pay twice—I've already paid.

Mine was a ham sandwich and a whiskey.

TICHOMI: Was it a small one, sir?

Minute.

(*Coming out of lavatory.*) What a pigsty!

I only hope, Don Lucio, we play to a better house tonight.

DON LUCIO: If we got rid of the guests, the critics, the police and the gate-crashers, what would we have? Two hundred people a performance, that's all.

There he goes . . . always going on about the same thing: houses packed with paper.

Last night wasn't so bad. Three quarters of 'em paid, anyway.

I reckon this rain smells me out, you know. I suffer bloody agonies with my corns.

There's only one way out: wash your feet more often.

ROBERT: Come on, everybody . . . back to the bus.

(*There are still a few waiting to go to the toilets. Barto and Londeque enter from the right to spy out the land.*)

BARTO: Not so bad. They're on their way.

LONDEQUE: Who d'you think they are?

BARTO: I dunno. Damn peculiar lot, if you ask me.

LONDEQUE: Ah, queer-looking bunch.

BARTO: D'you think it's true they stopped here for a pee and nothing else? Anyway, come on. We'll come back as soon as the bus starts up.

(*They leave.*)

## SCENE 6

(*Salvador enters from the street door. He is a bit-part player of the company. The other actors despise him because he is a "poor study." He doubles and trebles parts, forever changing costume. He is dressed as a Capucine monk and has a long, full, artificial beard. Middle-aged, small, something of a dreamer, he has been asleep at the back of the bus and has just woken up. He enters precipitately.*)

SALVADOR (*searching among the actors. He taps someone on the back*): Don Lucio?

What?

SALVADOR: Sorry, my mistake. (*To another.*) Have you seen Don Lucio?

(*Laughing.*) Don Lucio's gone.

SALVADOR: Gone? Don Lucio's gone? Why? (*Loudly.*) Anybody seen Don Lucio?

Where have you been hiding yourself?

SALVADOR: I was asleep.

Hey, look what's turned up.

Him again. (*Singing.*) "He's lost his way and don't know where to roam."

SALVADOR: You left me there. I opened my eyes and there I was, alone in the bus. God help me, the thunder and lightning! Where's Don Lucio? He hasn't gone, has he? Ah, there he is! (*He moves to Don Lucio and touches him on the shoulder almost caressingly, as if he feels secure at last.*)

DON LUCIO (*almost dryly*): What do you want? (*Salvador smiles and shrugs his shoulders.*) Come on, out with it. What do you want?

SALVADOR: Nothing.

DON LUCIO: Now then, none of your funny stuff. What are you after?

SALVADOR: Nothing . . . nothing.

DON LUCIO: Well, what have you interrupted me for?

SALVADOR: It's just that I want . . . (*He whispers in Don Lucio's ear.*)

DON LUCIO (*pointing to lavatory*): It's over there. You're just like a child. You want to grow up now you've got your beard on.

SALVADOR: It's not a real beard.

DON LUCIO: I know that. That's why I said it. Well, go on! (*Salvador joins the women's queue. They all laugh at him. He becomes nervous.*) The other one! The Gents! You're supposed to be a gent!

(*They all laugh at him. It makes him so nervous he loses his bearings. Men stand in front of the Gents, laughing, and in retreating from them, he fails to recognise where he ought to go. He approaches Tichomi and whispers to him.*)

SALVADOR: Where is it?

TICHOMI: If you're in such a hurry, go out in the yard there.

SALVADOR: Very well.

TICHOMI: Follow me, then.

(*Salvador and Tichomi leave by the door which leads to the yard.*)

ROBERT (*to those who remain*): If you've paid, d'you mind getting back on the bus? Come along, please. We've still got another seventy miles before Catirinada.

ACTOR: Where's he gone, the bartender . . . him with the apron?

ANOTHER: He's taken Salvador off somewhere or other.

ANOTHER: That Salvador is a damn nuisance.

FANI: We could manage it . . . and it wouldn't cost a lot of money, either. If we helped one another instead of opposing each other, we could share out the best footballers in the town . . . and do it for cheap.

(*The actors have gone. Only Don Lucio, the business manager of the company, and Robert are left. Tichomi returns. On entering, somebody pulls him by the shirt. Barto appears, half-hidden behind him.*)

BARTO: Who is he?

TICHOMI: Eh?

BARTO: The priest?

TICHOMI: Dunno.

BARTO (*menacing*): Don't lie.

TICHOMI: Let go of me, Barto. They're waiting for me.

BARTO: Let 'em wait. I happen to be more important.

TICHOMI: This is my bar.

BARTO: *Your* bar is in *our* town.

TICHOMI: The town belongs to everybody.

BARTO: No, it belongs to us. We won the cup.

TICHOMI: Yes, but it was a long time ago.

ROBERT (*to Tichomi*): Come on, we're in a hurry.

BARTO (*to Tichomi*): Why is that priest here? Tell me.

DON LUCIO (*calls*): How much do I owe you? (*Low voice.*) Who's that chap he's talking to?

ROBERT: He lives here.

DON LUCIO: He's got a chip on his shoulder, that one.

BARTO (*to Tichomi, who is trying to cross the stage*): If that priest doesn't come back here pretty soon, and I find out that he's spoken to anybody in this town, I tell you this: you're in for a very nasty time. A very nasty time, I warn you.

(*Tichomi moves behind the bar.*)

BUSINESS MANAGER: It's a sad life, Lucio.

DON LUCIO: What . . . at your age?

BUSINESS MANAGER: Young in body but not up here. I've seen it all.

TICHOMI (*counting mentally*): Right you are. What were they? Two coffees and three brandies.

BUSINESS MANAGER: I'm not stupid enough, that's my trouble. Just a bit more stupid and I'd be all right.

DON LUCIO: Eh?

BUSINESS MANAGER: I'd be happy then.

(*Robert leaves.*)

TICHOMI: I make it twenty-two seventy.

DON LUCIO: Leave it. I'll take care of it.

BUSINESS MANAGER: Thanks. There's a machine, you know . . . a machine to make people happy. It's perfectly adjusted, this machine is, to produce its optimum effect on the human heart encased in a chest measurement of thirty-six, thirty-seven, or thirty-eight.

ROBERT (*entering*): Hey, everybody's on board but you two.

DON LUCIO: Come on, Hector.

NESTOR: The future is ours.

FANI: The only certain thing about the future is its uncertainty.

DON LUCIO (*to Tichomi*): Good-bye. Hope we haven't troubled you too much.

TICHOMI: Good-bye, sir . . . good-bye.

(*Don Lucio and Hector leave. Tichomi continues reckoning up.*)

FANI: If we took them on, they might have a nostalgia for this place. I mean, the way they hang on to their club colors, wearing the same shorts day after day.

(*The bus starts up.*)

NESTOR: Our personnel department has started a course for our workers in the exercise of oblivion.

FANI: Oblivion?

NESTOR: Yes. The right degree of forgetfulness is remarkably necessary nowadays.

(*Robert enters.*)

ROBERT (*to Tichomi*): Hey! We've forgotten our little deal.

TICHOMI: Ah, your commission. I put it on one side. (*He shows him a small envelope.*)

ROBERT: Right.

TICHOMI: Here you are. (*He throws the envelope to Robert, who catches it.*)

ROBERT: So long, buddy. Thanks.

TICHOMI: And thank you. Take care on the road!

ROBERT: 'Bye. (*He leaves.*)

(*During the following, the bus moves off. Barto enters and remains near a wall.*)

TICHOMI: Wait a minute. . . . I've given him too much. Not much too much. All the same, too much. Well, I think so, anyway.

BARTO: Tichomi?

TICHOMI (*still doing his accounts*): Eh?

BARTO: Got rid of 'em, have you? Good.

TICHOMI (*vaguely*): Yes. (*Continues doing his accounts.*) Hey! Half a mo' . . . . the priest! (*Rises rapidly.*) . . . and the bus has gone! (*Runs to street door and returns.*) It's gone, Señor Barto! It was the accounts . . . adding up the accounts. That's what made me forget him.

BARTO (*sardonically*): Oh, so you've forgotten him, have you? That's going to be just too bad, isn't it, Tichomi? (*Barto leaves.*)

(*Tichomi moves into a room next to the bar which we imagine is a lumber room and returns with a brand-new, shining sports bicycle. The chain has come off. Tichomi tries to put it back.*)

TICHOMI: I might catch up with 'em. Goddammit, the chain's off!

(*Salvador appears in the doorway. His hands are folded and hidden in the sleeves of his habit. He moves slowly, in a beatific manner, like a Capucine in prayer.*)

SALVADOR: How beautiful a thing is a bicycle. A noble invention of the human mind! (*To Tichomi who is on the floor, urgently trying to fix the chain.*) Tell me, mine host, this charming brightness . . . is it double-plated? Moreover, should a traveler be in urgent haste, what maximum velocity may be granted him through the cunning manipulation of the three-speed gear?

TICHOMI (*throwing down the bike*): Oh, hell, I'll never catch 'em, not now!

SALVADOR (*picking up bike*): For the love of all the saints, have charity! Never abuse your bicycle, for even bicycles are creatures of God, just as the men who ride them are the creatures of God . . . or the brave bulls condemned to death by men. They too are creatures of God. And the fighting cocks, and the chimpanzees and the noble gorillas who one day will rise up in the African jungle, liberating themselves from the colonial yoke which the Negro has put upon them . . . unless, of course, unless . . . (*Wild eyed.*) . . . we have not first managed to put them all in orbit. Sweet creatures of God are the seas and the sandy shores and the motes of dust shining in the rays of God's good sunlight.

TICHOMI: And what about Señor Barto?

SALVADOR: Who?

TICHOMI: You'll soon find out what a nice creature of God he is.

SALVADOR: Do you know this poem? Let me see if I can remember it. (*He recites with boldness and emotion, continuing to appear ridiculous.*)

> Consider the stones and their feelings,
> Not the feeling of man, but of rock.
> For the stones have feelings,

Rivers and seas have feelings,
The wind has feelings,
Even those silent, infinite spaces can feel.
And when there is a time for tears,
For all who feel must weep,
Their tears fall on the ground,
Round, hard tears like grains of water.
If you can believe that the rain
Is the sigh of the suffering unknown,
If your mind can encompass all this,
Then be glad, I say it again, be glad,
For know it or not, you are good.

(*He continues in a normal tone.*) Did you like it? Pretty, wasn't it? (*He moves to the men's lavatory.*) Don Lucio, peep-o! . . . Don Lucio! It's me, Salvador! Going to be there long? . . . Eh? Nobody there! (*Tichomi tears his hair.*) Where are they . . . the rest of the company?

TICHOMI: They've gone.

SALVADOR (*horrified*): What?

TICHOMI: They've gone . . . moved off . . . gone.

SALVADOR: Gone?!

TICHOMI: They didn't realize you were still here. That driver you've got should have been counting the passengers instead of bothering about his ten percent.

SALVADOR: What am I going to do?

TICHOMI: What am *I* going to do is more like it.

SALVADOR: You?

TICHOMI: Yes, me. You don't know what a pile of trouble you might cause me.

SALVADOR: Can I get a taxi?

TICHOMI: Yes . . . we've got *one.*

SALVADOR: Well, go on! Ring for it.

TICHOMI: I haven't got a phone.

SALVADOR: Well, where does it park, then?

TICHOMI: God knows. It could be outside the co-op.

SALVADOR: How do I get there?

TICHOMI: You know the parish church?

SALVADOR: Eh?

TICHOMI: St. Anne's.

SALVADOR: Ah, Saint Anne! Saint Anne! (*He remains for a few moments in ecstasy.*) No, I'm afraid I don't know it.

TICHOMI: When you came into the town, it's on the left. It's a church with a tower.

SALVADOR: I . . . I was asleep.

TICHOMI (*remembering*): Yes, you were. Look, the best thing is, I'll go 'round and look for it. Wait here. (*He goes to leave, then wavers.*) I'm warning you, if he can manage to get the taxi started, it'll cost you a penny or two.

SALVADOR: That's all right. Don Lucio will pay. It was his fault, clearing off without me. Chucked aside, that's all I am . . . chucked aside.

(*Tichomi has taken off his apron. He adjusts his socks and pulls down his jersey.*)

SALVADOR: Hey, why have you got football togs on?

TICHOMI (*now at the door. To himself.*): What commission shall I ask the taxi? Let's make it twenty-five percent. (*He leaves.*)

SALVADOR: Just think! He's got football togs on. (*He thinks of the costume he has on underneath his monk's habit.*) Tut-tut-tut . . . what a coincidence! (*He approaches Fani and Nestor.*) Do you live here? Oh, first I should say, "Good afternoon" . . . or rather, "Good evening."

(*Fani takes off his hat. Nestor doesn't take kindly to Salvador's intrusion.*)

FANI: Good evening, Father.

NESTOR: Good evening.

SALVADOR: No, no, don't call me "Father."

FANI (*with sympathy*): Holy brother, then.

SALVADOR: No, don't call me that, either. I am not exactly what I seem.

NESTOR: Nobody is what they seem.

SALVADOR: Yes, but I'm *really* not what I seem. All this stuff (*indicating habit*) is stage costume. This beard (*pulls it off*) isn't mine. If I had a beard of my own, I think it would be very much like this one. But they won't let me grow one. No, this one belongs to Don Lucio. Everything belongs to Don Lucio.

NESTOR (*to Fani*): Somebody else who's trying to buy up Zapatoni.

(*Barto, Londeque, Youths A and B enter. Salvador has his back turned to Barto.*)

BARTO: There you are . . . what did I tell you? They've all gone except him with the beard.

SALVADOR (*to Nestor*): What did you say? I come from the Anthropophagi? What Anthropophagi?

YOUTH A: Tichomi is up to something.

BARTO: Tichomi is a traitor . . . that's what Tichomi is.

LONDEQUE: Perhaps he's the new church organist.

BARTO: We want no more organists. It's bad enough trying to stop the priest from shoving his nose in.

SALVADOR (*to Fani*): Zapatoni? Never heard of him. Who is he?

YOUTH B (*to Barto*): Which is the one with the beard?

BARTO: Him.

YOUTH B: But he hasn't got a beard.

SALVADOR: Hey! Why is everybody dressed up as footballers?

FANI (*threateningly*): Ah!

NESTOR (*inquisitorially*): Don't you know? And why are you in disguise? Why have you come dressed in disguise?

SALVADOR: It's a long story. (*He drinks from a glass of beer on the table.*) May I? (*In doing so, he turns around.*)

YOUTH A: You're right. He hasn't got a beard!

LONDEQUE: Then there must be two of them.

BARTO: It's a conspiracy . . . a Jesuit conspiracy!

YOUTH A: They're plotting against us!

BARTO: No time to be lost. You—go to the Club and bring 'em here. Everybody what's there. We've got to get our hands on the other one.

YOUTH A: Right. (*He leaves.*)

BARTO (*to Youth B*): Have a look in the yard.

SALVADOR: I took you to be tourists at first.

NESTOR: Tourists! Never! I'm a big-game hunter and he's prospecting for oil.

TICHOMI (*entering out of breath*): No taxi. It's gone to a wedding in Bocejunillas. (*He wipes the sweat from his face. Seeing Salvador without a beard.*) Who are you?

SALVADOR: Oh, God!

TICHOMI: Where's the one with the beard?

BARTO: Come inside, the lot of you.

(*All those who appeared earlier enter, except Youth A and B. They move toward Salvador threateningly. He backs to the bar. Barto and the Athletic Members bounce their footballs. In the hearts of Londeque and the United Club, there is growing an unexpected hope.*)

FANI: See? See how they make common cause against the foreigner. You can't stop it.

TICHOMI: Let me explain, Barto. Let me explain. He missed the bus.

ATHLETIC MEMBER: Are you going to get the Brads?

BARTO: No need. I can settle this one . . . me!

(*Salvador's back is firmly against the bar. He is terrified, constantly crossing himself, acting to perfection a Capucine.*

*The scene darkens, with the light centering on the face of Salvador. The music backing the prophecy is heard.*)

BARTO: The other monk . . . where is he?

TICHOMI: Yes, where is he?

(*Youth B enters, running.*)

YOUTH B: There's nobody out there.

SALVADOR (*putting on his beard*): I'm the other monk...me! Why are you all dressed as footballers?

TICHOMI: It's him ... no doubt of it.

BARTO: What's the meaning of all this? H'mmm?

FANI: Perhaps he's a monk after all. He looks so harmless.

NESTOR: Don't you believe it.

BARTO: Answer!

SALVADOR: You tell me why you're all dessed up as footballers. Some of you are too old for the game, aren't you?

LONDEQUE: We dress as we please.

SALVADOR (*laughs*): What a coincidence! I can't help laughing. What a coincidence!

BARTO: Be quiet. Here we've got an enemy in our midst and you (*To Tichomi.*) . . . you've been aiding and abetting him, haven't you?

TICHOMI: Me?

SALVADOR (*laughing*): What a coincidence!

LONDEQUE: What are you laughing about?

BARTO: Yes, what are you laughing about? Out with it!

SALVADOR: I'll tell you what I'm laughing about. It's this! (*He pulls off his habit.*) This! (*He appears dressed as a football referee.*) Eh? What d'you think? It's a laugh, isn't it?

(*Barto and his acolytes move backwards, full of surprise and terror. Fani and Nestor have risen. The United Members glow with joy.*

*The light centers upon Salvador's face. He blows a whistle and signals an imaginary foul to an imaginary side.*)

SALVADOR: Corner! Penalty! Offside! Half-time! (*He laughs.*) Coincidence, eh?

(*Darkness. A single spot picks out the group surrounding Salvador. The United Members put their arms around each oth-*

*er's shoulders and begin to sing their song. It acts as a musical background which is heard through the loudspeakers.)*

BARTO: Who are you?

YOUTH B: Who are you?

LONDEQUE: It's you . . . you, the long-awaited! The man who would come on a rainy afternoon in May. He'd have his face half-hidden . . . half-hidden! Do you realize, when he came in here, his face was half-hidden. The prophecy has been fulfilled!

BARTO: So you think you're going to bring us peace, do you? Never . . . not him!

LONDEQUE: Yes, Barto . . . he'll bring us peace, you'll see!

BARTO: No! . . . Brads! Brads!

*(A young United Member waves a United flag.)*

TICHOMI *(angrily)*: Why have you come? Who sent you?

SALVADOR: Me?

*(The United Members blow up their beach balls to the size of the Athletic Members' footballs. At a signal from Barto, the Athletic Members throw themselves on Salvador and knock him down. Suddenly Zapatoni leaps onto a table, brandishing a stick.)*

ZAPATONI: Quiet! *(Barto is about to leap upon him, but Zapatoni menaces him with the stick.)* Stay where you are, Barto.

BARTO *(conciliatory for the first time, as if justifying himself)*: This man . . . is the devil!

LOSING OPTIMIST: Always the devil . . . the devil. It's your one big excuse. Anything you don't agree with is the work of the devil.

BARTO: He is the devil!

LONDEQUE: Yes . . . for *you!*

ZAPATONI: But for us, he is our salvation.

SALVADOR: There is but one God.

BARTO: He's the devil! You'll soon see he's the devil, too!

FANI: See that lad on the table?

NESTOR: Yes.

FANI: It's Zapatoni!!!

> (*The characters freeze for ten seconds. Rapid curtain for end of act.*)

# ACT TWO

## A SIDE EVENT

(*As the curtain rises, we see the same actors who appeared at the end of Act I in the same postures, motionless. The lighting will also be identical to the end of Act I. Three children cross the stage in single file. They are dressed as soldiers in battle dress, equipped with machine guns. The first child carries a placard which reads: "Can the problem be solved?"; the second carries one which reads: "What solution?"; the third carries one which reads: "What do you think?" The actors remain still for two or three seconds after the last child has left.*

*Fani and Nestor (who are standing at the end of Act I) start moving to their seats. The light on Salvador's group fades. At the same time the light on Fani and Nestor increases.*

*Darkness on Salvador's group. Nestor and Fani continue looking toward the invisible group. Fani serves Nestor with beer, then serves himself.*)

NESTOR: Thank you, Fani.

> (*Fani lifts his glass and invites Nestor to do the same.*)

FANI: To a free world.

NESTOR: To equality of mankind.

> (*Nestor and Fani sit.*)

FANI: What we have just witnessed has made me ponder . . . ponder upon so many things.

NESTOR: Me, too.

FANI: What do you think is going to happen to this town?

NESTOR (*shrugs his shoulders*): How do I know? There's a lot could happen.

FANI: Yes, but in the circumstances . . . the rain, the month of May, the face half-hidden . . . don't you think the Blind Man's prophecy—

NESTOR: Prophecy?

FANI: Well, the song, then.

NESTOR: Are you trying to make me believe there's something supernatural in these events? Something miraculous?

FANI: Something along those lines.

NESTOR: You actually think that the monk has been sent by God? That he has come out of the sky to bring peace to this town?

FANI: Why not?

(*They look at each other in silence.*)

NESTOR: Bah. I neither believe in miracles nor prophecies. Neither do you. Men's desire for justice is so great that if a hero doesn't appear to lead them toward it, then they will invent a magician. I don't know whether this monk is merely an actor or not. What I do know is this: if he has enough courage to make himself heard, then the members of the United will do exactly what he tells them.

FANI: You believe that?

NESTOR: I'm certain of it.

FANI: It could be interesting . . . (*To himself.*) . . . very interesting indeed.

NESTOR: What are you plotting now?

(*We hear Salvador sneeze.*)

FANI: Salvador! (*He sneezes again.*) Salvador!

(*Spotlight goes up on Salvador's face. He is lying on the ground.*)

SALVADOR: Yes . . . yes, I'm here. I'm frozen stiff.

FANI (*paternally*): Put on your habit.

SALVADOR: You don't mind?

FANI: Not at all. Put it on.

SALVADOR: Right you are. (*Salvador drags himself toward the habit and puts it on. He then approaches Fani and Nestor.*) I shall put on the beard as well. Very warm and protecting, the beard. (*He puts it on.*) Very strange people in this town. Don't you think so? Very aggressive. Here, why do they all dress up as footballers?

NESTOR: There's an epidemic of reciprocating schizophrenia.

SALVADOR: Never! Is it catching?

NESTOR: Those who don't live here are immune.

(*A drop has been coming down slowly so the actors are now on the forestage.*)

SALVADOR: Ah well, that's not so bad. And you belong to the town, do you?

NESTOR: We're foreigners.

FANI: We happen to be here on a very important scientific mission. (*He stands to attention, with a click of his heels.*) Fani Gou, at your service.

SALVADOR: Salvador Venturina.

NESTOR (*with click of heels*): Nestor Popo.

SALVADOR: Delighted to meet you. (*To himself.*) What peculiar names!

FANI: H'mmm! You're on your way then, Nestor?

NESTOR (*getting up reluctantly*): Thank you for reminding me. . . . But a little later, I shall be having a chat with Don Salvador. (*To Fani.*) Understand? (*Nestor leaves.*)

SALVADOR: What I'd like to know is why so many people are interested in who I am. I'm simply an actor, that's all.

FANI (*admiringly*): Tut-tut-tut!

SALVADOR: Honestly. And the only thing I'm interested in is getting out of here as soon as possible. . . . Here, tell me: why did everybody go stark, staring mad? It was when I took off this habit, wasn't it? That's what did it. Screaming and banging away at me! Why?

FANI (*smiling*): Let me explain it to you . . . let me explain everything

INCIDENTAL NEWS
(*Darkness. Projected on the curtain at the back
is the following:* "SERIOUS DISTURBANCE IN DUN-
GUTA. GUERILLAS FROM THE UNBI AND SILUSI
TRIBES ARE ADVANCING ON CARLOSTOWN. THE
COMMITTEE OF SECURE NATIONS HAS DECIDED TO
SEND A MEDIATOR. BENJAMIN SEGAL HAS DEPARTED
FOR DUNGUTA.")

*The side event continues. Fani's solution begins.*

SALVADOR: Do you think I could hire a motor bike? Or perhaps just
a bike? It would have to have a lamp, though.

FANI: What for?

SALVADOR: To get away from here.

FANI: Get away? But you are the man they've been waiting for. . . .
Waiting and waiting year upon year.

SALVADOR: Waiting for me? Why?

FANI: You've even got the right name . . . Salvador, the savior.
"Peace on earth amongst men of goodwill."

SALVADOR: Yes, but—

FANI: A very important role lies before you.

SALVADOR: Important role? I've never had an important role, on the
stage or anywhere else. Anywhere else doesn't matter, because
people who take on important roles usually come to a sticky
end. But as for the stage . . . trouble is, I've got a bad memory. That's why I always get tiny parts. D'you know what my
part was in *The Duke of Braganza*? In the third act, I peeped
in through a window and shouted, "They're coming, they're
coming!" . . . And that was it. And as far as *The Merry Wives
of Windsor* was concerned, I didn't even get that much! I
acted the Merry Comrade. One short laugh and off! Mind you,
I'm very busy. Whenever you see the end of the cast list, saying, "Also Crowd, Soldiers, Pages and Ladies in Waiting" . . .
it's me. Plus anybody going spare, but always me. There I am,
night after night, swapping my moustache for an abbess's wim-

ple. True, you know. I'm the backbone of the nun's chorus. Twenty-five years in the profession and I've never been more than five minutes on the stage at any given time. No, wait a minute, I'm a liar. When we did *Richard III*, I was on for half an hour as a horse.

FANI: You don't say!

SALVADOR (*nods*): The back end of the horse.

FANI: Tut-tut-tut.

SALVADOR: Don Lucio says I've got no personality.

FANI: How can Don Lucio say that? You're overflowing with personality.

SALVADOR: You think so?

FANI: And what's more, my dear Salvador, you are a very great actor—a fabulous actor! Who but you would have been able to deceive everybody as you've done? The whole town believes you are the messiah they've been waiting for.

SALVADOR: Waiting for what?

FANI: You heard. They believe he'll come down from heaven.

SALVADOR: Amazing!

FANI: They're waiting for a referee, sent by the Lord God to bring peace into the home of each and every one of them.

SALVADOR: A football referee?

FANI: Yes, you could put it that way.

SALVADOR: I get it . . . that's why they're all dressed up as footballers.

FANI: Right! Thirty years ago there was a very important and historic football match in this little town. In it the town's two teams clashed: the Athletic on one side and the United on the other.

SALVADOR: Who won?

FANI: The Athletic . . . one-nothing.

SALVADOR: Go on, go on!

FANI: God, how those two sides hated each other's guts! So, right after the match, the Athletics banned the other club and didn't allow them to play football any more. And because of the Brads, the United haven't played from that day to this.

SALVADOR: Brads? Who are the Brads?

FANI: Well, up to that time, the Brads were the bouncers at the football matches. They've always had pretty high-spirited fellows around here, and the Brads used to keep them in order. Well, when the Athletic took over the football field, the Brads didn't want to give up their jobs so they joined the winning side. Result: they now carry out to the letter any absurd decision made by the Athletic, including the bursting of the United's footballs.

SALVADOR: You don't say!

FANI: Certainly. Mind you, the United supporters are not exactly resigned to their overthrow. They want to go on playing football and get that Cup Final decision annulled. The Athletic, however, stick to what happened all those years ago. And there you have it: always quarreling, always bad-tempered, always unhappy.

SALVADOR: And that's all that stands between them?

FANI: That's all. But you haven't heard everything yet. Get this, will you? A hundred years ago . . . or maybe two hundred—who knows? . . . somebody around here composed a ballad . . . you know, a sort of folk song. It was passed down, father to son, and you know what? The Blind Man in this town goes around singing this song and pretty well nothing else. It's all about a savior who's coming one day . . . a mediator, a referee. Now the Athletic Club's really scared he might arrive. The United are crazy for his arrival. And suddenly, you appear . . . you, my friend Salvador. Shhh! Shhhh!

(*The opposite side of the stage is lit and the Blind Man appears with his stick and guitar.*)

BLIND MAN (*singing*):
He'll arrive with his face half-hidden . . .

FANI: Like you, with your beard and your hood.

SALVADOR: I see.

BLIND MAN:
> On a rainy afternoon in May.

FANI: We happen to be in the month of May.

SALVADOR: And it's pouring cats and dogs.

BLIND MAN:
> He'll come down from the heavens, the savior . . .

(*Fani and Salvador look at each other.*)

FANI: Got it?

BLIND MAN:
> Who'll bring peace to my people and my town.

FANI: You understand now.

(*Salvador, deeply moved, makes a gesture of agreement.*)

BLIND MAN (*moving off*):
> Referee, referee,
> Referee, mediator, referee . . . (*The Blind Man moves into darkness and leaves.*)

SALVADOR: And what's more, I've got a referee's costume on.

FANI: Wouldn't you like to be this savior? (*Salvador sits, very moved.*) Wouldn't you like to take on the role of this long-awaited messenger of God, showing everybody, Don Lucio included, that you are every inch an actor?

SALVADOR: Yes.

FANI: What's more, you'd bring peace and brotherhood to this town. The hearts of these innocent townsfolk will overflow with gratitude. For centuries upon centuries your illustrious name will be venerated by the people. Streets and squares will be named after you. . . . And perhaps we should refer to more tangible things: (*Imagining it.*) The town council in plenary session agrees unanimously to offer you the finest residence within its borders, with your own orchards, your own stable, your own beach. And there, whenever you wish, you can live in luxury . . . always granted that your engagements as first actor of this land will permit you to have time off.

SALVADOR: Can I have my mother come as well?

FANI: Certainly.

SALVADOR: And Uncle Frederick?

FANI: And Uncle Frederick!

SALVADOR: And Uncle Frederick's children?

FANI: And Uncle Frederick's children!

SALVADOR: Uncle Frederick hasn't got any children ... but Uncle Jeremy has ... only we've fallen out with him. Besides, Uncle Frederick is not too fond of the seaside. All the same, we could arrange things, couldn't we? If the worst comes to the worst, I'll tell them to build me my house half an hour from the beach. (*Pointing.*) There are some nice hills back there.

FANI: Wherever you wish. Well, Salvador? Do you accept?

SALVADOR: Of course I accept. It's been my lifelong dream: *be* somebody ... do some good ... make my mark!

FANI: Then I might safely say it's all within your reach.

SALVADOR: How do I go about it?

FANI: Talk to them. That's all ... simply talk to them. Your very own words spoken with faith and hope ... will produce the miracle.

SALVADOR: What do I say, exactly?

FANI: You'll see. The main thing is not to arouse them too much. Simply encourage them to give up this stupid mania for football ... and open up their doors to the visitors. But don't overdo things ... always remember the preservation of order is essential for the common good. Let them see how much time is being wasted with their interminable arguments on the way to kick a ball. Tell them to think about doing some work instead. Eight, ten, twelve hours a day, if necessary. Only through work can you get happiness ... because work means production and production means a higher standard of living. Give them the good things of life and they'll forget their dear old football. ... A taste of well-being and they'll soon calm down. ... Once again, they will all live as brothers ... with the proviso, of course, that some brothers are naturally more deserving than other brothers. ... Ah, yes! Should the opportunity present itself, I should like you to distribute among the public my visiting card. ... (*Gives him a packet.*) You'll find enclosed four thousand of them. ... Here's a sample.

SALVADOR (*reading*): "Metacarpis Co. Ltd." . . . What's that?

FANI: Actually it's a football club which boasts of a philanthropic attitude. I'm its representative. Should this town settle down to normal working schedules . . . we are disposed to establish in these parts a huge modern factory plant which will give employment to your entire labor force: men, women, old folks and children. Backing this, we shall provide immense hospital blocks for the rapid treatment of those folks who get themselves sick through working too hard. We shall also build six-lane highways cutting through the territory and bringing to your doors the benefits of importation, exportation and the tourist trade. In short, a club dedicated to raise the living standards of every single member of this community.

SALVADOR: What a marvelous institution!

FANI: You said it!

SALVADOR: And you think I'll manage to play the part . . . like you said? It's not all that easy. A bit terrifying, really.

FANI (*smiling reassuringly*): You can do anything. You just come along with me and we'll finalize the details. Let's have dinner together. Do you like champagne?

SALVADOR: Never tasted it. . . . Onstage they give you fizzy water.

FANI: Well, you're going to get the genuine stuff tonight. . . . And we'll thrash the whole project out, eh? You're a lucky guy, Mr. Salvador!

## SCENE 1

(*The same characters and situation as at the end of Act I. No time has elapsed since the act ended. The Side Event should be regarded as having been dreamed by the audience, which cannot bear to have things left unexplained and insists on reducing pure farce to concrete reality.*)

ZAPATONI: Leave him alone! (*He threatens Salvador's assailants with a stick. He is still standing on the table.*) I said, "Leave him alone!" (*The three Athletic Members, intimidated by*

*Zapatoni's manner, let go of Salvador, who remains stretched out on the floor.)* If anybody lays another finger on him . . .

BARTO (*excitedly*): What's going on here? Eh? You realize you're committing an act of rebellion, don't you? I take it you're aware of the penalty for that? (*To Youth B, taking advantage of the impact of his words.*) Call the Brads!

(*Youth B runs toward the door. Zapatoni leaps from the table, reaches the door before him and, stretching his arms out with his back to the door, bars the way.*)

ZAPATONI: Hold it! . . . Celestino, lock the door. (*The Losing Optimist moves toward the door.*) Tichomi, give him the key!

TICHOMI: Now don't drag me into it. . . . Calm down, will you? For the love of God, calm down!

ZAPATONI: For the love of my *father!* Say that, and we'll agree. Now give him the key!

TICHOMI: Bear witness, Señor Barto. . . . I'm being forced to hand it over. (*He does so.*)

ZAPATONI (*to the Losing Optimist*): Lock the door. . . . (*Referring to key.*) . . . and let's have it. (*He takes it.*)

BARTO: Come on! Come on! I'm waiting. Touch me! That's all I want you to do. . . . Touch me!

ZAPATONI: I wouldn't soil my hands!

BARTO: You're going to suffer for this. . . . I pity you.

ZAPATONI: I'm not going to stand by and see you beat up an innocent man. Got that?

BARTO: I give the orders around here. What I say, goes!

ZAPATONI: Oh, yes? And what if we think your orders stink? Are we obliged to carry them out, eh?

BARTO: I demand utter obedience.

ZAPATONI: On what grounds? Well?

BARTO: I am the manager of the Athletic Club . . . and the Athletic won the cup!

LONDEQUE: Oh no, it didn't!

ZAPATONI: It was before my time . . . got it? When that cup final was played . . . I wasn't even born! All I know is . . . this man's done nothing wrong . . . and my conscience tells me he's got to be defended.

LOSING OPTIMIST (*moving to Zapatoni's side*): We're with you, lad . . . every word.

BARTO (*with enormous violence*): You can keep your goddam consciences and shove 'em . . .

LONDEQUE (*interrupting him*): Barto! I've waited thirty years for this man to arrive. Don't you know what that means to me? At least, let him speak, will you?

BARTO: Thirty years for this man to arrive . . . tut-tut-tut. (*He smiles.*)

LONDEQUE: It's been foretold . . . he'll come down from the heavens on a rainy afternoon in May.

BARTO: I thought you didn't believe in anything, Londeque. What's all this nonsense about people coming down from Heaven?

UNITED MEMBER: There was a flash of lightning when he came in. You saw it, didn't you?

YOUTH A: What the hell's that got to do with it?

UNITED MEMBER: He's come down from heaven, I tell you!

BARTO: What . . . on a flash of lightning? (*He bursts out laughing. The situation eases a little. To Zapatoni:*) All right . . . just give me the key, clear off, and I'll forget it for once.

ZAPATONI: I'm not budging, Señor Barto. And I shan't hand over the key, either.

BARTO (*angry*): I'm losing my patience. . . .

ZAPATONI (*cutting in*): We're going to hear him! He's going to talk and we're going to hear him out! Nobody's going to stop us—understand?

BARTO: He's not going to talk!

LONDEQUE: Why not? . . . Because you're scared of what he might say! You laughed at me, Barto, for believing in the Blind Man's prophecy . . . but *you* believe in it, don't you? You believe that it'll all take place!

BARTO: No! I *don't* believe it! It's just a fairy tale. That Blind Man's as bad as a gypsy. He's been kidding you along with those prophecies. . . . Think of the money he's made out of you, you fools! All right then, you want him to talk? (*Moves closer to Zapatoni.*) Want to hear him talk, eh? Well, I guess we'll have to humor you. Let's hear what he has to say. (*He laughs.*) "The savior who will bring peace to my town." . . . Come on, start talking!

YOUTH B: Señor Barto, are you serious?

BARTO: You heard me, didn't you? Or wasn't I speaking loud enough? Come on, let's hear you. Let's hear every word, shall we? Right from the horse's mouth. (*Barto forces Salvador to climb on the table.*) Come on—up you get! Now talk!

UNITED MEMBER: Courage, brother . . . we'll look after you.

BARTO: This "monk of high renown" doesn't need any looking after. You've come down from heaven, haven't you? Right, then, get started!

(*Barto has sat down on a chair next to the table on which Salvador is standing. Salvador bobs and crosses himself.*)

SALVADOR: Let's see now . . . let's see . . .

BARTO: Everybody happy? That's good! Here he is . . . the man who will bring peace to my people and my town. Right . . . what version of peace is it, then? The only peace I recognize is what the Athletic have brought about. Perhaps you'll all recognize it one day . . . but it might be too late. (*Sighs.*) Well, come on . . . if you're going to talk . . . talk!

SALVADOR: Very well. But promise me you'll let me leave the town straight afterwards.

BARTO: Let you leave the town? What's the point of that if you've brought us peace?

LONDEQUE (*after a brief pause*): Promise him, Barto.

BARTO (*after a long silence*): I promise. (*His tone is serious.*)

ZAPATONI: Say what you have to say.

(*Change of spot. A pause.*)

SALVADOR (*as if in ecstasy, arms crossed over his breast*): "And the Lord said unto Moses, Go get thee down; for thy people which thou broughtest out of the land of Egypt, have corrupted themselves."

UNITED MEMBER: Well said!

SALVADOR: "And moreover, the Lord said unto Moses, I have seen this people and, behold, it is a stiff-necked people. . . ." (*He hesitates, trying to remember.*) "They have turned aside quickly out of the way which I commanded them: they have made them a molten calf, and have worshiped it and have sacrificed thereunto, and have said, These be thy gods, which have brought thee up out of the land of Egypt."

LOSING OPTIMIST: Very nicely put!

SALVADOR: Thank you. . . . Let's see if I remember the next bit. . . . Ah, yes! "And the Lord said unto Moses, Speak thus unto the people of Israel: You are a stiff-necked people; therefore I say unto you, Throw off your raiment, make yourself naked before me, and I shall then know what I must do." (*He begins to take off his robe.*)

BARTO: And what will you do, eh? . . . You poor old bastard!

FANI (*rises and makes gestures to Salvador, telling him to stop*): Salvador, careful now . . . careful!

(*Salvador does up his robe again.*)

SALVADOR: "And I shall lift my hand from your eyes. . . ." (*He extends his left hand, palm open, toward an imaginary person in front of him.*) "And I will turn to you my back . . ." (*He turns his back*). "for thou shalt never look upon my face." (*He pulls on the elastic band which keeps his beard in place and explains*). I am referring to the face of God. (*The United Members begin to get restless.*) Are you with me?

YOUTH B: Oh, dry up!

BARTO (*sarcastically*): Shhh! Silence! Let him speak . . . the man who will bring peace to our people and our town.

YOUTH B: But he's just talking nonsense!

(*Nestor rises and claps for service.*)

NESTOR: Tichomi! (*He shows him an empty bottle.*)

TICHOMI: Right! (*He takes bottles from Fani and Nestor's table.*)

YOUTH A: He's not making any sense at all!

(*The three Athletic Members talk to each other.*)

BARTO: Quiet!

YOUTH B (*to Athletic Member*): Can you understand him?

ATHLETIC MEMBER: Well, it's got nothing to do with this town, has it? . . . Why we don't talk to the others . . . why we are all dressed up as footballers . . . why all this hatred. . . . That's what I want to hear from him.

YOUTH A: But what if he's on the side of the United? You heard what Barto said.

ATHLETIC MEMBER: Barto said no such thing. Barto said he came down from heaven.

YOUTH B: All right, then. The monk has been sent by God. Well, God doesn't support the United!

YOUTH A: Exactly! Either God's an Athletic Club fan or He's nothing!

ATHLETIC MEMBER: Aren't you curious to know what it is that happened here thirty years ago? I am. I want to know what happened.

YOUTH B: Well, I don't. We won the Final. We've had peace. We've had employment. We can play football. What more do you want?

ATHLETIC MEMBER: But *they* can't play football, can they? And down in the slums there are people who're starving.

YOUTH B: That's not true.

ATHLETIC MEMBER: Oh yes, it is. I've seen them.

YOUTH B: One or two, perhaps.

ATHLETIC MEMBER: It's enough for me if one single person suffers. If you've as much as got the end of your little toe on your left foot going gangrenous, then you run a temperature. . . . Right?

SALVADOR: "And when Moses had spoken unto them, he covered his face with a veil. And when Moses was come before Jehovah, he took off the veil and did stand barefaced until he did depart. And departing, he spoke unto the children of Israel those things which had been commanded him."

UNITED MEMBER: God's truth, what's he on about?

SALVADOR: "And the children of Israel looked upon the face of Moses, the complexion thereof . . . the face of Moses, the complexion thereof . . ." Ah, I don't remember! . . . "The complexion thereof . . ." That's my lot. . . . I don't remember! (*Out loud.*) I don't remember!

YOUTH B: You're telling us!

BARTO: And this is the man who's going to explain everything! Tut-tut-tut!

SALVADOR: "And once again Moses covered his face with a veil." . . . Wait a minute, I've jumped a speech, haven't I? Ah well! And I was going to have a little house by the seaside. . . . Well, it was worth trying for.

LONDEQUE: Can't you make it a bit clearer for us?

ZAPATONI (*pointing upward*): That's how they talk, where he comes from.

LOSING OPTIMIST: Let's have a bit of sense, shall we?

UNITED MEMBER: Let Zapatoni speak!

YOUTH B: Let Barto speak!

LOSING OPTIMIST: I don't understand a word.

UNITED MEMBER: He's real weird. Talks crazy!

LONDEQUE: Shut up!

ZAPATONI: Let the referee speak!

(*Meanwhile Salvador has produced a bible from underneath his monk's habit and searches through its pages.*)

SALVADOR: Now I've got here a nice little bit from the prophet Isaiah. It was in something we put on I don't know how many years ago, but I think you're going to like it. Very interesting . . . very interesting indeed. I shall have to read it; my memory's not all that good nowadays, see. (*Reading.*) "Hear the word of the Lord, ye rulers of Sodom; give ear unto the law of our God, ye people of Gomorrah. To what purpose is the multitude of your sacrifices unto me, saith the Lord. I am full of the burnt offerings of lambs and the fat of fed beasts; and I delight not in the blood of bullocks or of lambs, or of he-goats. Bring no more vain oblations; incense is an abomination unto me; your solemn meetings are an iniquity unto me. They are a trouble unto me and I am weary to bear them. And when ye spread forth your hands to make your prayers, I will hide mine eyes from you. Yea, when ye make many prayers, I will not hear; your hands are full of blood. Wash you, make you clean; put away the evil of your doings before mine eyes; cease to do evil. Learn to do well; make justice, relieve the oppressed, defend the rights of the fatherless, help the widow."

UNITED MEMBER: And what about the Cup Final? Didn't your Isaiah say anything about the Cup Final?

LONDEQUE: Quiet, you fool!

SALVADOR (*when all is silent once more*): "Come now, and let us reason together, saith the Lord. Though your sins be as scarlet, they shall be as white as snow; though they be red like crimson, they shall be as wool. If ye be willing and obedient, ye shall eat the good of the land; but if ye refuse and rebel, ye shall be devoured with the sword; for the mouth of the Lord has spoken it. How is the faithful city become an harlot! It was full of judgment; righteousness lodged in it; but now murderers. Thy silver has become dross, thy wine mixed with water. Thy princes are rebellious, and the companions of thieves: everyone loveth gifts and followeth after rewards. They do not give justice to the fatherless, neither doth the cause of the widow come unto them."

(*A silence.*)

UNITED MEMBER: Tell it to the parish priest!

ZAPATONI: I've never heard our priest talk like that.

SALVADOR: "Therefore, saith the Lord, the Lord of Hosts, the Mighty One of Israel, I will have satisfaction of mine enemies, I will turn my hand upon thee, and purely purge away thy dross and take away all thy tin; and I will restore thy judges as at the first, and thy counsellors as at the beginning; afterwards thou shalt be called the City of Righteousness, the Faithful City."

(*Darkness around Salvador. During the following the stage lighting returns to full coverage.*)

SALVADOR: These are the words of Holy Writ, the thoughts of Isaiah, the Great Prophet. There is but one thing I can say to you, then: Love one another as the Lord Himself has never ceased to love you. . . . Forget your rancor, your hatred, on the altar of this immense love which God has set before all of us. . . . Be of good cheer and make a sacrifice of your discord and your selfishness in the temple of that great virtue, which I fancy you have all forgotten . . . the temple of *charity*.

BARTO: Well spoken, sir.

YOUTH A: Well spoken.

YOUTH B: Yes . . . the last bit was all right.

UNITED MEMBER (*pulling on Salvador's habit*): Wait a minute, though. What about the final result?

SALVADOR: The final result?

UNITED MEMBER: }
LOSING OPTIMIST: } The Cup Final result.

SALVADOR (*shrugging his shoulders*): But you have heard the words of the great prophet, Isaiah.

TICHOMI: The Great Prophet was a Jew . . . and it was the Jews who killed our Lord.

SALVADOR: It was the Romans who killed our Salvador . . . I mean our Savior.

LONDEQUE (*arguing with Barto*): But why hasn't he mentioned the football match?

BARTO: Simple. . . . It's as he says: he's a messenger of God.

LONDEQUE: How do I know he's a messenger of God? . . . I'm not so sure.

BARTO (*laughing*): I see. So what it amounts to is this: if he'd said the Cup Final had been nullified, then he'd be God's messenger . . . but as all he's got to say is we've got to love one another, then he can't possibly be God's messenger.

SALVADOR: Can I go now?

BARTO: You can go whenever you like.

(*Salvador gets down from the table.*)

LONDEQUE: Oh no, you don't. You don't go yet. (*The United Members try to stop Salvador leaving. The Athletic Members argue with them, shouting insults.*)

ZAPATONI: Shut up!!! (*To Salvador.*) Are you from the F.F.F.F., by any chance? No need to be frightened. . . . Just answer.

SALVADOR: Answer? . . . All right, if you insist. But take things gently.

LONDEQUE: Who sent you to this town?

LOSING OPTIMIST: How did you get here?

UNITED MEMBER: It was a flash of lightning that brought you? . . . Well, wasn't it?

SALVADOR: Well, I wouldn't say Robert was all that slow as a driver. . . . but as far as—

BARTO: Who's Robert?

TICHOMI: The bus driver.

ZAPATONI (*gently*): Isn't it the F.F.F.F. who's sent you?

SALVADOR: The F.F.F.F.? What's the F.F.F.F.?

YOUTH B (*laughing*): Oh, come on!

LONDEQUE (*angrily*): The Fundamental Finalizated Football Federation.

SALVADOR: Good Lord! What a name!

BARTO: Did they send you?

SALVADOR: Me? No, sorry.

BARTO: Are you a referee of the first, second or third division?

ZAPATONI: Let's have it: the truth!

SALVADOR: What truth?

LONDEQUE (*serious and aggressive*): Are you a referee in the first, second, or third division?

SALVADOR: I'm afraid I don't understand.

ATHLETIC MEMBER: There you are—he doesn't understand!

ZAPATONI: Leave him alone . . . leave the referee alone!

YOUTH B: The referee! (*He laughs.*)

LONDEQUE: The F.F.F.F. has sent you here to arbitrate our objection to the previously declared result. . . . Right?

SALVADOR: Hold it, will you? Nobody's sent me . . . nobody! (*He moves away from the group.*) Oh dear, oh dear, I've got such a bellyache! The only thing that ever helps it is rice pudding and milk of magnesia—and not even that seems to do much good. I don't know what's set it off this time. Maybe that mushroom omelette . . . or perhaps it was that bit of fish I had with the prompter. . . .

LONDEQUE: The F.F.F.F has decided to wipe it off the record . . . yes or no?

SALVADOR: Perhaps it was those prawns in garlic sauce. . . . I'm fond of sea food, but . . . ouch! . . . it doesn't seem to suit me.

ZAPATONI (*paternally, moving over to him*): Salvador . . . Salvador?

SALVADOR (*turning*): Yes?

LONDEQUE: Why are you dressed up as a monk?

ZAPATONI: You're intimidating him! (*He puts his arm around Salvador's shoulders.*)

LONDEQUE: The man's a comic . . . a comic actor . . . a comedian.

SALVADOR: That's right.

LONDEQUE: Why have you got a referee's uniform on under your monk's outfit?

SALVADOR: Well, it's this way . . .

BARTO (*interrupting him*): Why have you got a false beard?

SALVADOR: Now look: Don Lucio has told me to—

LONDEQUE: Why did you go out into the yard?

(*Salvador moves rapidly to Barto to whisper in his ear. Barto takes him on one side.*)

BARTO: Never!

(*Salvador continues to whisper in his ear.*)

SALVADOR: D'you understand? I didn't think I was doing anything wrong. Besides, the doctor at the clinic has told me to—

LONDEQUE (*to Barto*): What's he whispering about?

BARTO: Nothing . . . nothing. (*To Salvador.*) But what about the disguise . . . the false beard?

LONDEQUE (*to Salvador*): What have you just said to him?

BARTO (*pushing Londeque*): Nothing, I tell you . . . nothing.

LONDEQUE: What did you say to Barto?

SALVADOR (*whining*): The lavatories were all occupied, so what could I do but go in the yard? (*Pause.*) I didn't think I was doing anything wrong. (*Pause.*) I couldn't wait. And so I explained to this gentleman about my "trouble." That's right, isn't it?

TICHOMI: Yes, quite right.

SALVADOR: And he said I could do it round the back. (*Pause.*) It's the first time I've ever had anyone take me to task about it. I mean, it's a natural weakness, isn't it? . . . And then all the things you've been pestering me with . . . all this football and stuff, and the F.F.F.F., and the Cup Final, and the wiping something or other from the records . . . and this climbing onto tables and jumping down again. . . . Oh dear!

BARTO: Why have you dressed up as a monk? Why have you put on a false beard?

SALVADOR: Look, I'll tell you all about it. We're doing that great play, *Secrets of the Vatican.* In the second act I come on as a Capucine monk. The Countess fixes me with her eye and says (*Mimicking.*) "Art thou sent from the king? Dost thou bring the . . . er . . . er." I've forgotten the line again, and it's my cue too! Anyway, she does a gesture with her hand, like that. . . . And I reply, (*Declaiming as if before the Countess.*) "Lady, thou sayest well. I come hotfoot from Rome. Sick at heart and burdened as I am, I bring the news." Etc., etc. Now, seeing as how *Secrets of the Vatican* is a bit on the short side, we follow it up with a little comedy called *Factory Football.*

BARTO: *Factory Football?*

SALVADOR: Yes, it's about a works' team . . . a satire on football fans. You see, this particular team tries to bribe the referee. I expect you've had that sort of thing happen, haven't you?

... When the referee declares it wasn't a goal even though the ball slammed into the back of the net because he had whistled for a penalty which wasn't really a penalty....

ZAPATONI: He's from the F.F.F.F.!

LOSING OPTIMIST: It's him!

LONDEQUE: Go on talking! Let's hear it!

SALVADOR: Hear what?

BARTO (*shaking Salvador*): You're talking nonsense, d'you hear me? Pure, utter nonsense! I don't want to hear anymore of your funny stuff. I know it all already. You can't fool me! Got that? So let's have it. . . . Why have you come? The penalty was a penalty, and Celestino's goal didn't count. Got that?

SALVADOR: Yes, sir, I've got it. Very well. What's it to do with me?

LONDEQUE: What's it to do with you? You're from the F.F.F.F., aren't you?

SALVADOR: Me? From the F.F.F.F.? Look, you're getting me all mixed up. If I'd known I'd have to go through all this, I'd have stayed in the bus and done it in my trousers! I'm an actor . . . a third-rate, badly paid actor. (*He weeps.*) A failure, d'you hear? A failure! I've been one all my life! First act of *Secrets of the Vatican* I'm a statue. Fifteen minutes on a pedestal without moving! Act Two, Scene One, I'm another statue, holding up a Roman pillar. At the end of the scene it falls on top of me. (*While saying this he kneels down.*) And then I come on as a Capucine monk, and after that I'm a referee. The trouble is they never give me a dressing room so I can change my costumes. What I do is wear my wardrobe one on top of the other. (*He sighs. Long pause.*) You tell them, will you, sir? (*He appeals to Tichomi.*) Isn't it true you've had a touring company in here? Tell him, will you? It's the truth!

TICHOMI: It's true, Señor Barto. This man is from a company of actors who were in here about an hour ago.

ZAPATONI (*disillusioned*): So you're not a referee, after all? You've nothing to do with the F.F.F.F.?

BARTO (*laughing*): Of course he isn't!

(*The Athletic Members laugh at the disillusionment of the United Members.*)

YOUTH B: He's on the stage.

YOUTH A: A lousy ham actor.

LONDEQUE (*shaking Salvador*): Are you or aren't you?

SALVADOR (*feelings hurt*): No . . . no, I'm not!

LONDEQUE: Coward!

ZAPATONI (*not losing hope*): Tell us the truth!

BARTO (*laughing*): But you've heard, haven't you?

LOSING OPTIMIST: Coward! Coward!

LONDEQUE: You coward!

SALVADOR: Coward? Why?

(*The question makes the Athletic Members burst into laughter. Salvador approaches Barto.*)

SALVADOR: Tell me why!

LONDEQUE: Thirty years we have waited for him. We've waited patiently. Full of hope! We've had nothing but dreams, thinking of you and the things you'd tell us, dreaming of what would happen to this town once you had arrived.

SALVADOR: Yes . . . well, I . . . er . . .

LONDEQUE: And what have you told us? What is the great message you have just delivered? Meaningless words which nobody understands.

SALVADOR: They're words from the Holy Scripture.

LONDEQUE: What do I care about the Holy Scripture? What have they got to do with it? There's nothing in 'em . . . not for us. They tell us nothing! D'you hear me? What have they got to do with us? Your Moses and Isaiah and the face of God and this calf made out of silver.

SALVADOR: It was a golden calf.

LONDEQUE: What does it matter what it was? What's it got to do with us? Nothing . . . absolutely nothing. We're not interested

in the history of the people of Israel. We don't want to know
what took place two thousand years ago. We're interested in
the history of our town. Problems that have been piled on us
and have got to be cleared up. And nothing will be settled
by yelling "Peace and goodwill" down our ears. Understand?

SALVADOR: I'm merely an actor, that's all.

BARTO: What you are is a comic turn. Just an old buffoon, aren't
you? (*To Londeque.*) Now then, I'd like to give you a little
lesson, Londeque. I'd like to convince you once and for all
that we're not to be played about with. So what shall we do,
eh? (*Jokingly.*) 'Cos we're a very lively lot, the Athletic. (*To
his followers who laugh triumphantly.*) And we like games as
well. So what games shall we play with this frightened little
rat you've been encouraging?

NESTOR: They're about to skin him alive.

SALVADOR: Now wait a minute. What can I say to you? How can
I make you understand? I'm an actor, that's all . . . nothing
else but an actor. I belong to that company that stopped here.
Honest! I swear it! I missed the bus. It was stupid of me, I
know, but I missed it. That's why I'm still here. I know
nothing about nothing! All I know is my lines—and I don't
know them very well. What do you want me to say to you . . .
What?

BARTO: Very well said. He's right, you know, he's right. . . . And
consequently, out of sheer admiration for you, I'm going to
decorate you. (*He looks at the United Members.*) What d'you
think? Just for once, this town has decided unanimously to
honor one of its visitors. (*To Salvador.*) I am about to decorate
you . . . or rather, I am about to give official recognition to
your being our one and only civic and honorary referee-*cum*-
comedian. (*Barto grabs at Salvador with his left hand. Salvador tries to free himself. He is horrified and guesses what is
coming. Barto becomes excited and loses control.*) For having
pissed in the yard without my permission . . . for wearing a
false beard . . . for daring to take it off . . . for missing the
bus . . . for taking off your monk's rig out in public . . . for
standing on the table and wasting ten minutes of our time with
a whole pile of bloody nonsense, . . . for actually saying the
penalty wasn't a penalty . . . take that! And that! (*He hits
him.*)

(*Nobody goes to his defense. There are slight movements from Zapatoni, Nestor and an Athletic Member. Barto takes the chair on which Nestor was seated and raises it over his head.*)

NESTOR: Careful, Barto. You're losing control.

BARTO (*chair above his head*): I decorate you with the ancient order of the chop!

(*Zapatoni, Nestor and the Athletic Member prevent Barto from bringing down the chair on Salvador.*)

ATHLETIC MEMBER: That's enough, Barto. We're not barbarians, you know.

BARTO: Yes, you're right. (*Long pause. He breathes heavily.*) This stupid fool has put me beside myself. (*Seeing various objects on the floor.*) Pick up your things and get out of here. Let's see the back of you.

(*The Athletic Member bends down to pick up a bible, a packet and the monk's hood which Salvador has dropped, but a United Member gets there first.*)

YOUTH B: You heard what Señor Barto said.

FANI: Dear oh dear, he's ruined it. He should never have told them he was an actor. Tut-tut-tut.

NESTOR: Give him what you promised and forget about it.

FANI: I haven't promised him anything. I haven't even spoken to him.

(*Salvador staggers to the street door, supported by the Athletic Member and the United Member.*)

UNITED MEMBER (*giving him the hood*): I should put it on. It's raining out there.

ATHLETIC MEMBER: He could catch pneumonia, Señor Barto.

LONDEQUE: Let him catch it, then. I hope he catches it and dies!

(*Salvador refuses the glass which Tichomi offers.*)

TICHOMI: Drink it. It's brandy. It'll do you good.

SALVADOR: Thank you, no. (*Turning.*) Why are the people of this town so cruel?

BARTO (*to Youth B*): I told you to throw him out! He's wasting our time, the damn fool!

SALVADOR: Fight for peace? You're all wrong. What you must fight for is justice—

LONDEQUE: Yes . . . fight for justice; you're right. But you haven't got the courage for it, have you? (*To United Member.*) Leave him alone. Let him clear out by himself. Can't you see he's on their side? When he's stopped beating about the bush, what have you got? You're back where you started. The Athletic won and we've got to go on and on just as we are now.

BARTO (*to Youth A*): Is that what he says? In that case, let him go on talking. (*He rubs his hands.*)

SALVADOR: Why is it that you must have enemies? You can't live without enemies. And if you haven't got them, you have to invent them. Why is it that you all want peace. . . . but only in order to exploit it? Why is it that in this town nobody thinks about his neighbor? Why is it that everybody thinks he is right? And when somebody says to them, "Yes, all of you are right . . . all of you" . . . then nobody believes him and they join together to throw him out of the place?

FANI: Ah, that's a bit better. If only he'd spoken like that earlier.

BARTO (*approaching*): Who do you think you are? Jesus Christ? Well, as far as I've heard, when Jesus Christ was swiped across the cheek, he turned the other.

SALVADOR: So did I. . . . But you kept on hitting me on the same side. What I said to you was in good faith.

LONDEQUE: Well, you can keep your good faith and clear off. You're not from the F.F.F.F. and you're not a referee, so just get out of here, will you?

TICHOMI: All the same, it's acting a bit rough, don't you think, with this rain coming down?

LONDEQUE: Oh, is it? Well, let him get drenched. He's the one who's told us to our face that that lot can go on playing football while we . . . oh, God help me, don't let's talk about it! He wants me to swallow down this "peace," as he calls it, wholesale. Well, I'll tell you what his kind of peace means: keep

your trap shut and toe the line! Why, he's worse than they
are. He not only wants us to go on and on as we have been
doing, but he tries to convince us that they have been right,
are right and always will be right.

SALVADOR: All of you, *all* are right.

LONDEQUE: Very well; if you like, all of us are right. . . . So what
we want you to do, all of us, is to clear off out of here. Why
the hell don't you go?

SALVADOR: Because I still have a faint hope that my being here
might be of some value to you. I'd rather not go through life
realizing I haven't done what I can for others. Now if everybody here could only forget about football, I'm quite sure you
would all be happy.

LONDEQUE: Yes, but some would be much happier than others.

SALVADOR: What does that matter? The misfortunes of the many
are the comfort of fools.

LONDEQUE (*sarcastically*): And the fortunes of the few are the
comfort of idiots. . . . What do you want, anyway?

SALVADOR: I want to open your eyes.

LONDEQUE: Well, I say, "Shut 'em!"

SALVADOR: I know of a certain philanthropic organization which
is wanting to pour millions upon millions into this town. It
would build factories, highways, hospitals, schools. It would
raise the standard of living. It would make everybody happy.
All it asks is for this town to be at peace.

LONDEQUE: I'm afraid you don't have to talk to me about it,
Salvador. We haven't got any influence in this town.

SALVADOR: But you are the ones who refused this peace that's
offered to you. You keep hoping for this miracle man who will
put himself at the head of the United and destroy the Athletic.

LONDEQUE: I don't know if we'll go on hoping—not after what's
happened today.

SALVADOR: Why can't you accept peace?

LONDEQUE: Because it's a peace imposed upon us by the Athletic.
And because they wish to be the ones, them alone, who rule

this town. We don't object to working to their orders, if necessary, as long as we can share in the organization and direction of where this town ought to go. But that's what they don't want . . . or daren't let us have. And that's why we're not disposed to share our work with them. . . . I've heard speak of this philanthropic society you mention. It's called the Metacarpis, isn't it?

SALVADOR: Yes, that's what they call themselves. (*He searches under his habit.*) Now I happen to have here a packet which they gave me, containing their business cards. Ah, here it is . . . no, that's the bible. They're round about the same size. Ah, here you are. . . . Take them. Do what you like with them.

LONDEQUE: We shall burn the lot, don't you worry.

SALVADOR: But . . . but why?

LONDEQUE: Because the factories and highways which this company would build, and the benefits we would derive from them, would establish an unfair difference of rights and privileges which we reject straight off. It'll be like building nice, new, modern flats on top of a building whose shape and structure we know to be rotten.

YOUTH B: It's stopped raining. Come on.

SALVADOR: Very well. I'll go. (*To everybody.*) I'm sorry I haven't been able to do anything for you.

LONDEQUE: Don't worry. . . . And forgive me if I've been a bit rough, won't you?

SALVADOR: That doesn't matter. (*We hear the March of the Slaves. Salvador, now in the doorway, cannot contain his tears. Everybody, except Londeque, turn their backs to him. Then the United Member and the Athletic Member look at him.*) Good-bye . . . good-bye, everybody. May God bless you. (*He puts on his hood, opens the door and leaves. At the moment of leaving, he stumbles against the Blind Man, who enters with his white stick and his dog. The music stops.*) Sorry. I didn't see you.

BLIND MAN: Well, that's something I can never say. I'm lucky. (*Entering the bar.*) Lord above, haven't the heavens opened this afternoon? Talk about rain!

BARTO: Shut up, will you?

BLIND MAN: Ah, we've got Señor Barto here. Is Señor Londeque here as well?

LONDEQUE: Yes. What do you want?

BLIND MAN: I suspect there's been a bit of an argument. (*Breathing in deeply.*) Yes, there is still the smell in the air. Very common smell in this town. And are the foreign gentlemen here as well . . . the ones who look for oil fields and go killing wild beasts?

FANI: Yes.

NESTOR: Yes, Blind Man, we are here.

BLIND MAN: There's a stuffiness about the bar. You've got a lot of people in here tonight, haven't you? Who are they? Eh? (*Pause.*) There's been a bit of novelty in the town today. A coachload of visitors stopped here. Very happy-go-lucky and excitable, they were. I heard the laughter and the shouting. . . . They've gone now, haven't they? I heard the bus move off. . . . Who was this fellow who bumped into me? Who was he? . . . Have you all gone dumb? . . . You've turned nasty again, is that it? Trust . . . trust and faith . . . that's what you're lacking.

(*From the moment of the Blind Man's entrance, the lights around him start dimming, leaving him in a pool of light. On his last line there is a blackout which lasts three seconds.*

*When the lights go up again, the table where Fani and Nestor are sitting is illuminated. Salvador stands near them.*)

FANI (*who half gets up from his chair*): You don't have to go, Nestor.

NESTOR: I think you'll talk more freely if you're alone together.

FANI: We've got nothing to say to each other. . . . (*To Salvador.*) Have we?

SALVADOR: Not very much. I'd like you to tell me, though . . . how was I?

FANI: You really want to know?

SALVADOR: Well, yes . . . seeing that I did all I could.

FANI: Appalling! Absolutely appalling!

SALVADOR: I was?

FANI: You couldn't have done it worse.

SALVADOR: As bad as that? I distributed your business cards . . . like you told me.

FANI: Distributed them? Are you out of your mind? You handed the whole lot over to Señor Londeque. . . . You didn't even open the packet! He'll throw it on the fire.

SALVADOR: I didn't realize he might do that.

FANI: You should have. I said, "Distribute them." One by one.

SALVADOR: There wasn't much time. Weigh it up yourself. . . . They were about to throw me out of the town.

FANI: An absolute disaster!

SALVADOR: That's what you think. Anyway, what about the little house by the seaside? (*Fani laughs.*) . . . with orchards and dairy cattle?

FANI: Don't make me laugh . . . please!

SALVADOR: And my name written up on all the streets and squares? (*Fani guffaws.*) No? Not even a cul-de-sac called after me? A little alleyway? Don't you think so?

FANI: Not a sausage! It's quite clear to me, Salvador, that oratory is not your strong suit.

SALVADOR: I did everything possible. But you saw it; they're not all that welcoming. If I'd come to this town a few years ago, I might have been able to manage things. But now they don't want to know . . . 'specially as far as peace is concerned. It's a pity . . . 'cos they're all nice people, really. (*Nestor smiles sympathetically.*) If only I could have got them to patch up their differences once and for all. . . . Then it wouldn't have mattered if I got that house and that stable . . . and had streets named after me . . . or not. . . . But to throw me out as they tried to do! And for you to say to me now there's no house . . . no streets with my name . . . not even a sausage!

FANI: That's life, Salvador. . . . And believe me, I'm mighty sorry about it. (*Rising and offering his hand which Salvador shakes mechanically.*) You'll excuse me, won't you? I'm rather busy at the moment. Another time, perhaps.

SALVADOR: Another time? When? . . . And how am I going to get to Catirinada? (*He looks at his watch.*) In two hours' time we're going up on *Secrets of the Vatican*. If I'm not there as a statue as soon as the curtain rises . . . Don Lucio will go raving mad. He'll give me the sack, that's certain.

FANI: I assure you I'm very sorry . . . but nothing can be done, I'm afraid.

SALVADOR: Can't you give me a lift in your car?

FANI: What? To Catirinada!

SALVADOR: Well, just as far as the main highway, then. Perhaps I can catch a bus at Protik.

FANI: Sorry again . . . but the car is being repaired.

SALVADOR: But it's just outside the door!

FANI: That one belongs to this gentleman.

NESTOR: I don't possess a car. The car outside is *his*.

SALVADOR: I see. You don't want to take me, then. (*Fani sits, puffs out a mouthful of smoke and drinks some beer.*) Good-bye . . . I'm sorry to have bothered you.

(*Nestor rises and offers him his hand.*)

NESTOR: Somebody is always responsible, Salvador . . . don't forget that. Every care, trouble, pain, grief . . . there's always somebody responsible. The wretch whose job it is to carry out orders diligently and loyally, bringing misery to his brothers . . . he's not your responsible one. No! Those who are really responsible glide through life unnoticed . . . their faces beaming with charm and kindness. You are a sincere man . . . and you want the truth, don't you? Then don't be deceived by the smiling mask . . . search them out . . . tear the mask from them. Do it publicly so all can see what lies beneath the surface. . . . And the day you manage that . . . that day peace will blossom in this town.

(*Darkness for three seconds. Then general overall lighting. The Blind Man is now center stage.*)

BLIND MAN: We are in the month of May. It is raining . . . the rain doesn't stop. The prophecy is about to be fulfilled.

ATHLETIC MEMBER: Shut up!

BARTO: Let him go on if he wants to. . . . Come on, let's have a drink.

BLIND MAN (*singing*):
  He'll arrive with his face half-hidden . . .

LONDEQUE: Shut up, will you!

LOSING OPTIMIST: Don't let's have that one again. . . .

BLIND MAN:
  On a rainy afternoon in May . . .

ZAPATONI: That's enough.

BLIND MAN:
  He'll come down from the heavens, the savior . . .

LOSING OPTIMIST: Hey, Blind Man! Go and fetch me your mother so I can shit on her!

ZAPATONI: You damned old billy goat!

LONDEQUE: We've had thirty years of your goddam lies! So we'll settle your hash once and for all! (*He hits him.*)

UNITED MEMBER: You bastard!

ZAPATONI: You swine!

(*The United Member, Londeque, Zapatoni and the Losing Optimist punch and kick the Blind Man. He cowers and tries to defend himself. They hurl insults at him.*)

BLIND MAN: Ouch! O, God! Ouch! Let me be! Don't hit me! I'm blind! What have I done? Ouch! What have I done to you, eh? Señor Barto! Señor Nestor! Barto! Londeque! Pity, will you? Pity! Bartooo!

BARTO: Fight back, Blind Man! Go on! Fight back!

(*Barto and Youths A and B are amused by the situation.*)

YOUTH B: Whack 'em with your stick!

YOUTH A: Go on! Use your stick! Lay into 'em!

(*The Blind Man starts lashing about with his stick.*)

BARTO: Harder! Harder!

YOUTH A: Lash into 'em!

BARTO: On your right! Go on! Get him!

YOUTH B: Lovely!

BARTO: Mind out . . . behind you!

(*The Blind Man flings vituperations at the attackers as he attempts to hit them.*)

BARTO: You see now, don't you. . . . That'll teach you to get us all wound up with your stupid songs.

SALVADOR (*resolved. He has now removed his beard*): That's enough! (*All stand still except the Blind Man who continues waving his stick in the air.*) And you, Blind Man! (*The Blind Man stops.*)

BLIND MAN: Who is it? Who speaks? Is it the man I bumped into?

(*Salvador slowly, solemnly and deliberately takes off his monk's habit and appears as a referee but now with long trousers, the same tone and color as the jacket. While Salvador is "changing," the following dialogue is said rapidly.*)

FANI (*to Nestor*): I see your game. . . . You've got 'round him. . . . He's in your pay.

NESTOR: No. . . . It's you who's made him come to his senses. It's you who's shown him the light.

FANI: What light?

NESTOR: Surely you know that our very best footballers . . . those who are the most enthusiastic . . . started their careers playing on your side?

SALVADOR (*to United Members*): Aren't you ashamed? . . . Aren't you ashamed to have fallen so low? Four men, four human beings beating up a defenseless blind man? . . . (*Turning to Barto's crowd.*) And you there . . . another quartet from the human race looking on and cheering!

BARTO: Are you off again?

SALVADOR: Yes, but this time I'll say what *I* think . . . what I believe to be the only true way of peace and goodwill.

BLIND MAN: He has come from the heavens!

SALVADOR: I haven't come from the heavens. . . . I've come in a bus. There's nothing magic about me. I'm a human being, like you are. I work. . . . I receive pay. . . . I try to eke it out on food and clothes. (*Pause.*) But how can you be so indifferent to another person's suffering? How did you manage to stoop lower than the beasts?

BARTO: Out of the town with you! Out of the town!

(*Fani is in a highly excited state.*)

SALVADOR: I'm not going. And don't try to throw me out. . . . because I refuse to leave. I have something to tell you.

BARTO: We've heard enough.

SALVADOR: But you haven't heard this: animals, wild beasts, when they wound and kill do it to some purpose. (*The March of the Slaves starts playing.*) They *know* why they wound, why they kill . . . but you don't! You're cruel and savage without knowing why. Your cruelty isn't even for the pleasure of it . . . because I'm certain you're all sorry in your hearts for what you've done to me and the blind man here. (*Silence. The Athletic and The United Members lower their heads.*) No! Don't bow your heads. Lift them up! Lift them up with pride! The blame is not with you. So be conscious of what you are: human beings! Men! And until it is proved to the contrary, consider yourselves the finest, the highest, the most noble thing in the whole universe. (*Pause. Broken voice.*) And yet . . . and yet some of you have attacked the blind . . . and others have looked on without moving a finger to defend him. Worse still . . . you have reveled in his torment, urging him to fight back with his stick . . . his blind man's stick. Why? Why? Who is it who gains from your cruelty? Who benefits from your attitude? Who lurks behind your actions? Who is responsible for all this? Or haven't you bothered to ask yourselves the question?

FANI: Why didn't he talk like this before?

NESTOR: You wanted an actor. All I want is a man.

BARTO: Fate! That's your answer, Salvador. Fate!

SALVADOR: That is a lie! It isn't fate. . . . It's men! . . . A handful
of men . . . a little clique! I used to make that mistake as
well; I once thought my own misery and the misery of those
around me were all part and parcel of the human condition . . .
that all struggle was useless . . . that nothing could change.
But it is not true! They teach us a lot, don't they? They fill
our heads with dates and data. They distract our attention.
They give us diplomas, certificates, titles, and qualifications.
They confer upon us an official wisdom . . . so that our
spontaneity, our open curiosity is lost and our ignorance is
forgotten. But we should ask ourselves: Why am I not happy?
Why are we not happy? The answer is always the same: fate,
destiny, man's lot. I tell you again, it's a lie! Man has a
concept of happiness, hasn't he? He has a potential for
happiness, he knows it. Then why is it not fulfilled? Because
it doesn't suit the book of the "few." How can we make
permanent that happiness we are only allowed a glimpse of
. . . that should be our main preoccupation. . . . But no, we
clutter up our minds with trivia, pettiness.

TICHOMI: For example?

SALVADOR (*with a mounting rhythm*): The commercial catalog of
top of the pops . . . politicians' names without their politics
. . . who'll be first on the moon? . . . the divorces of film stars
. . . TV serials . . . the sex and the violence of "Double-O-
Seven" . . . the bingo jackpot . . . and football. Oh yes, above
all, *football!*

ALL: *Football!!*

SALVADOR: Yes. It separates and it undermines. Every single town
has its Athletic and its United. . . . in every town the people
are divided. Naked we're equal . . . so they dress us up in
different costumes. Aren't we divided enough already? Our
heritage has been isolated pockets of civilization. Five conti-
nents, two hundred nations, four hundred races, a thousand
religions, and three thousand languages tug at us . . . but a
man and a woman, tribes and tribes apart can meet and fall
in love. (*The young people giggle. He rebukes them.*) No, my
young friends . . . their tenderness and gentleness in the act
can defy biology. If two men should meet by chance . . . they
greet each other with smiles. . . . Forgive me, if by error I

seem to be directing these words only to you. (*He looks at the United Members.*) I speak to all of you . . . because all of you are victims . . . workers and victims of a consumer world. (*He turns to the audience.*) And you, too . . . I speak to you. According to my calculations, three in every thousand men are responsible . . . *three!* And for those three, I desire with all my heart . . . an immediate death!

FANI: He's gone mad . . . the man's gone mad! (*He moves to left.*)

NESTOR: Where are you going?

FANI: I have an appointment.

NESTOR: Whatever you're going to do, think it over carefully, won't you?

(*Fani leaves.*)

SALVADOR: Today they will say to you: "Your town is in danger . . . you must go to war . . . your duty is to kill. There is our enemy!" And they will point their finger at a stranger. (*Pause.*) But tomorrow it's different. They will say: "We must live at peace. All pull together. Let's have mutual aid and a common market . . . that man is your friend so take him by the hand. . . ." And they point their finger at the same stranger! One day they say: "Procreate . . . increase your families . . . we want more people." Another, "We have too many mouths to feed; we must have living-room . . . so we'll kill and we'll kill to get it." In the morning, they say: "Eat and eat till you explode. Your duty is to consume." . . . At night we hear: "Tighten your belts . . . we've underestimated our productivity margin." . . . And those are the ones who decide on peace and war, freedom and slavery, love and hate, beauty and ugliness, life and death. . . . And they do it in cold blood, seated around their board room tables. . . . And between you and them is the electronic brain, the impartial computer turning your sweat and your humanity into punch card classifications. They make their ideas your ideas . . . for theirs is the press, the editorials, the radio, the television, the theatre, the cinema and the top twenty! Ideas may only be transmitted through their closely knit, all-pervading network.

LONDEQUE: How can we retain our freedom, then?

SALVADOR: "Retain your freedom"? We never have been free. But slowly . . . a few of us are beginning to realize that if the pretty flowers on the tree are really poisonous . . . it's no good cutting off the flowers . . . *we chop down the trunk!* . . . And what else must we do? We must band together and be vigilant. He who works as you work is your brother. Trust nobody else. When your two hands lift a sack of corn . . . there are two more hands at the other corners . . . and they are the hands of your brother. . . . When you push the truck along the pit rails, the hands that push with you are those of a brother. . . . The fingers that hit at the keys of typewriters are all of one family, brothers and sisters. . . . And when your hands switch on a motor, other hands twelve hours back on the other side of the world have switched off a motor . . . it's your brother handing over to you. . . . When your hands move, make, push, crush, sleep and heal their wounds . . . then remember they are not simply yours. . . . They are the hands of a brother.

(*Rabit and Kopas enter through the street door. They are both middle aged. Kopas wears a cutaway coat and a Basque beret. Rabit wears a traditional ringmaster's costume. His left breast is covered entirely with medals and decorations.*)

KOPAS: An entire afternoon without working.

RABIT: Without producing.

KOPAS: Without sweating.

RABIT: Without earning our livelihood.

KOPAS: Like yesterday.

RABIT: And the day before.

KOPAS: Disgusting.

RABIT: Absolutely disgusting.

SALVADOR: . . . And when you have cut the wedge into the tree and it is half-hewn and ready to fall . . . do not trust those pallid and poker-faced men who arrive on the scene and say to you: "You have done well. . . . How powerful you must be. . . . Please let me help you to do the rest."

KOPAS: Barto!

BARTO: At your service.

KOPAS: Why are you all here . . . joined together? Why is he permitted to speak? Who is he?

SALVADOR: I have no need to ask who you are. You are the honorable president of the Athletic Club. . . . Yes or no?

KOPAS: What impudence!

BARTO (*without relish*): Yes. Señor Kopas is our president.

SALVADOR: And the gentleman who accompanies him . . . there is no doubt who he once was. He was the president of the one-time United Club. Am I right?

LONDEQUE (*with pride, but unsmiling*): Yes. This is Señor Rabit. Our president.

SALVADOR: And the town's wickerwork company? Does that belong to Señor Kopas or Señor Rabit?

(*The following is said rapidly.*)

BARTO: Señor Kopas.

SALVADOR: And the Banderillas Company?

BARTO: Señor Rabit.

SALVADOR: And the bullring?

BARTO: Señor Kopas.

SALVADOR: And the olive groves?

BARTO: Señor Rabit.

SALVADOR: And the orange groves?

BARTO: Señor Kopas.

LONDEQUE: Señor Rabit.

BARTO: No, Señor Kopas.

LONDEQUE: Barto, they belong to Señor Rabit.

KOPAS: Neither of us . . . but don't let's talk about it.

BARTO:   ⎫ Eh?
LONDEQUE: ⎭

KOPAS: They belonged to me . . . but I sold them to the Linkomin Estate Company.

LONDEQUE: You sold our orange grove to the Linkomin Estate Company?

RABIT: Afraid so, my son. I can hardly tell you how sorry I am. The orange grove . . . the banderilla factory . . . the fields of olives . . . the lot. But they took me for a ride, Londeque . . . robbed me, they did. Do you know what Linkomin paid me? Twelve thousand an acre. . . . A week later they sold the orange grove to Consolidated Developments for a hundred and twenty a square yard!

LONDEQUE: You sold the orange grove without consulting us? . . . To a foreign company! I planted that grove twenty years ago. . . . These hands of mine have fed and watered the trees year after year. How can you do this? What will happen to them now?

RABIT: I don't exactly know. I believe they are thinking of constructing an oil refinery. . . . But they robbed me, Londeque. They paid me next to nothing.

LONDEQUE: I don't give a damn what they paid you. What about my orange trees? I carried sand . . . bit by bit, a mountain of sand to give them some protection from the east wind. Don't you know that?

BARTO: Come on, Londeque! Let's hear you shout, "Long live the United!" now! Come on! Let's hear you!

RABIT: Perhaps you ought to know, Barto, that Señor Kopas has disposed of certain properties in which you may feel you have some moral interest.

BARTO: Mmm? (*A delay in comprehending. Then:*) You haven't sold the wickerwork factory?

KOPAS: Yes.

BARTO: And the straw hat company?

KOPAS: To Mechanical Engineering, Inc. They're knocking it down and putting up an automobile factory.

BARTO (*seizing Kopas by the lapels*): Kopas! You're a dirty, stinking, lousy bastard! (*He takes off his shirt.*) Here—you can have it . . . you can have your filthy shirt back. . . . I'm not going to go around decked out in your fancy colors anymore! I've slaved in that damn factory ever since I was a kid. And now you go and sell it out from under us? Without us having anything to do with it at all?

YOUTH A: Where do we stand now? That's what I want to know.

YOUTH B: Who'll employ us? What work is there?

KOPAS: Don't start worrying. There'll be plenty of work for every-one. We're building a feed road off the main highway. Thou-sands of tourists will stop off here. We'll sell as much wickerwork as we want!

BARTO: My factory! My father built the walls . . . he got me my job there. It was me who carved up the willows, made the baskets. . . .

(*All those dressed in football shirts take them off.*)

SALVADOR (*in mounting rhythm*):
    It is now you are beginning . . .
    beginning to learn . . .
    beginning to learn the facts . . .
    the facts of life!
    Neither you . . .
    nor you . . .
    nor any of you . . .
    mean a jot . . .
    a ha'porth . . .
    a grain of sand on the seashores of this world . . .
    when these men . . .
    these top men . . .
    these top gentlemen . . .
    see the chance . . .
    the occasion . . .
    the opportunity . . .
    of doing *big business!!!*

(*We hear two rifle shots. Salvador falls.*)

BARTO: Down, all of you! Down!

(*They lie down.*)

LONDEQUE: He's wounded! Salvador's wounded.

LOSING OPTIMIST: Look at the blood . . . the blood!

NESTOR (*dragging himself forward*): Dying?

LONDEQUE: I think so.

(*Pause.*)

BARTO: No more shots.

KOPAS (*to Barto*): Wait!

TICHOMI: What lousy bastard's done this?

BARTO: (*to Nestor who is rising*): Down, for Christ's sake! Down!

NESTOR: No. There's nothing to fear. Lift your heads, will you? . . .
Stand on your two legs. . . . Face 'em. . . . Face up to 'em! . . .

(*A few have already risen with Nestor.*)

YOUTH B: Are you sure it's all right? Are you quite sure?

ZAPATONI: He's dying. Salvador's dying.

NESTOR: Where did the shots come from? (*He looks above the
mud wall which encloses the window.*) They could only fire
from this angle.

BARTO: If you make a straight line, it's Salvador, this window . . .
and the tower of our holy parish church.

LONDEQUE: The arrow slits . . . there are arrow slits in our church
tower!

BARTO (*to Youth B*): Find the Brads! Tell them to get to the
church . . . anybody suspect, hold 'em! (*Pause.*) Right, then
. . . which of you can use a rifle?

ZAPATONI: I'm a crack shot, Barto.

LONDEQUE: You can count on me, Barto.

BARTO (*to Youth B*): Tell the Chief Brad . . . that from now on he
takes his orders from Celestino . . . Go on! Quick!

RABIT (*referring to Salvador*): He's on the way out. He's had it.

KOPAS: What's happening to all of us? What's happening?

BARTO (*to Zapatoni*): Help me, will you. . . . Lift him up. . . .
Try and get him on this chair.

(*They do so.*)

ZAPATONI: He wants to say something. . . . What is it?

SALVADOR (*face in spot*): A little house . . . the seaside . . . Blind
Man! Blind Man!

ZAPATONI: He wants the Blind Man.

LONDEQUE: Come over to him, Blind Man.

BLIND MAN: Lead me . . . lead me!

(*They lead him to Salvador.*)

SALVADOR (*gripping the Blind Man's hand*): You with no eyes . . . you cannot read . . . they can't deceive you ever. . . . Guide them! . . . Love one another . . . as I have loved you.

ZAPATONI: Dead!

TICHOMI: The bastards!

(*Pause. The March of the Slaves is heard.*)

LONDEQUE: The town will never be the same. No orange groves . . . no olives.

BARTO: No more willow baskets . . . no more straw hats.

KOPAS: The town is on the way up, I promise you.

RABIT: You just see what it'll be like tomorrow.

BARTO: Get out of here! Get out of here, the pair of you!

LONDEQUE: Out! Go on! Out!

(*They leave.*)

BARTO: I've got nothing against you, Londeque.

LONDEQUE: I've nothing against you. . . . If you like, Barto . . . if you think it's a good idea . . . let's go and look for work together, shall we . . . look for work for all these people here?

BARTO: Look for work . . . look for a better way.

(*They shake hands.*)

BLIND MAN: They're shaking hands. Sightless though I am, I know it. . . . They're shaking hands. True?

BARTO: Yes.

BLIND MAN: Peace has come to the town. The prophecy has been fulfilled.

LONDEQUE: No, Blind Man . . . not peace to this town . . . only peace between us . . . we who are assembled here. But to win the real peace, the true peace, the lasting peace, there is much to do. It is a long way off, but we shall get there. . . . The unhappy thing is this: before we can attain it, we must fight! . . . We must fight! . . . We must fight

(*The March of the Slaves stops, all the lights go up and we now hear at full volume over the loudspeakers the March from the opening scene. There now enter from the rear: The Losing Optimist, Youth B, The Brads and finally Fani, with his rifle slung over his shoulder. Salvador gets up from his chair and asks for a cigarette which somebody gives him. The actors, now relaxed, chat with each other. Walking on stage rhythmically to the march is a man dressed as a referee. He smiles and shows a placard which reads: "Game Abandoned after 85 minutes."*

*A few yards behind him is another man similarly dressed with a placard reading: "Was the ground unfit for play?"*

*A third carries a placard reading: "Or did the referee violate the rules?"*

*As at the beginning of the play, the placard carriers go off and two of them return with fresh notices reading: "There'll be a replay."*

*The following one reads: "Spot the winner?"*

*On the reverse side is the same phrase in larger letters. The lights are lowered and Salvador shows a placard on which is written: "END."*

*Alone on stage, he holds it for a few moments. He then shows the other side which reads:*

"FOOTBALL."

CURTAIN.
END OF TRAGEDY.